Bond Market
Securities

Bond Market Securities

MOORAD CHOUDHRY

FINANCIAL TIMES
Prentice Hall

An imprint of **Pearson Education**

London ▪ New York ▪ San Francisco ▪ Toronto ▪ Sydney
Tokyo ▪ Singapore ▪ Hong Kong ▪ Cape Town ▪ Madrid
Paris ▪ Milan ▪ Munich ▪ Amsterdam

PEARSON EDUCATION LIMITED
Head Office:
Edinburgh Gate
Harlow CM20 2JE
Tel: +44 (0)1279 623623
Fax: +44 (0)1279 431059

London Office:
128 Long Acre
London WC2E 9AN
Tel: +44 (0)20 7447 2000
Fax: +44 (0)20 7240 5771
Website: www.financialminds.com

First published in Great Britain in 2001

The views, thoughts and opinions expressed in this book are those of the author in his
individual capacity and should not in any way be attributed to JPMorgan Chase &
Co, or to Moorad Choudhry as a representative, officer, or employee of JPMorgan
Chase & Co.

Whilst every effort has been made to ensure accuracy, no responsibility for loss
occasioned to any person acting or refraining from action as a result of any material in
this book can be accepted by the author, the publishers or any named person or entity.

Note
To save endless repetition of 'he or she', we have mainly used the male gender
indiscriminately to denote both genders.

ISBN 0 273 65408 X

British Library Cataloguing in Publication Data
A CIP catalogue record for this book can be obtained from the British Library

10 9 8 7 6 5 4 3 2 1

Typeset by Pantek Arts Ltd, Maidstone, Kent
Printed and bound in Great Britain by Bookcraft, Midsomer Norton, Bath

The Publishers' policy is to use paper manufactured from sustainable forests.

About the author

Moorad Choudhry is a vice-president with JPMorgan in London. He started his City career in 1989 at the London Stock Exchange, before joining the sterling Eurobond desk at Hoare Govett Fixed Interest. He was later employed as a Gilt-edged market maker and treasury trader at ABN Amro Hoare Govett Sterling Bonds Limited, where he ran the short-dated Gilt book, the gilt repo book and the sterling money markets book, and was also responsible for stock borrowing and lending and interbank funding. From there he moved to Hambros Bank Limited, where he set up and ran the Treasury division's sterling proprietary trading desk. He worked as a strategy and risk management consultant to some of the world's leading investment banks, before joining JPMorgan in 2000.

Moorad has an MA in Econometrics from Reading University and an MBA from Henley Management College. He has taught courses on bond and money markets subjects for organizations both in the City of London and abroad, including the International Faculty of Finance and FinTuition Limited, and has lectured at City University Business School. He is a member of the Chartered Institute of Bankers and the Global Association of Risk Professionals, and sits on the examination panel of the Securities Institute Bond and Fixed Income Markets Diploma paper.

For my Mum

Contents

PART II

Selected market instruments

PART IV

*Selected market
trading considerations*

Foreword

In a world of ever-changing parameters such as those in financial markets, one thing is certain; the need for constant study. What occurs in any given market, at any given moment, or in any given economic environment is relevant for all other markets, moments and environments. Our learning requirements offer us no respite. This book is dedicated to that educational purpose. It serves as more than just a 'user's guide', it aims to give the reader a fuller understanding of the nuances of the various components of the fixed income markets and a grasp of the fundamental theory involved.

Since my career began in the City, I have witnessed many changes within the markets as participants constantly endeavoured to out-think one another in the search for, at times elusive, profit. Then, as various trading strategies and techniques were exploited to the full, the search would continue on to more complex ones, and so on. The search for higher yields led many into markets where the diverse economic, financial and cultural environments all have a major influence. For example the establishment of domestic bond markets in what were typically regarded as emerging markets promised further opportunities and returns, but at the same time posed many concerns about credit status and transparency. These risks came home to roost in the late 1990s and encouraged a return to the core markets for many investors in fixed income, the so-called 'flight to quality'. Participants are slowly rediscovering their appetite for risk of this nature and are gradually returning to select markets such as Latin America and certain eastern European countries in an attempt to secure asset diversification, relative value and the possibility of enhanced returns.

With the euro's inception at the start of 1999, certain risks inherent within the European bond markets diminished and with them the chances for profit for those skilled enough to react to the opportunities as they appeared. This has caused traders and investors to explore other avenues in the search for revenue. But increasingly, those same market participants are recognizing that the new opportunities are bringing new complexities and new risks. It is essential to appreciate and understand these risks fully, and to limit exposure to them if necessary. The introduction of the new currency transformed the international debt capital markets with the issuance during the first quarter of 1999 proving extremely prodigious as borrowers sought to establish benchmarks and investors sought to ensure that their portfolios represented a suitable exposure to the new market.

Looking forward, the euro spells huge opportunities in European bond markets. Investors have a larger supply of bonds to choose from and issuers a bigger market within which to sell securities. However, the growth in debt securities markets is almost inevitably associated with a parallel rise in the level of credit risk.

While the adoption of the single currency will lead to more uniformity in market practices and bond structures, there will still be diversity in the way bonds are structured, valued and traded. Investors will need to be fully conversant in these differences to avoid the obvious pitfalls. Adoption of a single investment strategy in this regard would clearly lead to ruin. Also the barriers to financial services competition have crumbled, thus creating an environment in which financial innovation is likely to accelerate further. So once again we see how flexibility and a willingness for constant education is vital for successful navigation through the markets. This book assists one in properly gauging and managing these various hazards and is suitable for beginners and more experienced traders alike. It contains a wide range of methodologies that will help the reader to gain a good understanding of fixed income securities and some of their associated derivatives.

I first met Moorad Choudhry back in 1994 in the good old days of ABN AMRO Hoare Govett Sterling Bonds Limited when we worked together on the Gilt Desk under the watchful eye of Sean Baguley. Moorad always showed such propensity for the continual learning that I have been advocating within these brief words, and when our paths separated a few years later he went on to produce some fine books on diverse aspects of the financial markets. These books sit in pride of place on the bookshelves by the desk in my office right now! So it comes as no surprise to me that he has produced another exceptional example of writing that nestles in your hands at this moment. If you're looking for the answers to the mysteries of fixed income I can assure you, some of the ones you seek are contained in the following pages.

Graham 'Harry' Cross
European Government Trading
Spear, Leeds & Kellogg

Preface

The market in bond market securities – also known as the fixed income market – is incredibly large and diverse, and one that plays an irreplaceable part in global economic development. The vast majority of securities in the world today are debt instruments, with outstanding volume estimated at over $13 trillion. In this book we provide a concise and accessible description of the main elements of the markets, concentrating on the instruments used and their applications. As it has been designed to be both succinct and concise, the major issues are introduced and described, and where appropriate certain applications are also analyzed. So, for instance there is little or no description of specific markets, exchanges or trading conventions; such topics would result in a very large book and is abundantly covered in existing literature. Therefore, very detailed treatment is left out, as required in a book of this size, but interested readers can access the references listed in the bibliography, which are also recommended to various degrees by the author. Where possible these references are indicated for their level of analysis and technical treatment. All items listed are personally familiar to the author, which serves to makes bibliographies relevant and not over-long.

The global bond markets are very diverse, and it would not be possible to cover every single instrument and application. Our intention is to cover the most important areas. This book is aimed at those with little or no previous understanding of or exposure to the bond markets; however it also investigates the markets to sufficient depth to be of use to the more experienced practitioner. It is primarily aimed at front office, middle office and back office banking and fund management staff who are involved to some extent with fixed income securities. Others including corporate and local authority treasurers, bank auditors and consultants, risk managers and legal department staff may also find the contents useful.

The book is divided into four parts, covering introduction to bonds, selected market instruments and derivatives and trading strategy. The highlights include:

- detailed treatment of bond mathematics, including pricing and yield analytics. This includes modified duration and convexity;

- the concept of spot (zero-coupon) and forward rates, and the rates implied by market bond prices and yields;

- a description of yield curve fitting techniques, and an account of spline fitting using regression techniques;

- introductory discussion of term structure models;
- coverage of money market instruments;
- analysis of instruments that feature embedded options such as callable bonds;
- a discussion of mortgage-backed securities;
- the use and applications of credit derivatives by participants in the fixed income markets;
- a chapter on trading techniques based on the author's personal experience in the gilt market.

A number of subjects are deliberately *not* covered. Some of these, such as option instruments and pricing, and structured products, are left out because they are very well researched and there are innumerable books and articles covering them. Other subjects that have been omitted for reasons of space but which are very relevant for bond market participants include:

- a detailed analysis of bond futures, the basis and determination of the cheapest-to-deliver bond;
- risk management techniques such as the use of value-at-risk by banks to measure risk exposure;
- government bond markets including the Treasury and Gilt markets.

These subjects are covered in detail in other publications, some of them in the author's own, *The Repo Handbook* (Butterworth 2001) and *An Introduction to Value-at-Risk* (SI Services 1999).

Comments on the text are most welcome and should be sent to the author care of FT Prentice Hall.

Some of the content of this book was originally written as courses notes, and used to form part of bond market courses taught at a number of professional bodies and teaching institutions, including the Securities Institute, International Faculty of Finance, City University Business School and FinTuition Limited. From these courses, a number of Microsoft Powerpoint slides have been made available for use as teaching aids, and may be downloaded from the author's website at www.mchoudhry.co.uk. This website also holds sample lecture notes. In addition, there are details of bond and other training courses that are available on market topics, run by the author and his associates.

A word on the mathematics

Financial subjects such as the debt capital markets are essentially quantitative disciplines, and as such it is not possible to describe them, let alone analyze them, without recourse to a certain amount of numerical input. However, to maintain the accessibility of this book, we have limited the level of mathematics used; as a result many topics could not be reviewed in full detail. This is not, after all, a maths book; there are very few derivations for example, and fewer proofs. This does not impair the analysis, as the reader is still left with an understanding of the techniques required in the context of market instruments.

At the other end of the scale we have sought to make the book as succinct and concise as possible, so a certain amount of general familiarity with the financial markets is assumed. In addition, there is no coverage of specific market conventions. Complete beginners may wish to review an introductory text, for example the course companion for the SFA Registered Representatives exam or the securities part of Level I of the CFA qualification, before tackling this book. Generally, the writing style is designed to make the content accessible to a very wide readership. Finally, a certain amount of economic analysis is fairly relevant to a complete understanding of the debt markets, and it would do no harm for market participants to have an elementary grounding in this subject. There is a vast literature on this subject, and readers may wish to familiarize themselves with some of this as part of their learning.

Acknowledgements

Thanks to Jonathan Agbenyega at FT Prentice Hall, a gentleman and someone who has faith that I can deliver something halfway decent ... that's appreciated for a start!

A big thank you to Brian Eales at London Guildhall University for taking the trouble to review some of the chapters and offer constructive comment and criticism, which was much appreciated. Any errors or omissions are of course my responsibility alone.

Thanks to Harry for the foreword. Working on the desk with you and the others and still making close two-way prices immediately after the Bank had stung the market with a surprise rate hike ... aaah, the good old days!

Thanks also to Gurminder Bhachu at the UK Debt Management Office, very helpful when I rang up with obscure questions about the term structure or gilt strip yields ... if you spot any errors in the text please let me know! And thanks to Paul Darbyshire at the Institute of Physics, for that excellent course on quantitative finance, and to Jas Singh Ghag for taking time to help improve my footy skills, it's appreciated.

A warm thank you to Bogey for help with figures and diagrams.

There are some truly brilliant writers on financial economics out there, none of whom I've had the pleasure yet to meet. However, I've learnt a lot from (and been greatly inspired by) reading their work ... in no particular order my personal favourite works include those by Frank Fabozzi, Sheldon Ross, Satyajit Das, Jonathan Ingersoll, Damodar Gujarati, John Campbell, Suresh Sundaresan, Donald van Deventer, Bruce Tuckman and Robert Shiller.

For pure inspiration I'd like to thank J.E. 'Johnnie' Johnson, Hergé, Charles Schultz, David Gower, 'Keep It' by Dexy's Midnight Runners, Felt, and that song by the Sultans of Ping FC about the incomparable Nigel Clough, entitled 'Give him a ball and a yard of space'.

Moorad Choudhry
Surrey, England

Part I

Introduction to bonds

In Part I, we describe the building blocks of fixed income market analysis, which cover the basic concept of the bond instrument. The building blocks described here are generic and should be applicable in any market. The analysis is simplest when restricted to plain vanilla *default-free* bonds; as the instruments become more complex we are required to introduce additional techniques and assumption.

Part I comprises five chapters. We begin with bond pricing and yield, followed by traditional interest-rate risk measures such as modified duration and convexity. This is followed by a look at spot and forward rates, the derivation of such rates from market yields, and the concept of the yield curve. Yield curve analysis and the modelling of the term structure of interest rates is one of the most heavily-researched areas of financial economics.

The treatment here is kept as concise as possible, which sacrifices some detail, but bibliographies at the end of each chapter will direct interested readers on to what the author feels are the most accessible and readable references in this area.

CHAPTER 1

The bond instrument

Bonds are capital market debt instruments that represent a cash flow payable during a specified time period into the future. These cash flows represent the interest payable on the loan and the loan redemption. So a bond essentially is a loan, albeit one that is tradeable in a secondary market. This differentiates bond market securities from commercial bank loans.

For some considerable time, the analysis of bonds was frequently presented in what might be termed 'traditional' terms, with description limited to gross redemption yield or *yield to maturity*. Basic bond maths analysis is now presented in slightly different terms, as described in a range of books and articles such as those by Ingersoll (1987), Shiller (1990), Neftci (1996), Jarrow (1996), Van Deventer (1997) and Sundaresan (1997), among others.[1] For this reason we review the basic elements, strictly in overview fashion only, in this chapter. The academic approach and description of bond pricing, and a review of the term structure of interest rates, is considered in Chapter 3. Interested readers may wish to consult the texts in the bibliography for further information.

In the analysis that follows bonds are assumed to be *default free*, which means that there is no possibility that the interest payments and principal repayment will not be made. Such an assumption is accurate when one is referring to government bonds such as US Treasuries, UK gilts and so on. However it is unreasonable when applied to bonds issued by corporates or lower-rated sovereign borrowers. Nevertheless it is still relevant to understand the valuation and analysis of bonds that are default free, as the pricing of bonds that carry default risk is based on the price of risk-free government securities. Essentially the price investors charge borrowers that are not of risk-free credit standing is the price of government securities plus some *credit risk* and *liquidity* premium.

---

[1] This area of fixed income analytics has been extensively researched. The references given are, in the opinion of the author, some of the very best. In fact a reader could make do with reading and understanding the Jarrow, Shiller and Ingersoll references only, which are excellent. These references and others stated are given at the end of Chapter 3.

Time value of money

The principles of pricing in the bond market are exactly the same as those in other financial markets, which states that the price of any financial instrument is equal to the present value today of all the future cash flows emanating from the instrument. Bond prices are expressed as per 100 nominal of the bond, or 'per cent'. So, for example, if the price of a US dollar denominated bond is quoted as '98.00', this means that for every $100 nominal of the bond a buyer would pay $98.[2] The interest rate or discount rate used as part of the present value (price) calculation is key, as it reflects where the bond is trading in the market and how it is perceived by the market. All the determining factors that identify the bond, including the nature of the issuer, the maturity, the coupon and the currency, influence the interest rate at which a bond's cash flows are discounted. This discount rate will be similar to the rate used for comparable bonds. First, we consider the traditional approach to bond pricing for a plain vanilla instrument, making certain assumptions to keep the analysis simple, and then we present the more formal analysis commonly encountered in academic texts.

Introduction

Bonds or *fixed income*[3] instruments are debt capital market securities and therefore have maturities longer than one year. This differentiates them from money market securities. Bonds have more intricate cash flow patterns than money market securities, which usually have just one cash flow at maturity. This makes bonds more complex to price than money market instruments, and their prices more responsive to changes in the general level of interest rates. There are a large variety of bonds. The most common type is the *plain vanilla* (or *straight, conventional* or *bullet*) bond. This is a bond paying a regular (annual or semi-annual) fixed interest payment or *coupon* over a fixed period to maturity or *redemption*, with the return of principal (the par or nominal value of the bond) on the maturity date. All other bonds are variations on this.

The crucial identifying feature of a bond is its issuer, the entity that is borrowing funds by issuing the bond into the market. Issuers are generally categorized as one of four types: governments (and their agencies), local governments (or municipal authorities), supranational bodies such as the World Bank, and corporates. Within the municipal and corporate markets there are a wide range of issuers, each assessed as having differing

---

[2] The convention in certain markets is to quote a price per 1000 nominal.

[3] The term fixed income originated at a time when bonds were essentially plain vanilla instruments paying a fixed coupon per year. In the UK the term *fixed interest* was used. These days many bonds do not necessarily pay a fixed coupon each year, for instance asset-backed bond issues are invariably issued in a number of tranches, with each tranche paying a different fixed or floating coupon. The market is still commonly referred to as the fixed income market however (and certain sterling market diehards will even still call it the fixed interest market).

abilities to maintain the interest payments on their debt and repay the full loan on maturity. This ability is identified by a *credit rating* for each issuer. The *term to maturity* of a bond is the number of years over which the issuer has promised to meet the conditions of the debt obligation. The *maturity* of a bond refers to the date that the debt will cease to exist, at which time the issuer will redeem the bond by paying the principal. The practice in the bond market is to refer to the 'term to maturity' of a bond as simply its 'maturity' or 'term'. Some bonds contain provisions that allow either the issuer or the bondholder to alter a bond's term. The term to maturity of a bond is its other key feature. First, it indicates the time period over which the bondholder can expect to receive coupon payments and the number of years before the principal is paid back. Second, it influences the yield of a bond. Finally, the price of a bond will fluctuate over its life as yields in the market change. The volatility of a bond's price is dependent on its maturity. All else being equal, the longer the maturity of a bond, the greater its price volatility resulting from a change in market yields.

The *principal* of a bond is the amount that the issuer agrees to repay the bondholder on maturity. This amount is also referred to as the *redemption value, maturity value, par value* or *face value*. The coupon rate, or *nominal rate*, is the interest rate that the issuer agrees to pay each year during the life of the bond. The annual amount of interest payment made to bondholders is the *coupon*. The cash amount of the coupon is the coupon rate multiplied by the principal of the bond. For example, a bond with a coupon rate of eight per cent and a principal of £1000 will pay annual interest of £80. In the UK, the usual practice is for the issuer to pay the coupon in two semi-annual instalments. All bonds make periodic coupon payments, except for one type that makes none. These bonds are known as *zero-coupon bonds*. Such bonds are issued at a discount and redeemed at par. The holder of a zero-coupon bond realizes interest by buying the bond at this discounted value, below its principal value. Interest is therefore paid on maturity, with the exact amount being the difference between the principal value and the discounted value paid on purchase.

There are also *floating rate* bonds (FRNs). With these bonds, coupon rates are reset periodically according to a pre-determined benchmark, such as 3-month or 6-month LIBOR. For this reason FRNs typically trade more as money market instruments than conventional bonds.

A bond issue may include a provision that gives either the bondholder and/or the issuer an option to take some action against the other party. The most common type of option embedded in a bond is a *call feature*. This grants the issuer the right to call the debt, fully or partially, before the maturity date. A *put provision* gives bondholders the right to sell the issue back to the issuer at par on designated dates. A *convertible bond* is an issue giving the bondholder the right to exchange the bond for a specified number of shares (equity) in the issuing company. The presence of embedded options makes the valuation of such bonds more complex when compared with plain vanilla bonds.

Present value and discounting

As fixed income instruments are essentially a collection of cash flows, we begin by reviewing the key concept in cash flow analysis, that of discounting and *present value*. It is essential to have a firm understanding of the main principles before moving on to other areas. When reviewing the concept of the time value of money, assume that the interest rates used are the market determined rates of interest.

Financial arithmetic has long been used to illustrate that £1 received today is not the same as £1 received at a point in the future. Faced with a choice between receiving £1 today or £1 in one year's time we would not be indifferent given a rate of interest of say, ten per cent that was equal to our required nominal rate of interest. Our choice would be between £1 today or £1 plus 10p – the interest on £1 for one year at ten per cent per annum. The notion that money has a time value is a basic concept in the analysis of financial instruments. Money has time value because of the opportunity to invest it at a rate of interest. A loan that has one interest payment on maturity is accruing *simple interest*. On short-term instruments there is usually only the one interest payment on maturity, hence simple interest is received when the instrument expires. The terminal value of an investment with simple interest is given by (1.1) below.

$$F = P(1 + r) \tag{1.1}$$

where

F is the terminal value or *future value*;
P is the initial investment or *present value*;
r is the interest rate.

The market convention is to quote interest rates as *annualized* interest rates, which is the interest that is earned if the investment term is one year. Consider a three-month deposit of £100 in a bank, placed at a rate of interest of six per cent. In such an example the bank deposit will earn six per cent interest for a period of 90 days. As the annual interest gain would be £6, the investor will expect to receive a proportion of this, which is calculated below:

$$£6.00 \times \frac{90}{365}$$

Therefore the investor will receive £1.479 interest at the end of the term. The total proceeds after the three months is therefore £100 plus £1.479. If we wish to calculate the terminal value of a short-term investment that is accruing simple interest we use the following expression (1.2):

$$F = P\left(1 + r \times \frac{\text{days}}{\text{year}}\right). \tag{1.2}$$

The fraction $\frac{\text{days}}{\text{year}}$ refers to the numerator, which is the number of days the investment runs, divided by the denominator which is the number of days in the year. In the sterling markets the number of days in the year is taken to be 365, however most other markets (including the dollar and euro markets) have a 360-day year convention. For this reason we simply quote the expression as 'days' divided by 'year' to allow for either convention.

Let us now consider an investment of £100 made for three years, again at a rate of six per cent, but this time fixed for three years. At the end of the first year the investor will be credited with interest of £6. Therefore for the second year the interest rate of six per cent will be accruing on a principal sum of £106, which means that at the end of year two, the interest credited will be £6.36. This illustrates how *compounding* works, which is the principle of earning interest on interest. The outcome of the process of compounding is the *future value* of the initial amount. The expression is given in (1.3).

$$FV = PV (1 + r)^n \tag{1.3}$$

where

    FV is the future value;

    PV is initial outlay or *present value*;

    r is the periodic rate of interest (expressed as a decimal);

    n is the number of periods for which the sum is invested.

When we compound interest we have to assume that the reinvestment of interest payments during the investment term is at the same rate as the first year's interest. That is why we stated that the six per cent rate in our example was *fixed* for three years. We can see however that compounding increases our returns compared to investments that accrue only on a simple interest basis.

Now let us consider a deposit of £100 for one year, at a rate of six per cent but with quarterly interest payments. Such a deposit would accrue interest of £6 in the normal way but £1.50 would be credited to the account every quarter, and this would then benefit from compounding. Again assuming that we can reinvest at the same rate of six per cent, the total return at the end of the year will be:

$$100 \times [(1 + 0.015) \times (1 + 0.015) \times (1 + 0.015) \times (1 + 0.015)] = 100 \times [(1 + 0.015)^4]$$

which gives us 100×1.06136, a terminal value of £106.136. This is some 13 pence more than the terminal value using annual compounded interest.

In general if compounding takes place m times per year, then at the end of n years mn interest payments will have been made and the future value of the principal is given by (1.4) below.

$$FV = PV\left(1 + \frac{r}{m}\right)^{mn} \qquad (1.4)$$

As we showed in our example the effect of more frequent compounding is to increase the value of the total return when compared to annual compounding. The effect of more frequent compounding is shown below, where we consider the annualized interest rate factors, for an annualized rate of six per cent.

$$\text{Interest rate factor} = \left(1 + \frac{r}{m}\right)^{m}$$

Compounding frequency	Interest rate factor	
Annual	$(1 + r)$	$= 1.060000$
Semi-annual	$\left(1 + \frac{r}{2}\right)^{2}$	$= 1.060900$
Quarterly	$\left(1 + \frac{r}{4}\right)^{4}$	$= 1.061364$
Monthly	$\left(1 + \frac{r}{12}\right)^{12}$	$= 1.061678$
Daily	$\left(1 + \frac{r}{365}\right)^{365}$	$= 1.061831$

This shows us that the more frequent the compounding the higher the interest rate factor. The last case also illustrates how a limit occurs when interest is compounded continuously. Equation (1.4) can be rewritten as follows:

$$FV = PV\left[\left(1 + \frac{r}{m}\right)^{m/r}\right]^{rn}$$

$$= PV\left[\left(1 + \frac{1}{m/r}\right)^{m/r}\right]^{rn} \qquad (1.5)$$

$$= PV\left[\left(1 + \frac{1}{n}\right)^{n}\right]^{rn}$$

where $n = m/r$. As compounding becomes continuous and m and hence n approach infinity, the expression in the square brackets in (1.5) approaches a value known as e, which is shown below.

$$e = \lim_{n \to \infty} \left(1 + \frac{1}{n}\right)^{n} = 2.718281\ldots$$

If we substitute this into (1.5) this gives us:

$$FV = PVe^{rn} \tag{1.6}$$

where we have continuous compounding. In (1.6) e^{rn} is known as the *exponential function* of rn and it tells us the continuously compounded interest rate factor. If $r = 6\%$ and $n = 1$ year then:

$$e^r = (2.718281)^{0.05} = 1.061837$$

This is the limit reached with continuous compounding. It is close to daily compounding and is used for ease of analysis in financial markets.

The convention in both wholesale and personal (retail) markets is to quote an annual interest rate. A lender who wishes to earn the interest at the rate quoted has to place his funds on deposit for one year. Annual rates are quoted irrespective of the maturity of a deposit, from overnight to ten years or longer. For example if one opens a bank account that pays interest at a rate of 3.5% but then closes it after six months, the actual interest earned will be equal to 1.75% of the sum deposited. The actual return on a three-year building society bond (fixed deposit) that pays 6.75% fixed for three years is 21.65% after three years. The quoted rate is the annual one-year equivalent. An overnight deposit in the wholesale or *interbank* market is still quoted as an annual rate, even though interest is earned for only one day.

The convention of quoting annualized rates is to allow deposits and loans of different maturities and different instruments to be compared on the basis of the interest rate applicable. We must be careful when comparing interest rates for products that have different payment frequencies. As we have seen from the foregoing paragraphs the actual interest earned will be greater for a deposit earning six per cent on a semi-annual basis compared to six per cent on an annual basis. The convention in the money markets is to quote the equivalent interest rate applicable when taking into account an instrument's payment frequency.

We saw how a *future value* could be calculated given a known *present value* and rate of interest. For example £100 invested today for one year at an interest rate of six per cent will generate $100 \times (1 + 0.06) = £106$ at the end of the year. The future value of £100 in this case is £106. We can also say that £100 is the *present value* of £106 in this case.

In equation 1.3 we established the following future value relationship:

$$FV = PV (1 + r)^n$$

By reversing this expression we arrive at the present value calculation given in (1.7).

$$PV = \frac{FV}{(1 + r)^n} \tag{1.7}$$

where the symbols represent the same terms as before. Equation (1.7) applies in the case of annual interest payments and enables us to calculate the present value of a known future sum.

To calculate the present value for a short-term investment of less than one year we will need to adjust what would have been the interest earned for a whole year by the proportion of days of the investment period. Rearranging the basic equation, we can say that the present value of a known future value is:

$$PV = \frac{FV}{\left(1 + r \times \frac{days}{year}\right)} \qquad (1.8)$$

Given a present value and a future value at the end of an investment period, what then is the interest rate earned? We can rearrange the basic equation again to solve for the *yield*.

When interest is compounded more than once a year, the formula for calculating present value is modified, as shown at (1.9).

$$PV = \frac{FV}{\left(1 + \frac{r}{m}\right)^{mn}} \qquad (1.9)$$

where as before FV is the cash flow at the end of year n, m is the number of times a year interest is compounded, and r is the rate of interest or discount rate. Illustrating this therefore, the present value of £100 that is received at the end of five years at a rate of interest of five per cent, with quarterly compounding is:

$$PV = \frac{100}{\left(1 + \frac{00.5}{4}\right)^{(4)(5)}}$$

$$= £78.00$$

Interest rates in the money markets are always quoted for standard maturities, for example overnight, 'tom next' (the overnight interest rate starting tomorrow, or 'tomorrow to the next'), spot next (the overnight rate starting two days forward), 1 week, 1 month, 2 months and so on up to 1 year. If a bank or corporate customer wishes to deal for non-standard periods, an interbank desk will calculate the rate chargeable for such an 'odd date' by *interpolating* between two standard period interest rates. If we assume that the rate for all dates in between two periods increases at the same steady state, we can calculate the required rate using the formula for *straight line* interpolation, shown at (1.10).

$$r = r_1 + (r_2 - r_1) \times \frac{n - n_1}{n_2 - n_1} \qquad (1.10)$$

where

r is the required odd-date rate for n days;
r_1 is the quoted rate for n_1 days;
r_2 is the quoted rate for n_2 days.

Let us imagine that the 1-month (30-day) offered interest rate is 5.25% and that the 2-month (60-date) offered rate is 5.75%. If a customer wishes to borrow money for a 40-day period, what rate should the bank charge? We can calculate the required 40-day rate using the straight line interpolation process. The increase in interest rates from 30 to 40 days is assumed to be 10/30 of the total increase in rates from 30 to 60 days. The 40-day offered rate would therefore be:

5.25% + (5.75% − 5.25%) × 10/30 = 5.4167%.

What about the case of an interest rate for a period that lies just before or just after two known rates and not roughly in between them? When this happens we *extrapolate* between the two known rates, again assuming a straight line relationship between the two rates and for a period after (or before) the two rates. So if the 1-month offered rate is 5.25% while the 2-month rate is 5.75%, the 64-day rate is:

5.25 + (5.75 − 5.25) × 34/30 = 5.8167%.

Discount factors

An n-period discount factor is the present value of 1 unit of currency (£1 or $1) that is payable at the end of period n. Essentially it is the present value relationship expressed in terms of £1. If $d(n)$ is the n-year discount factor, then the five-year discount factor at a discount rate of six per cent is given by:

$$d(5) = \frac{1}{(1 + 0.06)^5} = 0.747258.$$

The set of discount factors for every time period from 1 day to 30 years or longer is termed the *discount function*. Discount factors may be used to price any financial instrument that is made up of a future cash flow. For example what would be the value of £103.50 receivable at the end of six months if the six-month discount factor is 0.98756? The answer is given by:

0.98756 × 103.50 = 102.212.

In addition, discount factors may be used to calculate the future value of any present investment. From the example above, £0.98756 would be worth £1 in six months' time, so by the same principle a present sum of £1 would be worth:

1 / $d(0.5)$ = 1 / 0.98756 = 1.0126

at the end of six months.

It is possible to obtain discount factors from current bond prices. Assume an hypothetical set of bonds and bond prices as given in table 1.1 below, and assume further that the first bond in the table matures in precisely six months time (these are semi-annual coupon bonds).

TABLE 1.1 ■ Hypothetical set of bonds and bond prices

Coupon	Maturity date	Price
7%	7-Jun-01	101.65
8%	7-Dec-01	101.89
6%	7-Jun-02	100.75
6.50%	7-Dec-02	100.37

Taking the first bond, this matures in precisely six months' time, and its final cash flow will be 103.50, comprised of the £3.50 final coupon payment and the £100 redemption payment. The price or present value of this bond is 101.65, which allows us to calculate the six-month discount factor as:

$$d(0.5) \times 103.50 = 101.65$$

which gives $d(0.5)$ equal to 0.98213.

From this first step we can calculate the discount factors for the following six-month periods. The second bond in table 1.1, the 8% 2001 has the following cash flows:

■ £4 in six months' time;

■ £104 in one year's time.

The price of this bond is 101.89, which again is the bond's present value, and consists of the sum of the present values of the bond's total cash flows. So we are able to set the following:

$$101.89 = 4 \times d(0.5) + 104 \times d(1)$$

However, we already know $d(0.5)$ to be 0.98213, which leaves only one unknown in the above expression. Therefore we may solve for $d(1)$ and this is shown to be 0.94194.

If we carry on with this procedure for the remaining two bonds, using successive discount factors, we obtain the complete set of discount factors as shown in table 1.2. The continuous function for the two-year period from today is shown as the discount function, at figure 1.1.

TABLE 1.2 ■ Discount factors calculated using bootstrapping technique

Coupon	Maturity date	Term (years)	Price	d(n)
7%	7-Jun-01	0.5	101.65	0.98213
8%	7-Dec-01	1.0	101.89	0.94194
6%	7-Jun-02	1.5	100.75	0.92211
6.50%	7-Dec-02	2.0	100.37	0.88252

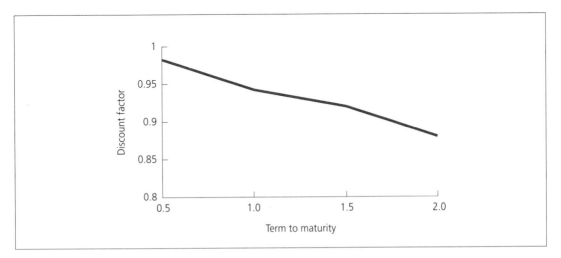

FIGURE 1.1 ■ Hypothetical discount function

This technique, which is known as *bootstrapping*, is conceptually neat but problems arise when we do not have a set of bonds that mature at precise six-month intervals. In addition, liquidity issues connected with specific individual bonds can also cause complications. Nevertheless, it is still worth being familiar with this approach.

Note from figure 1.1 how discount factors decrease with increasing maturity: this is intuitively obvious, since the present value of something to be received in the future diminishes the further into the future we go.

Bond pricing and yield: the traditional approach

Bond pricing

The interest rate that is used to discount a bond's cash flows (called the *discount* rate) is the rate required by the bondholder. It is therefore known as the bond's *yield*. The yield on the bond will be determined by the market and is the price demanded by investors for buying it, which is why it is sometimes called the bond's *return*. The required yield for any bond will depend on a number of political and economic factors, including what yield is being earned by other bonds of the same class. Yield is always quoted as an annualized interest rate, so that for a semi-annually paying bond exactly half of the annual rate is used to discount the cash flows.

The *fair price* of a bond is the present value of all its cash flows. Therefore, when pricing a bond, we need to calculate the present value of all the coupon interest payments and the present value of the redemption payment, and sum these. The price of a conventional bond that pays annual coupons can be given therefore by (1.11).

$$P = \frac{C}{(1 + r)} + \frac{C}{(1 + r)^2} + \frac{C}{(1 + r)^3} + \ldots\ldots + \frac{C}{(1 + r)^N} + \frac{M}{(1 + r)^N}$$

$$= \sum_{n=1}^{N} \frac{C}{(1 + r)^n} + \frac{M}{(1 + r)^N}$$

(1.11)

where

P is the price;
C is the annual coupon payment;
r is the discount rate (therefore, the required yield);
N is the number of years to maturity (therefore, the number of interest periods in an annually-paying bond; for a semi-annual bond the number of interest periods is $N \times 2$); and an adjustment to r must be made);
M is the maturity payment or par value (usually 100 per cent of currency).

For long-hand calculation purposes the first half of (1.11) is usually simplified and is sometimes encountered in one of the two ways shown in (1.12).

$$P = C \left[\frac{1 - \left[\frac{1}{(1 + r)^N} \right]}{r} \right]$$

or

(1.12)

$$P = \frac{C}{r} \left[1 - \frac{1}{(1 + r)^N} \right]$$

The price of a bond that pays semi-annual coupons is given by the expression at (1.13), which is our earlier expression modified to allow for the twice-yearly discounting:

$$P = \frac{C/2}{\left(1 + \frac{1}{2} r\right)} + \frac{C/2}{\left(1 + \frac{1}{2} r\right)^2} + \frac{C/2}{\left(1 + \frac{1}{2} r\right)^3} + \ldots\ldots + \frac{C/2}{\left(1 + \frac{1}{2} r\right)^{2N}} + \frac{M}{\left(1 + \frac{1}{2} r\right)^{2N}}$$

$$= \sum_{t=1}^{2T} \frac{C/2}{(1 + \frac{1}{2}r)^n} + \frac{M}{(1 + \frac{1}{2}r)^{2N}} \tag{1.13}$$

$$= \frac{C}{r}\left[1 - \frac{1}{(1 + \frac{1}{2}r)^{2N}}\right] + \frac{M}{(1 + \frac{1}{2}r)^{2N}}.$$

Note how we set $2N$ as the power to which to raise the discount factor, as there are two interest payments every year for a bond that pays semi-annually. Therefore, a more convenient function to use might be the number of interest periods in the life of the bond, as opposed to the number of years to maturity, which we could set as n, allowing us to alter the equation for a semi-annually paying bond as:

$$P = \frac{C}{r}\left[1 - \frac{1}{(1 + \frac{1}{2}r)^n}\right] + \frac{M}{(1 + \frac{1}{2}r)^n}. \tag{1.14}$$

The formula at (1.14) calculates the fair price on a coupon payment date, so that there is no *accrued interest* incorporated into the price. It also assumes that there is an even number of coupon payments dates remaining before maturity. The concept of accrued interest is an accounting convention, and treats coupon interest as accruing every day that the bond is held; this amount is added to the discounted present value of the bond (the *clean price*) to obtain the market value of the bond, known as the *dirty price*.

The date used as the point for calculation is the *settlement date* for the bond, the date on which a bond will change hands after it is traded. For a new issue of bonds, the settlement date is the day when the stock is delivered to investors and payment is received by the bond issuer. The settlement date for a bond traded in the *secondary market* is the day that the buyer transfers payment to the seller of the bond and when the seller transfers the bond to the buyer. Different markets will have different settlement conventions, for example, UK gilts normally settle one business day after the trade date (the notation used in bond markets is 'T + 1') whereas Eurobonds settle on T + 3. The term *value date* is sometimes used in place of settlement date, however the two terms are not strictly synonymous. A settlement date can only fall on a business date, so that a gilt traded on a Friday will settle on a Monday. A value date can however sometimes fall on a non-business day, for example when accrued interest is being calculated.

If there is an odd number of coupon payment dates before maturity the formula at (1.14) is modified as shown in (1.15).

$$P = \frac{C}{r}\left[1 - \frac{1}{(1 + \frac{1}{2}r)^{2N+1}}\right] + \frac{M}{(1 + \frac{1}{2}r)^{2N+1}} \tag{1.15}$$

The standard formula also assumes that the bond is traded for settlement on a day that is precisely one interest period before the next coupon payment. The price formula is adjusted if dealing takes place in between coupon dates. If we take the *value date* for any transaction, we then need to calculate the number of calendar days from this day to the next coupon date. We then use the following ratio i when adjusting the exponent for the discount factor:

$$i = \frac{\text{Days from value date to next coupon date}}{\text{Days in the interest payment}}.$$

The number of days in the interest period is the number of calendar days between the last coupon date and the next one, and it will depend on the day count basis used for that specific bond. The price formula is then modified as shown at (1.16).

$$P = \frac{C}{(1 + r)^i} + \frac{C}{(1 + r)^{1+i}} + \frac{C}{(1 + r)^{2+i}} + \dots\dots + \frac{C}{(1 + r)^{n-1+i}} + \frac{M}{(1 + r)^{n-1+i}} \tag{1.16}$$

where the variables C, M, n and r are as before. Note that (1.16) assumes r for an annually-paying bond and is adjusted to $r/2$ for a semi-annual coupon paying bond.

EXAMPLE *1.1*

In these examples we illustrate the long-hand price calculation, using both expressions for the calculation of the present value of the annuity stream of a bond's cash flows.

1.1 (a) Calculate the fair pricing of a UK gilt, the 9% Treasury 2008, which pays semi-annual coupons, with the following terms:

C = £9.00 per £100 nominal
M = £100
N = 10 years (that is, the calculation is for value 13 October 1998)
r = 4.98%

$$P = \frac{£9.00}{0.0498}\left\{ 1 - \frac{1}{[1 + \frac{1}{2}(0.0498)]^{20}} \right\} + \frac{£100}{[1 + \frac{1}{2}(0.0498)]^{20}}$$

$$= £70.2175 + £61.1463$$
$$= £131.3638$$

The fair price of the gilt is £131.3638, which is composed of the present value of the stream of coupon payments (£70.2175) and the present value of the return of the principal (£61.1463).

1.1(b) What is the price of a 5% coupon sterling bond with precisely 5 years to maturity, with semi-annual coupon payments, if the yield required is 5.40%?

As the cash flows for this bond are 10 semi-annual coupons of £2.50 and a redemption payment of £100 in 10 six-month periods from now, the price of the bond can be obtained by solving the following expression, where we substitute $C = 2.5$, $n = 10$ and $\frac{1}{2}r = 0.027$ into the price equation (the values for C and r reflect the adjustments necessary for a semi-annual paying bond).

$$P = 2.5 \left[\frac{1 - \left[\frac{1}{(1.027)^{10}} \right]}{0.027} \right] + \frac{100}{(1.027)^{10}}$$

$$= 21.65574 + 76.61178$$
$$= £98.26752$$

The price of the bond is £98.2675 per £100 nominal.

1.1(c) What is the price of a 5% coupon euro bond with five years to maturity paying annual coupons, again with a required yield of 5.4%?

In this case there are five periods of interest, so we may set $C = 5$, $n = 5$, with $r = 0.05$.

$$P = 5 \left[\frac{1 - \left[\frac{1}{(1.054)^{5}} \right]}{0.054} \right] + \frac{100}{(1.054)^{5}}$$

$$= 21.410121 + 76.877092$$
$$= £98.287213$$

Note how the annual-paying bond has a slightly higher price for the same required annualized yield. This is because the semi-annual paying sterling bond has a higher *effective* yield than the euro bond, resulting in a lower price.

1.1(d) Consider our 5% sterling bond again, but this time the required yield has risen and is now 6%. This makes $C = 2.5$, $n = 10$ and $r = 0.03$.

$$P = 2.5 \left[\frac{1 - \left[\frac{1}{(1.03)^{10}} \right]}{0.03} \right] + \frac{100}{(1.03)^{10}}$$

$$= 21.325507 + 74.409391$$
$$= £95.7349$$

As the required yield has risen, the discount rate used in the price calculation is now higher, and the result of the higher discount is a lower present value (price).

1.1(e) Calculate the price of our sterling bond, still with five years to maturity but offering a yield of 5.1%.

$$P = 2.5 \left[\frac{1 - \left[\frac{1}{(1.0255)^{10}} \right]}{0.0255} \right] + \frac{100}{(1.0255)}$$

$$= 21.823737 + 77.739788$$
$$= £99.563525$$

Then to satisfy the lower required yield of 5.1% the price of the bond has fallen to £99.56 per £100.

1.1(f) Calculate the price of the 5% sterling bond one year later, with precisely four years left to maturity and with the required yield still at the original 5.40%. This sets the terms in 2.2(a) unchanged, except now $n = 8$.

$$P = 2.5 \left[\frac{1 - \left[\frac{1}{(1.027)^{8}} \right]}{0.027} \right] + \frac{100}{(1.027)^{8}}$$

$$= 17.773458 + 80.804668$$
$$= £98.578126$$

The price of the bond is £98.58. Compared to 1.1(b) this illustrates how, other things being equal, the price of a bond will approach par (£100 per cent) as it approaches maturity.

There also exist *perpetual* or *irredeemable* bonds which have no redemption date, so that interest on them is paid indefinitely. They are also known as *undated* bonds. An example of an undated bond is the 3.5% War Loan, a UK gilt originally issued in 1916 to help pay for the 1914–1918 war effort. Most undated bonds date from a long time in the past and it is unusual to see them issued today. In structure the cash flow from an undated bond can be viewed as a continuous annuity. The fair price of such a bond is given from (1.11) by setting $N = \infty$, such that:

$$P = \frac{C}{r} \tag{1.17}$$

In most markets bond prices are quoted in decimals, in minimum increments of $1/100^{ths}$. This is the case with Eurobonds, euro-denominated bonds and gilts, for example. Certain markets including the US Treasury market, South African and Indian government bond markets for example quote prices in *ticks*, where the minimum increment is $1/32^{nd}$. One tick is therefore equal to 0.03125. A US Treasury might be priced at '98–05' which means '98 and 5 ticks'. This is equal to 98 and $5/32^{nds}$ which is 98.15625.

EXAMPLE *1.2*

What is the consideration for £5 million nominal of a gilt, where the price is 114.50?

The price of the gilt is £114.50 per £100, so the consideration is:

$1.145 \times 5,000,000 = £5,725,000$

What consideration is payable for $5 million nominal of a US Treasury, quoted at an all-in price of 99–16?

The US Treasury price is 99–16, which is equal to 99 and 16/32, or 99.50 per $100. The consideration is therefore:

$0.9950 \times 5,000,000 = \$4,975,000$

If the price of a bond is below par the total consideration is below the nominal amount, whereas if it is priced above par the consideration will be above the nominal amount.

Bonds that do not pay a coupon during their life are known as *zero-coupon* bonds or *strips*, and the price for these bonds is determined by modifying (1.11) to allow for the fact that $C = 0$. We know that the only cash flow is the maturity payment, so we may set the price as:

$$P = \left(\frac{M}{(1 + r)^N} \right) \tag{1.18}$$

where M and r are as before and N is the number of years to maturity. The important factor is to allow for the same number of interest periods as coupon bonds of the same currency. That is, even though there are no actual coupons, we calculate prices and yields on the basis of a *quasi-coupon* period. For a US dollar or a sterling zero-coupon bond, a five-year zero-coupon bond would be assumed to cover ten quasi-coupon periods, which would set the price equation as:

$$P = \left(\frac{M}{\left(1 + \frac{1}{2}r\right)^{2n}} \right)$$

(1.19)

We have to note carefully the quasi-coupon periods in order to maintain consistency with conventional bond pricing.

EXAMPLE *1.3*

1.3(a)   Calculate the price of a gilt *strip* with a maturity of precisely 5 years, where the required yield is 5.40%.

These terms allow us to set $N = 5$ so that $n = 10$, $r = 0.054$ (so that $r/2 = 0.027$), with $M = 100$ as usual.

$$P = \frac{100}{(1.027)^{10}}$$

$= £76.611782$

1.3(b)   Calculate the price of a French government zero-coupon bond with precisely five years to maturity, with the same required yield of 5.40%.

$$P = \frac{100}{(1.054)^{5}}$$

$= £76.877092$

An examination of the bond price formula tells us that the yield and price for a bond are closely related. A key aspect of this relationship is that the price changes in the opposite direction to the yield. This is because the price of the bond is the net present value of its cash flows; if the discount rate used in the present value calculation increases, the present values of the cash flows will decrease. This occurs whenever the yield level required by bondholders increases. In the same way, if the required yield decreases, the price of the bond will rise. This property was observed in example 1.2. As the required yield decreased the price of the bond increased, and we observed the same relationship when the required yield was raised.

   The relationship between any bond's price and yield at any required yield level is illustrated in figure 1.2, which is obtained if we plot the yield against the corresponding price; this shows a *convex* curve.

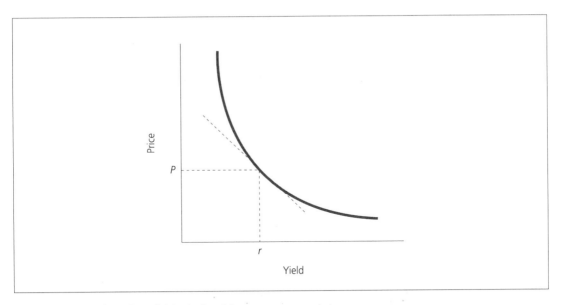

FIGURE 1.2 ■ The price/yield relationship

Summary of the price/yield relationship

■ At issue if a bond is priced at par, its coupon will equal the yield that the market requires from the bond.

■ If the required yield rises above the coupon rate, the bond price will decrease.

■ If the required yield goes below the coupon rate, the bond price will increase.

Bond yield

We have observed how to calculate the price of a bond using an appropriate discount rate known as the bond's *yield*. We can reverse this procedure to find the yield of a bond where the price is known, which would be equivalent to calculating the bond's *internal rate of return*. The IRR calculation is taken to be a bond's *yield to maturity* or *redemption yield* and is one of various yield measures used in the markets to estimate the return generated from holding a bond. In most markets bonds are generally traded on the basis of their prices but because of the complicated patterns of cash flows that different bonds can have, they are generally compared in terms of their yields. This means that a market-maker will usually quote a two-way price at which he will buy or sell a particular bond, but it is the *yield* at which the bond is trading that is important to the market-maker's customer. This is because a bond's price does not actually tell us anything useful about what we are getting. Remember that in any market there will be a number of bonds with different issuers, coupons and terms to maturity. Even in a homogenous market such as the gilt market, different gilts will trade according to their own specific characteristics. To compare bonds in the market, therefore, we need the yield on any bond and it is yields that we compare, not prices.

The yield on any investment is the interest rate that will make the present value of the cash flows from the investment equal to the initial cost (price) of the investment. Mathematically the yield on any investment, represented by r, is the interest rate that satisfies equation (1.20) below, which is simply the bond price equation we have already reviewed.

$$P = \sum_{n=1}^{N} \left(\frac{C_n}{(1 + r)^n} \right) \tag{1.20}$$

But as we have noted there are other types of yield measure used in the market for different purposes. The simplest measure of the yield on a bond is the *current yield*, also know as the *flat yield, interest yield* or *running yield*. The running yield is given by (1.21).

$$rc = \frac{C}{P} \times 100 \qquad \frac{5}{100} \times 100 = 5\ PCT. \tag{1.21}$$

where rc is the current yield.

In (1.21) C is not expressed as a decimal. Current yield ignores any capital gain or loss that might arise from holding and trading a bond and does not consider the time value of money. It essentially calculates the bond coupon income as a proportion of the price paid for the bond, and to be accurate would have to assume that the bond was more like an annuity rather than a fixed-term instrument.

The current yield is useful as a 'rough-and-ready' interest rate calculation; it is often used to estimate the cost of or profit from a short-term holding of a bond. For example, if other short-term interest rates such as the one-week or three-month rates are higher than the current yield, holding the bond is said to involve a *running cost*. This is also known as *negative carry* or *negative funding*. The term is used by bond traders and market makers and *leveraged* investors. The *carry* on a bond is a useful measure for all market practitioners as it illustrates the cost of holding or *funding* a bond. The funding rate is the bondholder's short-term cost of funds. A private investor could also apply this to a short-term holding of bonds.

The *yield to maturity* or *gross redemption* yield is the most frequently used measure of return from holding a bond.[4] Yield to maturity (YTM) takes into account the pattern of coupon payments, the bond's term to maturity and the capital gain (or loss) arising over

---

[4] In this book the terms *yield to maturity* and *gross redemption yield* are used synonymously. The latter term is encountered in sterling markets.

the remaining life of the bond. We saw from our bond price formula in the previous section that these elements were all related and were important components determining a bond's price. If we set the IRR for a set of cash flows to be the rate that applies from a start-date to an end-date we can assume the IRR to be the YTM for those cash flows. The YTM therefore is equivalent to the *internal rate of return* on the bond, the rate that equates the value of the discounted cash flows on the bond to its current price. The calculation assumes that the bond is held until maturity and therefore it is the cash flows to maturity that are discounted in the calculation. It also employs the concept of the time value of money.

As we would expect the formula for YTM is essentially that for calculating the price of a bond. For a bond paying annual coupons the YTM is calculated by solving equation (1.11). Note that the expression at (1.11) has two variable parameters, the price P and yield r. It cannot be rearranged to solve for yield r explicitly and in fact the only way to solve for the yield is to use numerical iteration. The process involves estimating a value for r and calculating the price associated with the estimated yield. If the calculated price is higher than the price of the bond at the time, the yield estimate is lower than the actual yield, and so it must be adjusted until it converges to the level that corresponds with the bond price.[5] For the YTM of a semi-annual coupon bond we have to adjust the formula to allow for the semi-annual payments, shown at (1.13).

To differentiate redemption yield from other yield and interest rate measures described in this book, we henceforth refer to it as *rm*.

EXAMPLE *1.4 Yield to maturity for semi-annual coupon bond*

A semi-annual paying bond has a dirty price of £98.50, an annual coupon of 6% and there is exactly one year before maturity. The bond therefore has three remaining cash flows, comprising two coupon payments of £3 each and a redemption payment of £100. Equation (1.13) can be used with the following inputs:

$$9850 = \frac{3.00}{\left(1 + \frac{1}{2}\, rm\right)} + \frac{103.00}{\left(1 + \frac{1}{2}\, rm\right)^2}$$

Note that we use half of the YTM value *rm* because this is a semi-annual paying bond. The expression above is a quadratic equation, which is solved using the standard solution for quadratic equations, which is noted below.

---

[5] Bloomberg also uses the term *yield-to-workout* where 'workout' refers to the maturity date for the bond.

$$ax^2 + bx + c = 0$$

$$x = \frac{-b \pm \sqrt{b^2 - 4ac}}{2a}$$

In our expression if we let $x = (1 + rm/2)$, we can rearrange the expression as follows:

$$98.50x^2 - 3.0x - 103.00 = 0$$

We then solve for a standard quadratic equation, and as such there will be two solutions, only one of which gives a positive redemption yield. The positive solution is $rm/2 = 0.037929$ so that $rm = 7.5859\%$.

As an example of the iterative solution method, suppose that we start with a trial value for rm of $r_1 = 7\%$ and plug this into the right-hand side of equation (1.13). This gives a value for the right-hand side of:

$$\text{RHS}_1 = 99.050$$

which is higher than the left-hand side (LHS = 98.50); the trial value for rm was therefore too low. Suppose then that we try next $r_2 = 8\%$ and use this as the right-hand side of the equation. This gives:

$$\text{RHS}_2 = 98.114$$

which is lower than the LHS. Because RHS_1 and RHS_2 lie on either side of the LHS value we know that the correct value for rm lies between 7% and 8%. Using the formula for linear interpolation,

$$rm = r_1 + (r_2 - r_1) \frac{\text{RHS}_1 - \text{LHS}}{\text{RHS}_1 - \text{RHS}_2}$$

our linear approximation for the redemption yield is $rm = 7.587\%$, which is near the exact solution.

Note that the redemption yield as calculated as discussed in this section is the *gross redemption yield,* the yield that results from payment of coupons without deduction of any withholding tax. The *net redemption yield* is obtained by multiplying the coupon rate C by (1 − marginal tax rate). The net yield is what will be received if the bond is traded in a market where bonds pay coupon *net*, which means net of a withholding tax. The net redemption yield is always lower than the gross redemption yield.

We have already alluded to the key assumption behind the YTM calculation, namely that the rate rm remains stable for the entire period of the life of the bond. By assuming the same yield we can say that all coupons are reinvested at the same yield *rm*. For the bond in example 1.4, this means that if all the cash flows are discounted at 7.59% they will have a total net present value of 98.50. This is patently unrealistic since we can predict with virtual certainty that interest rates for instruments of similar maturity to the bond at each coupon date will not remain at this rate for the life of the bond. In practice, however, investors require a rate of return that is equivalent to the price that they are paying for a bond and the redemption yield is, to put it simply, as good a measurement as any. A more accurate measurement might be to calculate present values of future cash flows using the discount rate that is equal to the markets view on where interest rates will be at that point, known as the *forward* interest rate. However, forward rates are *implied* interest rates, and a YTM measurement calculated using forward rates can be as speculative as one calculated using the conventional formula. This is because the *actual* market interest rate at any time is invariably different from the rate implied earlier in the forward markets. So a YTM calculation made using forward rates would not be realized in practice either.[6] We shall see later how the *zero-coupon* interest rate is the true interest rate for any term to maturity, however the YTM is, despite the limitations presented by its assumptions, the main measure of return used in the markets.

We have noted the difference between calculating redemption yield on the basis of both annual and semi-annual coupon bonds. Analysis of bonds that pay semi-annual coupons incorporates semi-annual discounting of semi-annual coupon payments. This is appropriate for most UK and US bonds. However, government bonds in most of continental Europe and most Eurobonds pay annual coupon payments, and the appropriate method of calculating the redemption yield is to use annual discounting. The two yields measures are not therefore directly comparable. We could make a Eurobond directly comparable with a UK gilt by using semi-annual discounting of the Eurobond's annual coupon payments. Alternatively we could make the gilt comparable with the Eurobond by using annual discounting of its semi-annual coupon payments. The price/yield formulae for different discounting possibilities we encounter in the markets are listed below (as usual we assume that the calculation takes place on a coupon payment date so that accrued interest is zero).

Semi-annual discounting of annual payments:

$$P_d = \frac{C}{(1 + \frac{1}{2}rm)^2} + \frac{C}{(1 + \frac{1}{2}rm)^4} + \frac{C}{(1 + \frac{1}{2}rm)^6} + \ldots + \frac{C}{(1 + \frac{1}{2}rm)^{2N}} + \frac{M}{(1 + \frac{1}{2}rm)^{2N}} \quad (1.22)$$

Annual discounting of semi-annual payments:

$$P_d = \frac{C/2}{(1 + rm)^{1/2}} + \frac{C/2}{(1 + rm)} + \frac{C/2}{(1 + rm)^{3/2}} + \ldots + \frac{C/2}{(1 + rm)^N} + \frac{M}{(1 + rm)^N} \quad (1.23)$$

---

[6] Such an approach is used to price interest-rate swaps, however.

Consider a bond with a dirty price of 97.89, a coupon of 6% and five years to maturity. This bond would have the following gross redemption yields under the different yield calculation conventions:

Discounting	Payments	Yield to maturity (%)
Semi-annual	Semi-annual	6.500
Annual	Annual	6.508
Semi-annual	Annual	6.428
Annual	Semi-annual	6.605

This proves what we have already observed, namely that the coupon and discounting frequency will impact the redemption yield calculation for a bond. We can see that increasing the frequency of discounting will lower the yield, while increasing the frequency of payments will raise the yield. When comparing yields for bonds that trade in markets with different conventions it is important to convert all the yields to the same calculation basis.

Intuitively we might think that doubling a semi-annual yield figure will give us the annualized equivalent; in fact this will result in an inaccurate figure due to the multiplicative effects of discounting and one that is an underestimate of the true annualized yield. The correct procedure for producing an annualized yield from semi-annual and quarterly yields is given by the expressions below.

The general conversion expression is given by (1.24):

$$rm_a = (1 + \text{interest rate})^m - 1 \tag{1.24}$$

where m is the number of coupon payments per year.

Specifically we can convert between yields using the expressions given at (1.25) and (1.26).

$$rm_a = \left[(1 + \tfrac{1}{2}rm_s)^2 - 1\right]$$
$$rm_s = \left[(1 + rm_a)^{\frac{1}{2}} - 1\right] \times 2 \tag{1.25}$$

$$rm_a = \left[(1 + \tfrac{1}{4}rm_q)^4 - 1\right]$$
$$rm_q = \left[(1 + rm_a)^{\frac{1}{4}} - 1\right] \times 4 \tag{1.26}$$

where rm_q, rm_s and rm_a are respectively the quarterly, semi-annually and annually compounded yields to maturity.

EXAMPLE *1.5*

A UK gilt paying semi-annual coupons and a maturity of 10 years has a quoted yield of 4.89%. A European government bond of similar maturity is quoted at a yield of 4.96%. Which bond has the higher effective yield?

The effective annual yield of the gilt is:

$$rm = (1 + \tfrac{1}{2} \cdot 0.0489)^2 - 1 = 4.9498\%$$

Therefore the gilt does indeed have the lower yield.

The market convention is sometimes simply to double the semi-annual yield to obtain the annualized yields, despite the fact that this produces an inaccurate result. It is only acceptable to do this for rough calculations. An annualized yield obtained by multiplying the semi-annual yield by two is known as a *bond equivalent yield*.

While yield to maturity (YTM) is the most commonly used measure of yield, it has one major disadvantage. The disadvantage is that implicit in the calculation of the YTM is the assumption that each coupon payment as it becomes due is reinvested at the rate *rm*. This is clearly unlikely, due to the fluctuations in interest rates over time and as the bond approaches maturity. In practice, the measure itself will not equal the actual return from holding the bond, even if it is held to maturity. That said, the market standard is to quote bond returns as yields to maturity, bearing the key assumptions behind the calculation in mind.

Another disadvantage of the yield to maturity measure of return is where investors do not hold bonds to maturity. The redemption yield will not be of great use where the bond is not being held to redemption. Investors might then be interested in other measures of return, which we can look at later.

To reiterate then, the redemption yield measure assumes that:

■ the bond is held to maturity;

■ all coupons during the bond's life are reinvested at the same (redemption yield) rate.

Therefore the YTM can be viewed as an *expected* or *anticipated* yield and is closest to reality perhaps where an investor buys a bond on first issue and holds it to maturity. Even then the actual realized yield on maturity would be different from the YTM figure because of the inapplicability of the second condition above.

In addition, as coupons are discounted at the yield specific for each bond, it actually becomes inaccurate to compare bonds using this yield measure. For instance the coupon cash flows that occur in two years' time from both a two-year and five-year bond will be discounted at different rates (assuming we do not have a flat yield curve). This would occur because the YTM for a five-year bond is invariably different to the YTM for a two-year bond. However it would clearly not be correct to discount a two-year cash flow at different rates, because we can see that the present value calculated today of a cash flow in two years' time should be the same whether it is sourced from a short- or long-dated bond. Even if the first condition noted above for the YTM calculation is satisfied, it is clearly unlikely for any but the shortest maturity bond that all coupons will be reinvested at the same rate. Market interest rates are in a state of constant flux and hence this would affect money reinvestment rates. Therefore although yield to maturity is the main market measure of bond levels, it is not a true interest rate. This is an important result and we shall explore the concept of a true interest rate in Chapter 2.

Accrued interest, clean and dirty bond prices

Our discussion of bond pricing up to now has ignored coupon interest. All bonds (except zero-coupon bonds) accrue interest on a daily basis, and this is then paid out on the coupon date. The calculation of bond prices using present value analysis does not account for coupon interest or *accrued interest*. In all major bond markets the convention is to quote price as a *clean price*. This is the price of the bond as given by the net present value of its cash flows, but excluding coupon interest that has accrued on the bond since the last dividend payment. As all bonds accrue interest on a daily basis, even if a bond is held for only one day, interest will have been earned by the bondholder. However we have referred already to a bond's *all-in* price, which is the price that is actually paid for the bond in the market. This is also known as the *dirty price* (or *gross price*), which is the clean price of a bond plus accrued interest. In other words the accrued interest must be added to the quoted price to get the total consideration for the bond.

Accruing interest compensates the seller of the bond for giving up all of the next coupon payment even though he will have held the bond for part of the period since the last coupon payment. The clean price for a bond will move with changes in market interest rates; assuming that this is constant in a coupon period, the clean price will be constant for this period. However the dirty price for the same bond will increase steadily from one interest payment date until the next one. On the coupon date the clean and dirty prices are the same and the accrued interest is zero. Between the coupon payment date and the next *ex dividend* date the bond is traded *cum dividend*, so that the buyer gets the next coupon payment. The seller is compensated for not receiving the next coupon payment by receiving accrued interest instead. This is positive and increases up to the next ex dividend date, at which point the dirty price falls by the present value of the amount of the coupon payment. The dirty price at this point is below the clean price, reflecting the fact that accrued interest is now negative. This is because after the ex dividend date the bond is traded 'ex dividend'; the seller not the buyer receives the next coupon and the buyer has to be compensated for not receiving the next coupon by means of a lower price for holding the bond.

The net interest accrued since the last ex dividend date is determined as follows:

$$AI = C \times \left[\frac{N_{xt} - N_{xc}}{\text{DayBase}} \right] \tag{1.27}$$

where:

AI	is the next accrued interest;
C	is the bond coupon;
N_{xc}	is the number of days between the *ex dividend* date and the coupon payment date (7 business days for UK gilts);
N_{xt}	is the number of days between the *ex dividend* date and the date for the calculation;
Day Base	is the day count base (365 or 360).

Interest accrues on a bond from and including the last coupon date up to and excluding what is called the *value date*. The value date is almost but not quite always the *settlement* date for the bond, or the date when a bond is passed to the buyer and the seller receives payment. Interest does not accrue on bonds whose issuer has subsequently gone into default. Bonds that trade without accrued interest are said to be trading *flat* or *clean*. By definition therefore:

clean price of a bond = dirty price − accrued interest.

For bonds that are trading ex-dividend, the accrued coupon is negative and would be subtracted from the clean price. The calculation is given by (1.28) below.

$$AI = -C \times \frac{\text{days to } \textit{next} \text{ coupon}}{\text{Day Base}} \qquad (1.28)$$

Certain classes of bonds, for example US Treasuries and Eurobonds, do not have an *ex dividend* period and therefore trade *cum dividend* right up to the coupon date.

The accrued interest calculation for a bond is dependent on the day-count basis specified for the bond in question. When bonds are traded in the market the actual consideration that changes hands is made up of the clean price of the bond together with *the accrued interest* that has accumulated on the bond since the last coupon payment; these two components make up the dirty price of the bond. When calculating the accrued interest, the market will use the appropriate day-count convention for that bond. A particular market will apply one of five different methods to calculate accrued interest; these are:

- actual/365   Accrued = Coupon × days/365;
- actual/360   Accrued = Coupon × days/360;
- actual/actual Accrued = Coupon × days/actual number of days in the interest period;
- 30/360   (see below);
- 30E/360   (see below).

When determining the number of days in between two dates, include the first date but not the second; thus, under the actual/365 convention, there are 37 days between 4 August and 10 September. The last two conventions assume 30 days in each month, so for example there are '30 days' between 10 February and 10 March. Under the 30/360 convention, if the first date falls on the 31st, it is changed to the 30th of the month, and if the second date falls on the 31st *and* the first date is on the 30th or 31st, the second date is changed to the 30th. The difference under the 30E/360 method is that if the second date falls on the 31st of the month it is automatically changed to the 30th.

Van Deventer (1997) presents an effective critique of the accrued interest concept, believing essentially that is an arbitrary construct that has little basis in economic reality. He states:

'The amount of accrued interest bears no relationship to the current level of interest rates.'

(Van Deventer, 1997, p.11)

This is quite true, the accrued interest on a bond that it is traded in the secondary market at any time is not related to the current level of interest rates, and is the same irrespective of where current rates are. As example 1.6 makes clear, the accrued interest on a bond is a function of its coupon, which reflects the level of interest rates at the time the bond was issued. Accrued interest is therefore an accounting concept only, but at least it serves to recompense the holder for interest earned during the period the bond was held. It is conceivable that the calculation could be adjusted for present value, but at the moment accrued interest is the convention that is followed in the market.

EXAMPLE *1.6 Accrual calculation for 7% Treasury 2002*

This gilt has coupon dates of 7 June and 7 December each year. £100 nominal of the bond is traded for value 27 August 1998. What is accrued interest on the value date?

On the value date 81 days has passed since the last coupon date. Under the old system for gilts, act/365, the calculation was:

$$7 \times \frac{81}{365} = 1.55342$$

Under the current system of act/act, which came into effect for gilts in November 1998, the accrued calculation uses the actual number of days between the two coupon dates, giving us:

$$7 \times \frac{81}{183} \times 0.5 = 1.54918$$

EXAMPLE *1.7*

Mansur buys £25,000 nominal of the 7% 2002 gilt for value on 27 August 1998, at a price of 102.4375. How much does he actually pay for the bond?

The clean price of the bond is 102.4375. The dirty price of the bond is:

102.4375 + 1.55342 = 103.99092

The total consideration is therefore 1.0399092 × 25,000 = £25,997.73

EXAMPLE *1.8*

A Norwegian government bond with a coupon of 8% is purchased for settlement on 30 July 1999 at a price of 99.50. Assume that this is 7 days before the coupon date and therefore the bond trades ex-dividend. What is the all-in price?

The accrued interest $= -8 \times \dfrac{7}{365} = -0.153424$

The all-in price is therefore 99.50 − 0.1534 = 99.3466

EXAMPLE *1.9*

A bond has coupon payments on 1 June and 1 December each year. What is the day-base count if the bond is traded for value date on 30 October, 31 October and 1 November 1999 respectively? There are 183 days in the interest period.

	30 October	*31 October*	*1 November*
Act/365	151	152	153
Act/360	151	152	153
Act/Act	151	152	153
30/360	149	150	151
30E/360	149	150	150

```
<HELP> for explanation.                              DL24 Corp   WB
Screen Printed
    World Bond Markets - Yield Curves
                            Yield: Conventional
```

Country	2yr	5yr	10yr	30yr
1) US Treasury	4.707	4.730	5.093	5.485
2) Canada	5.045	5.184	5.383	5.666
3) UK	5.179	5.166	4.928	4.355
4) France	4.433	4.535	4.935	5.466
5) Germany	4.360	4.484	4.795	5.373
6) Italy	4.499	4.758	5.174	5.815
7) Spain	4.489	4.707	5.121	5.638
8) Sweden	4.205	4.796	4.949	
9) Netherland	4.473	4.584	4.925	5.415
10) Switzerland	3.176	3.166	3.448	3.990
11) Norway	7.076	6.223	5.947	
12) Denmark	4.878	4.914	5.087	5.526
13) Greece	4.541	4.886	5.363	
14) Portugal	4.578	4.771	5.140	
15) Belgium	4.452	4.698	5.158	
16) So. Africa	10.499	11.884	12.590	12.128
17) Austria	4.496	4.723	5.096	5.683
18) Japan	.350	.810	1.530	2.405
19) Australia	5.174	5.032	5.380	
20) New Zealand	6.400	5.900	6.020	

```
Copyright 2000 BLOOMBERG L.P.   Frankfurt:69-920410   Hong Kong:2-977-6000   London:207-330-7500   New York:212-318-2000
Princeton:609-279-3000   Singapore:65-212-1000   Sydney:2-9777-8686   Tokyo:3-3201-8900   Sao Paulo:11-3048-4500
                                                                          I432-212-0 18-Jan-01 15:37:48
```

Bloomberg PROFESSIONAL

FIGURE 1.3 ■ Bloomberg world bond markets – yield curves screen, December 2000

SELECTED BIBLIOGRAPHY AND REFERENCES

Readers are often put off when confronted with a seemingly never-ending list of references. In this book we shall try to limit the book list to only the most essential references, all of which are familiar personally to the author. The following readings are recommended, but there is no need to look up every single one. For a general introduction and accessible account of more difficult topics, Tuckman (1996) is excellent. Sundaresan (1997) presents a high quality overview of the debt markets as a whole, and there is much practical application as well as theoretical treatment. Higson (1995) is a very accessible treatment that places fixed income instruments in the context of the capital markets as a whole, and is also very good for an introduction to financial arithmetic. However, any one book should always be supplemented by one or two Fabozzi titles, the benchmark for excellence in fixed income writing.

Allen, S.L., Kleinstein, A.D., *Valuing Fixed Income Investments and Derivative Securities*, New York Institute of Finance 1991

Fabozzi, F., *Bond Markets, Analysis and Strategies*, Prentice Hall 1989, chapter 2

Fabozzi, F., *Bond Markets, Analysis and Strategies*, 2nd edition, Prentice Hall 1993

Fabozzi, F., *Fixed Income Mathematics*, 3rd edition, McGraw-Hill 1997, pp. 190–192

Fabozzi, F. (ed.), *The Handbook of Fixed Income Securities*, 5th edition, McGraw-Hill 1997

Fabozzi, F., *Valuation of Fixed Income Securities and Derivatives*, 3rd edition, FJF Associates 1998

Fabozzi, F., *Treasury Securities and Derivatives*, FJF Associates 1998

Higson, C., *Business Finance*, Butterworth 1995

Questa, G., *Fixed Income Analysis for the Global Financial Market*, Wiley 1999

Stigum, M., Robinson, F., *Money Market and Bond Calculations*, Irwin 1996

Sundaresan, S., *Fixed Income Markets and their Derivatives*, South-Western 1997

Tuckman, B., *Fixed Income Securities*, Wiley 1996

Van Deventer, D., Imai, K., *Financial Risk Analytics*, Irwin 1997, pp. 9–11

Weston, J.F., Copeland, T.E., *Managerial Finance*, Dryden, 1986

CHAPTER 2

Bond instruments and interest-rate risk

Chapter 1 described the basic concepts in bond pricing. This chapter is really a continuity of the first, but has been placed on its own in order to make Chapter 1 tolerable. Here we discuss the sensitivity of bond prices to changes in market interest rates, the key concepts of duration and convexity.

Duration, modified duration and convexity

Bonds pay a part of their total return during their lifetime, in the form of coupon interest, so that the term to maturity does not reflect the true period over which the bond's return is earned. Additionally if we wish to gain an idea of the trading characteristics of a bond, and compare this to other bonds of say, similar maturity, term to maturity is insufficient and so we need a more accurate measure. A plain vanilla coupon bond pays out a proportion of its return during the course of its life, in the form of coupon interest. If we were to analyze the properties of a bond, we should conclude quite quickly that its maturity gives us little indication of how much of its return is paid out during its life, nor any idea of the timing or size of its cash flows, and hence its sensitivity to moves in market interest rates. For example, if comparing two bonds with the same maturity date but different coupons, the higher coupon bond provides a larger proportion of its return in the form of coupon income than does the lower coupon bond. The higher coupon bond provides its return at a faster rate; its value is theoretically therefore less subject to subsequent fluctuations in interest rates.

We may wish to calculate an average of the time to receipt of a bond's cash flows, and use this measure as a more realistic indication of maturity. However, cash flows during the life of a bond are not all equal in value, so a more accurate measure would be to take the average time to receipt of a bond's cash flows, but weighted in the form of the cash flows' present value. This is, in effect, *duration*. We can measure the speed of payment of a bond, and hence its price risk relative to other bonds of the same maturity by measuring the average maturity of the bond's cash flow stream. Bond analysts use duration to measure this property (it is sometimes known as *Macaulay's duration*, after its inventor, who first introduced it in 1938).[1] Duration is the weighted average time until the receipt of cash flows from a bond, where the weights are the present values of the cash flows, measured in years. At the time that he introduced the concept, Macaulay used the duration measure as an alternative for the length of time that a bond investment had remaining to maturity.

Duration

Recall that the price/yield formula for a plain vanilla bond is as given at (2.1) below, assuming complete years to maturity paying annual coupons, and with no accrued interest at the calculation date. The yield to maturity reverts to the symbol r in this section.

$$P = \frac{C}{(1 + r)} + \frac{C}{(1 + r)^2} + \frac{C}{(1 + r)^3} + ...+ \frac{C}{(1 + r)^n} + \frac{M}{(1 + r)^n} \qquad (2.1)$$

If we take the first derivative of this expression we obtain (2.2).

$$\frac{dP}{dr} = \frac{(-1)C}{(1 + r)^2} + \frac{(-2)C}{(1 + r)^3} + ...+ \frac{(-n)C}{(1 + r)^{n+1}} + \frac{(-n)M}{(1 + r)^{n+1}} \qquad (2.2)$$

If we rearrange (2.2) we will obtain the expression at (2.3), which is our equation to calculate the approximate change in price for a small change in yield.

$$\frac{dP}{dr} = -\frac{1}{(1 + r)}\left[\frac{1C}{(1 + r)} + \frac{2C}{(1 + r)^2} + ...+ \frac{nC}{(1 + r)^n} + \frac{nM}{(1 + r)^n}\right] \qquad (2.3)$$

Readers may feel a sense of familiarity regarding the expression in brackets in equation (2.3) as this is the weighted average time to maturity of the cash flows from a bond, where the weights are, as in our example above, the present values of each cash flow. The expression at (2.3) gives us the approximate measure of the change in price for a small change in yield. If we divide both sides of (2.3) by P we obtain the expression for the approximate percentage price change, given at (2.4).

---

[1] Macaulay, F., *Some theoretical problems suggested by the movements of interest rates, bond yields and stock prices in the United States since 1865*, National Bureau of Economic Research, NY 1938. Although frequently quoted, it is rare to meet someone who has actually read this work. However, it remains a fascinating treatise and is well worth reading; it is available from Risk Classics publishing, under the title *Interest Rates, bond yields and stock prices in the United States since 1856*.

$$\frac{dP}{dr} \frac{1}{P} = -\frac{1}{(1+r)} \left[\frac{1C}{(1+r)} + \frac{2C}{(1+r)^2} +.....+ \frac{nC}{(1+r)n} + \frac{nM}{(1+r)^n} \right] \frac{1}{P} \qquad (2.4)$$

If we divide the bracketed expression in (2.4) by the current price of the bond P we obtain the definition of Macaulay duration, given at (2.5).

$$D = \frac{\frac{1C}{(1+r)} + \frac{2C}{(1+r)^2} +.....+ \frac{nC}{(1+r)^n} + \frac{nM}{(1+r)^n}}{P} \qquad (2.5)$$

Equation (2.5) is simplified using Σ as shown by (2.6).

$$D = \frac{\sum_{n=1}^{N} \frac{nC_n}{(1+r)^n}}{P} \qquad (2.6)$$

where C represents the bond cash flow at time n.

Example 2.1 (overleaf) calculates the Macaulay duration for a hypothetical bond, the 8% 2009 annual coupon bond.

The Macaulay duration value given by (2.6) is measured in years. An interesting observation by Galen Burghardt in *The Treasury Bond Basis* is that, 'measured in years, Macaulay's duration is of no particular use to anyone' (Burghardt, 1994, page 90). This is essentially correct. However, as a risk measure and hedge calculation measure, duration transformed into *modified duration* is the primary measure of interest rate risk used in the markets, and is still widely used despite the advent of the *value-at-risk* measure for market risk.

If we substitute the expression for Macaulay duration (2.5) into equation 2.4 for the approximate percentage change in price we obtain (2.7).

$$\frac{dP}{dr} \frac{1}{P} = -\frac{1}{(1 + r)} D \qquad (2.7)$$

This is the definition of modified duration, given as (2.8).

$$MD = \frac{D}{(1 + r)} \qquad (2.8)$$

Modified duration is clearly related to duration then, in fact we can use it to indicate that, for small changes in yield, a given change in yield results in an inverse change in bond price. We can illustrate this by substituting (2.8) into (2.7), giving us (2.9).

$$\frac{dP}{dr} \frac{1}{P} = -MD \qquad (2.9)$$

EXAMPLE *2.1*

Calculating the Macaulay duration for an 8% 2009 annual coupon bond

Issued	30 September 1999
Maturity	30 September 2009
Price	102.497
Yield	7.634%

TABLE 2.1 ▪ Duration calculation for the 8% 2009 bond

Period (n)	Cash flow	PV at current yield *	n × PV
1	8	7.43260	7.4326
2	8	6.90543	13.81086
3	8	6.41566	19.24698
4	8	5.96063	23.84252
5	8	5.53787	27.68935
6	8	5.14509	30.87054
7	8	4.78017	33.46119
8	8	4.44114	35.529096
9	8	4.12615	37.13535
10	108	51.75222	517.5222
Total		102.49696	746.540686

*Calculated as $C/(1 + r)n$

Macaulay duration = 746.540686/102.497
  = 7.283539998 years

Modified duration = 7.28354/1.07634
  = 6.76695

If we are determining duration long-hand, there is another arrangement we can use to shorten the procedure. Instead of equation (2.1) we use (2.10) as the bond price formula, which calculates price based on a bond being comprised of an annuity stream and a redemption payment, and summing the present values of these two elements. Again we assume an annual coupon bond priced on a date that leaves a complete number of years to maturity and with no interest accrued.

$$P = C\left[\frac{1 - \dfrac{1}{(1 + r)^n}}{r}\right] + \frac{M}{(1 + r)^n}$$

(2.10)

This expression calculates the price of a bond as the present value of the stream of coupon payments and the present value of the redemption payment. If we take the first derivative of (2.10) and then divide this by the current price of the bond P, the result is another expression for the modified duration formula, given at (2.11).

$$MD = \frac{\dfrac{C}{r^2}\left[1 - \dfrac{1}{(1 + r)^n}\right] + \dfrac{n\left(M - \frac{C}{r}\right)}{(1 + r)^{n+1}}}{P} \tag{2.11}$$

We have already shown that modified duration and duration are related; to obtain the expression for Macaulay duration from (2.11) we multiply it by $(1 + r)$. This short-hand formula is demonstrated in example (2.2) for a hypothetical bond, the annual coupon 8% 2009.

EXAMPLE *2.2*

8% 2009 bond: using equation (2.11) for the modified duration calculation

Coupon	8%, annual basis
Yield	7.634%
n	10
Price	102.497

Substituting the above terms into the equation we obtain:

$$MD = \frac{\dfrac{8}{(0.07634^2)}\left[1 - \dfrac{1}{(1.07634)^{10}}\right] + \dfrac{10\left(100 - \dfrac{8}{0.07634}\right)}{(1.07634)^{11}}}{102.497}$$

$MD = 6.76695$

To obtain the Macaulay duration we multiply the modified duration by $(1 + r)$, in this case 1.07634, which gives us a value of 7.28354 years.

For an irredeemable bond duration is given by:

$$D = \frac{1}{rc} \tag{2.12}$$

where $rc = (C/P_d)$ is the *running yield* (or *current yield*) of the bond. This follows from equation (2.6) as $N \to \infty$, recognizing that for an irredeemable bond $r = rc$. Equation (2.12) provides the limiting value to duration. For bonds trading at or above par, duration increases with maturity and approaches this limit from below. For bonds trading at a discount to par duration increases to a maximum at around 18 years and then declines towards the limit given by (2.12). So in general, duration increases with maturity, with an upper bound given by (2.12).

Properties of Macaulay duration

A bond's duration is always less than its maturity. This is because some weight is given to the cash flows in the early years of the bond's life, which brings forward the average time at which cash flows are received. In the case of a zero-coupon bond, there is no present value weighting of the cash flows, for the simple reason that there are no cash flows, and do duration for a zero-coupon bond is equal to its term to maturity. Duration varies with coupon, yield and maturity. The following three factors imply higher duration for a bond:

- the lower the coupon;
- the lower the yield;
- broadly, the longer the maturity.

Duration increases as coupon and yield decrease. As the coupon falls, more of the relative weight of the cash flows is transferred to the maturity date and this causes duration to rise. Because the coupon on index-linked bonds is generally much lower than on vanilla bonds, this means that the duration of index-linked bonds will be much higher than for vanilla bonds of the same maturity. As yield increases, the present values of all future cash flows fall, but the present values of the more distant cash flows fall relatively more than those of the nearer cash flows. This has the effect of increasing the relative weight given to nearer cash flows and hence of reducing duration.

The effect of the coupon frequency

As we have already stated, certain bonds such as Eurobonds pay coupon annually compared to say, gilts which pay semi-annual coupons. Thinking of a duration *fulcrum*, if we imagine that every coupon is divided into two parts, with one part paid a half-period earlier than the other, this will represent a shift in weight to the left, as part of the coupon is paid earlier. Thus increasing the coupon frequency shortens duration, and of course decreasing coupon frequency has the effect of lengthening duration.

Duration as maturity approaches

Using our definition of duration we can see that initially it will decline slowly, and then at a more rapid pace as a bond approaches maturity.

Duration of a portfolio

Portfolio duration is a weighted average of the duration of the individual bonds. The weights are the present values of the bonds divided by the full price of the entire portfolio, and the resulting duration calculation is often referred to as a 'market-weighted' duration. This approach is in effect to the duration calculation for a single bond. Portfolio duration has the same application as duration for a individual bond, and can be used to structure an *immunized* portfolio.

Modified duration

Although it is common for newcomers to the market to think intuitively of duration much as Macaulay originally did, as a proxy measure for the time to maturity of a bond, such an interpretation is to miss the main point of duration, which is a measure of price volatility or interest rate risk.

Using the first term of a Taylor's expansion of the bond price function[2] we can show the following relationship between price volatility and the duration measure, which is expressed as (2.13),

$$\Delta P = -\left[\frac{1}{(1 + r)}\right] \times \text{Macaulay duration} \times \text{Change in yield} \tag{2.13}$$

where r is the yield to maturity for an annual-paying bond (for a semi-annual coupon bond, we use $\frac{r}{2}$). If we combine the first two components of the right-hand side, we obtain the definition of modified duration. Equation (2.13) expresses the approximate percentage change in price as being equal to the modified duration multiplied by the change in yield. We saw in the previous section how the formula for Macaulay duration could be modified to obtain the *modified duration* for a bond. There is a clear relationship between the two measures. From the Macaulay duration of a bond can be derived its modified duration, which gives a measure of the sensitivity of a bond's price to small changes in yield. As we have seen, the relationship between modified duration and duration is given by (2.14).

$$MD = \frac{D}{1 + r} \tag{2.14}$$

where MD is the modified duration in years. However, it also measures the approximate change in bond price for a 1% change in bond yield. For a bond that pays semi-annual coupons, the equation becomes:

---

[2] For an accessible explanation of the Taylor expansion, see Butler, C., *Mastering Value-at-Risk*, FT Prentice Hall, 1998, pp. 112–114.

$$MD = \left(\frac{D}{(1 + \frac{1}{2}r)}\right).$$
(2.15)

This means that the following relationship holds between modified duration and bond prices:

$$\Delta P = MD \times \Delta r \times P.$$
(2.16)

In the UK markets, the term *volatility* is sometimes used to refer to modified duration but this is becoming increasingly uncommon in order to avoid confusion with option markets use of the same term, which there often refers to *implied volatility* and is something different.

EXAMPLE *2.3 Using modified duration*

An 8% annual coupon bond is trading at par with a duration of 2.85 years. If yields rise from 8% to 8.50%, then the price of the bond will fall by:

$$\Delta P = - D \times \frac{\Delta(r)}{1 + r} \times P$$

$$= - (2.85) \times \left(\frac{0.005}{1.080}\right) \times 100$$

$$= - £1,3194$$

That is, the price of the bond will now be £98.6806.
The modified duration of a bond with a duration of 2.85 years and yield of 8% is obviously:

$$MD = \frac{2.85}{1.08}$$

which gives us *MD* equal to 2.537 years.

Consider a five-year 8% annual coupon bond with a duration of 4.31 years, the modified duration can be calculated to be 3.99. This tells us that for a 1% move in the yield to maturity, the price of the bond will move (in the opposite direction) by 3.99%.

We can use modified duration to approximate bond prices for a given yield change. This is illustrated with the following expression introduced above as (2.16):

$$\Delta P = - MD \times (\Delta r) \times P$$
(2.17)

For a bond with a modified duration of 3.99, priced at par, an increase in yield of 1 basis point (100 basis = 1%) leads to a fall in the bond's price of:

$\Delta P = (-3.24 \, / \, 100) \times (+ \, 0.01) \times 100.00$

$\Delta P = £0.0399$, or 3.99 pence

In this case 3.99 pence is the *basis point value* of the bond, which is the change in the bond price given a 1 basis point change in the bond's yield. The basis point value of a bond can be calculated using (2.18).

$$BPV = \frac{MD}{100} \cdot \frac{P}{100} \qquad (2.18)$$

Basis point values (BPVs) are used in hedging bond positions. To hedge a bond position requires an opposite position to be taken in the hedging instrument. So if we are long a 10-year bond, we may wish to sell short a similar 10-year bond as a hedge against it. Similarly a short position in a bond will be hedged through a purchase of an equivalent amount of the hedging instrument. In fact there are a variety of hedging instruments available, both on- and off-balance sheet. Once the hedge is put on, any loss in the primary position should in theory be offset by a gain in the hedge position, and vice versa. The objective of a hedge is to ensure that the price change in the primary instrument is equal to the price change in the hedging instrument. If we are hedging a position with another bond, we use the BPVs of each bond to calculate the amount of the hedging instrument required. This is important because each bond will have different BPVs, so that to hedge a long position in say £1 million nominal of a 30-year bond does not mean we simply sell £1 million of another 30-year bond. This is because the BPVs of the two bonds will almost certainly be different. Also there may not be another 30-year bond in that particular bond. What if we have to hedge with a 10-year bond? How much nominal of this bond would be required?

We need to know the ratio given at (2.19) to calculate the nominal hedge position,

$$\frac{BPV_p}{BPV_b} \qquad (2.19)$$

where

BPV_p is the basis point value of the primary bond (the position to be hedged);

BPV_b is the basis point value of the hedging instrument.

The *hedge ratio* is used to calculate the size of the hedge position and is given at (2.20).

$$\frac{BPV_p}{BPV_b} \times \frac{\text{Change in yield for primary bond position}}{\text{Change in yield for hedge instrument}} \qquad (2.20)$$

The second ratio in (2.20) is known as the *yield beta*.

Example 2.4 illustrates using the hedge ratio.

EXAMPLE *2.4 Calculating hedge size using basis point value*

A trader holds a long position of £1 million of the 8% 2019 bond. The modified duration of the bond is 11.14692 and its price is 129.87596. The basis point value of this bond is therefore 0.14477. The trader decides, to protect against a rise in interest rates, to hedge the position using the 0% 2009 bond, which has a BPV of 0.05549. If we assume that the yield beta is 1, what nominal value of the zero-coupon bond must be sold in order to hedge the position?

The hedge ratio is:

$$\frac{0.14477}{0.05549} \times 1 = 2.60894.$$

Therefore to hedge £1 million of the 20-year bond the trader shorts £2,608,940 of the zero-coupon bond. If we use the respective BPVs to see the net effect of a 1 basis point rise in yield, the loss on the long position is approximately equal to the gain in the hedge position.

EXAMPLE *2.5 The nature of the modified duration approximation*

Table 2.2 ■ Nature of the modified duration approximation

Bond	Maturity (years)	Modified duration	Price duration of basis point	Yield									
				6.00%	6.50%	7.00%	7.50%	7.99%	8.00%	8.01%	8.50%	9.00%	10.00%
8% 2009	10	6.76695	0.06936	114.72017	110.78325	107.02358	103.43204	100.0671311	100.00000	99.932929	96.71933	93.58234	87.71087

Yield change	Price change	Estimate using price duration
down 1 bp	0.06713	0.06936
up 1 bp	0.06707	0.06936
down 200 bp	14.72017	13.872
up 200 bp	12.28913	13.872

Table 2.2 shows the change in price for one of our hypothetical bonds, the 8% 2009, for a selection of yields. We see that for a 1 basis point change in yield, the change in price given by the dollar duration figure, while not completely accurate, is a reasonable estimation of the actual change in price. For a large move however, say 200 basis points, the approximation is significantly in error and analysts would not use it. Notice also for our hypothetical bond how the dollar duration value, calculated from the modified duration measurement, underestimates the change in price resulting from a fall in yields but overestimates the price change for a rise in yields. This is a reflection of the price/yield relationship for this bond. Some bonds will have a more pronounced convex relationship between price and yield and the modified duration calculation will underestimate the price change resulting from both a fall or a rise in yields.

Convexity

Duration can be regarded as a first-order measure of interest rate risk: it measures the *slope* of the present value/yield profile. It is, however, only an approximation of the actual change in bond price given a small change in yield to maturity. Similarly for modified duration, which describes the price sensitivity of a bond to small changes in yield. However as figure 2.1 illustrates, the approximation is an underestimate of the actual price at the new yield. This is a weakness of the duration measure.

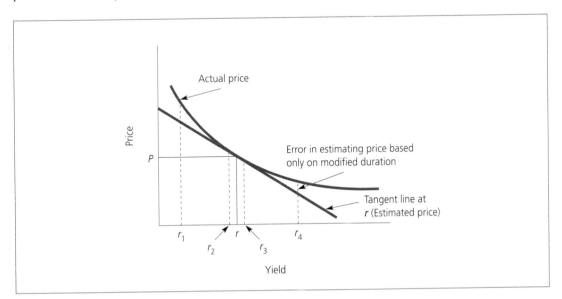

FIGURE 2.1 ■ Approximation of the bond price change using modified duration

Convexity is a second-order measure of interest rate risk; it measures the *curvature* of the present value/yield profile. Convexity can be regarded as an indication of the error we make when using duration and modified duration, as it measures the degree to which the curvature of a bond's price/yield relationship diverges from the straight-line estimation. The convexity of a bond is positively related to the dispersion of its cash flows thus, other things being equal, if one bond's cash flows are more spread out in time than another's, then it will have a higher *dispersion* and hence a higher convexity. Convexity is also positively related to duration.

The second-order differential of the bond price equation with respect to the redemption yield *r* is:

$$\frac{\Delta P}{P} = \frac{1}{P}\frac{\Delta P}{\Delta r}(\Delta r) + \frac{1}{2P}\frac{\Delta^2 P}{\Delta r^2}(\Delta r)^2 \tag{2.21}$$

$$= -MD(\Delta r) = \frac{CV}{2}(\Delta r)^2$$

where *CV* is the convexity.

From equation (2.21), convexity is the rate at which price variation to yield changes with respect to yield. That is, it describes a bond's modified duration changes with respect to changes in yield. It can be approximated by expression (2.22).

$$CV = 10^8 \left(\frac{\Delta P'}{P} + \frac{\Delta P''}{P} \right) \tag{2.22}$$

where:

$\Delta P'$ is the change in bond price if yield increases by 1 basis point (0.01);
$\Delta P''$ is the change in bond price if yield decreases by 1 basis point (0.01).

Appendix 2.2 provides the mathematical derivation of the formula.

EXAMPLE *2.6*

A 5 per cent annual coupon is trading at par with three years to maturity. If the yield increases from 5.00 to 5.01 per cent, the price of the bond will fall (using the bond price equation) to:

$$P'_d = \frac{5}{(0.0501)}\left[1 - \frac{1}{(1.0501)^3}\right] + \frac{100}{(1.0501)^3}$$
$$= 99.97277262$$

or by $\Delta P'_d = -0.02722738$. If the yield falls to 4.99 per cent, the price of the bond will rise to:

$$P''_d = \frac{5}{(0.0499)}\left[1 - \frac{1}{(1.0499)^3}\right] + \frac{100}{(1.0499)^3}$$

$$= 100.02723695$$

or by $\Delta P''_d = 0.02723695$. Therefore

$$CV = 10^8\left(\frac{-0.02722738}{100} + \frac{0.02723695}{100}\right)$$

$$= 9.57,$$

that is, a convexity value of approximately 9.57.

The unit of measurement for convexity using (2.22) is the number of interest periods. For annual coupon bonds this is equal to the number of years; for bonds paying coupon on a different frequency we use (2.23) to convert the convexity measure to years.

$$CV_{years} = \frac{CV}{C^2} \tag{2.23}$$

The convexity measure for a zero-coupon bond is given by (2.24).

$$CV = \frac{n(n+1)}{(1+r)^2} \tag{2.24}$$

Convexity is a second-order approximation of the change in price resulting from a change in yield. This is given by (2.21), reproduced below for convenience:

$$\Delta P = \tfrac{1}{2} \times CV \times (\Delta r)^2 \tag{2.25}$$

The reason we multiply the convexity by $\tfrac{1}{2}$ to obtain the convexity adjustment is because the second term in the Taylor expansion contains the coefficient $\tfrac{1}{2}$. The convexity approximation is obtained from a Talyor expansion of the bond price formula. An illustration of Taylor expansion of the bond price/yield equation is given at Appendix 2.3.

The formula is the same for a semi-annual coupon bond.

Note that the value for convexity given by the expressions above will always be positive, that is the approximate price change due to convexity is positive for both yield increases and decreases.

EXAMPLE *2.7 Second-order interest risk rate*

A 5 per cent annual coupon bond is trading at par with a modified duration of 2.639 and convexity of 9.57. If we assume a significant market correction and yields rise from 5 to 7 per cent, the price of the bond will fall by:

$$\Delta P_d = -MD \times (\Delta r) \times P_d + \frac{CV}{2} \times (\Delta r)^2 \times P_d$$

$$= -(2.639) \times (0.02) \times 100 + \frac{9.57}{2} \times (0.02)^2 \times 100$$

$$= -5.278 + 0.1914$$

$$= -£5.0866$$

to £94.9134. The first-order approximation, using the modified duration value of 2.639, is −£5.278, which is an overestimation of the fall in price by £0.1914.

EXAMPLE *2.8*

The 5% 2009 bond is trading at a price of £96.23119 (a yield of 5.50%) and has precisely 10 years to maturity. If the yield rises to 7.50%, a change of 200 basis points, the percentage price change due to the convexity effect is given by:

$(0.5) \times 96.23119 \times (0.02)^2 \times 100 = 1.92462\%$

If we use an HP calculator to find the price of the bond at the new yield of 7.50% we see that it is £82.83980, a change in price of 13.92%. The convexity measure of 1.92462% is an approximation of the error we would make when using the modified duration value to estimate the price of the bond following the 200 basis point rise in yield.

If the yield of the bond were to fall by 200 basis points, the convexity effect would be the same, as given by the expression at (2.25).

In example 2.8 we saw that the price change estimated using modified duration will be quite inaccurate, and that the convexity measure is the approximation of the size of the inaccuracy. The magnitude of the price change as estimated by both duration and convexity is obtained by summing the two values. However, it only makes any significant difference if the change in yield is very large. If we take our hypothetical bond again, the 5% 2009 bond, its modified duration is 7.64498. If the yield rises by 200 basis points, the approximation of the price change given by modified duration and convexity is:

Modified duration   = 7.64498 × 2   = –15.28996
Convexity   = 1.92462

Note that the modified duration is given as a negative value, because a rise in yields results in a fall in price. This gives us a net percentage price change of 13.36534. As we saw in example 2.8, the actual percentage price change is 13.92%. So in fact using the convexity adjustment has given us a noticeably more accurate estimation. Let us examine the percentage price change resulting from a fall in yields of 1.50% from the same starting yield of 5.50%. This is a decrease in yield of 150 basis points, so our convexity measurement needs to be re-calculated. The convexity value is:

$$(0.5) \times 96.23119 \times (0.0150)^2 \times 100 = 1.0826\%$$

So the price change is based on:

Modified duration   = 7.64498 × 1.5   = 11.46747
Convexity   = 1.0826

This gives us a percentage price change of 12.55007. The actual price change was 10.98843%, so here the modified duration estimate is actually closer! This illustrates that the convexity measure is effective for larger yield changes only; example 2.9 shows us that for very large changes, a closer approximation for bond price volatility is given by combining the modified duration and convexity measures.

EXAMPLE 2.9

The hypothetical bond is the 5% 2009, again trading at a yield of 5.50% and priced at 96.23119. If the yield rises to 8.50%, a change of 300 basis points, the percentage price change due to the convexity effect is given by:

$$(0.5) \times 96.23119 \times (0.03)^2 \times 100 = 4.3304\%$$

Meanwhile as before the modified duration of the bond at the initial yield is 7.64498. At the new yield of 8.50% the price of the bond is 77.03528 (check using an HP calculator).

The price change can be approximated using:

Modified duration   = 7.64498 × 3.0   = –22.93494
Convexity   = 4.3304

This gives a percentage price change of 18.60454%. The actual percentage price change was 19.9477%, but our estimate is still closer than that obtained using only the modified duration measure. The continuing error reflects the fact that convexity is also a dynamic measure and changes with yield changes; the effect of a large yield movement compounds the inaccuracy given by convexity.

Convexity is an attractive property for a bond to have. What level of premium will be attached to a bond's higher convexity? This is a function of the current yield levels in the market as well as market volatility. Remember that modified duration and convexity are functions of yield level, and that the effect of both is magnified at lower yield levels. As well as the relative level, investors will value convexity higher if the current market conditions are volatile. The cash effect of convexity is noticeable only for large moves in yield. If an investor expects market yields to move only by relatively small amounts, he will attach a lower value to convexity; and vice versa for large movements in yield. Therefore the yield premium attached to a bond with higher convexity will vary according to market expectations of the future size of interest rate changes.

The convexity measure increases with the square of maturity, and it decreases with both coupon and yield. As the measure is a function of modified duration, index-linked bonds have greater convexity than conventional bonds. We discussed how the price/yield profile will be more convex for a bond of higher convexity, and that such a bond will outperform a bond of lower convexity whatever happens to market interest rates. High convexity is therefore a desirable property for bonds to have. In principle, a more convex bond should fall in price less than a less convex one when yields rise, and rise in price more when yields fall. That is, convexity can be equated with the potential to outperform. Thus other things being equal, the higher the convexity of a bond the more desirable it should in principle be to investors. In some cases investors may be prepared to accept a bond with a lower yield in order to gain convexity. We noted also that convexity is in principle of more value if uncertainty, and hence expected market volatility, is high, because the convexity effect of a bond is amplified for large changes in yield. The value of convexity is therefore greater in volatile market conditions.

For a conventional vanilla bond, convexity is almost always positive. Negative convexity resulting from a bond with a concave price/yield profile would not be an attractive property for a bondholder; the most common occurrence of negative convexity in the cash markets is with callable bonds.

We illustrated that for most bonds, and certainly when the convexity measure is high, the modified duration measurement for interest rate risk becomes more inaccurate for large changes in yield. In such situations it becomes necessary to use the approximation given by our convexity equation, to measure the error we have made in estimating the price change based on modified duration only. The expression was given earlier in this chapter.

The following points highlight the main convexity properties for conventional vanilla bonds.

A fall in yields leads to an increase in convexity

A decrease in bond yield leads to an increase in the bond's convexity; this is a property of positive convexity. Equally a rise in yields leads to a fall in convexity.

For a given term to maturity, higher coupon results in lower convexity

For any given redemption yield and term to maturity, the higher a bond's coupon, the lower its convexity. Therefore among bonds of the same maturity, zero-coupon bonds have the highest convexity.

For a given modified duration, higher coupon results in higher convexity

For any given redemption yield and modified duration, a higher coupon results in a higher convexity. Contrast this with the earlier property; in this case, for bonds of the same modified duration, zero-coupon bonds have the lowest convexity.

APPENDICES

Appendix 2.1: Formal derivation of modified duration measure

Given that duration is defined as:

$$D = \frac{\displaystyle\sum_{n=1}^{N} \frac{nC_n}{(1+r)^n}}{P},$$

(2.1.1)

if we differentiate P with respect to r we obtain:

$$\frac{dP}{dr} = -\sum_{n=1}^{N} nC_n (1+r)^{-n-1}$$

(2.1.2)

Multiplying (2.1.2) by $(1+r)$ we obtain:

$$(1+r)\frac{dP}{dr} = -\sum_{n=1}^{N} nC_n (1+r)^{-n}$$

(2.1.3)

We then divide the expression (2.13) by P giving us:

$$\frac{dP}{dr}\frac{1+r}{P} = -\sum_{n=1}^{N} \frac{nC_n}{(1+r)^n P} = -D.$$

(2.1.4)

Having defined modified duration as $D/(1+r)$ then it can be shown that:

$$-\frac{dP}{dr}\frac{1}{P} = MD$$

(2.1.5)

Therefore modified duration measures the effect on bond price of a change in its yield. The sign in (2.1.5) is negative because of the inverse relationship between bond prices and yields.[3] So if a bond has a modified duration of 4.0, then a rise in yield of 1% means that the price of the bond will fall by 4%. As we discuss in the main text however, this is an approximation only and is progressively more inaccurate for greater changes in yield.

---

[3] That is, rising yields result in falling prices.

Appendix 2.2: Measuring convexity

The modified duration of a plain vanilla bond is:

$$MD = \frac{D}{(1 + r)}$$
(2.2.1)

We know that:

$$\frac{dP}{dr} \frac{1}{P} = - MD$$
(2.2.2)

This shows that for a percentage change in the yield we have an inverse change in the price by the amount of the modified duration value.

If we multiply both sides of (2.2.2) by any particular change in the bond yield, given by dr, we obtain expression (2.2.3).

$$\frac{dP}{P} = - MD \times dr$$
(2.2.3)

Using the first two terms of a Taylor expansion, we obtain an approximation of the bond price change, given by (2.2.4).

$$dP = \frac{dP}{dr} dr + \frac{1}{2} \frac{d^2P}{dr^2} (dr)^2 + \text{approximation error}$$
(2.2.4)

If we divide both sides of (2.2.4) by P to obtain the percentage price change, the result is the expression at (2.2.5)

$$\frac{dP}{P} = \frac{dP}{dr} \frac{1}{P} dr + \frac{1}{2} \frac{d^2P}{dr^2} \frac{1}{P} (dr)^2 + \frac{\text{approximation error}}{P}$$
(2.2.5)

The first component of the right-hand side of (2.2.4) is the expression at (2.2.3), which is the cash price change given by the duration value. Therefore equation (2.2.4) is the approximation of the price change. Equation (2.2.5) is the approximation of the price change as given by the modified duration value. The second component in both expressions is the second derivative of the bond price equation. This second derivative captures the convexity value of the price/yield relationship and is the cash value given by convexity. As such it is referred to as *dollar convexity* in the US markets. The dollar convexity is stated as (2.2.6).

$$CV_{dollar} = \frac{d^2P}{dr^2}$$
(2.2.6)

If we multiply the dollar convexity value by the square of a bond's yield change we obtain the approximate cash value change in price resulting from the convexity effect. This is shown by (2.2.7).

$$dP = (CV_{dollar}) (dr)^2 \tag{2.2.7}$$

If we then divide the second derivative of the price equation by the bond price, we obtain a measure of the percentage change in bond price as a result of the convexity effect. This is the measure known as *convexity* and is the convention used in virtually all bond markets. This is given by the expression at (2.2.8).

$$CV = \frac{d^2P}{dr^2} \frac{1}{P} \tag{2.2.8}$$

To measure the amount of the percentage change in bond price as a result of the convex nature of the price/yield relationship we can use (2.2.9).

$$\frac{dP}{P} = \frac{1}{2} CV (dr)^2 \tag{2.2.9}$$

For long-hand calculations note that the second derivative of the bond price equation is (2.2.10), which can be simplified to (2.2.12). The usual assumptions apply to the expressions, that the bond pays annual coupons and has a precise number of interest periods to maturity. If the bond is a semi-annual paying one the yield value r is replaced by $r/2$.

$$\frac{d^2P}{dr^2} = \sum_{n=1}^{N} \frac{n(n + 1)C}{(1 + r)^{n+2}} + \frac{n(n + 1)M}{(1 + r)^{n+2}} \tag{2.2.10}$$

Alternatively we differentiate to the second order the bond price equation as given by (2.2.11), giving us the alternative expression (2.2.12).

$$P = \frac{C}{r} = \left[1 - \frac{1}{(1 + r)^n}\right] + \frac{100}{(1 + r)^n} \tag{2.2.11}$$

$$\frac{d^2P}{dr^2} = \frac{2C}{r^3} \left[1 - \frac{1}{(1 + r)^n}\right] - \frac{2C}{r^2(1 + r)^{n+1}} + \frac{n(n + 1)(100 - \frac{C}{r})}{(1 + r)^{n+2}} \tag{2.2.12}$$

Appendix 2.3: Taylor expansion of the price/yield function

We summarize the bond price formula as (2.3.1) where C represents all the cash flows from the bond, including the redemption payment.

$$P = \sum_{n=1}^{N} \frac{C_n}{(1 + r)^n} \qquad (2.3.1)$$

We therefore derive the following:

$$\frac{dP}{dr} = - \sum_{n=1}^{N} \frac{C_n \cdot n}{(1 + r)^{n+1}} \qquad (2.3.2)$$

$$\frac{d^2P}{dr^2} = \sum_{n=1}^{N} \frac{C_n \cdot n(n + 1)}{(1 + r)^{n+2}} \qquad (2.3.3)$$

This then gives us:

$$\Delta P = \left[\frac{dP}{dr} \Delta r \right] + \left[\frac{1}{2!} \frac{d^2P}{dr^2} (\Delta r)^2 \right] + \left[\frac{1}{3!} \frac{d^3P}{dr^3} (\Delta r)^3 \right] + \dots \qquad (2.3.4)$$

The first expression in (2.3.4) is the modified duration measure, while the second expression measures convexity. The more powerful the changes in yield, the more expansion is required to approximate the change to greater accuracy. Expression (2.3.4) therefore gives us the equations for modified duration and convexity, shown by (2.3.5) and (2.3.6) respectively.

$$MD = - \frac{dP/dr}{P} \qquad (2.3.5)$$

$$CV = - \frac{d^2P/dr^2}{P} \qquad (2.3.6)$$

We can therefore state the following:

$$\frac{\Delta P}{P} = [-(MD)\Delta r] + [\tfrac{1}{2} (CV)(\Delta r)^2] + \text{residual error} \qquad (2.3.7)$$

$$\Delta P = - [P(MD)\Delta r] + \left[\frac{P}{2} (CV)(\Delta r)^2 \right] + \text{residual error} \qquad (2.3.8)$$

EXAMPLE *2.3.1*

Consider a three-year bond with (annual) coupon of 5% and yield of 5%. At a price of par we have:

$$\frac{dP}{dr} = -\left[\frac{5}{(1.05)^2} + \frac{5(2)}{(1.05)^3} + \frac{105(3)}{(1.05)^4}\right] = 263.9048$$

$$D = \frac{dP}{dr} = \left[\frac{1+r}{P}\right] = 263.9048\left[\frac{1.05}{100}\right] = 2.771$$

$$MD = \frac{2.771}{1.05} = 2.639$$

$$\frac{d^2P}{dr^2} = \left[\frac{5(1)(2)}{(1.05)^3} + \frac{5(2)(3)}{(1.05)^4} + \frac{105(3)(4)}{(1.05)^5}\right] = 957.3179$$

$$CV = \frac{d^2P/dr^2}{P} = \frac{957.3179}{100} = 9.573$$

SELECTED BIBLIOGRAPHY AND REFERENCES

The references given in Chapter 1 are also very useful for duration, modified duration and convexity. Readers nevertheless may wish to have a look at the following texts. Burghardt's book, although on a specialized subject not concentrating on interest-rate risk, nevertheless contains many useful insights and will help assist the reader to develop a deeper understanding of bond instruments; it is an excellent text. The same can be applied to Garbade (1996), another very high-quality work that contains many valuable insights on (among other things) duration, convexity and the practicalities of risk and hedging from a trader's perspective. It is well worth purchasing.

Finally, true *aficionados* may want to take a look at Macaulay (1999), the original work from 1938, now once more available as part of the RISK Classics library and still a fascinating read.

Bierwag, G.O., 'Immunization, duration and the term structure of interest rates,' *Journal of Financial and Quantitative Analysis*, December 1977, pp. 725–741

Bierwag, G.O., 'Measures of duration,' *Economic Inquiry 16*, October 1978, pp. 497–507

Burghardt, G., *The Treasury Bond Basis*, McGraw-Hill 1994

Garbade, K., *Fixed Income Analytics,* MIT Press 1996, chapters 3, 4, 12

Macaulay, F., *The Movements of Interest Rates, Bond Yields and Stock Prices in the United States Since 1856*, RISK Classics Library 1999

CHAPTER 3

Bond pricing, spot and forward rates

In this chapter we present a brief overview of fixed income analysis as it appears in the current literature. Basic concepts are outlined, followed by a discussion of yield curve analysis and the term structure of interest rates.

Basic concepts

We are familiar with two types of fixed income security – *zero-coupon bonds*, also known as *discount bonds* or *strips*, and *coupon bonds*. A zero-coupon bond makes a single payment on its maturity date, while a coupon bond makes regular interest payments at regular dates up to and including its maturity date. A coupon bond may be regarded as a set of strips, with each coupon payment and the redemption payment on maturity being equivalent to a zero-coupon bond maturing on that date. This is not a purely academic concept, witness events before the advent of the formal market in US Treasury strips, when a number of investment banks had traded the cash flows of Treasury securities as separate zero-coupon securities.[1] The literature we review in this section is set in a market of default-free bonds, whether they are zero-coupon bonds or coupon bonds. The market is assumed to be liquid so that bonds may be freely bought and sold. Prices of bonds are determined by the economy-wide supply and demand for the bonds at any time, so they are *macroeconomic* and not set by individual bond issuers or traders.

---

[1] These banks included Merrill Lynch, Lehman Brothers and Salomon Brothers, among others (see Fabozzi 1993). The term 'strips' comes from Separate Trading of Registered Interest and Principal of Securities, the name given when the official market was introduced by the US Treasury. The banks would purchase Treasuries which would then be deposited in a safe custody account. Receipts were issued against each cash flow from each Treasury, and these receipts traded as individual zero-coupon securities. The market making banks earned profit due to the arbitrage difference in the price of the original coupon bond and the price at which the individual strips were sold. The US Treasury formalized trading in strips after 1985, after legislation had been introduced that altered the tax treatment of such instruments. The market in UK gilt strips trading began in December 1997. Strips are also traded in France, Germany, the Netherlands, among other countries.

Zero-coupon bonds

A zero-coupon bond is the simplest fixed income security. It is an issue of debt, the issuer promising to pay the face value of the debt to the bondholder on the date the bond matures. There are no coupon payments during the life of the bond, so it is a discount instrument, issued at a price that is below the face or *principal* amount. We denote as $P(t, T)$ the price of a discount bond at time t that matures at time T, with $T \geq t$. The term to maturity of the bond is denoted with n, where $n = T - t$. The price increases over time until the maturity date when it reaches the maturity or *par* value. If the par value of the bond is £1, then the *yield to maturity* of the bond at time t is denoted by $r(t, T)$, where r is actually 'one plus the percentage yield' that is earned by holding the bond from t to T. We have:

$$P(t, T) = \frac{1}{[r(t, T)]^n} \tag{3.1}$$

The yield may be obtained from the bond price and is given by

$$r(t, T) = \left[\frac{1}{P(t, T)} \right]^{1/n} \tag{3.2}$$

which is sometimes written as

$$r(t, T) = P(t, T)^{-(1/n)} \tag{3.3}$$

Analysts and researchers frequently work in terms of logarithms of yields and prices, or continuously compounded rates. One advantage of this is that it converts the non-linear relationship in (3.2) into a linear relationship.[2]

The bond price at time t_2 where $t \leq t_2 \leq T$ is given by

$$P(t_2, T) = P(t, T)e^{(t_2 - t)r(t, T)} \tag{3.4a}$$

which is natural given that the bond price equation in continuous time is

$$P(t, T) = e^{-r(t, T)(T - t)} \tag{3.4b}$$

so that the yield is given by

---

[2] A linear relationship in X would be a function $Y = f(X)$ in which the X values change via a power or index of 1 only and are not multiplied or divided by another variable or variables. So for example terms such as X^2, $\sqrt{X}$ and other similar functions are not linear in X, nor are terms such as XZ or X/Z where Z is another variable. In econometric analysis, if the value of Y is solely dependent on the value of X, then its rate of change with respect to X, or the derivative of Y with respect to X, denoted dY/dX, is independent of X. Therefore if $Y = 5X$, then $dY/dX = 5$, which is independent of the value of X. However if $Y = 5X^2$, then $dY/dX = 10X$, which is not independent of the value of X. Hence this function is not linear in X. The classic regression function $E(Y | X_i) = \alpha + \beta X_i$ is a linear function with slope β and intercept α and the regression 'curve' is represented geometrically by a straight line.

$$r(t, T) = -\log\left(\frac{P(t, T)}{n}\right) \tag{3.5}$$

which is sometimes written as

$$\log r(t, T) = -\left(\frac{1}{n}\right)\log P(t, T) \tag{3.6}$$

The expression in (3.4) includes the exponential function, hence the use of the term 'continuously compounded'.

The *term structure of interest rates* is the set of zero-coupon yields at time t for all bonds ranging in maturity from $(t, t + 1)$ to $(t, t + m)$ where the bonds have maturities of $\{0, 1, 2, \ldots, m\}$. A good definition of the term structure of interest rates is given in Sundaresan, who states that it

> '… refers to the relationship between the yield to maturity of default-free zero coupon
> securities and their maturities.'   *(Sundaresan, 1997, p. 176)*

The *yield curve* is a plot of the set of yields for $r(t, t + 1)$ to $r(t, t + m)$ against m at time t. For example, figures 3.1–3.3 show the log zero-coupon yield curve for US Treasury strips, UK gilt strips and French OAT strips on 27 September 2000. Each of the curves exhibit peculiarities in their shape, although the most common type of curve is gently upward sloping, as is the French curve. The UK curve is *inverted*. We explore further the shape of the yield curve later in this chapter.

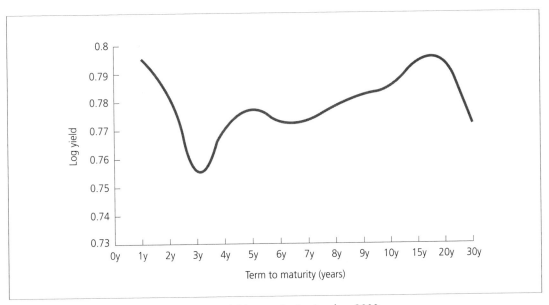

FIGURE 3.1 ▪ US Treasury zero-coupon yield curve in September 2000

Source: Bloomberg

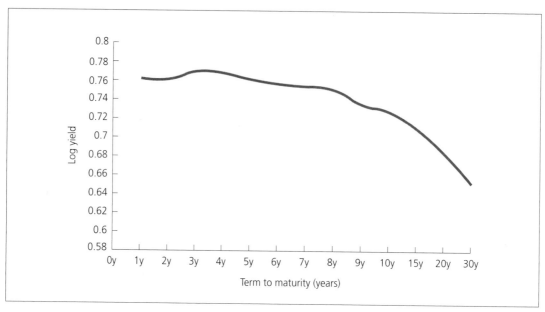

FIGURE 3.2 ■ UK gilt zero-coupon yield curve

Source: Bloomberg

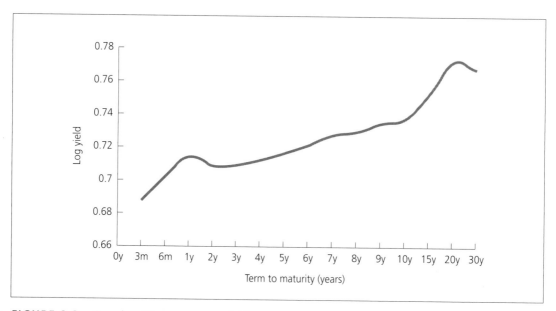

FIGURE 3.3 ■ French OAT zero-coupon yield curve

Source: Bloomberg

Coupon bonds

The majority of bonds in the market make periodic interest or *coupon* payments during their life, and are known as coupon bonds. We have already noted that such bonds may be viewed as a package of individual zero-coupon bonds. The coupons have a nominal value that is a percentage of the nominal value of the bond itself, with steadily longer maturity dates, while the final redemption payment has the nominal value of the bond itself and is redeemed on the maturity date. We denote a bond issued at time i and maturing at time T as having a w-element vector of payment dates $(t_1, t_2, ..., t_{w-1}, T)$ and matching date payments $C_1, C_2, ..., C_{w-1}, C_w$. In the academic literature these coupon payments are assumed to be made in continuous time, so that the stream of coupon payments is given by a positive function of time $C(t)$, $i < t \leq T$. An investor that purchases a bond at time t that matures at time T pays $P(t, T)$ and will receive the coupon payments as long as he continues to hold the bond.[3]

The yield to maturity at time t of a bond that matures at T is the interest rate that relates the price of the bond to the future returns on the bond, that is, the rate that *discounts* the bond's cash flow stream C_w to its price $P(t, T)$. This is given by

$$P(t, T) = \sum_{t_i > t} C_i e^{-(t_i - t)r(t, T)} \tag{3.7}$$

which says that the bond price is given by the present value of the cash flow stream of the bond, discounted at the rate $r(t, T)$. For a zero-coupon bond (3.7) reduces to (3.5). In the academic literature where coupon payments are assumed to be made in continuous time, the $\sum$ summation in (3.7) is replaced by the $\int$ integral. (A very brief overview summary of the integral is given at Appendix 3.1.) We will look at this in a moment.

In some texts, the plot of the yield to maturity at time t for the term of the bonds m is described as the term structure of interest rates but it is generally accepted that the term structure is the plot of zero-coupon rates only. Plotting yields to maturity is generally described as graphically depicting the yield curve, rather than the term structure. Of course, given the law of one price, there is a relationship between the yield to maturity yield curve and the zero-coupon term structure, and given the first one can derive the second.

The expression at (3.7) obtains the continuously compounded yield to maturity $r(t, T)$. It is the use of the exponential function that enables us to describe the yield as continuously compounded.

Earlier we noted that the market frequently uses the measure known as *current yield,* which is

---

[3] In theoretical treatment this is the discounted clean price of the bond. For coupon bonds in practice, unless the bond is purchased for value on a coupon date, it will be traded with interest accrued. The interest that has accrued on a pro-rata basis from the last coupon date is added to the clean price of the bond, to give the market 'dirty' price that is actually paid by the purchaser.

$$rc = \frac{C}{P_d} \times 100 \qquad\qquad (3.8)$$

where P_d is the dirty price of the bond. The measure is also known as the *running yield* or *flat yield*. Current yield is not used to indicate the interest rate or discount rate and therefore should not be mistaken for the yield to maturity.

Bond price in continuous time[4]

Fundamental concepts

In this section we present an introduction to the bond price equation in continuous time. The necessary background on price processes is introduced in Chapter 4, readers will see the logic in this as we introduce term structure modelling there.

Consider a trading environment where bond prices evolve in a *w*-dimensional process

$$X(t) = [X_1(t),\ X_2(t),\ X_3(t),\ .....,\ X_w(t)],\ t > 0 \qquad\qquad (3.9)$$

where the random variables are termed *state variables* that reflect the state of the economy at any point in time. The markets assume that the state variables evolve through a process described as *geometric Brownian motion* or a *Weiner process*. It is therefore possible to model the evolution of these variables, in the form of a stochastic differential equation.

The market assumes that the cash flow stream of assets such as bonds and (for equities) dividends is a function of the state variables. A bond is characterized by its coupon process

$$C(t) = \tilde{C}\,[X_1(t),\ X_2(t),\ X_3(t),\ .....,\ X_w(t),\ t] \qquad\qquad (3.10)$$

The coupon process represents the cash flow that the investor receives during the time that he holds the bond. Over a small incremental increase in time of dt from the time t the investor can purchase $1 + C(t)dt$ units of the bond at the end of the period $t + dt$. Assume that there is a very short-term discount security such as a Treasury bill that matures at $t + dt$, and during this period the investor receives a return of $r(t)$. This rate is the annualized short-term interest rate or *short rate*, which in the mathematical analysis is defined as the rate of interest charged on a loan that is taken out at time t and which matures almost immediately. For this reason, the rate is also known as the *instantaneous rate*. The short rate is given by

---

[4] This section follows the approach adopted in such texts as Avellaneda (2000), Baxter and Rennie (1996), Neftci (2000), Campbell *et al.* (1997), Ross (1999) and Shiller (1990). These are all excellent texts of very high quality, and strongly recommended. For an accessible and highly readable introduction Ross's book is worth buying for chapter 4 alone, as is Avellaneda's for his chapter 12. For a general introduction to the main pricing concepts see Campbell *et al.* (1997), chapter 10. Chapter 3 in Jarrow (1996) is an accessible introduction for discrete-time bond pricing. Sundaresan (1997) is an excellent overview text on the fixed income market as a whole, and is highly recommended. Further recommended references are given in the bibliography.

$$r(t) = r(t, t) \tag{3.11}$$

and

$$r(t) = -\frac{\partial}{\partial T} \log P(t, t) \tag{3.12}$$

With regard to the terminology, let $r(t, s)$ be the continuously compounded interest rate for the term starting at t and of term to maturity s, so that it has a maturity of $t + s$. If the price of a zero-coupon bond of maturity term s is denoted $P(t, t + s)$, then the rate $r(t, s)$ is defined by

$$P(t, t + s) = \exp[-sr(t, s)]. \tag{3.12a}$$

As the time period s approaches zero, the rate $r(t, s)$ becomes the spot rate $r(t, t)$ or $r(t)$. This would then be the continuously compounded interest rate payable on a zero-coupon bond of zero maturity, in other words the rate of interest payable on a borrowing that was repaid instantaneously.

If we continuously reinvest the short-term security such as the T-bill at this short rate, we obtain a cumulative amount that is the original investment multiplied by (3.13).[5]

$$M(t) = \exp\left[\int_t^T r(s)ds\right] \tag{3.13}$$

where M is a money market account that offers a return of the short rate $r(t)$.

If we say that the short rate is constant, making $r(t) = r$, then the price of a risk-free bond that pays £1 on maturity at time T is given by

$$P(t, T) = e^{-r(T-t)} \tag{3.13a}$$

What (3.13a) states is that the bond price is simply a function of the continuously compounded interest rate, with the right-hand side of (3.13a) being the discount factor at time t. At $t = T$ the discount factor will be 1, which is the redemption value of the bond and hence the price of the bond at this time.

Consider the following scenario; a market participant may undertake the following:

■ it can invest $e^{-r(T-t)}$ units cash in a money market account today, which will have grown to a sum of £1 at time T;

■ it can purchase the risk-free zero-coupon bond today, which has a maturity value of £1 at time T.

---

[5] This expression uses the integral operator. The integral is the tool used in mathematics to calculate sums of an infinite number of objects, that is where the objects are uncountable. This is different to the Σ operator which is used for a countable number of objects. For a readable and accessible review of the integral and its use in quantitative finance, see Neftci (2000), pp. 59–66, a summary of which is given at appendix 3.1.

The market participant can invest in either instrument, both of which we know before-hand to be risk-free, and both of which have identical payouts at time T and have no cash flow between now and time T. As interest rates are constant, a bond that paid out £1 at T must have the same value as the initial investment in the money market account, which is $e_t^{-r(T-t)}$. Therefore equation (3.13a) must apply. This is a restriction placed on the zero-coupon bond price by the requirement for markets to be arbitrage-free.

If the bond was not priced at this level, arbitrage opportunities would present them-selves. Consider if the bond was priced higher than $e_t^{-r(T-t)}$. In this case, an investor could sell short the bond and invest the sale proceeds in the money market account. On maturity at time T, the short position will have a value of –£1 (negative, because the investor is short the bond) while the money market will have accumulated £1, which the investor can use to pay the proceeds on the zero-coupon bond. However the investor will have surplus funds because at time t

$$P(t, T) - e^{-r(T-t)} > 0$$

and so will have profited from the transaction at no risk to himself.

The same applies if the bond is priced below $e_t^{-r(T-t)}$. In this case the investor borrows $e_t^{-r(T-t)}$ and buys the bond at its price $P(t, T)$. On maturity the bond pays £1 which is used to repay the loan amount, however the investor will gain because

$$e^{-r(T-t)} - P(t, T) > 0$$

Therefore the only price at which no arbitrage profit can be made is if

$$P(t, T) = \exp^{-r(T-t)} \tag{3.13b}$$

In the academic literature the price of a zero-coupon bond is given in terms of the evolu-tion of the short-term interest rate rate, in what is termed the *risk-neutral measure*.[6] The short rate $r(t)$ is the interest rate earned on a money market account or short-dated risk-free security such as the T-bill suggested above, and it is assumed to be continuously compounded. This makes the mathematical treatment simpler. With a zero-coupon bond we assume a payment on maturity of 1 (say $1 or £1), a one-off cash flow payable on maturity at time T. The value of the zero-coupon bond at time t is therefore given by

$$P(t, T) = \exp\left(-\int_t^T r(s)ds\right) \tag{3.14}$$

which is the redemption value of 1 divided by the value of the money market account, given by (3.13).

The bond price for a coupon bond is given in terms of its yield as

$$P(t, T) = \exp(-(T-t)r(T-t)) \tag{3.15}$$

---

[6] This is part of the *arbitrage pricing theory*. For detail on this see Cox *et al.* (1985), while Duffie (1992) is a fuller treatment for those with a strong grounding in mathematics.

Expression (3.14) is very commonly encountered in the academic literature. Its derivation is not so frequently occurring however; we present it in appendix 3.2, which is a summary of the description given in Ross (1999). This reference is highly recommended reading. It is also worth referring to Neftci (2000), chapter 18.

The expression (3.14) represents the zero-coupon bond pricing formula when the spot rate is continuous or *stochastic*, rather than constant. The rate $r(s)$ is the risk-free return earned during the very short or *infinitesimal* time interval $(t, t + dt)$. The rate is used in the expressions for the value of a money market account (3.13) and the price of a risk-free zero-coupon bond (3.15).

Stochastic rates in continuous time

In the academic literature, the bond price given by (3.15) evolves as a *martingale* process under the risk-neutral probability measure $\tilde{P}$. This is an advanced branch of fixed income mathematics, and is outside the scope of this book; however, an introduction to the concept is provided in Chapter 4.[7] However, under this analysis the bond price is given as

$$P(t, T) = E_t^{\tilde{P}}\left[e^{-\int_t^T r(s)ds}\right] \tag{3.16}$$

where the right-hand side of (3.16) is viewed as the randomly evolved *discount factor* used to obtain the present value of the £1 maturity amount. Expression (3.16) also states that bond prices are dependent on the entire spectrum of short-term interest rates $r(s)$ in the future during the period $t < s < T$. This also implies that the term structure at time t contains all the information available on short rates in the future.[8]

From (3.16) we say that the function $T \rightarrow P_t^T$, $t < T$ is the discount curve (or *discount function*) at time t. Avellaneda (2000) notes that the markets usually replace the term $(T - t)$ with a term meaning *time to maturity*, so the function becomes

$\tau \rightarrow P_t^{t+\tau}$, $\tau > 0$, where $\tau = (T - t)$.

Under a constant spot rate, the zero-coupon bond price is given by

$$P(T - t) = e^{-r(t, T)(T - t)} \tag{3.17}$$

From (3.16) and (3.17) we can derive a relationship between the yield $r(t, T)$ of the zero-coupon bond and the short rate $r(t)$, if we equate the two right-hand sides, namely

$$e^{-r(T, t)(T - t)} = E_t^{\tilde{P}}\left[e^{-\int_t^T r(s)ds}\right] \tag{3.18}$$

Taking the logarithm of both sides we obtain

[7] Interested readers should consult Nefcti (2000), chapters 2, 17–18, another accessible text is Baxter and Rennie (1996) while Duffie (1992) is a leading-edge reference for those with a strong background in mathematics.
[8] This is related to the view of the short rate evolving as a martingale process. For a derivation of (3.16) see Neftci (2000), page 417.

$$r(t, T) = \frac{-\log E_t^{\tilde{P}}\left[e^{-\int_t^T r(s)ds}\right]}{T - t}$$

(3.19)

This describes the yield on a bond as the average of the spot rates that apply during the life of the bond, and under a constant spot rate the yield is equal to the spot rate.

With a zero-coupon bond and assuming that interest rates are positive, $P(t, T)$ is less than or equal to 1. The yield of the bond is, as we have noted, the continuously compounded interest rate that equates the bond price to the discounted present value of the bond at time t. This is given by

$$r(t, T) = -\frac{\log(P(t, T))}{T - t}$$

(3.20)

so we obtain

$$P(t, T) = e^{-(T-t)r(T-t)}$$

(3.21)

In practice, this means that an investor will earn $r(t, T)$ if he purchases the bond at t and holds it to maturity.

Coupon bonds

Using the same principles as in the previous section, we can derive an expression for the price of a coupon bond in the same terms of a risk-neutral probability measure of the evolution of interest rates. Under this analysis, the bond price is given by

$$P_c = 100.E_t^{\tilde{P}}\left(e^{-\int_t^{t_N} r(s)ds}\right) + \sum_{n:t_n > t}^{N} \frac{C}{w}E_t^{\tilde{P}}\left(e^{-\int_t^{t_n} r(s)ds}\right)$$

(3.22)

where

P_c is the price of a coupon bond;
C is the bond coupon;
t_n is the coupon date, with $n \leq N$, and $t = 0$ at the time of valuation;
w is the coupon frequency;[9]

and where 100 is used as the convention for *principal* or bond nominal value (that is, prices are quoted per cent, or per 100 nominal).

Expression (3.22) is written in some texts as

$$P_c = 100e^{-rN} + \int_n^N Ce^{-rn}dt$$

(3.23)

---

[9] Conventional or *plain vanilla* bonds pay coupon on an annual or semi-annual basis. Other bonds, notably certain floating-rate notes and mortgage- and other asset-backed securities also pay coupon on a monthly basis, depending on the structuring of the transaction.

We can simplify (3.22) by substituting Df to denote the discount factor part of the expression and assuming an annual coupon, which gives us

$$P = 100.Df_N + \sum_{n:t_n \geq t}^{N} C.Df_n \qquad (3.24)$$

which states that the market value of a risk-free bond on any date is determined by the discount function on that date.

We know from Chapter 2 that the actual price paid in the market for a bond includes accrued interest from the last coupon date, so that price given by (3.24) is known as the *clean price,* and the traded price, which includes accrued interest, is known as the *dirty price.*

Forward rates

An investor can combine positions in bonds of differing maturities to guarantee a rate of return that begins at a point in the future. That is, the trade ticket would be written at time t but would cover the period T to $T + 1$ where $t < T$ (sometimes written as beginning at T_1 and ending at T_2, with $t < T_1 < T_2$). The interest rate earned during this period is known as the *forward rate.*[10] The mechanism by which this forward rate can be guaranteed is described in the box, following Jarrow (1996) and Campbell *et al.* (1997).

The forward rate

An investor buys at time t, 1 unit of a zero-coupon bond maturing at time T, priced at $P(t, T)$ and simultaneously sells $P(t, T)/P(t, T + 1)$ bonds that mature at $T + 1$. From table 3.1 we see that the net result of these transactions is a zero cash flow. At time T there is a cash inflow of 1, and then at time $T + 1$ there is a cash outflow of $P(t, T)/P(t, T + 1)$. These cash flows are identical to a loan of funds made during the period T to $T + 1$, contracted at time t. The interest rate on this loan is given by $P(t, T)/P(t, T + 1)$, which is therefore the forward rate. That is,

$$f(t, T) = \frac{P(t, T)}{P(t, T + 1)} \qquad (3.25)$$

Together with our earlier relationships on bond price and yield, from (3.25) we can define the forward rate in terms of yield, with the return earned during the period $(T, T + 1)$ being

▶

---

[10] See the footnote on page 639 of Shiller (1990) for a fascinating insight on the origin of the term 'forward rate', which Shiller ascribes to John Hicks in his book *Value and Capital* (2nd edition, Oxford University Press 1946).

$$f(t, T, T+1) = \frac{1}{(P(t, T+1)/P(t, T))} = \frac{(r(t, T+1))^{(T+1)}}{r(t, T)^T} \quad (3.26)$$

TABLE 3.1

	Time		
Transactions	t	T	$T+1$
Buy 1 unit of T-period bond	$-P(t,T)$	$+1$	
Sell $P(t,T)/P(t,T+1)$ $T+1$ period bonds	$+[(P(t,T)/P(t,T+1)]P(t,T+1)$		$-P(t,T)/P(t,T+1)$
Net cash flows	0	$+1$	$-P(t,T)/P(t,T+1)$

From (3.25) we can obtain a bond price equation in terms of the forward rates that hold from t to T,

$$P(t, T) = \frac{1}{\prod_{k=t}^{T-1} f(t, k)}. \quad (3.27)$$

A derivation of this expression can be found in Jarrow (1996), chapter 3. Equation (3.27) states that the price of a zero-coupon bond is equal to the nominal value, here assumed to be 1, receivable at time T after it has been discounted at the set of forward rates that apply from t to T.[11]

When calculating a forward rate, it is as if we are writing an interest rate today that is applicable at the forward start date; in other words we trade a forward contract. The law of one price, or no-arbitrage, is used to calculate the rate. For a loan that begins at T and matures at $T+1$, similarly to the way we described in the box above, consider a purchase of a $T+1$ period bond and a sale of p amount of the T-period bond. The cash net cash position at t must be zero, so p is given by

$$p = \frac{P(t, T+1)}{P(t, T)}$$

and to avoid arbitrage the value of p must be the price of the $T+1$-period bond at time T. Therefore the forward yield is given by

---

[11] The symbol $\prod$ means 'take the product of', and is defined as $\prod_{i=1}^{n} x_i = x_1 \cdot x_2 \cdot \ldots \cdot x_n$, so that $\prod_{k=t}^{T-1} f(t, k) = f(t, t) \cdot f(t, t+1) \cdot \ldots \cdot f(t, T-1)n$ which is the result of multiplying the rates that obtain when the index k runs from t to $T-1$.

$$f(t, T + 1) = -\frac{\log P(t, T + 1) - \log P(t, T)}{(T + 1) - T} \tag{3.28}$$

If the period between T and the maturity of the later-dated bond is reduced, so we now have bonds that mature at T and T_2, and $T_2 = T + \Delta t$, then as the incremental change in time Δt becomes progressively smaller we obtain an instantaneous forward rate, which is given by

$$f(t, T) = -\frac{\partial}{\partial T} \log P(t, T). \tag{3.29}$$

This rate is defined as the forward rate and is the price today of forward borrowing at time T. The forward rate for borrowing today where $T = t$ is equal to the instantaneous short rate $r(t)$. At time t the spot and forward rates for the period (t, t) will be identical, at other maturity terms they will differ.

For all points other than at (t, t) the forward rate yield curve will lie above the spot rate curve if the spot curve is positively sloping. The opposite applies if the spot rate curve is downward sloping. Campbell *et al.* (1997, pages 400–401) observe that this property is a standard one for marginal and average cost curves. That is, when the cost of a marginal unit (say, of production) is above that of an average unit, then the average cost will increase with the addition of a marginal unit. This results in the average cost rising when the marginal cost is above the average cost. Equally, the average cost per unit will decrease when the marginal cost lies below the average cost.

EXAMPLE *3.1 The spot and forward yield curves*

From the discussion in this section we see that it is possible to calculate bond prices, spot and forward rates provided that one has a set of only one of these parameters. Therefore given the following set of zero-coupon rates, observed in the market, given in table 3.2, we calculate the corresponding forward rates and zero-coupon bond prices as shown using the spot and forward equations just described. The initial term structure is upward sloping. The two curves are illustrated in figure 3.4.

There are technical reasons why the theoretical forward rate has a severe kink in at the later maturity.

Essentially the relationship between the spot and forward rate curve is as stated by Campbell *et al.* (ibid.) The forward rate curve will lie above the spot rate curve if the latter is increasing, and will lie below it if the spot rate curve is decreasing. This relationship can be shown mathematically; the forward rate or *marginal rate*

TABLE 3.2 ▪ Hypothetical zero-coupon yield and forward rates

Term to maturity (0,T)	Spot rate r(0,T)*	Forward rate f(0,T)*	Bond price P(0,T)
0			1
1	1.054	1.054	0.94877
2	1.055	1.056	0.89845
3	1.0563	1.059	0.8484
4	1.0582	1.064	0.79737
5	1.0602	1.068	0.7466
6	1.0628	1.076	0.69386
7	1.06553	1.082	0.64128
8	1.06856	1.0901	0.58833
9	1.07168	1.0972	0.53631
10	1.07526	1.1001	0.48403
11	1.07929	1.1205	0.43198

*Interest rates are given as (1+r)

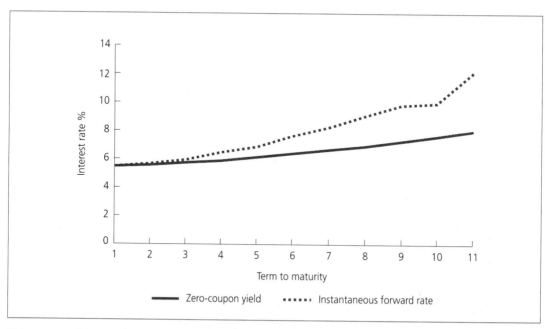

FIGURE 3.4(a) ▪ Hypothetical zero-coupon and forward yield curves

of return is equal to the spot rate or *average rate of return* plus the rate of increase of the spot rate, multiplied by the sum of the increases between t and T. If the spot rate is constant (a flat curve), the forward rate curve will be equal to it.

However an increasing spot rate curve does not always result in an increasing forward curve, only one that lies above it. It is possible for the forward curve to be increasing or decreasing while the spot rate is increasing. If the spot rate reaches a maximum level and then stays constant, or falls below this high point, the forward curve will begin to decrease at a maturity point *earlier* than the spot curve high point. In the example in figure 3.4(a), the rate of increase in the spot rate in the last period is magnified when converted to the equivalent forward rate; if the last spot rate had been below the previous-period rate, the forward rate curve would look like that in figure 3.4(b).

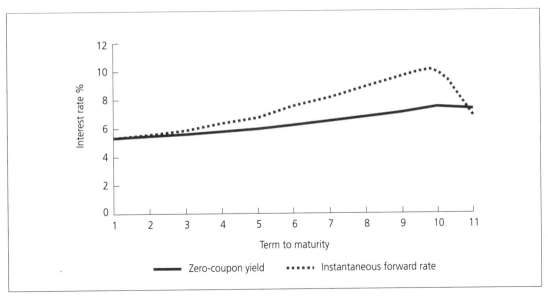

FIGURE 3.4(b) ■ Hypothetical spot and forward yield curves

The term structure

We have already referred to the yield curve or *term structure of interest rates*. Strictly speaking, only a spot rate yield curve is a term structure, but the two expressions are sometimes used synonymously. At any time t there will be a set of coupon and/or zero-coupon bonds with different terms to maturity and cash flow streams. There will be certain fixed maturities that are not represented by actual bonds in the market, as there will be more than one bond maturing at or around the same redemption date. The debt capital markets and the pricing of debt instruments revolves around the term structure, and for this reason this area has been extensively researched in the academic literature. There are a number of ways to estimate and interpret the term structure, and in this section we review the main highlights.

The bootstrapping approach using bond prices[12]

In this section we describe how to obtain zero-coupon and forward rates from the yields available from coupon bonds, using the *boot-strapping* technique. In a government bond market such as that for US Treasuries or gilts, the bonds are considered to be *default-free*. The rates from a government bond yield curve describe the risk-free rates of return available in the market *today*, however, they also *imply* (risk-free) rates of return for *future time periods*. These implied future rates, known as *implied forward rates*, or simply *forward rates,* can be derived from a given spot yield curve using boot-strapping. This term reflects the fact that each calculated spot rate is used to determine the next period spot rate, in successive steps.

Table 3.3 shows an hypothetical benchmark yield curve for value as at 2 January 2000. The observed yields of the benchmark bonds that compose the curve are displayed in the last column. All rates are annualized and assume semi-annual compounding. The bonds all pay on the same coupon dates of 2 January and 2 July, and as the value date is a coupon date, there is no accrued interest. Note also that all the bonds are priced at par.

TABLE 3.3 ■ Hypothetical coupon bond yields

Bond	Term to maturity (years)	Coupon	Maturity date	Price	Gross redemption yield
6-month	0.5	4%	02-Jul-00	100	4%
1-year	1	5%	02-Jan-01	100	5%
1.5-year	1.5	6%	02-Jul-01	100	6%
2-year	2	7%	02-Jan-02	100	7%
2.5-year	2.5	8%	02-Jul-02	100	8%
3-year	3	9%	02-Jan-03	100	9%

Hypothetical government benchmark bond yields as at 2 January 2000

---

[12] This section demonstrates the bootstrapping approach using the par yield curve, and follows the approach described in Windas (1993).

The gross redemption yield or *yield-to-maturity* of a coupon bond describes the single rate that present-values each of its future cash flows to a given price. This yield measure suffers from a fundamental weakness in that each cash-flow is present-valued at the same rate, an unrealistic assumption in anything other than a flat yield curve environment. The bonds in table 3.3 pay semi-annual coupons on 2 January and 2 July and have the same time period – six months – between 2 January 2000, their valuation date and 2 July 2000, their next coupon date. However, since each issue carries a different yield, the next six-month coupon payment for each bond is present-valued at a different rate. In other words, the six-month bond present-values its six-month coupon payment at its 4% yield to maturity, the one-year at 5%, and so on.

Because each of these issues uses a different rate to present-value a cash flow occurring at the same future point in time, it is unclear which of the rates should be regarded as the true interest rate or benchmark rate for the six-month period from 2 January 2000 to 2 July 2000. This problem is repeated for all other maturities. We require a set of true interest rates however, and so these must be derived from the redemption yields that we can observe from the benchmark bonds trading in the market. These rates we designate as rs_i, where rs_i is the *implied spot rate* or *zero-coupon rate* for the term beginning on 2 January 2000 and ending at the end of period i.

We begin calculating implied spot rates by noting that the six-month bond contains only one future cash flow, the final coupon payment and the redemption payment on maturity. This means that it is in effect trading as a zero-coupon bond. Since this cash flow's present value, future value and maturity term are known, the unique interest rate that relates these quantities can be solved using the compound interest equation (3.30) below.

$$FV = P \times \left(1 + \frac{rs_i}{m}\right)^{(nm)}$$

$$rs_i = m \times \left(\sqrt[(nm)]{\frac{FV}{P}} - 1\right) \tag{3.30}$$

where

    FV is the future value;
    P is the present value (or price);
    rs_i is the implied *i*-period spot rate;
    m is the number of interest periods per year;
    n is the number of years in the term.

The first rate to be solved is referred to as the implied six-month spot rate and is the true interest rate for the six-month term beginning on 2 January and ending on 2 July 2000.

Equation (3.30) relates a cash flow's present value and future value in terms of an associated interest rate, compounding convention and time period. Of course if we rearrange it, we may use it to solve for an implied spot rate. For the six-month bond the final cash flow on maturity is £102, comprised of the £2 coupon payment and the par redemption amount. So we have for the first term, $i = 1$, $FV = £102$, $P = £100$, $n = 0.5$ years and $m = 2$. This allows us to calculate the spot rate as follows:

$$rs_i = m \times \left({}^{(nm)}\!\sqrt{FV/P} - 1 \right)$$
$$rs_1 = 2 \times \left({}^{(0.5 \times 2)}\!\sqrt{£102/£100} - 1 \right) \tag{3.31}$$
$$rs_1 = 0.04000$$
$$rs_1 = 4.000\%$$

Thus the implied six-month spot rate or zero-coupon rate is equal to 4%.[13] We now need to determine the implied one-year spot rate for the term from 2 January 2000 to 2 January 2001. We note that the one-year issue has a 5% coupon and contains two future cash flows: a £2.50 six-month coupon payment on 2 July 2000 and a £102.50 one-year coupon and principal payment on 2 January 2001. Since the first cash flow occurs on 2 July – six months from now – it must be present-valued at the 4 per cent six-month spot rate established above. Once this present value is determined, it may be subtracted from the £100 total present value of the one-year issue to obtain the present value of the one-year coupon and cash flow. Again we then have a single cash flow with a known present value, future value and term. The rate that equates these quantities is the implied one-year spot rate. From equation (3.30) the present value of the six-month £2.50 coupon payment of the one-year benchmark bond, discounted at the implied six-month spot rate, is:

$$P_{\text{6-mo cash flow, 1-yr bond}} = £2.50/(1 + 0.04/2)^{(0.5 \times 2)}$$
$$= £2.45098$$

The present value of the one-year £102.50 coupon and principal payment is found by subtracting the present value of the six-month cash flow, determined above, from the total present value (current price) of the issue:

$$P_{\text{1-yr cash flow, 1-yr bond}} = £100 - £2.45098$$
$$= £97.54902$$

The implied one-year spot rate is then determined by using the £97.54902 present value of the one-year cash flow determined above:

---

[13] Of course intuitively we would have concluded that the six-month spot rate was 4%, without the need to apply the arithmetic, as we had already assumed that the six-month bond was a quasi-zero-coupon bond.

$$rs_2 = 2 \times \left(\sqrt[(1 \times 2)]{£102.50/£97.54902} - 1 \right)$$
$$= 0.0501256$$
$$= 5.01256\%$$

The implied 1.5 year spot rate is solved in the same way:

$$P_{\text{6-mo cash flow, 1.5-yr bond}} = £3.00/(1 + 0.04/2)^{(0.5 \times 2)}$$
$$= £2.94118$$

$$P_{\text{1-yr cash flow, 1.5-yr bond}} = £3.00/(1 + 0.0501256/2)^{(1 \times 2)}$$
$$= £2.85509$$

$$P_{\text{1.5-yr cash flow, 1.5-yr bond}} = £100 - £2.94118 - £2.85509$$
$$= £94.20373$$

$$rs_3 = 2 \times \left(\sqrt[(1.5 \times 2)]{£103/£94.20373} - 1 \right)$$
$$= 0.0604071$$
$$= 6.04071\%$$

Extending the same process for the remaining bonds, we calculate the implied two-year spot rate rs_4 to be 7.0906%, and rates rs_5 and rs_6 to be 8.1614% and 9.25403% respectively.

The interest rates rs_1, rs_2, rs_3, rs_4, rs_5 and rs_6 describe the true zero-coupon or spot rates for the 6-month, 1-year, 1.5-year, 2-year, 2.5-year and 3-year terms that begin on 2 January 2000 and end on 2 July 2000, 2 January 2001, 2 July 2001, 2 January 2002, 2 July 2002 and 2 January 2003 respectively. They are also called implied spot rates because they have been calculated from redemption yields observed in the market from the benchmark government bonds that were listed in table 3.3.

Note that the 1-, 1.5-, 2-, 2.5- and 3-year implied spot rates are progressively greater than the corresponding redemption yields for these terms. This is an important result, and occurs whenever the yield curve is positively sloped. The reason for this is that the present values of a bond's shorter-dated cash flows are discounted at rates that are lower than the redemption yield; this generates higher present values that, when subtracted from the current price of the bond, produce a lower present value for the final cash flow. This lower present value implies a spot rate that is greater than the issue's yield. In an inverted yield curve environment we observe the opposite result, that is implied rates that lie below the corresponding redemption yields. If the redemption yield curve is flat, the implied spot rates will be equal to the corresponding redemption yields.

Once we have calculated the spot or zero-coupon rates for the 6-month, 1-year, 1.5-year, 2-year, 2.5-year and 3-year terms, we can determine the rate of return that is implied by the yield curve for the sequence of six-month periods beginning on 2 January 2000,

2 July 2000, 2 January 2001, 2 July 2001 and 2 January 2002. These period rates are referred to as *implied forward rates* or *forward-forward rates* and we denote these as rf_i, where rf_i is the implied six-month forward interest rate today for the ith period.

Since the implied six-month zero-coupon rate (spot rate) describes the return for a term that coincides precisely with the first of the series of six-month periods, this rate describes the risk-free rate of return for the first six-month period. It is therefore equal to the first period spot rate. Thus we have $rf_1 = rs_1 = 4.0\%$, where rf_1 is the risk-free forward rate for the first six-month period beginning at period 1. The risk-free rates for the second, third, fourth, fifth and sixth six-month periods, designated rf_2, rf_3, rf_4, rf_5 and rf_6 respectively may be solved from the implied spot rates.

The benchmark rate for the second semi-annual period rf_2 is referred to as the one-period forward six-month rate, because it goes into effect one six-month period from now ('one-period forward') and remains in effect for six months ('six-month rate'). It is therefore the six-month rate in six months' time, and is also referred to as the six-month forward-forward rate. This rate in conjunction with the rate from the first period rf_1, must provide returns that match those generated by the implied one-year spot rate for the entire one-year term. In other words, £1 invested for six months from 2 January 2000 to 2 July 2000 at the first period's benchmark rate of 4% and then reinvested for another six months from 2 July 2000 to 2 January 2001 at the second period's (as yet unknown) implied *forward* rate must enjoy the same returns as £1 invested for one year from 2 January 2000 to 2 January 2001 at the implied one-year *spot* rate. This reflects the law of no-arbitrage.

A moment's thought will convince us that this must be so. If this were not the case, there might exist an interest rate environment in which the return over any given term would depend on whether an investment is made at the start period for the entire maturity term, or over a succession of periods within the whole term and reinvested at points in between. If there were any discrepancies between the returns received from each approach, there would exist an unrealistic arbitrage opportunity, in which investments for a given term carrying a lower return might be sold short against the simultaneous purchase of investments for the same period carrying a higher return, thereby locking in a risk-free, cost-free profit. Therefore forward interest rates must be calculated so that they are *arbitrage-free*. Excellent mathematical explanations of the no-arbitrage property of interest-rate markets are contained in Ingersoll (1987), Jarrow (1996) and Shiller (1990) among others.

The existence of a no-arbitrage market of course makes it straightforward to calculate forward rates; we know that the return from an investment made over a period must equal the return made from investing in a shorter period and successively reinvesting to a matching term. If we know the return over the shorter period, we are left with only one unknown – the full-period forward rate, which is then easily calculated. In our example, having established the rate for the first six-month period, the rate for the second six-month period – the one-period forward six-month rate – is determined below.

The future value of £1 invested at rf_1, the period 1 forward rate, at the end of the first six-month period is calculated as follows:

$$FV_1 = £1 \times \left(1 + \frac{rf_1}{2}\right)^{(0.5 \times 2)}$$

$$= £1 \times \left(1 + \frac{0.04}{2}\right)^{1}$$

$$= £1.02000$$

The future value of £1 at the end of the one-year term, invested at the implied benchmark one-year spot rate is determined as follows:

$$FV_2 = £1 \times \left(1 + \frac{rf_2}{2}\right)^{(1 \times 2)}$$

$$= £1 \times \left(1 + \frac{0.0501256}{2}\right)^{1}$$

$$= £1.050754$$

The implied benchmark one-period forward rate rf_2 is the rate that equates the value of FV_1 (£1.02) on 2 July 2000 to FV_2 (£1.050754) on 2 January 2001. From equation (3.31) we have:

$$rf_2 = 2 \times \left((0.5 \times 2)\sqrt{\frac{FV_2}{FV_1}} - 1\right)$$

$$= 2 \times \left(\frac{0.0501256}{2} - 1\right)$$

$$= 0.060302$$

$$= 6.0302\%$$

In other words £1 invested from 2 January to 2 July at 4.0% (the implied forward rate for the first period) and then reinvested from 2 July to 2 January 2001 at 6.0302% (the implied forward rate for the second period) would accumulate the same returns as £1 invested from 2 January 2000 to 2 January 2001 at 5.01256% (the implied one-year spot rate).

The rate for the third six-month period – the two-period forward six-month interest rate – may be calculated in the same way:

$$FV_2 = \pounds1.050754$$

$$
\begin{aligned}
FV_3 &= \pounds1 \times (1 + rs_3/2)^{(1.5 \times 2)} \\
&= \pounds1 \times (1 + 0.0604071/2)^3 \\
&= \pounds1.093375
\end{aligned}
$$

$$rf_3 = 2 \times \left({}^{(0.5 \times 2)}\sqrt{\frac{FV_3}{FV_4}} - 1 \right)$$

$$
\begin{aligned}
&= 2 \times \left({}^1\sqrt{\pounds1.093375 / \pounds1.050754} - 1 \right) \\
&= 0.081125 \\
&= 8.1125\%
\end{aligned}
$$

In the same way the three-period forward six-month rate rf_4 is calculated to be 10.27247%, and rates rf_5 and rf_6 are shown to be 12.59% and 15.23% respectively.

The results of the implied spot (zero-coupon) and forward rate calculations along with the given yield curve are displayed in table 3.4, and illustrated graphically in figure 3.5. This methodology can be applied using a spreadsheet for actual market redemption yields, although in practice we will not have a set of bonds with exact and/or equal periods to maturity and coupons falling on the same date. In designing a spreadsheet spot rate calculator therefore, the coupon rate and maturity date is entered as standing data and usually interpolation is used when calculating the spot rates for bonds with uneven maturity dates.

TABLE 3.4 ■ Implied spot and forward rates

Term to maturity (years)	Cash market yield	Implied spot rate	Implied one-period forward rate
0.5	4.00000%	4.00000%	4.00000%
1	5.00000%	5.01256%	6.03023%
1.5	6.00000%	6.04071%	8.11251%
2	7.00000%	7.09062%	10.27247%
2.5	8.00000%	8.16140%	12.59782%
3	9.00000%	9.25403%	15.23100%

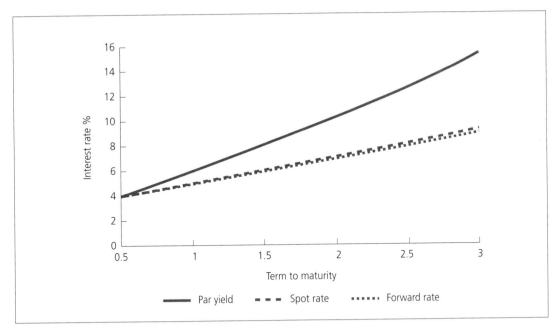

FIGURE 3.5 ■ Implied spot and forward rates

The theoretical approach described above is neat and appealing, but in practice there are a number of issues that will complicate the attempt to extract zero-coupon rates from bond yields. The main problem is that it is highly unlikely that we will have a set of bonds that are both precisely six months (or one interest) apart in maturity and priced precisely at par. We also require our procedure to fit as smooth a curve as possible. Setting our coupon bonds at a price of par simplified the analysis in our illustration of bootstrapping, so in reality we need to apply more advanced techniques. A basic approach for extracting zero-coupon bond prices is described in the next section.

Calculating spot rates in practice

Researchers have applied econometric techniques to the problem of extracting a zero-coupon term structure from coupon bond prices. The most well-known approaches are described in McCulloch (1971, 1975), Schaefer (1981), Nelson and Siegel (1987), Deacon and Derry (1994), Adams and Van Deventer (1994) and Waggoner (1997), to name but a few. The most accessible article is probably the one by Deacon and Derry.[14] In addition, a good overview of all the main approaches is contained in James and Webber (2000), and chapters

---

[14] This is the author's opinion. Those with a good grounding in econometrics will find all these references both readable and accessible. Further recommended references are given in the bibliography.

15–18 of their book provide an excellent summary of the research highlights to date.

We have noted that a coupon bond may be regarded as a portfolio of zero-coupon bonds. By treating a set of coupon bonds as a larger set of zero-coupon bonds, we can extract an (implied) zero-coupon interest rate structure from the yields on the coupon bonds.

If the actual term structure is observable, so that we know the prices of zero-coupon bonds of £1 nominal value P_1, P_2, ..., P_N then the price P_C of a coupon bond of nominal value £1 and coupon C is given by

$$P_C = P_1 C + P_2 C + ... + P_N (1 + C) \qquad (3.32)$$

Conversely if we can observe the coupon bond yield curve, so that we know the prices P_{C1}, P_{C2}, ..., P_{CN}, then we may use (3.32) to extract the implied zero-coupon term structure. We begin with the one-period coupon bond, for which the price is

$$P_{C1} = P_1(1 + C)$$

so that

$$P_1 = \frac{PC_1}{(1 + C)} \qquad (3.33)$$

This process is repeated. Once we have the set of zero-coupon bond prices P_1, P_2, ..., P_{N-1} we obtain P_N using

$$P_N = \frac{P_{CN} - P_{N-1}C - ...... - P_1 C}{1 + C}. \qquad (3.34)$$

At this point we apply a regression technique known as *ordinary least squares* (OLS) to fit the term structure. Chapter 4 discusses this area in greater detail; we have segregated this so that readers who do not require an extensive familiarity with this subject may skip that chapter. Interested readers should also consult the references at the end of Chapter 4.

Expression (3.32) restricts the prices of coupon bonds to be precise functions of the other coupon bond prices. In fact, this is unlikely in practice because specific bonds will be treated differently according to liquidity, tax effects and so on. For this reason we add an *error term* to (3.32) and estimate the value using cross-sectional regression against all the other bonds in the market. If we say that these bonds are numbered $i = 1, 2, ..., I$ then the regression is given by

$$P_{C_i N_i} = P_1 C_i + P_2 C_i + ... + P_{N_i}(1 + C_i) + u_i \qquad (3.35)$$

for $i = 1, 2, ..., I$ and where C_i is the coupon on the ith bond and N_i is the maturity of the ith bond. In (3.35) the regressor parameters are the coupon payments at each interest period date, and the coefficients are the prices of the zero-coupon bonds P_1 to P_N where $j = 1, 2, ..., N$. The values are obtained using OLS as long as we have a complete term structure and that $I \geqslant N$.

In practice we will not have complete term structure of coupon bonds and so we are not able to identify the coefficients in (3.35). McCulloch (1971, 1975) described a *spline estimation* method, which assumes that zero-coupon bond prices vary smoothly with term to maturity. In this approach we define P_N, a function of maturity $P(N)$, as a *discount function* given by

$$P(N) = 1 + \sum_{j=1}^{J} a_j f_j(N) \tag{3.36}$$

The function $f_j(N)$ is a known function of maturity N, and the coefficients a_j must be estimated. We arrive at a regression equation by substituting (3.36) into (3.35) to give us (3.37), which can be estimated using OLS.

$$\Pi_i = \sum_{j=1}^{J} a_j X_{ij} + u_i, \qquad i = 1, 2, ..., I \tag{3.37}$$

where

$$\Pi_i \equiv P_{C_i N_i} - 1 - C_i N_i$$
$$X_{ij} \equiv f_j(N_i) + C_i \sum_{l=1}^{Ni} f_j(l)$$

The function $f_j(N)$ is usually specified by setting the discount function as a polynomial. In certain texts, including McCulloch, this is carried out by applying what is known as a *spline* function. Considerable academic research has gone into the use of spline functions as a yield curve fitting technique; however, we are not able to go into the required level of detail here, which is left to Chapter 4. Please refer to the bibliography for further information. For a specific discussion on using regression techniques for spline curve fitting methods see Suits *et al.* (1978).

Term structure hypotheses

As befits a subject that has been the target of extensive research, a number of hypotheses have been put forward that seek to explain the term structure of interest rates. These hypotheses describe why yield curves assume certain shapes, and relate maturity terms with spot and forward rates. These hypotheses are briefly reviewed in this section.

The expectations hypothesis

Simply put, the *expectations hypothesis* states that the slope of the yield curve reflects the market's expectations about future interest rates. There are in fact four main versions of the hypothesis, each distinct from the other and each not compatible with the others. The expectations hypothesis has a long history, first being described in 1896 by Fisher and later developed by Hicks (1946) among others.[15] As Shiller (1990) describes, the thinking behind it probably stems from the way market participants discuss their view on future interest rates when assessing whether to purchase long-dated or short-dated bonds. For instance, if interest rates are expected to fall, investors will purchase long-dated bonds in order to 'lock in' the current high long-dated yield. If all investors act in the same way, the yield on long-dated bonds will of course decline as prices rise in response to demand, and this yield will remain low as long as short-dated rates are expected to fall, and will revert to a higher level only once the demand for long-term rates is reduced. Therefore, downward-sloping yield curves are an indication that interest rates are expected to fall, while an upward-sloping curve reflects market expectations of a rise in short-term interest rates.

Let us briefly consider the main elements of the discussion. The *unbiased expectations hypothesis* states that current forward rates are unbiased predictors of future spot rates. Let $f_t(T, T+1)$ be the forward rate at time t for the period from T to $T+1$. If the one-period spot rate at time T is r_T then according to the unbiased expectations hypothesis

$$f_t(T, T+1) = E_t[r_T] \tag{3.38}$$

which states that the forward rate $f_t(T, T+1)$ is the expected value of the future one-period spot rate given by r_T at time T.

The *return-to-maturity expectations hypothesis* states that the return generated from an investment of term t to T by holding a $(T - t)$-period bond will be equal to the expected return generated by a holding a series of one-period bonds and continually rolling them over on maturity. More formally we write

$$\frac{1}{P(t, T)} = E_t[(1 + r_t)(1 + r_{t+1})\ldots\ldots(1 + r_{T-1})]. \tag{3.39}$$

The left-hand side of (3.39) represents the return received by an investor holding a zero-coupon bond to maturity, which is equal to the expected return associated with rolling over £1 from time t to time T by continually reinvesting one-period maturity bonds, each of which has a yield of the future spot rate r_t. A good argument for this hypothesis is contained in Jarrow (1996, page 52), which states that essentially in an environment of *economic equilibrium* the returns on zero-coupon bonds of similar maturity cannot be significantly different, otherwise investors would not hold the bonds with the lower return. A similar argument can be put forward with relation to coupon bonds of differing maturities. Any difference in yield would not therefore disappear as equilibrium was re-

---

[15] See the footnote on page 644 of Shiller (1990) for a fascinating historical note on the origins of the expectations hypothesis. An excellent overview of the hypothesis itself is contained in Ingersoll (1987, pages 389–392).

established. However there are a number of reasons why investors will hold shorter-dated bonds, irrespective of the yield available on them, so it is possible for the return-to-maturity version of the hypothesis not to apply. A good explanation in this regard is contained in Rubinstein (1999, pages 84–85). In essence, this version represents an equilibrium condition in which expected *holding period returns* are equal, although it does not state that this return is the same from different bond holding strategies.

From (3.38) and (3.39) we can determine that the unbiased expectations hypothesis and the return-to-maturity hypothesis are not compatible with each other, unless there is no correlation between future interest rates. As Ingersoll (1987) notes, although it would be both possible and interesting to model such an economic environment, it is not related to reality, as interest rates are highly correlated. Given positive correlation between rates over a period of time, bonds with maturity terms longer than two periods will have a higher price under the unbiased expectations hypothesis than under the return-to-maturity version. Bonds of exactly two-period maturity will have the same price.

The *yield-to-maturity expectations hypothesis* is described in terms of yields. It is given by

$$\left[\frac{1}{P(t, T)}\right]^{\frac{1}{T-t}} = E_t\left[\{(1 + r_t)(1 + r_{t+1}).....(1 + r_{T-1})\}^{\frac{1}{T-t}}\right] \tag{3.40}$$

where the left-hand side specifies the yield-to-maturity of the zero-coupon bond at time t. In this version, the expected holding period *yield* on continually rolling over a series of one-period bonds will be equal to the yield that is guaranteed by holding a long-dated bond until maturity.

The *local expectations hypothesis* states that all bonds will generate the same expected rate of return if held over a small term. It is given by

$$\frac{E_t[P(t + 1, T)]}{P(t, T)} = 1 + r_t \tag{3.41}$$

This version of the hypothesis is the only one that is consistent with no-arbitrage, because the expected rates of return on all bonds are equal to the risk-free interest rate. For this reason the local expectations hypothesis is sometimes referred to as *the risk-neutral expectations hypothesis*.

Liquidity premium hypothesis

The liquidity premium hypothesis arises from the natural desire for borrowers to borrow long while lenders prefer to lend short. It states that current forward rates differ from future spot rates by an amount that is known as the *liquidity premium*. It is expressed as

$$f_t(T, T + 1) = E_t[r_T] + \pi_t(T, T + 1) \tag{3.42}$$

Expression (3.42) states that the forward rate $f_t(T,T+1)$ is the expected value of the future one-period spot rate given by r_T at time T plus the liquidity premium, which is a function of the maturity of the bond (or term of loan). This premium reflects the conflicting requirements of borrowing and lenders, while traders and speculators will borrow short and lend long, in an effort to earn the premium. The liquidity premium hypothesis has been described in Hicks (1946).

Segmented markets hypothesis

The *segmented markets hypothesis* seeks to explain the shape of the yield curve by stating that different types of market participants invest in different sectors of the term structure, according to their requirements. So for instance the banking sector has a requirement for short-dated bonds, while pension funds will invest in the long end of the market. This was first described in Culbertson (1957). There may also be regulatory reasons why differ-ent investors have preferences for particular maturity investments. A *preferred habitat* theory was described in Modigliani and Sutch (1967), which states not only that investors have a preferred maturity but also that they may move outside this sector if they receive a premium for so doing. This would explain 'humped' shapes in yield curves. The preferred habitat theory may be viewed as a version of the liquidity preference hypothesis, where the preferred habitat is the short-end of the yield curve, so that longer-dated bonds must offer a premium in order to entice investors to hold them. This is described in Cox, Ingersoll and Ross (1981).

APPENDICES

Appendix 3.1: The integral

The approach used to define integrals begins with an approximation involving a count-able number of objects, which is then gradually transformed into an uncountable number of objects. A common form of integral is the Riemann integral.

Given a calculable or *deterministic* function that has been graphed for a period of time, let us say we require the area represented by this graph. The function is $f(t)$ and it graphed over the period $[0, T]$. The area of the graph is given by the integral

$$\int_0^T f(s)ds \qquad\qquad (3.1.1)$$

which is the area represented by the graph. This can be calculated using the Riemann integral, for which the area represented is shown at figure 3.1.1.

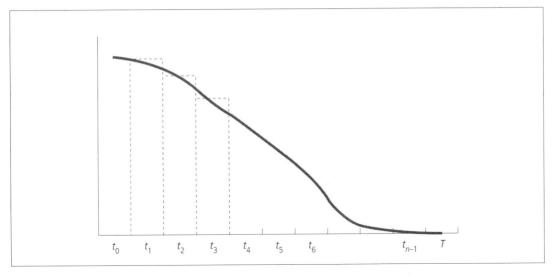

FIGURE 3.1.1

The general definition

To make the calculation the time interval is separated into a set of n intervals, given by

$$t_0 = 0 < t_1 < t_2 < \ldots < t_{n-1} < t_n < T$$

The approximate area under the graph is given by the sum of the area of each of the rect-angles, for which we assume each segment outside the graph is compensated by the area under the line that is not captured by any of the rectangles. Therefore we can say that an approximating measure is described by

$$\sum_{i=0}^{n} f\left(\frac{t_i + t_{i-1}}{2}\right)(t_i - t_{i-1})$$

(3.1.2)

This states that the area under the graph can be approximated by taking the sum of the n rectangles, which are created from the base x-axis which begins from t_0 through to T_n and the y-axis as height, described as

$$f((t_i + t_{i-1})/2)$$

This approximation only works if a sufficiently small base has been used for each interval, and if the function $f(t)$ is a smooth function, that is it does not experience sudden swings or kinks.

The definition of the Riemann integral is, given that

$$\max_i |t_i - t_{i-1}| \rightarrow 0,$$

defined by the limit

$$\sum_{i=0}^{n} f\left(\frac{t_i + t_{i-1}}{2}\right)(t_i - t_{i-1}) \rightarrow \int_0^T f(s)ds$$

(3.1.3)

If the approximation is not sufficiently accurate we can adjust it by making the intervals smaller still, which will make the approximation closer. This approach cannot be used if the function is not smooth; in mathematics this requirement is stated by saying that the function must be integrable or Riemann integrable.

Other integral forms are also used, a good introduction to these is given in Neftci (2000), chapter 4.

Appendix 3.2: The derivation of the bond price equation in continuous time

This section summarizes with permission the approach described in Ross (1999), on pages 54–56. This is an excellent reference, very readable and accessible, and is highly recommended. We replace Ross's use of investment at time 0 for maturity at time t with the terms t and T respectively, which is consistent with the price equations given in the main text. We also use the symbol M for the maturity value of the money market account, again to maintain consistency with the expressions used in Chapters 2–4 of this book.

Assume a continuously compounded interest rate $r(s)$ that is payable on a money market account at time s. This is the instantaneous interest rate at time s. Assume further that an investor places x in this account at time s; after a very short time period of time h, the account would contain

$$x_h \approx x(1 + r(s)h) \tag{3.2.1}$$

Say that $M(T)$ is the amount that will be in the account at time T if an investor deposits £1 at time t. To calculate $M(T)$ in terms of the spot rate $r(s)$, where $t \leq s \leq T$, for an incremental change in time of h, we have

$$M(s + h) \approx M(s)(1 + r(s)h) \tag{3.2.2}$$

which leads us to

$$M(s + h) - M(s) \approx M(s)r(s)h \tag{3.2.3}$$

and

$$\frac{M(s + h) - M(s)}{h} \approx M(s)r(s) \tag{3.2.4}$$

The approximation given by (3.2.4) turns into an equality as the time represented by h becomes progressively smaller. At the limit given as h approaches zero, we say

$$M'(s) = M(s)r(s) \tag{3.2.5}$$

which can be rearranged to give

$$\frac{M'(s)}{M(s)} = r(s) \tag{3.2.6}$$

From expression (3.2.6) we imply that in a continuous time process

$$\int_t^T \frac{M'(s)}{M(s)} ds = \int_t^T r(s)ds \tag{3.2.7}$$

and that

$$\log(M(T)) - \log(M(t)) = \int_t^T r(s)ds \qquad (3.2.8)$$

However we deposited £1 at time t, that is $M(t) = 1$, so from (3.2.8) we obtain the value of the money market account at T to be

$$M(T) = \exp\left(\int_t^T r(s)ds\right) \qquad (3.2.9)$$

which was our basic equation shown as (3.13).

Let us now introduce a risk-free zero-coupon bond that has a maturity value of £1 when it is redeemed at time T. If the spot rate is constant, then the price at time t of this bond is given by

$$P(t, T) = e^{-r(T-t)} \qquad (3.2.10)$$

where r is the continuously compounded instantaneous interest rate. The right-hand side of (3.2.10) is the expression for the present value of £1, payable at time T, discounted at time t at the continuously compounded, constant interest rate r.

So we say that $P(t, T)$ is the present value at time t of £1 to be received at time T. Since a deposit of $1/M(T)$ at time t will have a value of 1 at time T, we are able to say that

$$P(t, T) = \frac{1}{M(T)} = \exp\left(-\int_t^T r(s)ds\right) \qquad (3.2.11)$$

which is our bond price equation in continuous time.

If we say that the *average* of the spot interest rates from t to T is denoted by $rf(T)$, so we have $rf(T) = \frac{1}{T}\int_t^T r(s)ds$, then the function $rf(T)$ is the term structure of interest rates.

SELECTED BIBLIOGRAPHY AND REFERENCES

Adams, K., Van Deventer, D., 'Fitting Yield Curves and Forward Rate Curves with Maximum Smoothness', *Journal of Fixed Income* 4, 1994, pp. 52–62

Avellaneda, M., Laurence, P., *Quantitative Modelling of Derivative Securities*, Chapman & Hall/CRC 2000, chapters 10–12

Baxter, M., Rennie, A., *Financial Calculus*, Cambridge University Press 1996, Chapter 5

Campbell, J., Lo, A., MacKinlay, A., *The Econometrics of Financial Markets,* Princeton University Press 1997, chapters 10–11

Cox, J., Ingersoll, J., Ross, S., 'An Inter-Temporal General Equilibrium Model of Asset Prices', *Econometrica* 53, 1985

Deacon, M., Derry, A., 'Estimating the Term Structure of Interest Rates', *Bank of England Working Paper Series* No 24, July 1994

Duffie, D., *Dynamic Asset Pricing Theory*, Princeton University Press 1992

Fabozzi, F., *Bond Markets, Analysis and Strategies*, 2nd edition, Prentice Hall 1993, chapter 5

Fabozzi, F., *Fixed Income Mathematics*, McGraw-Hill 1997

Guajarati, D., *Basic Econometrics,* 3rd edition, 1995

Hicks, J., *Value and Capital*, 2nd edition, Oxford University Press 1946

Ingersoll, J. Jr., *Theory of Financial Decision Making,* Rowman & Littlefied 1987, chapter 18

James, J., Webber, N., *Interest Rate Modelling,* Wiley 2000

Jarrow, R., *Modelling Fixed Income Securities and Interest Rate Options,* McGraw-Hill 1996, chapter 3

Kitter, G., *Investment Mathematics for Finance and Treasury Professionals*, Wiley 1999, chapters 3, 5

McCulloch, J., 'Measuring the Term Structure of Interest Rates', *Journal of Business* 44, 1971, pp. 19–31

McCulloch, J., 'The Tax-Adjusted Yield Curve', *Journal of Finance* 30, 1975, pp. 811–830

Neftci, S., *An Introduction to the Mathematics of Financial Derivatives,* 2nd edition, Academic Press 2000, chapter 18

Nelson, C., Siegel, A., 'Parsimonious Modelling of Yield Curves', *Journal of Business* 60(4), 1987, pp. 473–489

Ross, Sheldon M., *An Introduction to Mathematical Finance*, Cambridge University Press 1999

Rubinstein, M., *Rubinstein on Derivatives*, RISK 1999

Schaefer, S., 'Measuring a Tax-Specific Term Structure of Interest Rates in the Market for British Government Securities', *Economic Journal* 91, 1981, pp. 415–438

Shiller, R., 'The Term Structure of Interest Rates', in Friedman, B., Hanh, F. (eds), *Handbook of Monetary Economics*, Volume 1, North Holland 1990, chapter 13

Suits, D., Mason, A., Chan, L., 'Spline Functions Fitted by Standard Regression Methods', *Review of Economics and Statistics* 60, 1978, pp. 132–139

Sundaresan, S., *Fixed Income Markets and Their Derivatives*, South-Western 1997

Van Deventer, D., Imai, K., *Financial Risk Analytics,* Irwin 1997

Van Horne, J., *Financial Management and Policy*, 10th edition, Prentice Hall 1995

Waggoner, D., 'Spline Methods for Extracting Interest Rate Curves from Coupon Bond Prices', *Working Paper, Federal Reserve Bank of Atlanta*, 97/10, 1997

Windas, T., *An Introduction to Option-Adjusted Spread Analysis*, Bloomberg, 1993

In addition to the publications listed above, interested readers may wish to consult the following recommended references on term structure analysis.

Constantinides, G., 'A Theory of the Nominal Term Structure of Interest Rates', *The Review of Financial Studies* 5 (4), 1992, pp. 531–552

Cox, J., Ingersoll, J., Ross, S., 'A Re-examination of Traditional Hypotheses about the Term Structure of Interest Rates', *Journal of Finance* 36, 1981, pp. 769–799

Cox, J., Ingersoll, J., Ross, S., 'A Theory of the Term Structure of Interest Rates', *Econometrica* 53, pp. 385–407, 1985

Culbertson, J., 'The Term Structure of Interest Rates', *Quarterly Journal of Economics* LXXI, 1957, pp. 489–504

McCulloch, J.H., 'A Re-examination of Traditional Hypotheses about the Term Structure: A Comment', *Journal of Finance* 63 (2), 1993, pp. 779–789

Stambaugh, R., 'The Information in Forward Rates: Implications for Models of the Term Structure', *Journal of Financial Economics* 21, 1988, pp. 41–70

Shiller, R., Cambell, J., Schoenholtz, K., 'Forward Rates and Future Policy: Interpreting the Term Structure of Interest Rates', *Brookings Papers on Economic Activity* 1, 1983, pp. 173–223

CHAPTER 4

Interest rate modelling

Chapter 3 introduced the basic concepts of bond pricing and analysis. We build on these concepts in this chapter and in Chapter 5, which is a review of the initial and subsequent work conducted in this field. Term structure modelling has been extensively researched in the financial economics literature; it is perhaps the most heavily covered subject in that field. It is not possible to deliver a comprehensive summary in just two chapters, but we aim to cover the main topics to a sufficient level. As ever, interested readers are directed to the bibliography listing, which contains the more accessible titles in this area.

In this chapter we review a number of interest-rate models, generally the more well-known ones. In Chapter 5 we discuss some of the techniques used to fit a smooth yield curve to market-observed bond yields.

Introduction

Term structure modelling is based on theory describing the behaviour of interest rates. A model would seek to identify the elements or *factors* that are believed to explain the dynamics of interest rates. These factors are random or *stochastic* in nature, so that we cannot predict with certainty the future level of any particular factor.[1] An interest-rate model must therefore specify a statistical process that describes the stochastic property of these factors, in order to arrive at a reasonably accurate representation of the behaviour of interest rates.

The first term structure models described in the academic literature described the interest-rate process as one where the *short rate*[2] follows a stochastic process and where all other interest rates are a function of the short rate. So the dynamics of the short rate drive all other term interest rates. These models are known as *one-factor models*. A one-factor model assumes that all term rates follow on from when the short rate is specified,

---

[1] The word stochastic is derived from a term in ancient Greek, the word stokhos which means 'a bull's eye'. The connection? Throwing darts at a board and aiming for the bull's eye is a stochastic process, as it will contain a number of misses.
[2] We came across this expression in Chapter 3.

that is they are not randomly determined. Two-factor interest-rate models have also been described. For instance the model described by Brennan and Schwartz (1979) specified the factors as the short rate and a long-term rate, while a model described by Fong and Vasicek (1991) specified the factors as the short rate and short-rate volatility.

Basic concepts

The original class of interest-rate models describe the dynamics of the short rate; the later class of models known as 'HJM' models describe the dynamics of the forward rate, and we will introduce these later. The foundation of interest-rate models is grounded in probability theory, so readers may wish to familiarize themselves with this subject. An excellent introduction to this is given in Ross (1999), which we referred to in Chapter 3, while a fuller treatment is given in the same author's better known book, *Probability Models* (2000).

In a one-factor model of interest rates, the short rate is assumed to be a random or stochastic variable, with the dynamics of its behaviour being uncertain and acting in an unpredictable manner. A random variable such as the short rate is defined as a variable whose future outcome can assume more than one possible value. Random variables are either *discrete* or *continuous*. A discrete variable moves in identifiable breaks or jumps. So for example while time is continuous, the trading hours of an exchange-traded future are not continuous, as the exchange will be shut outside business hours. Interest rates are treated in academic literature as being continuous, whereas in fact rates such as central bank base rates move in discrete steps. A continuous variable moves in a manner that has no breaks or jumps. So if an interest rate can move in a range from 5% to 10%, if it is continuous it can assume any value between this range, for instance a value of 5.671291%. Although this does not reflect market reality, assuming that interest rates and the processes they follow are continuous allows us to use calculus to derive useful results in our analysis.

The short rate is said to follow a stochastic process, so although the rate itself cannot be predicted with certainty, as it can assume a range of possible values in the future, the process by which it changes from value to value can be assumed, and hence modelled. The dynamics of the short rate therefore are a stochastic process or *probability distribution*. A one-factor model of the interest rate actually specifies the stochastic process that describes the movement of the short rate.

The analysis of stochastic processes employs mathematical techniques originally used in physics. An instantaneous change in value of a random variable x is written as dx. The changes in the random variable are assumed to be normally distributed. The shock to this random variable that generates it to change value, also referred to as *noise*, follows a randomly generated process known as a *Weiner process* or *geometric Brownian motion* (this is described in Appendix 4.1). A variable following a Weiner process is a random variable, termed x or z, whose value alters instantaneously, but whose patterns of change follow a normal distribution with mean 0 and standard deviation 1. If we assume that the yield r of a zero-coupon bond follows a continuous Weiner process with mean 0 and standard deviation 1, this would be written

$$dr = dz$$

Changes or 'jumps' in the yield that follow a Weiner process are scaled by the volatility of the stochastic process that drives the interest rate, which is given by σ. So the stochastic process for the change in yields is given by

$$dr = \sigma dz$$

The value of this volatility parameter is user-specified, that is it is set at a value that the user feels most accurately describes the current interest-rate environment. Users often use the volatility implied by the market price of interest-rate derivatives such as caps and floors.

So far we've said that the zero-coupon bond yield is a stochastic process following a geometric Brownian motion that drifts with no discernible trend; however, under this scenario, over time the yield would continuously rise to a level of infinity or fall to infinity, which is not an accurate representation of reality. We need to add to the model a term that describes the observed trend of interest rates moving up and down in a cycle. This expected direction of the change in the short rate is the second parameter in an interest-rate model, which in some texts is referred to by a letter such as a or b and in other texts is referred to as μ.

The short-rate process can therefore be described in the functional form given by (4.1).

$$dr = a\, dt + \sigma dz \tag{4.1}$$

where

dr is the change in the short rate;
a is the expected direction of change of the short rate or *drift*;
dt is the incremental change in time;
σ is the standard deviation of changes in the short rate;
dz is the random process.

Equation (4.1) is sometimes seen with dW or dx in place of dz. It assumes that on average the instantaneous change in interest rates is given by the function adt, with random shocks specified by σdz. It is similar to a number of models, such as those first described by Vasicek (1977), Ho and Lee (1986), Hull and White (1991) and others.

To reiterate then, (4.1) states that the change in the short rate r over an infinitesimal period of time dt, termed dr, is a function of:

■ the drift rate or expected direction of change in the short rate a;

■ a random process dz.

The two significant properties of the geometric Brownian motion are that:

- the drift rate is equal to the expected value of the change in the short rate. Under a zero drift rate, the expected value of the change is also zero and the expected value of the short rate is given by its current value;

- the variance of the change in the short rate over a period of time T is equal to T, while its standard deviation is given by $\sqrt{T}$.

The model given by (4.1) describes a stochastic short rate process, modified with a drift rate to influence the direction of change. However, a more realistic specification would also build in a term that describes the long-run behaviour of interest rates to drift back to a long-run level. This process is known as *mean reversion*, and perhaps is best known from the Hull-White model. A general specification of mean reversion would be a modification given by (4.2).

$$dr = a(b - r)\, dt + \sigma dz \tag{4.2}$$

where b is the long-run mean level of interest rates and where a now describes the speed of mean reversion. Equation (4.2) is known as an *Ornstein-Uhlenbeck process*. When r is greater than b, it will be pulled back towards b, although random shocks generated by dz will delay this process. When r is below b the short rate will be pulled up towards b.

Ito's lemma

Having specified a term structure model, for market practitioners it becomes necessary to determine how security prices related to interest rates fluctuate. The main instance of this is where we wish to determine how the price P of a bond moves over time and as the short rate r varies. The formula used for this is known as *Ito's lemma*. For the background on the application of Ito's lemma see Hull (1997) or Baxter and Rennie (1996). Ito's lemma transforms the dynamics of the bond price P in terms of the internet rate into a stochastic process in the following form:

$$dP + P_r dr + \tfrac{1}{2} P_{rr} (dr)^2 + P_t \tag{4.3}$$

The subscripts indicate partial derivatives.[3] The terms dr and $(dr)^2$ are dependent on the stochastic process that is selected for the short rate r. If this process is the Ornstein-Uhlenbeck process that was described in (4.2), then the dynamics of P can be specified as (4.4).

$$\begin{aligned}
dP &= P_r \, [a(b - r)dt + \sigma dz] + \tfrac{1}{2} P_{rr} \, \sigma^2 \, dt + P_t dt \\
&= \left[P_r \, a(b - r) + \tfrac{1}{2} P_{rr} \, \sigma^2 + P_t \right] dt + P_r \sigma dz \\
&= a(r,\ t)dt + \sigma(r,\ t) dz
\end{aligned} \tag{4.4}$$

---

[3] This is the great value of Ito's lemma, a mechanism by which we can transform a partial differential equation.

What we have done is to transform the dynamics of the bond price in terms of the drift and volatility of the short rate. Equation (4.4) states that the bond price depends on the drift of the short rate, and the volatility.

Ito's lemma is used as part of the process of building a term structure model. The generic process this follows involves the following steps:

■ specify the random or stochastic process followed by the short rate, for which we must make certain assumptions about the short rate itself;

■ use Ito's lemma to transform the dynamics of the zero-coupon bond price in terms of the short rate;

■ impose no-arbitrage conditions, based on the principle of hedging a position in one bond with one in another of bond of a different maturity (for a one-factor model), in order to derive the partial differential equation of the zero-coupon bond price. We note for a one-factor model: for a two-factor model we would require two bonds as hedging instrument;

■ solve the partial differential equation for the bond price, which is subject to the condition that the price of a zero-coupon bond on maturity is 1.

In the next section we review some of the models that are used in this process.

One-factor term structure models

In this section we discuss briefly a number of popular term structure models and attempt to summarize the advantages and disadvantages of each, which renders them useful or otherwise under certain conditions and user requirements.

The Vasicek model

The Vasicek model (1977) was the first term structure model described in the academic literature, and is a yield-based one-factor equilibrium model. It assumes that the short rate process follows a normal distribution. The model incorporates mean reversion and is popular with certain practitioners as well as academics because it is analytically tractable.[4] Although it has a constant volatility element, the mean reversion feature means that the model removes the *certainty* of a negative interest rate over the long term. However, other practitioners do not favour the model because it is not necessarily arbitrage-free with respect to the prices of actual bonds in the market.

So the instantaneous short rate described in the Vasicek model is

---

[4] *Tractability* is much prized in a yield curve model, and refers to the ease with which a model can be implemented, that is, with which yield curves can be computed.

$$dr = a(b - r)dt + \sigma dz \tag{4.5}$$

where a is the speed of the mean reversion and b is the mean reversion level or the long-run value of r.

In (4.5), z is the standard Weiner process or Brownian motion with a 0 mean and 1 standard deviation. In Vasicek's model, the price at time t of a zero-coupon bond that matures at time T is given by

$$P(t, T) = A(t,T)e^{-B(t, T)r(t)} \tag{4.6}$$

where $r(t)$ is the short rate at time t and

$$B(t, T) = \frac{1 - e^{-a(T - t)}}{a}$$

and

$$A(t, T) = \exp\left[\frac{(B(t, T) - T + t)(a^2b - \sigma^2/2)}{a^2} - \frac{\sigma^2 B(t, T)^2}{4a}\right]$$

The derivation of (4.6) is given in a number of texts (not least the original article!); we recommend section 5.3 in Van Deventer and Imai (1997) for its accessibility.

Note that in certain texts the model is written as

$$dr = \kappa(\theta - r)dt + \sigma dz$$

or

$$dr = \alpha(\mu - r)dt + \sigma dZ$$

but it just depends on which symbols the particular text is using. We use the form shown at (4.5) because it is consistent with our introductory discussion in the previous section.

In Vasicek's model the short rate r is normally distributed so, therefore, it *can* be negative with positive probability. The occurrence of negative rates is dependent on the initial interest rate level and the parameters chosen for the model, and is an extreme possibility. For instance, a very low initial rate, such as that observed in the Japanese economy for some time now, and volatility levels set with the market, have led to negative rates when using the Vasicek model. This possibility, which also applies to a number of other interest rate models, is inconsistent with a no-arbitrage market because investors will hold cash rather than opt to invest at a negative interest rate.[5] However, for most applications the model is robust and its tractability makes it popular with practitioners.

[5] This is stated in Black (1995).

The Ho and Lee model

The Ho and Lee model (1986) was an early arbitrage-free yield-based model. It is often called the extended Merton model as it is an extension of an earlier model described by Merton (1970).[6] It is called an arbitrage model as is it used to fit a given initial yield curve. The model assumes a normally distributed short rate, and the drift of the short rate is dependent on time, which makes the model arbitrage-free with respect to observed prices in the market, as these are the inputs to the model.

The model is given at (4.7).

$$dr = a(t)dt + \sigma dz \tag{4.7}$$

The bond price equation is given as

$$P(t, T) = A(t, T)e^{-r(t)(T-t)} \tag{4.8}$$

where $r(t)$ is the rate at time t and

$$\ln A(t, T) = \ln \left(\frac{P(0, T)}{P(0, t)} \right) - (T - t) \frac{\partial \ln P(0, t)}{\partial t} - \frac{1}{2} \sigma^2 (T - t)^2$$

There is no mean reversion feature incorporated so that interest rates can fall to negative levels, which is a cause for concern for market practitioners.

The Hull and White model

The model described by Hull and White (1993) is another well-known model. It fits the theoretical yield curve that one would obtain using Vasicek's model extracted from the actual observed market yield curve. As such, it is sometimes referred to as the 'extended Vasicek model', with time-dependent drift.[7] The model is popular with practitioners precisely because it enables them to calculate a theoretical yield curve that is identical to yields observed in the market, which can then be used to price bonds, bond derivatives and also calculate hedges.

The model is given at (4.9).

$$dr = a \left(\frac{b(t)}{a} - r \right) dt + \sigma dz \tag{4.9}$$

where a is the rate of mean reversion and $\frac{b(t)}{a}$ is a time-dependent mean reversion.

The price at time t of a zero-coupon bond with maturity T is

$$P(t, T) = A(t, T)e^{-B(t, T)r(t)}$$

---

[6] The reference in the bibliography is a later publication that is a collection of Merton's earlier papers.
[7] Haug (1998) also states that the Hull-White model is essentially the Ho and Lee model with mean reversion.

where $r(t)$ is the short rate at time t and

$$B(t, T) = \frac{1-e^{-a(T-t)}}{a}$$

$$\ln A(t, T) = \ln \left[\frac{P(0, T)}{P(0, t)}\right] - B(T, t)\frac{\partial\, P(0, t)}{\partial t} - \frac{v(t, T)^2}{2}$$

and

$$v(t, T)^2 = \frac{1}{2a^3}\, \sigma^2\, (e^{-aT} - e^{-at})^2(e^{2at} - 1)$$

Further one-factor term structure models

The academic literature and market application have thrown up a large number of term structure models as alternatives to the Vasicek model, and models based on it such as the
Hull-White model. As with these two models, each possess a number of advantages and disadvantages. As discussed in the previous section, the main advantage of Vasicek-type models is
their analytic tractability, with the assumption of the dynamics of the interest-rate allowing the
analytical solution of bonds and bond instruments. The main weakness of these models is that
they permit the possibility of negative interest rates. While negative interest rates are not a
market impossibility,[8] the thinking would appear to be that they are a function of more than
one factor, therefore, modelling them using Vasicek-type models is not tenable. This aspect of
the models does not necessarily preclude their use in practice, and will depend on the state of
the economy at the time. To consider an example, during 1997–1998, Japanese money market
interest rates were frequently below 0.5%, and at this level, even low levels of volatility below
5% will imply negative interest rates with high probability if using Vasicek's model. In this environment, practitioners may wish to use models that do not admit the possibility of negative
interest rates, perhaps those that model more than the short rate alone, so-called 'two-factor'
and 'multi-factor' models. We look briefly at these in the next section. First, we consider, again
briefly, a number of other one-factor models. As usual, readers are encouraged to review the
bibliography articles for the necessary background and further detail on application.

The Cox, Ingersoll and Ross model

Although published officially in 1985, the Cox-Ingersoll-Ross model was apparently
described in academic circles in 1977 or perhaps earlier, which would make it the first
interest-rate model. Like the Vasicek model, it is a one-factor model that defines interest
rate movements in terms of the dynamics of the short rate. However, it incorporates an

---

[8] Negative interest rates manifest themselves most obviously in the market for specific bonds in repo which
have gone excessively special. However, academic researchers often prefer to work with interest rate
environments that do not consider negative rates a possibility (for example see Black (1995)).

additional feature whereby the variance of the short rate is related to the level of interest rates, and this feature has the effect of not allowing negative interest rates. It also reflects a higher interest rate volatility in periods of relatively high interest rates, and corresponding lower volatility when interest rates are lower. The model is given at (4.10).

$$dr = k(b - r)dt + \sigma \sqrt{r}dz \tag{4.10}$$

The derivation of the zero-coupon bond price equation given at (4.11) is contained in Ingersoll (1987), chapter 18. The symbol τ represents the term to maturity of the bond or $(T - t)$.

$$P(r, \tau) = A(\tau)e^{-B(\tau)r} \tag{4.11}$$

where

$$A(\tau) = \left[\frac{2\gamma e^{(\gamma + \lambda + k)\frac{\tau}{2}}}{g(\tau)} \right]^{\frac{2kb}{\sigma^2}}$$

$$B(\tau) = \frac{-2(1 - e^{-\gamma\tau})}{g(\tau)}$$

$$g(\tau) = 2\gamma + (k + \lambda + \gamma)(e^{\gamma\tau} - 1)$$

$$\gamma = \sqrt{(k + \lambda)^2 + 2\sigma^2}$$

Some researchers have stated that the difficulties in determining parameters for the CIR model have limited its use among market practitioners.[9]

The Black, Derman and Toy model

The Black-Derman-Toy model (1990) also removes the possibility of negative interest rates and is commonly encountered in the markets. The parameters specified in the model are time-dependent, and the dynamics of the short rate process incorporate changes in the level of the rate. The model is given at (4.12).

$$d[\ln(r)] = [\vartheta(t) - \phi(t)\ln(r)]dt + \sigma(t)dz \tag{4.12}$$

The popularity of the model among market practitioners reflects the following:

■ it fits the market-observed yield curve, similar to the Hull-White model;

■ there is no allowance for negative interest rates;

■ it models the volatility levels of interest rates in the market.

---

[9] For instance see Van Deventer and Imai (1997) citing Fleseker (1993) on page 336, although the authors go on to state that the CIR model is deserving of futher empirical analysis and remains worthwhile for practical application.

Against this, the model is not considered particularly tractable or able to be programmed for rapid calculation. Nevertheless, it is important in the market, particularly for interest-rate derivative market makers. An excellent and accessible description of the Black-Derman-Toy model is contained in Sundaresan (1997) on pages 240–244; Tuckman (1996) pages 102–106 is also recommended.

Two-factor interest-rate models

As their name suggests, two-factor interest-rate models specify the yield curve in terms of two factors, one of which is usually the short rate. There are a number of possible factors that could be modelled when describing the dynamics of interest rates. For example, if defining the corporate bond term structure, an additional factor might be the spread of identical-rated bonds over the equivalent-maturity Treasury bond, known as the *credit spread*. The additional factors that could be modelled are listed below; note that models also exist that specify more than two factors, which are known as multi-factor models. Possible factors include:

- the short-term or instantaneous interest rate;
- the long-term (say ten-year) interest rate;
- short- and long-term real rates of interest;
- the spread between the short-term and long-term interest rates, either the current level or the expected long-term level;
- the corporate credit spread, either the current level or the long-term expected level;
- the current rate of inflation;
- the long-term average expected rate of inflation.

The choice of factors is dependent on the uses to which the model is being put, for example whether for the pricing or hedging of derivative instruments or arbitrage trading. Other considerations will also apply, for instance the ease and readiness with which model parameters can be determined. A particular issue in the use of two-factor and multi-factor models is the choice of factor. This section briefly introduces a number of two-factor models, with references for readers who wish to learn about their derivation and application.

The Brennan and Schwartz model

The Brennan-Schwartz model (1979) is a two-factor model that specifies the term structure in terms of the short rate and the long-term interest rate. The long-term rate is defined as the market yield observed on an irredeemable or perpetual bond, also known as an undated or consol bond. Both interest rates are assumed to follow what is known as a Gaussian-Markov process.[10] In the model, the dynamics of the logarithm of the short rate is defined as:

$$d[\ln(r)] = a[\ln(l) - \ln(p) - \ln(r)]dt + \sigma_1 dz_1 \tag{4.13}$$

where p is a parameter that describes the relationship between the short rate and the long-term rate. The short rate r is related to the long-term rate and changes in response to moves in the level of the long-term rate l, which has the stochastic process of the following form:

$$dl = l[l - r + \sigma_2^2 + \lambda_2 \sigma_2]dt + l\sigma_2 dz_2 \tag{4.14}$$

where λ is the premium placed by the market on the risk associated with the long-term interest rate. In a later study by Longstaff and Schwartz (1992) the Brennan-Schwartz model was fitted with accurate results to market bond yields.

The extended Cox, Ingersoll and Ross model

In further academic research[11] the Cox-Ingersoll-Ross model has been transformed into a two-factor model which specifies the interest rate as the function of two uncorrelated variables, both of which are assumed to follow a stochastic process. The model states:

$$dy_i = k_i(\theta_i - y_i)dt + \sigma_i \sqrt{y_i}dz_i \tag{4.15}$$

where y_i are the independent variables. Under this model, the authors derive the formula for the price of a zero-coupon bond as:

$$P(y_1, y_2, t, T) = A_1 A_2 e^{-B_1 y_1 - B_2 y_2} \tag{4.16}$$

where A and B are defined as before. In the 1992 article by Chen and Scott this two-factor Cox-Ingersoll-Ross model is shown to possess a number of advantages with a number of useful applications.

The Heath, Jarrow and Morton model

We have devoted a separate section to the approach described by Heath, Jarrow and Morton (1992) because it is a radical departure from the earlier family of interest rate models. As usual, a fuller exposition can be found in the references listed in the bibliography.

The Heath-Jarrow-Morton (HJM) approach to the specification of stochastic state variables is different to that used in earlier models. The previous models describe interest-rate

---

[10] A Markov process is one whose future behaviour is independent of its past behaviour, and is conditional on present behaviour only. A Gaussian process is one whose marginal distribution, where marginals are random variables, is normal in behaviour.
[11] See Chen and Scott (1992).

dynamics in terms of the short rate as the single or (in two- and multi-factor models) key state variable. With multi-factor models, the specification of the state variables is the fundamental issue in practical application of the models themselves. In the HJM model, the entire term structure and not just the short rate is taken to be the state variable. In Chapter 3, it was shown how the term structure can be defined in terms of default-free zero-coupon bond prices, yields, spot rates or forward rates. The HJM approach uses forward rates. So in the single-factor HJM model the change in forward rates at current time t, with a maturity at time u, is captured by:

- a volatility function;
- a drift function;
- a geometric Brownian or Weiner process which describes the shocks or *noise* experienced by the term structure.

We present here a brief introduction to the HJM model. A recommended fuller treatment is presented in chapter 8 of James and Webber (2000) and chapter 5 of Baxter and Rennie (1996). The author suggests reading James and Webber first; both accounts, while presented as an 'introduction', nevertheless require a good grounding in financial calculus.

The single-factor HJM model

To establish the HJM framework we present our familiar simple interest-rate model. If we have a forward-rate term structure $f(0, T)$ that is T-integrable, the dynamics of the forward term structure may be described by:

$$df(t, T) = a(t, T)dt + \sigma dz \tag{4.17}$$

where a is the drift rate and σ the constant volatility level. The expression dz represents the geometric Brownian motion or Weiner process and is written as dW in some texts, or dW_t to represent the expression as applicable to the current time t. This is the stochastic differential equation for the forward rate. To transform this expression into the equation for the price of an asset we would apply Ito calculus, but this is something that we shall leave to specialized texts on financial mathematics. The forward rate expressed as an integral equivalent of (4.17) is

$$f(t, T) = f(0, T) + \int_0^t a(s, T)ds + \sigma dz \tag{4.18}$$

which assumes that the forward rate is normally distributed. Crucially the different forward rates of maturity $f(0,1), f(0,2)....f(0, T)$ are assumed to be perfectly correlated. The random element is the Brownian motion dz, and the impact of this process is felt over time, rather than over different maturities.

As we noted, the term structure can be defined in terms of bond prices, yields, spot rates and forward rates. The HJM model is based on the instantaneous forward rate $f(t, T)$, and the single-factor version states that, given an initial forward-rate term structure $f(0, T)$ at time t the forward rate for each maturity T is given by

$$df(t, T) = a(t, T)dt + \sigma(t, T)dz \tag{4.19}$$

in the differential form, but which is usually seen in integral form:

$$f(t, T) = f(0, T) + \int_0^t a(s, T)ds + \int_0^t \sigma(s, T)dz_{(s)} \tag{4.20}$$

where s is an incremental move forward in time (so that $0 \leq t \leq T$ and $t \leq s \leq T$). Note that the expressions at (4.19) and (4.20) are simplified versions of the formal model.

Under (4.19) and (4.20) the forward rate for any maturity period T will develop as described by the drift and volatility parameters $a(t, T)$ and $\sigma(t, T)$. In the single-factor HJM model the random character of the forward-rate process is captured by the Brownian motion dz.[12] Under HJM, the primary assumption is that for each T the drift and volatility processes are dependent only on the history of the Brownian motion process up to the current time t, and on the forward rates themselves up to time t.

The multi-factor HJM model

Under the single-factor HJM model, the movement in forward rates of all maturities are perfectly correlated. This can be too much of a restriction for market application, for example when pricing an interest-rate instrument that is dependent on the yield spread between two points on the yield curve. In the multi-factor model, each of the state variables is described by its own Brownian motion process.[13] So for example in an m-factor model there would be m Brownian motions in the model, $dz_1, dz_2, \ldots, dz_m$. This allows each T-maturity forward rate to be described by its own volatility level $\sigma_i(t, T)$ and Brownian motion process dz_i. Under this approach, the different forward rates given by the different maturity bonds that describe the current term structure evolve under more appropriate random processes, and different correlations between forward rates of differing maturities can be accommodated. The multi-factor HJM model is given at (4.21).

$$f(t, T) = f(0, T) + \int_0^t a(s, T)ds + \sum_{i=1}^{m} \int_0^t \sigma_i(s, T)dz_i(s) \tag{4.21}$$

Equation (4.21) states that the dynamics of the forward rate process, beginning with the initial rate $f(0, T)$, are specified by the set of Brownian motion processes and the drift parameter.

---

[12] Note that certain texts use α for the drift term and W_t for the random term.
[13] For a good introduction see chapter 6 in Baxter and Rennie (1996).

For practical application, the evolution of the forward-rate term structure is usually carried out as a binomial-type path-dependent process. However, path-independent processes have also been used. The HJM approach has become popular in the market, both for yield curve modelling as well as for pricing derivative instruments, due to the realistic effect of matching yield curve maturities to different volatility levels, and it is reasonably tractable when applied using the binomial-tree approach. Simulation modelling based on Monte Carlo techniques are also used. For further detail on the former approach see Jarrow (1996).

Choosing a term structure model

Selection of an appropriate term structure model is more of an art than a science. The different types of model available, and the different applications and user requirements, mean that it is not necessarily clear-cut which approach should be selected. For example, a practitioner's requirements will determine whether a single-factor model or two- or multi-factor model is more appropriate. The Ho-Lee and Black-Dorman-Toy models for example, are *arbitrage* models, which means that they are designed to match the current term structure. With arbitrage (or arbitrage-free) models, assuming that the specification of the evolution of the short rate is correct, the law of no-arbitrage can be used to determine the price of interest-rate derivatives. There are also the class of interest-rate models known as *equilibrium* models, which make an assumption of the dynamics of the short rate in the same as arbitrage models do, but are not designed to match the current term structure. With equilibrium models, therefore, the price of zero-coupon bonds given by the model-derived term structure is not required to (and does not) match prices seen in the market. This means that the prices of bonds and interest-rate derivatives are not given purely by the short rate process. Overall then, arbitrage models take the current yield curve as described by the market prices of default-free bonds as given, whereas equilibrium models do not.

Factors to consider

What considerations must be taken into account when deciding which term structure model to use? As described in Tuckman (1996, chapter 9), and elsewhere, some of the key factors include:

- ease of application;
- capturing market imperfections;
- pricing bonds and interest-rate derivatives;
- use of models over time.

These are considered below.

Ease of application

The key input to arbitrage models is the current spot rate term structure, which are straightforward to determine using the market price of bonds currently trading in the market. This is an advantage over equilibrium models, whose inputs are more difficult to obtain.

Capturing market imperfections

The term structure generated by an arbitrage model will reflect the current market term structure, which may include pricing irregularities due to liquidity and other considerations. If this is not desired, it is a weakness of the arbitrage approach. Equilibrium models would not reflect pricing imperfections.

Pricing bonds and interest-rate derivatives

Traditional 'seat-of-the-pants' market making often employs a combination of the trader's nous, the range of prices observed in the market (often from inter-dealer broker screens) and gut feeling to price bonds.[14] For a more scientific approach or for relative value trading[15] a yield curve model may well be desirable. In this case, an equilibrium model is clearly the preferred model, as the trader will want to compare the theoretical price given by the model compared to the actual price observed in the market. An arbitrage model would not be appropriate because it would take the observed yield curve, and hence the market bond price, as given, and so would assume that the market bond prices were correct. Put another way, using an arbitrage model for relative value trading would suggest to the trader that there was no gain to be made from entering into say, a yield curve spread trade. Pricing derivative instruments such as interest-rate options or swaptions requires a different emphasis. This is because the primary consideration of the derivative market maker is the technique and price of hedging the derivative. That is, upon writing a derivative contract, the market maker will simultaneously hedge the exposure using either the underlying asset or a combination of this and other derivatives such as exchange-traded futures. The derivative market maker generates profit through extracting premium and from the difference in price over time between the price of the derivative and the underlying hedge position. For this reason, only an arbitrage model is appropriate, as it would price the derivative relative to the market, which is important for a market maker; an equilibrium model would price the derivative relative to the theoretical market, which would not be appropriate since it is a market instrument that is being used as the hedge.

---

[14] Typified par excellence by the lads at Hoare Govett Fixed Interest during the author's time there! That includes you Tommo... .

[15] For example yield curve trades where bonds of different maturities are spread against each other, with the trader betting on the change in spread as opposed to the direction of interest rates, are a form of relative value trade.

Use of models over time

At initial use, the parameters used in an interest-rate model most notably the drift, volatility and (if applicable) mean reversion rate – reflect the state of the economy up to that point. This state is not constant, consequently, over time, any model must be continually *recalibrated* to reflect the current market state. That is, the drift rate used today when calculating the term structure may well be a different value tomorrow. This puts arbitrage models at a disadvantage, as their parameters will be changed continuously in this way. Put another way, use of arbitrage models is not consistent over time. Equilibrium model parameters are calculated from historic data or from intuitive logic, and so may not be changed as frequently. However, their accuracy over time may suffer. It is up to users to decide whether they prefer the continual tweaking of the arbitrage model over the more consistent use of the equilibrium model.

Conclusion

The above is just the beginning; there are a range of issues which must be considered by users when selecting an interest-rate model. For example, in practice it has been observed that models incorporating mean reversion work more accurately than those that do not feature this. Another factor is the computer processing power available to the user, and it is often the case that single-factor models are preferred precisely because processing is more straightforward. A good account of the different factors to be considered when assessing which model to use is given in chapter 15 of James and Webber (2000).

Appendix 4.1. Geometric Brownian motion

Brownian motion was described in 1827 by the English scientist Robert Brown, and defined mathematically by the American mathematician Norbert Weiner in 1918. As applied to the price of a security, consider the change in price of a security as it alters over time. The time now is denoted as 0, with $P(t)$ as the price of the security at time t from now. The collection of prices $P(t)$, $0 \leq t < \infty$ is said to follow a Brownian motion with *drift* parameter μ and variance parameter σ^2 if for all non-negative values of t and T the random variable

$$P(t + T) - P(t)$$

is independent of all the prices P that have been recorded up to time t. That is, the historic prices do not influence the value of the random variable. Also the random variable is normally distributed with a mean uT and variance $\sigma^2 T$.

Standard Brownian motion has two drawbacks when applied to model security prices. The first and most significant is that, as the security price is a normally distributed random variable, it can assume negative values with non-negative probability, a property of the normal distribution. This cannot happen with equity prices and only very rarely, under very special conditions, with interest rates. The second drawback of standard Brownian motion is that the difference between prices over an interval is assumed to follow a normal distribution irrespective of the price of the security at the start of the interval. This is not realistic, as the probabilities are affected by the initial price of the security.

For this reason, the *geometric Brownian motion* model is used in quantitative finance. Again, the time now is 0 and the security price at time t from now is given by $P(t)$. The collection of prices $P(t), 0 \leq t < \infty$ follows a geometric Brownian motion with drift μ and standard deviation or *volatility* σ if for non-negative values of t and T the random variable $P(t + T)/P(t)$ is independent of all prices up to time t. In addition the value

$$\log \left(\frac{P(t + T)}{P(t)} \right)$$

is a normally distributed random variable with mean μT and variance $\sigma^2 T$.

The significance of this is that once the parameters μ and σ have been ascertained, the present price of the security, and the present price only, determines the probabilities of future prices. The history of past prices has no impact. In addition, the probabilities of the ratio of the price at future time T to the price now are not dependent on the present price. The practical impact of this is that the probability that the price of a security doubles in price at some specified point in the future is identical whether the price now is 5 or 50.

For our purposes we need only be aware that at an initial price of $P(0)$, the expected price at time t is a function of the two parameters of geometric Brownian motion. The expected price, given an initial price $P(0)$, is given by

$$E[P(t)] = P_0 e^{t(\mu + \sigma^2/2)} \tag{4.1.1}$$

(4.1.1) above states that under geometric Brownian motion, the expected price of a security is the present price increasing at the rate of $\mu + \frac{\sigma^2}{2}$.

The evolution of a price process, including an interest rate, under varying parameters is shown at figure 4.1.1, with an initial price level at 100.

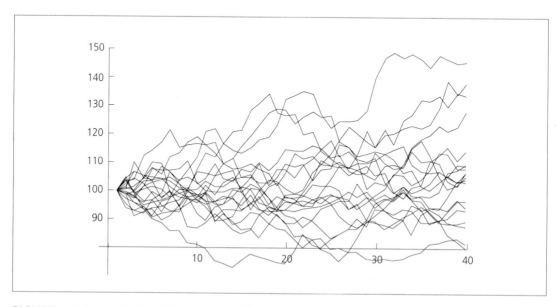

FIGURE 4.1.1 ■ Evolution of Brownian or Weiner process

SELECTED BIBLIOGRAPHY AND REFERENCES

This field is an extensively researched one. Readers are first directed to the specific references cited in this chapter. If your interest is a general treatment of term structure models, we suggest James and Webber (2000), while Baxter and Rennie (1996) is an excellent treatment of the mathematics involved. They call it an introduction, and to the rocket scientist this is true I'm sure, but a good basic grounding in calculus and probability theory would help the rest of us. For a general exposition of the theory of the yield curve, chapter 18 of Ingersoll (1987) is absolutely priceless and strongly recommended. Rebonato (1996) looks at the practical issues involved in implementing interest-rate models, and is a highly technical treatment. Finally, Van Deventer and Imai (1997) is an excellent accessible account of, among other things, term structure modelling and yield curve smoothing techniques.

Baxter, M., Rennie, A., *Financial Calculus*, Cambridge University Press 1996, pp. 57–62

Black, F., 'Interest Rates as Options', *Journal of Finance*, December 1995, pp. 1371–1376

Black, F., Derman, E., Toy, W., 'A One-Factor Model of Interest Rates and its Application to Treasury Bond Options', *Financial Analysts Journal*, Spring 1990, pp. 33–39

Brennan, M., Schwartz, E., 'A Continuous Time Approach to the Pricing of Bonds', *Journal of Banking and Finance*, July 1979, pp. 135–155

Campbell, J., 'A Defence of Traditional Hypotheses about the Term Structure of Interest Rates', *Journal of Finance* 41 (1986), pp. 183–193

Chen, R-R, Scott, L., 'Pricing Interest Rate Options in a Two-Factor Cox-Ingersoll-Ross Model of the Term Structure', *Review of Financial Studies*, Winter 1992, pp. 613–636

Cox, J., Ingersoll, J., Ross, S., 'A Theory of the Term Structure of Interest Rates', *Econometrica* 53, March 1985, pp. 385–407

Fong, H.G., Vasicek, O., 'Fixed Income Volatility Management', *Journal of Portfolio Management*, Summer 1991, pp. 41–46

Gibbons, M., Ramaswamy, K., 'The Term Structure of Interest Rates: Empirical Evidence', *Review of Financial Studies* 1994

Haug, E., *The Complete Guide to Option Pricing Formulas*, McGraw-Hill 1998, chapter 4

Heath, D., Jarrow, R., Morton, A., 'Bond Pricing and the Term Structure of Interest Rates: A New Methodology for Contingent Claims Valuation', *Econometrica* 60, January 1992, pp. 77–105

Ho, T., Lee, S-b., 'Term Structure Movements and Pricing Interest Rate Contingent Claims', *Journal of Finance*, December 1986, pp. 1011–1029

Hull, J., *Options, Futures and other Derivatives*, 3rd edition, Prentice Hall 1997, pp. 220–222

Hull, J., White, A., 'Pricing Interest Rate Derivative Securities', *Review of Financial Studies*, 1990, pp. 573–592

Ingersoll, J., Jr., *Theory of Financial Decision Making*, Rowman & Littlefield, 1987

James, J., Webber, N., *Interest Rate Modelling*, Wiley 2000, chapters 5–15

Jarrow, R., *Modelling Fixed Income Securities and Interest Rate Options*, McGraw-Hill 1996

Merton, R., *Continuous Time Finance*, Blackwell 1993, chapter 11

Rebonato, R., *Interest Rate Option Models*, Wiley 1996

Rebonato, R., Cooper, I., 'The Limitations of Simple Two-Factor Interest Rate Models', *Journal of Financial Engineering*, March 1996

Ross, S., *Probability Models*, 7th edition, Academic Press 2000

Sundaresan, S., *Fixed Income Markets and their Derivatives*, South Western Publishing 1997

Tuckman, B., *Fixed Income Securities*, Wiley 1996

Van Deventer, D., Imai, K., *Financial Risk Analytics*, Irwin 1997, chapter 5

Vasicek, O., 'An Equilibrium Characterization of the Term Structure', *Journal of Financial Economics*, 5, 1977, pp. 177–188

Fitting the yield curve

In this chapter, we consider some of the techniques used to actually fit the term structure. In theory we could use the bootstrapping approach described earlier (see Chapter 3). For a number of reasons however this does not produce accurate results, and so other methods are used instead. The term structure models described in Chapter 4 defined the interest rate process under various assumptions about the nature of the stochastic process that drives these rates. However, the zero-coupon curve derived by models such as those described by Vasicek (1977), Brennan and Schwartz (1979) and Cox, Ingersoll and Ross (1985) do not fit the observed market rates or spot rates implied by market yields, and generally market yield curves are found to contain more variable shapes than those derived using term structure models. Hence the interest rate models described in Chapter 4 are required to be *calibrated* to the market, and in practice they are calibrated to the market yield curve. This is carried out in two ways; the model is either calibrated to market instruments such as money market products and interest-rate swaps, which are used to construct the yield curve, or the yield curve is constructed from market instrument rates and the model is calibrated to this constructed curve. If the latter approach is preferred, there are a number of *non-parametric* methods that may be used. We will consider these later.

The academic literature contains a good deal of research into the empirical estimation of the term structure, the object of which is to fit a zero-coupon curve[1] that is a reasonably accurate fit to the market prices *and* is a smooth function. There is an element of trade-off between these two objectives. The second objective is as important as the first however, in order to derive a curve that makes economic sense. (It would be possible to fit the curve perfectly at the expense of smoothness, but this would be almost meaningless.)

In this chapter we present an overview of some of the methods used to fit the yield curve. An excellent account of the approaches used that we discuss in this chapter is given in Anderson *et al.* (1996), but unfortunately this book is now out of print.

---

[1] The zero-coupon or spot curve, or equivalently the forward rate curve or the discount function: all would be describing the same thing.

Fortunately an excellent working paper that formed part of the input to this book is still available, which is Deacon and Derry (1994). A selection of other useful references is provided in the bibliography at the end of this chapter.

Yield curve smoothing

An approach that has been used to estimate the term structure was described by Carleton and Cooper (1976) and which assumed that default-free bond cash flows are payable on specified discrete dates, with a set of unrelated discount factors that apply to each cash flow. These discount factors were then estimated as regression coefficients, with each bond cash flow acting as the independent variables, and the bond price for that date acting as the dependent variable.[2] Using simple linear regression in this way produces a discrete discount function, not a continuous one, and forward rates that are estimated from this function are very jagged. An approach more readily accepted by the market was described by McCulloch (1971), who fitted the discount function using polynomial splines. This method produces a continuous function, and one that is linear so that the *ordinary least squares* regression technique can be employed. In a later study, Langetieg and Smoot (1981) use an extended McCulloch method, fitting *cubic splines* to zero-coupon rates instead of the discount function, and using non-linear methods of estimation.[3]

That is a historical summary of early efforts. But let's get back to the beginning. We know that the term structure can be described as the complete set of discount factors, the discount function, that can be extracted from the price of default-free bonds trading in the market. The bootstrapping technique described in Chapter 3 may be used to extract the relevant discount factors. However, there are a number of reasons why this approach is problematic in practice. First, it is unlikely that the complete set of bonds in the market will pay cash flows at precise six-month intervals every six months from today to 30 years or longer. An adjustment is made for cash flows received at irregular intervals, and for the lack of cash flows available at longer maturities. Another issue is the fact that the technique presented earlier allowed practitioners to calculate the discount factor for six-month maturities, whereas it may be necessary to determine the discount factor for non-standard periods, such as four-month or 14.2-year maturities. This is often the case when pricing derivative instruments.

A third issue concerns the market price of bonds. These often reflect specific investor considerations, which include:

---

[2] The basic concepts regression are summarized briefly in Appendix 5.1.
[3] Reference in Vasicek and Fong (1982).

■ the liquidity or lack thereof of certain bonds, caused by issue sizes, market maker support, investor demand, non-standard maturity, and a host of other factors;

■ the fact that bonds do not trade continuously, so that some bond prices will be 'newer' than others;

■ the tax treatment of bond cash flows, and the effect that this has on bond prices;

■ the effect of the bid-offer spread on the market prices used.

The statistical term used for bond prices subject to these considerations is *error*. It is also common to come across the statement that these effects introduce *noise* into market prices.

To construct a fit to the yield curve that better handles the above considerations, *smoothing* techniques are used to derive the complete set of discount factors from market bond prices, known as the discount function. Using the simple technique presented in Chapter 3 we graph the discount function for the UK gilt prices as at 12 June 2000 (figure 5.2). The yield curve plotted from gilt redemption yields is shown at figure 5.1. Figure 5.3 shows the zero-coupon yield curve and forward rate curve that correspond to the discount function from the date.

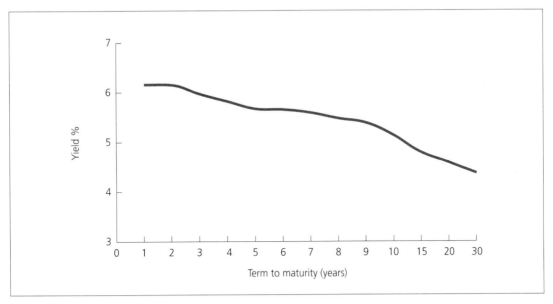

FIGURE 5.1 ■ Gilt gross redemption yields, 12 June 2000

Source: Bloomberg

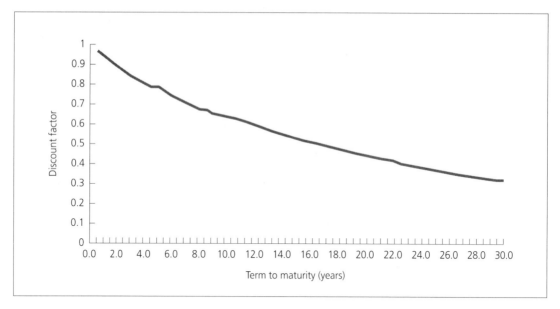

FIGURE 5.2 ■ Discount factors from gilt prices, 12 June 2000

Source: Bloomberg

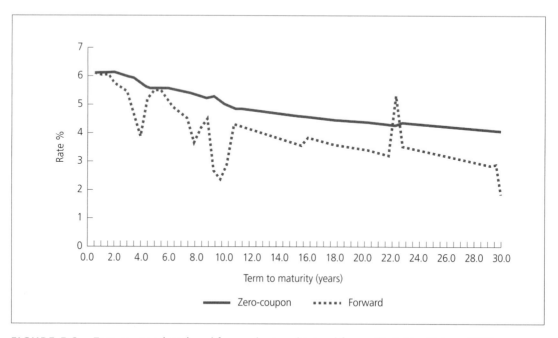

FIGURE 5.3 ■ Zero-coupon (spot) and forward rates obtained from gilt yields, 12 June 2000

Source: Bloomberg

From figure 5.2 we see that the discount function is quite smooth, while the zero-coupon curve is also relatively smooth, although not as smooth as the discount function. The forward rate curve is distinctly unsmooth, if the reader will permit such as an expression, and there is obviously something wrong. In fact, the jagged nature of implied forward rates is one of the main concerns of the fixed income analyst, and indicates in the first instance that the discount function and zero-coupon curve are not as smooth as they appear. Using the naïve estimation method here, the main reason why the forward rates oscillate wildly[4] is that minor errors at the discount factor stage are magnified many times over when translated into the forward rate. That is, any errors in the discount factors (which errors may stem from any of the reasons given above) are compounded when spot rates are calculated from them, and these are compounded into larger errors when calculating forward rates.

Smoothing techniques

A common technique that may be used, but which is not accurate and so not recommended, is *linear interpolation*. In this approach, the set of bond prices are used to graph a redemption yield curve (as in the previous section), and where bonds are not available for the required maturity term, the yield is interpolated from actual yields. Using gilt yields for 26 June 1997 we plot this as shown in figure 5.4. The interpolated yields are those that are not marked by a cross. Figure 5.4 looks reasonable for any practitioner's purpose. However, spot and forward yields that are obtained from this curve are apt to behave in unrealistic fashion, as shown in figure 5.5. The forward curve is very bumpy, and each bump will correspond to a bond used in the original set. The spot rate has a kink at 21.5 years, and so the forward curve jumps significantly at this point. This curve would appear to be particularly unrealistic.

For this reason, market analysts do not bother with linear interpolation and instead use multiple regression or spline-based methods. One approach might be to assume a functional form for the discount function and estimate parameters of this form from the prices of bonds in the market. We consider these approaches next.

Using a cubic polynomial

A simple functional form for the discount function is a *cubic polynomial*. This approach consists of approximating the set of discount factors using a cubic function of time. If we say that $d(t)$ is the discount factor for maturity t, we approximate the set of discount factors using the following cubic function.

---

[4] I've been looking for an excuse to use this expression, for the most obscure reason which we needn't go into here...

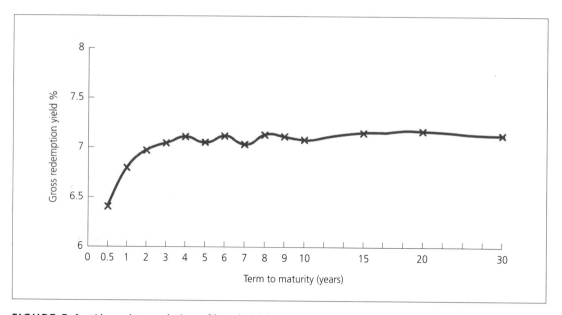

FIGURE 5.4 ■ Linear interpolation of bond yields, 26 June 1997

Yield source: Bloomberg

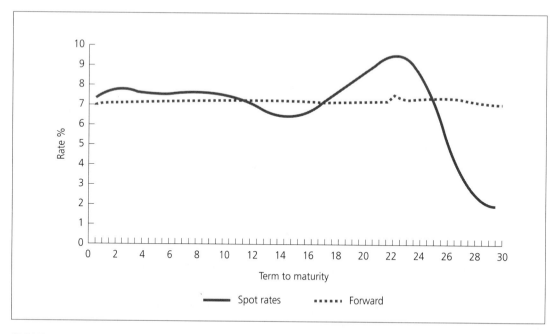

FIGURE 5.5 ■ Spot and forward rates implied from figure 5.4

Yield source: Bloomberg

$$\hat{d}(t) = a_0 + a_1(t) + a_2(t)^2 + a_3(t)^3 \tag{5.1}$$

In some texts the coefficients sometimes are written as a, b and c rather than a_1 and so on.

The discount factor for $t = 0$, that is at time now, is 1. Therefore $a_0 = 1$, and (5.1) can then be rewritten as:

$$\hat{d}(t) - 1 = a_1(t) + a_2(t)^2 + a_3(t)^3 \tag{5.2}$$

The market price of a traded coupon bond can be expressed in terms of discount factors. So at (5.3) we show the expression for the price of an N-maturity bond paying identical coupons C at regular intervals and redeemed at maturity at M.

$$P = d(t_1)C + d(t_2)C + \ldots + d(t_N)(C + M) \tag{5.3}$$

Using the cubic polynomial equation (5.2), expression (5.3) is transformed into:

$$P = C[1 + a_1(t_1) + a_2(t_1)^2 + a_3(t_1)^3] + \ldots + (C + M)[1 + a_1(t_N) + a_2(t_N)^2 + a_3(t_N)^3]. \tag{5.4}$$

We require the coefficients of the cubic function in order to start describing the yield curve, so we rearrange (5.4) in order to express it in terms of these coefficients. This is shown at (5.5).

$$P = M + \sum C + a_1[C(t_1) + \ldots + (C + M)(t_N)] + a_2[C(t_1)^2 + \ldots + (C + M)(t_N)^2]$$
$$+ a_3[C(t_1)^3 + \ldots + (C + M)(t_N)^3] \tag{5.5}$$

In the same way we can express the pricing equation for each bond in our data set in terms of the unknown parameters of the cubic function.

From (5.5) we may write

$$P - (M + \sum C) = a_1 X_1 + a_2 X_2 + a_3 X_3 \tag{5.6}$$

where X_i is the appropriate expression in square brackets in (5.5); this is the form in which the expression is encountered commonly in text books.

EXAMPLE 5.1

A benchmark semi-annual coupon four-year bond with a coupon of 8% is trading at a price of 101.25. Assume the first coupon is precisely six months from now, so that $t_1 = 0.5$ and so $t_N = 4$. Set up the cubic function expression.

We have $C = 4$ and $M = 100$ so therefore:

$100 + \sum C = 100 + (8 \times 4) = 132$

$P - (100 + \sum C) = 101.25 - 132 = -30.75$

$X_1 = (4 \times 0.5) + (4 \times 1) + (4 \times 1.5) + \ldots + (104 \times 4) = 472$

$X_2 = [4 \times (0.5)^2] + [4 \times (1)^2] + [4 \times (1.5)^2] + \ldots + [104 \times (4)^2] = 1{,}796$

$$X_3 = \left[4 \times (0.5)^3\right] + \left[4 \times (1)^3\right] + \left[4 \times (1.5)^3\right] + \ldots + \left[104 \times (4)^3\right] = 7,528$$

This means that we now have an expression for the three coefficients, which is:

$$472a_1 + 1796a_2 + 7528a_3 = -30.75$$

The prices for all other bonds are expressed in terms of the unknown parameters. To calculate the coefficient values, we use a statistical technique such as linear regression, for example *least squares* to find the best fit values of the cubic equation. An introduction to this technique is given at Appendix 5.1 which also considers this bond pricing equation further.

In practice, the cubic polynomial approach is too limited a technique, requiring one equation per bond, and does not have the required flexibility to fit market data satisfactorily. The resulting curve is not really a curve but rather a set of independent discount factors that have been fit with a line of best fit. In addition, the impact of small changes in the data can be significant at the non-local level, so for example a change in a single data point at the early maturities can result in badly behaved longer maturities. Alternatively, a *piecewise cubic polynomial* approach is used, whereby $d(t)$ is assumed to be a different cubic polynomial over each maturity range. This means that the parameters a_1, a_2 and a_3 will be different over each maturity range. We will look at a special case of this use, the cubic spline, a little later.

Non-parametric methods

Outside of the cubic polynomial approach described in the previous section there are two main approaches to fitting the term structure. These are usually grouped into *parametric* and *non-parametric* curves. Parametric curves are based on term structure models such as the Vasicek model or Longstaff and Schwartz model. Non-parametric curves are not derived from an interest-rate model and are general approaches, described using a set of parameters. They include spline-based methods. Another way to describe them would be as econometric techniques, a best fit with error conditions, while the parametric approach can be considered the analytical market method.

Spline-based methods

A spline is a statistical tool and a form of linear interpolation method. There is more than one way of applying them, and the most straightforward method to understand the process is the spline function fitted using regression techniques. For the purposes of yield curve construction, this method can cause curves to jump wildly and are over-sensitive to changes in parameters.[5]

---

[5] For instance see James and Webber (2000), section 15.3.

However, we feel it is the most accessible method to understand and an introduction to the basic technique, as described in Suits *et al.* (1978), is given at Appendix 5.2.[6]

An *n*-th order spline is a piecewise polynomial approximation with *n*-degree polynomials that are differentiable *n*-1 times. 'Piecewise' means that the different polynomials are connected at arbitrarily selected points known as *knot* points (see Appendix 5.2). A cubic spline is a three-order spline, and is a piecewise cubic polynomial that is differentiable twice along all its points.

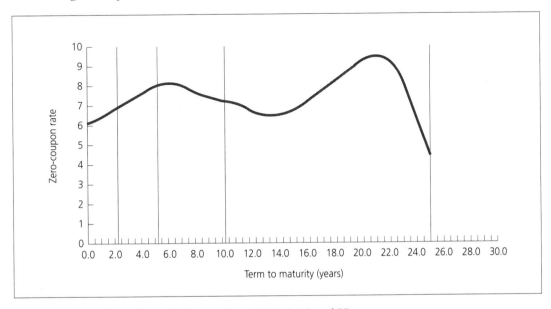

FIGURE 5.6 ■ Cubic spline with knot points at 0, 2, 5, 10 and 25

The *x*-axis in the regression is divided into segments at arbitrary points known as *knot points*. At each knot point, the slope of adjoining curves are required to match, as must the curvature. Figure 5.6 is a cubic spline. The knot points are selected at 0, 2, 5, 10 and 25 years. At each of these points the curve is a cubic polynomial, and with this function we could accommodate a high and low in each space bounded by the knot points.

Cubic spline interpolation assumes that there is a cubic polynomial that can estimate the yield curve at each maturity gap. One can think of a spline as a number of separate polynomials of $y = f(X)$ where X is the complete range, divided into user-specified segments, which are joined smoothly at the knot points. If we have a set of bond yields $r_0, r_1, r_2, ... r_n$ at maturity points $t_0, t_1, t_2, ...t_n$, we can estimate the cubic spline function in the following way:

■ the yield on bond i at time t is expressed as a cubic polynomial of the form $r_i(t) = a_i + b_i t + c_i t^2 + d_i t^3$ for the interval over t_i and t_{i-1};

---

[6] The original article by Suits *et al.* (1978) is excellent and highly recommended. Appendix 5.2 is a summary of some of their results.

- the coefficients of the cubic polynomial are calculated for all n intervals between the $n + 1$ data points, which results in $4n$ unknown coefficients that must be computed;

- these equations can be solved because they are made to fit the observed data. They are twice differentiable at the knot points, and these derivatives are equal at these points;

- the constraints specified are that the curve is instantaneously straight at the start of the curve (the shortest maturity) and instantaneously straight at the end of the curve, the longest maturity, that is $r(0) = 0$.

An accessible and readable account of this technique can be found in Van Deventer and Imai (1997).

The general formula for a cubic spline is:

$$s(\tau) = \sum_{i=0}^{3} a_i \tau^i + \frac{1}{3!} \sum_{p=1}^{n-1} b_p (\tau - X_p)^3 \tag{5.7}$$

where τ is the time of receipt of cash flows and where X_p refers to the points where adjacent polynomials are joined and which are known as knot points, with $\{X_0,.....,X_n\}, X_p < X_{p+1}$, $p = 0,.....,\ n - 1$. In addition $(\tau - X_p) = \max (\tau - X_p, 0)$. The cubic spline is twice differentiable at the knot points. In practice the spline is written down as a set of basis functions with the general spline being made up of a combination of these. One way to do this is by using what are known as *B-splines*. For a specified number of knot points $\{X_0,.....,X_n\}$ this is given by (5.8):

$$B_p(\tau) = \sum_{j=p}^{p+4} \left(\prod_{i=p, i \neq 1}^{p+4} \frac{1}{X_i - X_j} \right) (\tau - X_p)^3 \tag{5.8}$$

where $B_p(\tau)$ are cubic splines which are approximated on $\{X_0,.....,X_n\}$ with the following function:

$$\delta(\tau) = \delta (\tau | \lambda_{-3},\ ....,\ \lambda_{n-1}) = \sum_{p=-3}^{n-1} \lambda_p B_p(\tau) \tag{5.9}$$

with $\lambda = (\lambda_{-3},.....,\lambda_{n-1})$ the required coefficients. The maturity periods $\tau_1,.....,\tau_n$ specify the B-splines so that $B = \{B_p(\tau_j)\}_{p=-3,.....,n-1, j=1,.....,m}$ and $\hat{\delta} = (\delta(\tau_1),.....,\delta(\tau_m))$. This allows us to set

$$\hat{\delta} = B'\lambda \tag{5.10}$$

and therefore the regression equation

$$\lambda^* = \arg \min_{\lambda} \{\varepsilon'\varepsilon | \varepsilon = P - D\lambda\} \tag{5.11}$$

with $D = CB'$.

$\varepsilon'\varepsilon$ are the minimum errors. The regression at (5.11) is computed using ordinary least squares regression.

An illustration of the use of B-splines is given in Steeley (1991) and more recently, and with a complete methodology by Didier Joannas in Choudhry *et al.* (2001).

Appendix 5.2 provides background on splines fitted using regression methods.

Nelson and Siegel curves

The curve fitting technique first described by Nelson and Siegel (1985) has since been applied and modified by other authors, which is why they are sometimes described as a 'family' of curves. These curves provide a satisfactory rough fit of the complete term structure, with some loss of accuracy at the very short and very long end. In the original curve the authors specify four parameters. The approach is not a bootstrapping technique, rather a method for estimating the zero-coupon rate function from the yields observed on T-bills, under an assumed function for forward rates.

The Nelson and Spiegel curve states that the implied forward rate yield curve may be modelled along the entire term structure using the following function:

$$rf(m, \beta) = \beta_0 + \beta_1 \exp\left(\frac{-m}{t_1}\right) + \beta_2\left(\frac{m}{t_1}\right) \exp\left(\frac{-m}{t_1}\right) \tag{5.12}$$

where $\beta = (\beta_0, \beta_1, \beta_2, t_1)'$ is the vector of parameters describing the yield curve, and m is the maturity at which the forward rate is calculated. There are three components, the constant term, a decay term and term reflecting the 'humped' nature of the curve. The shape of the curve will gradually lead into an asymptote at the long end, the value of which is given by β_0, with a value of $\beta_0 + \beta_1$ at the short end.

A version of the Nelson and Siegel curve is the Svensson model (1994) with an adjustment to allow for the humped characteristic of the yield curve. This is fitted by adding an extension, as shown by (5.13).

$$rf(m, \beta) = \beta_0 + \beta_1 \exp\left(\frac{-m}{t_1}\right) + \beta_2\left(\frac{m}{t_1}\right) \exp\left(\frac{-m}{t_1}\right) + \beta_3\left(\frac{m}{t_2}\right) \exp\left(\frac{-m}{t_2}\right) \tag{5.13}$$

The Svensson curve is modelled therefore using six parameters, with additional input of β_3 and t_2.

Nelson and Siegel curves are popular in the market because they are straightforward to calculate. Jordan and Mansi (2000) state that one of the advantages of these curves is that they force the long-date forward curve into an horizontal asymptote, while another is that the user is not required to specify knot points, the choice of which determines the effectiveness or otherwise of cubic spline curves. The disadvantage they note is that these curves are less flexible than spline-based curves, and there is therefore a chance that they do not fit the observed data as accurately as spline models.[7] James and Webber (2000, pages 444–445) also suggest that Nelson and Siegel curves are slightly inflexible due to the limited number of parameters, and are accurate for yield curves that have only one

---

[7] This is an excellent article, strongly recommended, a good overview introduction to curve fitting is given in the introduction, and the main body of the article gives a good insight into the type of research that is currently being undertaken in yield curve analysis.

hump, but are unsatisfactory for curves that possess both a hump and trough. As they are only reasonable for approximations, Nelson and Siegel curves would not be appropriate for no-arbitrage applications.

Comparing curves

Whichever curve is chosen will depend on the user's requirements and the purpose for which the model is required. The choice of modelling methodology is usually a trade-off between simplicity and ease of computation and accuracy. Essentially, the curve chosen must fulfil the qualities of:

- *Accuracy.* Is the curve a reasonable fit of the market curve? Is it flexible enough to accommodate a variety of yield curve shapes?
- *Model consistency.* Is the curve fitting method consistent with a theoretical yield curve model such as Vasicek or Cox-Ingersoll-Ross?
- *Simplicity.* Is the curve reasonably straightforward to compute, that is, is it *tractable*?

The different methodologies all fit these requirements to greater or lesser extent. A good summary of the advantages and disadvantages of some popular modelling methods can be found in James and Webber (2000, chapter 15).

APPENDICES

Appendix 5.1: Linear regression: ordinary least squares

The main purpose of regression analysis is to estimate or predict the average value of a *dependent* variable given the known values of an independent or *explanatory* variable. In one way it measures the relationship between two sets of data. This data might be the relationship between family income and expenditure; here the income would be the independent variable and expenditure the dependent variable. More relevant for our purposes, it could also be the relationship between the change in price of a corporate bond, priced off the benchmark yield curve, and changes in the price of a short-dated benchmark bond and the price of a long-term bond. In this case, the price of the corporate bond is the dependent variable, while the prices of the short- and long-term government bonds are independent variables. If there is a linear relationship between the dependent and independent variables, we may use a regression function to determine the relationship between them.

This appendix provides a basic overview and introduction to regression and ordinary least squares. Regression analysis is a key part of financial econometrics, and advanced econometric analysis is extensively used in fixed income work. For a background in basic econometrics, we recommend the book of the same title by Damodar Gujarati, published by McGraw-Hill (3rd edition, 1995), which is excellent. Gujarati's book is very accessible and readable, and provides a good grounding in the topic. For more advanced applications we recommend *The Econometrics of Financial Markets* by Campbell, Lo and MacKinlay (Princeton 1997).

If our data set consists of the entire population, rather than a statistical sample of the population, we estimate the relationship between two data sets using the population regression function. Given an independent variable X and dependent variable Y it can be shown that the conditional mean $E(Y \mid X_i)$ is a function of X_i. This would be written

$$E(Y \mid X_i) = f(X_i) \tag{5.1.1}$$

where $f(X_i)$ is a function of the independent variable X_i. Equation (5.1.1) is termed the two-variable population regression function and states that average value of Y given X_i is a linear function of X_i. It can further be shown that

$$E(Y \mid X_i) = \alpha + \beta X_i \tag{5.1.2}$$

where α and β are the regression coefficients; they are unknown but fixed parameters. The α term is the intercept coefficient and β is the slope coefficient. These are shown at figure 5.7. The objective of regression analysis is to estimate the values of the regression coefficients using observations of the values of X and Y.

Equation (5.1.2) is a two-variable regression; it is sometimes written as

$$Y = \beta_1 + \beta_2 X_i \qquad\qquad (5.1.3)$$

Where there are more than two variables we use a multi-variable regression.

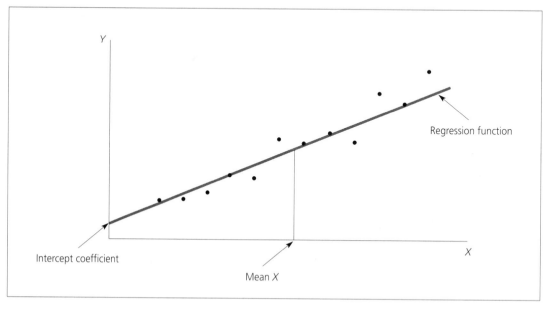

FIGURE 5.7 ■ Regression line passing through values of *X* and *Y*

It can be shown further that given a value for X_i, the independent variable value will be clustered around the average value for *Y* at that X_i, in other words around the conditional expectation. The deviation of an individual Y_i around its expected value is defined as

$$u_i = Y_i - E(Y|X_i) \qquad\qquad (5.1.4)$$

This is rearranged to give

$$Y_i = E(Y|X_i) + u_i \qquad\qquad (5.1.5)$$

where the term u_i is an unknown random variable and is known as the stochastic disturbance or stochastic error term, or simply *error term*. It is written as ε in some textbooks.

The value of the dependent variable is the sum of two elements; the systematic or deterministic element, which is given by the regression function above, and a random or non-systematic element which is the error term. Essentially the error term captures all those elements that have been missed out or left out of the regression model.

In practice it is most unlikely that we will have data sets available for the entire population, so we use statistical sample data instead. When regression is carried out on sample data we use the sample regression function (SRF), which is (5.1.6) below.

$$Y_i = \hat{\alpha} + \hat{\beta}X_i + \hat{u}_i \qquad (5.1.6)$$

where

$\hat{\alpha}$ is the *estimator* of α

$\hat{\beta}$ is the estimator of β

The SRF is determined using a statistical technique known as *ordinary least squares* or OLS. This approach is covered in any number of statistics and econometrics textbooks, we suggest chapter 3 in Gujarati (1995). A very brief description is given here.

Let us expand our regression model. Assume we have N observations and m independent variables. Say that Y_i is the ith observation on the dependent variable and X_{it} is the ith observation on the tth independent variable. The regression function of the relationship between the dependent and independent variables is given by

$$Y_i = \beta_1 X_{1i} + \beta_2 X_{2i} + \dots\dots + \beta_m X_{mi} + \varepsilon_i \qquad (5.1.7)$$

and where we must estimate the $\beta_1, \beta_2, \dots, \beta_m$ regression coefficients. This is done using OLS. From (5.1.7) ε_i is the error in the model, the random element that is left out in predicting the ith value of the dependent variable. From our earlier description we know that

$$e_i = Y_i \beta_1 X_{1i} - \beta_2 X_{2i} - \dots\dots - \beta_m X_{mi} \qquad (5.1.8)$$

We require the *sum of squared errors*, which is given by $\varepsilon_1^2 + \varepsilon_2^2 + \varepsilon_i^2$, and OLS is determining the coefficients that minimize this sum of squared errors.

Earlier in the chapter (Example 5.1), we illustrated a bond pricing equation, which was

$$472a_1 + 1796a_2 + 7528a_3 = -30.75$$

What this expression tells us is that -30.75 is the value of the dependent variable; there are three independent variables with values of 472, 1,796 and 7,528. As there are three unknowns, we require only four such bond price equations and we can solve for a_1, a_2 and a_3. This may appear slightly daunting if it is to be carried out by hand, and in fact software applications are used to speed the process. Using such a package, we can calculate the values that minimize the sum of squared errors on the model.

If we say that the values are a_1, a_2 and a_3, then the OLS estimate of the discount function, given the market bond prices used to derive the coefficient equations, is given by

$$\hat{d}(t) = 1 + a_1 t + a_2 t^2 + a_3 t^3 \qquad (5.1.9)$$

Appendix 5.2: Regression splines

This appendix is a summary part of Suits *et al.* (1978), an excellent account of how a spline function may be fitted using regression methods. The article is very accessible and strongly recommended.

A standard econometric approach is that of *piecewise linear regression*. This method is not suitable for fitting a relationship that is not purely linear however (such as a term structure), as illustrated by figure 5.8.

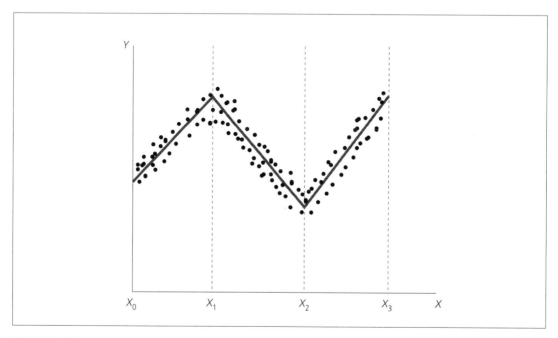

FIGURE 5.8

To get around this problem, one approach would be to join a series of linear regressions, at arbitrary points specified by the user. This is described by

$$Y = [a_1 + b_1(X - X_0)]D_1 + [a_2 + b_2(X - X_1)]D_2 + [a_3 + b_3(X - X_2)]D_3 + u \qquad (5.2.1)$$

In (5.2.1) D_i is what is known as a dummy variable, with a value of 1 for all observations whenever $X_{i-1} \leq X \leq X_i$ and a value of 0 at other times. As it stands (5.2.1) is discontinuous at X_1 and X_2 but this can be removed by imposing the following constraints:

$$a_2 = a_1 + b_1 (X_1 - X_0)$$
$$a_3 = a_2 + b_2 (X_2 - X_1) \qquad (5.2.2)$$

If (5.2.2) is substituted into (5.2.1) the following is obtained:

$$Y = a_1 + b_1[(X - X_0)]D_1 + (X_1 - X_0)D_2 + (X_2 - X_1)D_3] + b_2[(X - X_1)D_2$$
$$+ (X_2 - X_1)D_3] + b_3[(X - X_2)D_3] + u \qquad (5.2.3)$$

The expression at (5.2.3) has converted a piecewise linear regression into a multiple regression. Y is the dependent variable and is regressed on three *composite variables*, the values for which are obtained from:

■ the X data sets;

■ the values for X_i at the points at which the curve is required to 'bend';

■ the widths of the selected intervals;

■ the three dummy variables.

As Suits *et al.* state, it would be possible to calculate the coefficients by hand (!) but there are a number of standard software packages that the user can employ to solve the regression.

The disadvantages of piecewise linear regression if used for a number of applications, including yield curve fitting, are twofold. First, the derivatives of the function are not continuous, and this discontinuity can seriously distort the curve at the derivative points, which would make curve meaningless at these points. Second, and more crucial for yield curve applications, it may not be obvious where the linear segments should be placed: the scatter diagram of observations may indicate several possibilities. This situation may make it desirable to specify X_i at user-specified (arbitrary) points, and this makes linear regression unsuitable.

To get around these problems we use a *spline function*. For this the linear function described by (5.2.1) is replaced with a set of piecewise polynomial functions. It would be possible to polynomials of any degree, but the most common approach is to use cubic polynomials. The x-axis is divided into three intervals, at the points X_0, X_1, X_2 and X_3. These points are known as *knot points* and are illustrated at figure 5.9.

In figure 5.9 the segments chosen, following Suits *et al.*, are at equal intervals. This is not essential to the procedure, however, and for applications including yield curve modelling is not undertaken: instead the knots are placed at points where the user thinks the relationship changes most. For example, for the term structure the knots may be placed at 0-, 2-, 5- and 10-year maturities. If more than four knots are required, for instance to go beyond to 20- and 30-year maturities, then the analyst will require a greater number of composite variables, as discussed later. The downside associated with a greater number of intervals is that more composite variables are required to fit the curve and hence there is loss of additional degrees of freedom.

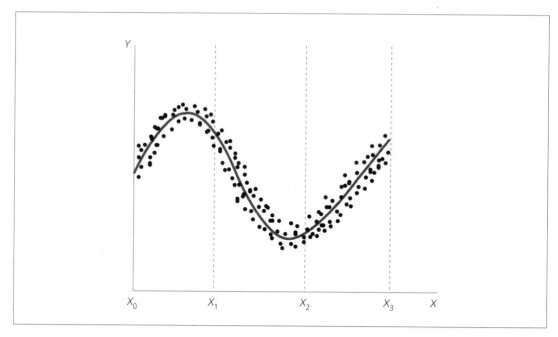

FIGURE 5.9

The regression relationship now becomes

$$Y = \lfloor a_1 + b_1(X - X_0) + c_1(X - X_0)^2 + d_1(X - X_0)^3 \rfloor D_1$$
$$+ \lfloor a_2 + b_2(X - X_1) + c_2(X - X_1)^2 + d_2(X - X_1)^3 \rfloor D_2 \qquad (5.2.4)$$
$$+ \lfloor a_3 + b_3(X - X_2) + c_3(X - X_2)^2 + d_3(X - X_2)^3 \rfloor D_3 + u$$

where D_i is a dummy variable specified by the interval i.

This time both the function described by (5.2.4) and its derivatives are discontinuous at the knot points, but this feature can be removed by applying constraints to the coefficients. The constraints ensure the following:

- for a_i the values of the very short-end and the very long-end are equal at the start and end knot points;

- for b_i the first derivatives, the slope of the left- and right-hand sides of each knot point, are equal;

- for c_i the second derivatives are equal.

The constraints are given by (5.2.5).

$$a_2 = a_1 + b_1(X_1 - X_0) + c_1(X_1 - X_0)^2 + d_1(X_1 - X_0)^3$$
$$a_3 = a_2 + b_2(X_2 - X_1) + c_2(X_2 - X_1)^2 + d_2(X_2 - X_1)^3$$
$$b_2 = b_1 + 2c_1(X_1 - X_0) + 3d_1(X_1 - X_1)^2$$
$$b_3 = b_2 + 2c_2(X_2 - X_1) + 3d_2(X_2 - X_1)^2 \qquad (5.2.5)$$
$$c_2 = c_1 + 3d_1(X_1 - X_0)$$
$$c_3 = c_2 + 3d_2(X_2 - X_1)$$

Using expression (5.2.5), a spline function becomes a multiple regression of the dependent variable Y on five composite variables and Suits *et al.* show this to be

$$Y = a_1 + b_1(X - X_0) + c_1(X - X_0)^2 + d_1(X - X_0)^3 + (d_2 - d_1)(X - X_1)^3 D_1^* + (d_3 - d_2)(X - X_2)^3 D_2^* \quad (5.2.6)$$

where D_1^* and D_2^* are dummy variables where $D_i^* = 1$ if $X \geq X_i$, at other times the dummy variable is equal to 0. To compute *the coefficients of the regression* we can use the least-squares procedure, available on standard software packages.

Finally, if we wish to select more than three intervals, that is more than four knot points, which is common in yield curve applications, we can use (5.2.7) below, derived from Suits *et al.* (1978). This is a multiple regression, a fitted spline function with $n + 1$ intervals, with knot points at $X_0, X_1, X_2, \ldots, X_{n+1}$ and corresponding dummy variables D_1^*, $D_2^*, \ldots, D_n^*$.

$$Y = a_1 + b_1(X - X_0) + c_1(X - X_0)^2 + d_1(X - X_0)^3 + \sum_{i=1}^{n} (d_{i+1} - d_i)(X - X_i)^3 D_i^* \qquad (5.2.7)$$

With each extra interval, an extra composite variable is required and this results in the loss of one more degree of freedom.

Appendix 5.3: United Kingdom gilt yields 1989–2000

The benchmark United Kingdom gilt gross redemption yields from 1989 to 2000 are given here, sourced from Bloomberg. The three-month rate is the T-bill yield. The implied spot and forward rates calculated from these bond yields are given alongside.

UK gilt gross redemption yields, and implied spot and forward rates

		GRY	*Spot rate*	*Forward rate*
9-Nov-00	3m	5.82	5.820	5.820
	1y	5.75	5.749	5.579
	2y	5.69	5.688	5.532
	3y	5.66	5.656	5.375
	4y	5.55	5.538	5.377
	5y	5.53	5.518	5.149
	6y	5.48	5.462	4.888
	7y	5.41	5.382	4.817
	8y	5.35	5.313	4.280
	9y	*5.25	5.196	4.014
	10y	5.15	5.075	4.570
	15y	4.93	4.814	4.033
	20y	4.70	4.514	4.319
	30y	4.50	4.253	3.390
9-Jun-00	3m	6.06	6.060	6.060
	1y	6.13	6.130	6.069
	2y	6.15	6.151	5.592
	3y	5.97	5.959	5.257
	4y	5.80	5.776	5.086
	5y	5.67	5.635	5.531
	6y	5.66	5.630	4.992
	7y	5.58	5.396	4.626
	8y	5.48	5.424	4.498
	9y	5.39	5.319	4.251
	10y	5.12	4.990	4.401
	15y	4.81	4.638	4.075
	20y	4.60	4.387	5.267
	30y	4.39	4.126	3.249

		GRY	Spot rate	Forward rate
10-Nov-99	3m	5.27	5.270	5.441
	1y	5.79	5.795	5.977
	2y	5.97	5.979	6.064
	3y	6.04	6.051	5.577
	4y	5.94	5.938	5.413
	5y	5.85	5.837	5.396
	6y	5.79	5.770	4.888
	7y	5.68	5.642	4.641
	8y	5.57	5.514	4.781
	9y	5.50	5.433	3.558
	10y	5.16	5.015	4.296
	15y	4.77	4.568	3.905
	20y	4.50	4.248	4.559
	30y	4.29	4.007	3.175
10-Jun-99	3m	5.12	5.120	5.140
	1y	5.10	5.100	5.535
	2y	5.31	5.316	5.310
	3y	5.31	5.314	5.223
	4y	5.29	5.291	5.180
	5y	5.27	5.269	5.961
	6y	5.34	5.384	5.371
	7y	5.37	5.382	4.883
	8y	5.32	5.320	4.648
	9y	5.26	5.245	4.080
	10y	5.11	5.057	5.230
	15y	5.12	5.088	4.794
	20y	5.05	4.990	4.654
	30y	4.93	4.798	4.301
10-Nov-98	3m	6.45	6.450	6.450
	1y	6.06	6.056	4.910
	2y	5.35	5.327	4.925
	3y	5.21	5.187	4.774
	4y	5.11	5.085	4.708
	5y	5.04	5.013	4.498

		GRY	Spot rate	Forward rate
	6y	4.96	4.927	5.485
	7y	5.04	5.024	4.978
	8y	5.04	5.026	3.975
	9y	4.94	4.906	5.460
	10y	4.99	4.972	5.032
	15y	5.03	5.031	4.301
	20y	4.88	4.806	4.336
	30y	4.70	4.524	3.648
10-Jun-98	3m	7.35	7.350	7.350
	1y	7.32	7.319	6.685
	2y	6.98	6.966	5.903
	3y	6.61	6.575	4.987
	4y	6.20	6.135	5.478
	5y	6.07	6.002	5.465
	6y	*5.985	5.915	5.270
	7y	5.90	5.825	5.467
	8y	5.86	5.785	4.956
	9y	5.78	5.694	4.646
	10y	5.69	5.587	5.612
	15y	5.69	5.008	5.224
	20y	5.60	5.497	5.071
	30y	5.44	5.233	4.4
10-Nov-97	3m	7.15	7.150	7.150
	1y	7.30	7.301	7.320
	2y	7.09	7.082	6.762
	3y	7.01	6.999	6.555
	4y	6.92	6.901	6.203
	5y	6.80	6.768	6.625
	6y	6.79	6.671	5.992
	7y	6.70	6.655	6.500
	8y	6.69	6.648	6.488
	9y	6.63	6.574	5.913
	10y	6.58	6.513	6.582
	15y	6.62	6.593	5.970

		GRY	Spot rate	Forward rate
	20y	6.51	6.4	6.194
	30y	6.47	6.357	6.231
10-Jun-97	3m	6.60	6.600	6.600
	1y	6.72	6.721	6.837
	2y	6.87	6.877	6.705
	3y*	6.85	6.853	7.382
	4y	7.02	7.042	6.850
	5y	7.01	7.026	7.468
	6y	7.10	7.131	6.821
	7y	7.08	7.102	7.431
	8y	7.13	7.164	7.119
	9y	7.14	7.174	6.757
	10y	7.12	7.142	7.238
	15y	7.20	7.257	6.962
	20y	7.18	7.205	7.35
	30y	7.17	7.171	7.01
10-May-96	3m	5.93	5.930	5.930
	1y	6.35	6.347	7.077
	2y	6.70	6.709	8.159
	3y	7.15	7.189	7.734
	4y*	7.28	7.324	8.043
	5y	7.41	7.466	8.808
	6y	7.60	7.688	9.333
	7y	7.79	7.920	9.881
	8y	7.98	8.163	8.368
	9y*	8.01	8.185	8.311
	10y	8.03	8.197	8.795
	15y	8.24	8.489	8.378
	20y	8.26	8.468	8.201
	30y	8.25	8.367	8.125
10-Nov-95	3m	6.61	6.610	6.610
	2y	6.63	6.627	7.406
	3y	6.87	6.884	8.173
	4y	7.16	7.204	7.861

		GRY	Spot rate	Forward rate
	5y	7.28	7.334	8.680
	6y	7.47	7.556	8.456
	7y*	7.58	7.684	8.663
	8y	7.68	7.805	8.829
	9y*	7.77	7.917	9.115
	10y	7.86	8.036	8.439
	15y	8.02	8.238	8.087
	20y	8.03	8.203	8.316
	30y	8.08	8.293	8.700
10-May-94	3m	4.93	4.930	4.930
	1y	5.95	5.948	8.492
	2y	7.17	7.211	7.851
	3y	7.38	7.423	9.210
	4y	7.78	7.864	8.496
	5y	7.90	7.989	10.088
	6y	8.19	8.335	8.466
	7y	8.22	8.353	11.147
	8y	8.48	8.697	6.922
	9y	8.36	8.497	6.565
	10y	8.24	8.303	8.625
	15y	8.35	8.461	7.957
	20y	8.29	8.306	8.131
	30y	8.26	8.212	7.903
10-May-93	3m	5.45	5.450	5.450
	2y	6.39	6.405	8.170
	3y	6.94	6.989	7.792
	4y	7.13	7.189	8.191
	5y	7.31	7.387	8.468
	6y	7.73	7.892	7.189
	7y	7.67	7.790	8.444
	8y	8.01	8.239	9.591
	9y	8.13	8.388	7.226
	10y	8.07	8.270	9.491
	15y	8.45	8.849	9.198

		GRY	Spot rate	Forward rate
	20y	8.55	8.977	8.894
	30y	8.60	9.003	9.321
10-May-92	3m	10.00	10.000	10.000
	6m	10.00	10.511	8.882
	1y	9.94	9.933	8.749
	2y	9.37	9.337	9.436
	3y	9.39	9.368	8.841
	4y	9.27	9.234	9.090
	5y	9.24	9.204	9.240
	6y	9.24	9.209	9.333
	7y	9.25	9.226	7.279
	8y	9.07	8.980	10.251
	9y	9.16	9.119	8.854
	10y	9.14	9.092	8.724
	15y	9.02	8.905	9.020
	20y	9.02	8.932	8.802
	30y	8.98	8.832	8.449
10-May-91	3m	11.50	11.500	11.500
	6m	11.19	11.820	1.967
	1y*	11.20	6.989	15.793
	2y*	11.05	11.280	10.102
	3y*	10.77	10.884	8.755
	4y*	10.34	10.347	9.422
	5y	10.19	10.160	10.578
	6y	10.24	10.228	10.530
	7y	10.27	10.270	10.504
	8y	10.29	10.298	7.851
	9y	10.11	10.022	11.895
	10y	10.22	10.207	9.921
	15y	10.14	10.064	8.528
	20y	9.91	9.544	7.477
10-May-90	3m	15.12	15.120	15.120
	6m	15.25	16.458	12.672
	1y	15.13	15.115	13.807

		GRY	Spot rate	Forward rate
	2y*	14.51	14.448	12.829
	3y*	14.02	13.905	11.466
	4y*	13.49	13.288	10.761
	5y*	13.06	12.777	11.846
	6y	12.91	12.619	12.406
	7y	12.86	12.586	11.379
	8y	12.74	12.435	11.851
	9y	12.68	12.369	9.655
	10y	12.32	11.782	10.686
	15y	11.86	11.092	9.345
	20y	11.48	10.363	7.264
5-Oct-89	3m			
	6m			
	1y			
	2y			
	3y			
	4y			
	5y			
	6y			
	7y	10.46	10.613	10.395
	8y	10.45	10.586	8.782
	9y	10.32	10.385	9.812
	10y	10.28	10.327	7.920
	15y	9.60	9.188	8.037
	20y	9.31	8.724	6.739

(GRY yields source: Bloomberg and author's records)

* Indicates interpolated yield

SELECTED BIBLIOGRAPHY AND REFERENCES

This is another heavily researched field. Questa (1999) is a good general introduction, see part two in his book. Chapter 2 of Van Deventer and Imai (1997) is also an excellent introduction to yield curve smoothing; the book itself is a good general text. James and Webber (2000) is an overview account of the main developments in yield curve modelling, but assumes a good grounding in calculus and econometrics. For a readable introduction to econometric techniques see Guajarati (1995). Choudhry *et al.* (2001) is accompanied by a CD-Rom that contains a yield curve calculator that allows users to calculate spot and forward yield curves from observed bond redemption yields. The journal articles we strongly recommend are Deacon and Derry (1994) and Jordan and Mansi (2000) for their accessibility and readability; both are very good accounts. Finally, Tuckman (1996) is an excellent general text, all of part one of his book is well worth reading.

Anderson, N., Breedon, F., Deacon, M., Derry, A., Murphy, M., *Estimating and Interpreting the Yield Curve*, Wiley 1996

Carleton, W., Cooper, I., 'Estimation and Uses of the Term Structure of Interest Rates', *Journal of Finance*, September 1976, pp. 1067–1083

Choudhry, M., Joannas, D., Pereira, R., Pienaar, R., *Capital Market Instruments: Valuation and Analysis*, FT Prentice Hall 2001

Deacon, M., Derry, A., 'Estimating the Term Structure of Interest Rates', *Bank of England Working Paper* No 24, July 1994

Gujarati, D., *Basic Econometrics,* 3rd edition, McGraw-Hill 1995

James, J., Webber, N., *Interest Rate Modelling*, Wiley 2000

Jordan, J., Mansi, S., 'How Well do Constant-Maturity Treasuries Approximate the On-The-Run Term Structure?', *Journal of Fixed Income* 10:2, September 2000, pp. 35–45

McCulloch, J.H., 'Measuring the Term Structure of Interest Rates', *Journal of Business*, January 1971, pp. 19–31

Questa, G., *Fixed Income Analysis for the Global Financial Market*, Wiley 1999

Steeley, J.M., 'Estimating the Gilt-Edged Term Structure: Basis Splines and Confidence Intervals', *Journal of Business Finance and Accounting* 18, 1991, pp. 513–530

Suits, D., Mason, A., Chan, L., 'Spline Functions Fitted by Standard Regression Methods', *Review of Economics and Statistics* 60, 1978, pp. 132–139

Tuckman, B., *Fixed Income Securities*, Wiley 1996

Van Deventer, D., Imai, K., *Financial Risk Analytics,* Irwin 1997

Vasicek, O., Fong, H.G., 'Term Structure Modelling Using Exponential Splines', *Journal of Finance* 37(2), May 1982, pp. 339–348

Part II

Selected market instruments

The second part of the book reviews selected instruments traded in the debt capital markets. The products have been chosen to give the reader an idea of the depth of variety in the market. So we consider money market instruments, followed by hybrid securities, mortgage-backed securities and callable bonds. Some of the techniques used to analyze these more complex products are also described and explained.

CHAPTER 6

The money markets

In terms of trading volume the *money markets* are the largest and most active market in the world. Money market securities are securities with maturities of up to 12 months, that is, they are short-term debt obligations. Money market debt is an important part of the global financial markets, and facilitates the smooth running of the banking industry as well as providing working capital for industrial and commercial corporate institutions. The market allows issuers, who are financial organizations as well as corporates, to raise funds for short-term periods at relatively low interest rates. These issuers include sovereign governments, who issue Treasury bills, corporates issuing commercial paper and banks issuing bills and certificates of deposit. At the same time, investors are attracted to the market because the instruments are highly liquid and carry relatively low credit risk. Investors in the money market include banks, local authorities, corporations, money market investment funds and individuals, however, the money market essentially is a wholesale market and the denominations of individual instruments are relatively large.

Although the money market has traditionally been defined as the market for instruments maturing in one year or less, frequently the money market desks of banks trade instruments with maturities of up to two year, both cash and off-balance sheet.[1] In addition to the cash instruments that go to make up the market, the money markets also consist of a wide range of over-the-counter off-balance sheet derivative instruments. These instruments are used mainly to establish future borrowing and lending rates, and to hedge or change existing interest rate exposure. This activity is carried out by banks, central banks and corporates. The main derivatives are short-term interest rate futures, forward rate agreements, and short-dated interest rate swaps.

In this chapter we review the cash instruments traded in the money market as well as the two main money market derivatives, interest-rate futures and forward-rate agreements.

---

[1] For instance, the author has experience in market-making on a desk that combined cash and derivative instruments of up to two years maturity as well as government bonds of up to three years maturity.

Overview

The cash instruments traded in the money market include the following:

- Treasury bill;
- time deposit;
- certificate of deposit;
- commercial paper;
- bankers acceptance;
- bill of exchange.

We can also add the market in repurchase agreements or *repo*, which are essentially secured cash loans, to this list.

A Treasury bill is used by sovereign governments to raise short-term funds, while certificates of deposit (CDs) are used by banks to raise finance. The other instruments are used by corporates and occasionally banks. Each instrument represents an obligation on the borrower to repay the amount borrowed on the maturity date together with interest if this applies. The instruments above fall into one of two main classes of money market securities: those quoted on a *yield* basis and those quoted on a *discount* basis. These two terms are discussed below.

The calculation of interest in the money markets often differs from the calculation of accrued interest in the corresponding bond market. Generally the day-count convention in the money market is the exact number of days that the instrument is held over the number of days in the year. In the sterling market the year base is 365 days, so the interest calculation for sterling money market instruments is given by expression (6.1).

$$i = \frac{n}{365} \qquad\qquad (6.1)$$

The majority of currencies including the US dollar and the euro calculate interest based on a 360-day base.

Settlement of money market instruments can be for value today (generally only when traded in before midday), tomorrow or two days forward, known as *spot*.

Securities quoted on a yield basis

Two of the instruments in the list above are yield-based instruments.

Money market deposits

These are fixed-interest term deposits of up to one year with banks and securities houses. They are also known as *time deposits* or *clean deposits*. They are not negotiable so cannot be liquidated before maturity. The interest rate on the deposit is fixed for the term and related to the London Interbank Offer Rate (LIBOR) of the same term. Interest and capital are paid on maturity.

LIBOR

The term LIBOR or 'Libor' means the London Interbank Offered Rate and is the interest rate at which one London bank offers funds to another London bank of acceptable credit quality in the form of a cash deposit. The rate is 'fixed' by the British Bankers Association at 1100 hours every business day morning (in practice the fix is usually about 20 minutes later) by taking the average of the rates supplied by member banks. The term LIBID is the bank's 'bid' rate, that is the rate at which it pays for funds in the London market. The quote spread for a selected maturity is therefore the difference between LIBOR and LIBID. The convention in London is to quote the two rates as LIBOR-LIBID, thus matching the yield convention for other instruments. In some other markets, the quote convention is reversed. EURIBOR is the interbank rate offered for euros as reported by the European Central Bank and fixed in Brussels. Other money centres also have their rates fixed, so for example STIBOR is the Stockholm banking rate, while pre-euro the Portuguese escudo rate fixing out of Lisbon was LISBOR.

The effective rate on a money market deposit is the annual equivalent interest rate for an instrument with a maturity of less than one year.

Certificates of Deposit

Certificates of Deposit (CDs) are receipts from banks for deposits that have been placed with them. They were first introduced in the sterling market in 1958. The deposits themselves carry a fixed rate of interest related to LIBOR and have a fixed term to maturity, so cannot be withdrawn before maturity. However, the certificates themselves can be traded in a secondary market, that is, they are negotiable.[2] CDs are therefore very similar to negotiable money market deposits, although the yields are about 0.15% below the equivalent deposit rates because of the added benefit of liquidity. Most CDs issued are of between

---

[2] A small number of CDs are non-negotiable.

one and three months maturity, although they do trade in maturities of one to five years. Interest is paid on maturity except for CDs lasting longer than one year, where interest is paid annually or occasionally, semi-annually.

Banks, merchant banks and building societies issue CDs to raise funds to finance their business activities. A CD will have a stated interest rate and fixed maturity date and can be issued in any denomination. On issue a CD is sold for face value, so the settlement proceeds of a CD on issue always equal its nominal value. The interest is paid, together with the face amount, on maturity. The interest rate is sometimes called the *coupon*, but unless the CD is held to maturity this will not equal the yield, which is of course the current rate available in the market and varies over time. In the US, CDs are available in smaller denomination amounts to retail investors.[3] The largest group of CD investors are banks, money market funds, corporates and local authority treasurers.

Unlike coupons on bonds, which are paid in rounded amounts, CD coupon is calculated to the exact day.

CD yields

The coupon quoted on a CD is a function of the credit quality of the issuing bank, and its expected liquidity level in the market, and of course the maturity of the CD, as this will be considered relative to the money market yield curve. As CDs are issued by banks as part of their short-term funding and liquidity requirement, issue volumes are driven by the demand for bank loans and the availability of alternative sources of funds for bank customers. The credit quality of the issuing bank is the primary consideration however; in the sterling market the lowest yield is paid by 'clearer' CDs, which are CDs issued by the clearing banks such as RBS NatWest, HSBC and Barclays plc. In the US market, 'prime' CDs, issued by highly rated domestic banks, trade at a lower yield than non-prime CDs. In both markets, CDs issued by foreign banks such as French or Japanese banks will trade at higher yields.

Euro-CDs, which are CDs issued in a different currency to the home currency, also trade at higher yields in the US because of reserve and deposit insurance restrictions.

If the current market price of the CD including accrued interest is P and the current quoted yield is r, the yield can be calculated given the price, using (6.2).

$$r = \left\{ \frac{M}{P} \times \left[1 + C\left(\frac{N_{im}}{B}\right) \right] - 1 \right\} \times \left(\frac{B}{N_{sm}}\right) \tag{6.2}$$

The price can be calculated given the yield using (6.3).

---

[3] This was first introduced by Merrill Lynch in 1982.

$$P = M \times \left[1 + C \left(\frac{N_{im}}{B} \right) \right] \Big/ \left[1 + r \left(\frac{N_{sm}}{B} \right) \right] \tag{6.3}$$

where

> C is the quoted coupon on the CD;
> M is the face value of the CD;
> B is the year day-basis (365 or 360);
> F is the maturity value of the CD;
> N_{im} is the number of days between issue and maturity;
> N_{sm} is the number of days between settlement and maturity;
> N_{is} is the number of days between issue and settlement.

After issue, a CD can be traded in the secondary market. The secondary market in CDs in the UK is very liquid, and CDs will trade at the rate prevalent at the time, which will invariably be different from the coupon rate on the CD at issue. When a CD is traded in the secondary market, the settlement proceeds will need to take into account interest that has accrued on the paper and the different rate at which the CD has now been dealt. The formula for calculating the settlement figure is given at (6.4), which applies to the sterling market and its 365-day count basis.

$$\text{Proceeds} = \frac{M \times \text{Tenor} \times C \times 100 + 36500}{\text{Days remaining} \times r \times 100 + 36500} \tag{6.4}$$

The *tenor* of a CD is the life of the CD in days, while *days remaining* is the number of days left to maturity from the time of trade.

The return on holding a CD is given by (6.5).

$$\text{Return} = \left[\frac{\left(1 + \text{purchase yield} \times \frac{\text{days from purchase to maturity}}{B} \right)}{1 + \text{sale yield} \times \frac{\text{days from sale to maturity}}{B}} - 1 \right] \times \frac{B}{\text{days held}} \tag{6.5}$$

Securities quoted on a discount basis

The remaining money market instruments are all quoted on a *discount* basis, and so are known as 'discount' instruments. This means that they are issued on a discount to face value, and are redeemed on maturity at face value. Hence Treasury bills, bills of exchange, bankers acceptances and commercial paper are examples of money market securities that are quoted on a discount basis, that is, they are sold on the basis of a discount to par. The difference between the price paid at the time of purchase and the redemption value (par) is the interest earned by the holder of the paper. Explicit interest is not paid on discount instruments, rather interest is reflected implicitly in the difference between the discounted issue price and the par value received at maturity. In some markets, CP is quoted on a yield basis, but not in the UK or in the US where they are discount instruments.

Treasury bills

Treasury bills or T-bills are short-term government 'IOUs' of short duration, often three-month maturity. For example if a bill is issued on 10 January it will mature on 10 April. Bills of one-month and six-month maturity are also issued, but only rarely in the UK market. On maturity, the holder of a T-bill receives the par value of the bill by presenting it to the Central Bank. In the UK, most such bills are denominated in sterling but issues are also made in euros. In a capital market, T-bill yields are regarded as the *risk free* yield, as they represent the yield from short-term government debt. In emerging markets, they are often the most liquid instruments available for investors.

For instance, a sterling T-bill with £10 million face value issued for 91 days will be redeemed on maturity at £10 million. If the three-month yield at the time of issue is 5.25%, the price of the bill at issue is:

$$P = \frac{10m}{(1 + 0.0525 \times \frac{91}{365}} = £9,870,800.69$$

In the UK and US markets, the interest rate on discount instruments is quoted as a *discount rate* rather than a yield. This is the amount of discount expressed as an annualized percentage of the face value, and not as a percentage of the original amount paid. By definition the discount rate is always lower than the corresponding yield. If the discount rate on a bill is d, then the amount of discount is given by (6.6) below.

$$d_{Value} = M \times d \times \frac{n}{B} \tag{6.6}$$

The price P paid for the bill is the face value minus the discount amount, given by (6.7).

$$P = 100 \times \left[1 - \frac{d.\left(\frac{N_{sm}}{365}\right)}{100} \right] \tag{6.7}$$

If we know the yield on the bill then we can calculate its price at issue by using the simple present value formula, as shown at (6.8).

$$P = M / \left[1 + r\left(\frac{N_{sm}}{365}\right) \right] \tag{6.8}$$

The discount rate d for T-bills is calculated using (6.9).

$$d = (1 - P) \times \frac{B}{n} \tag{6.9}$$

The relationship between discount rate and true yield is given by (6.10).

$$d = \frac{r}{(1 + r \times \frac{n}{B})} \qquad (6.10)$$

$$r = \frac{d}{1 - d \times \frac{n}{B}}$$

If a T-bill is traded in the secondary market, the settlement proceeds from the trade are calculated using (6.11).

$$\text{Proceeds} = M - \left(\frac{M \times \text{days remaining} \times d}{B \times 100} \right) \qquad (6.11)$$

Bond equivalent yield

In certain markets – including the UK and US markets – the yields on government bonds that have a maturity of less than one year are compared to the yields of Treasury bills; however the comparison is made, the yield on a bill must be converted to a 'bond equivalent' yield. Therefore, the bond equivalent yield of a US Treasury bill is the coupon of a theoretical Treasury bond trading at par that has an identical maturity date. If the bill has 182 days or less until maturity, the calculation required is the conventional conversion from discount rate to yield, with the exception that it is quoted on a 365-day basis (in the UK market, the quote basis is essentially the same unless it is a leap year, so the conversion element in (6.12) is not necessary). The calculation for the US market is given by (6.12),

$$r = \frac{d}{1 - d \times \frac{\text{days}}{360}} \times \frac{365}{360} \qquad (6.12)$$

where r is the bond-equivalent yield that is being calculated.

Note that if there is a bill and a bond that mature on the same day in a period under 182 days, the bond-equivalent yield will not precisely be the same as the yield quoted for the bond in its final coupon period, although it is a very close approximation. This is because the bond is quoted on actual/actual basis, so its yield is actually made up of 2 times the actual number of days in the interest period.

Bankers acceptances

A bankers acceptance is a written promise issued by a borrower to a bank to repay borrowed funds. The lending bank lends funds and in return accepts the bankers acceptance. The acceptance is negotiable and can be sold in the secondary market. The investor who buys the acceptance can collect the loan on the day that repayment is due. If the borrower defaults, the investor has legal recourse to the bank that made the first acceptance. Bankers acceptances are also known as *bills of exchange, bank bills, trade bills* or *commercial bills*.

Bankers acceptances are essentially instruments created to facilitate commercial trade transactions. The instrument is called a *bankers acceptance* because a bank accepts the ultimate responsibility to repay the loan to its holder. The use of bankers acceptances to finance commercial transactions is known as *acceptance financing*. The transactions for which bankers acceptances are created include import and export of goods, the storage and shipping of goods between two overseas countries, where neither the importer nor the exporter is based in the home country,[4] and the storage and shipping of goods between two entities based at home. Acceptances are discount instruments and are purchased by banks, local authorities and money market investment funds. The rate that a bank charges a customer for issuing a bankers acceptance is a function of the rate at which the bank thinks it will be able to sell it in the secondary market. A commission is added to this rate. For ineligible bankers acceptances (see below) the issuing bank will add an amount to offset the cost of the additional reserve requirements.

Eligible bankers acceptance

An accepting bank that chooses to retain a bankers acceptance in its portfolio may be able to use it as collateral for a loan obtained from the central bank during open market operations, for example the Bank of England in the UK and the Federal Reserve in the US. Not all acceptances are eligible to be used as collateral in this way, as they must meet certain criteria set by the central bank. The main requirement for eligibility is that the acceptance must be within a certain maturity band (a maximum of six months in the US and three months in the UK), and that it must have been created to finance a self-liquidating commercial transaction. In the US, eligibility is also important because the Federal Reserve imposes a reserve requirement on funds raised via bankers acceptances that are ineligible. Bankers acceptances sold by an accepting bank are potential liabilities of the bank, but reserve requirements impose a limit on the amount of eligible bankers acceptances that a bank may issue. Bills eligible for deposit at a central bank enjoy a finer rate than ineligible bills, and also act as a benchmark for prices in the secondary market.

Commercial paper

Commercial paper (CP) is a short-term money market funding instrument issued by corporates. In the UK and the US it is a discount instrument, with sterling paper being dealt with on a 365-day basis. They trade essentially as T-bills but with higher yields as they are

---

[4] A bankers acceptance created to finance such a transaction is known as a *third-party acceptance*.

unsecured corporate obligations. CP is an important part of the US money market, and began as a US instrument before being introduced in other money centres around the world. The instrument ranges in maturity from 30 to 270 days (although typical maturities are 30 to 90 days) and is usually issued in response to investor demand or for short-term working capital considerations. As the paper is unsecured investor sentiment usually requires that any issue be rated by a rating agency such as Moody's Investors Services or Standard & Poor's, and there is also a market in high-yield CP.

Another significant market exists in euro-commercial paper (ECP), which is similar in concept to CP but is not restricted to the 27-day maturity.[5] The market in ECP exists in money centres globally. Standard settlement of ECP is for spot value (which is two business days forward), whereas standard settlement of US and UK settlement is on a same-day basis. ECP can be issued both as a discount instrument or a yield-bearing instrument, although the latter is rarer.

For yield-bearing ECP the calculation of settlement proceeds in the secondary market is given by (6.13).

$$\text{Proceeds} = M \times \left[\frac{1 + \frac{C \times T}{36000}}{1 + \frac{r \times N}{36000}} \right] \tag{6.13}$$

where

M is the face amount;
C is the coupon;
r is the yield;
T is the paper's original maturity or *tenor*;
N is the time from settlement to maturity.

For paper issued on a discount basis the proceeds are given by

$$\text{Proceeds} = \left[\frac{M}{1 + \frac{r \times N}{36000}} \right]. \tag{6.14}$$

The majority of ECP is issued in US dollars, although euro, sterling, Japanese yen are also popular currencies.

---

[5] In the US market this is a Securities and Exchange Commission requirement.

Asset-backed commercial paper

The rise in securitisation has led to the growth of short-term instruments backed by the cash flows from other assets, known as *asset-backed commercial paper* (ABCP). Securitisation is looked at in greater detail elsewhere in this book, here we discuss briefly the basic concept of ABCP.

Generally securitisation is used as a funding instrument by companies for three main reasons: it offers lower-cost funding compared with traditional bank loan or bond financing; it is a mechanism by which assets such as corporate loans or mortgages can be removed from the balance sheet, thus improving the lender's return on assets or return on equity ratios; and it increases a borrower's funding options. When entering into securitisation, an entity may issue term securities against assets into the public or private market, or it may issue commercial paper via a special vehicle known as a *conduit*. These conduits are usually sponsored by commercial banks.

Entities usually access the commercial paper market in order to secure permanent financing, rolling over individual issues as part of a longer-term *programme* and using interest-rate swaps to arrange a fixed rate if required. Conventional CP issues are typically supported by a line of credit from a commercial bank, and so this form of financing is in effect a form of bank funding.

Money market derivatives

The market in short-term interest-rate derivatives is a large and liquid one, and the instruments involved are used for a variety of purposes. Here we review the two main contracts used in money markets trading, the short-term *interest rate future* and the *forward rate agreement*. The concept of the forward rate as introduced in Chapter 3. Money market derivatives are priced on the basis of the forward rate, and are flexible instruments for hedging against or speculating on forward interest rates. The forward rate agreement (FRA) and the exchange-traded interest-rate future both date from around the same time, and although initially developed to hedge forward interest-rate exposure, they now have a range of uses. Here the instruments are introduced and analyzed, and there is a review of the main uses that they are put to. Readers interested in the concept of *convexity* bias in swap and futures pricing may wish to refer to the chapter listed in the bibliography, which is by the author and is an accessible introduction.

US Treasury bills

The Treasury bill market in the US is one of the most liquid and transparent debt markets in the world. Consequently the bid-offer spread on them is very narrow. The Treasury issues bills at a weekly auction each Monday, made up of 91-day and 182-day bills. Every fourth week, the Treasury also issues 52-week bills. As a result, there are large numbers of Treasury bills outstanding at any one time. The interest earned on Treasury bills is not liable to state and local income taxes.

Federal funds

Commercial banks in the US are required to keep reserves on deposit at the Federal Reserve. Banks with reserves in excess of required reserves can lend these funds to other banks, and these interbank loans are called *federal funds* or *fed funds* and are usually overnight loans. Through the fed funds market, commercial banks with excess funds are able to lend to banks that are short of reserves, thus facilitating liquidity. The transactions are very large denominations, and are lent at the *fed funds rate*, which is a very volatile interest rate because it fluctuates with market shortages.

Prime rate

The *prime interest rate* in the US is often said to represent the rate at which commercial banks lend to their most creditworthy customers. In practice, many loans are made at rates below the prime rate, so the prime rate is not the best rate at which highly rated firms may borrow. Nevertheless the prime rate is a benchmark indicator of the level of US money market rates, and is often used as a reference rate for floating-rate instruments. As the market for bank loans is highly competitive, all commercial banks quote a single prime rate, and the rate for all banks changes simultaneously.

Forward rate agreements

A *forward rate agreement* (FRA) is an OTC derivative instrument that trades as part of the money markets. It is essentially a forward-starting loan, but with no exchange of principal, so that only the difference in interest rates is traded. Trading in FRAs began in the early 1980s and the market now is large and liquid; turnover in London exceeds $5 billion each day. So an FRA is a forward-dated loan, dealt at a fixed rate, but with no exchange of principal – only the interest applicable on the notional amount between the rate dealt at and the actual rate prevailing at the time of settlement changes hands. That is, FRAs are *off-balance sheet* (OBS) instruments. By trading today at an interest rate that is effective at some point in the future, FRAs enable banks and corporates to hedge interest rate exposure. They are also used to speculate on the level of future interest rates.

An FRA is an agreement to borrow or lend a *notional* cash sum for a period of time lasting up to 12 months, starting at any point over the next 12 months, at an agreed rate of interest (the FRA rate). The 'buyer' of an FRA is borrowing a notional sum of money while the 'seller' is lending this cash sum. Note how this differs from all other money market instruments. In the cash market, the party buying a CD or bill, or bidding for stock in the repo market, is the lender of funds. In the FRA market, to 'buy' is to 'borrow'. We use the term 'notional' because with an FRA no borrowing or lending of cash actually takes place, as it is an OBS product. The notional sum is simply the amount on which interest payment is calculated.

So when a FRA is traded, the buyer is borrowing (and the seller is lending) a specified notional sum at a fixed rate of interest for a specified period, the 'loan' to commence at an agreed date in the future. The *buyer* is the notional borrower, so if there is a rise in interest rates between the date that the FRA is traded and the date that the FRA comes into effect, he will be protected. If there is a fall in interest rates, the buyer must pay the difference between the rate at which the FRA was traded and the actual rate, as a percentage of the notional sum. The buyer may be using the FRA to hedge an actual exposure, that is an actual borrowing of money, or simply speculating on a rise in interest rates. The counterparty to the transaction, the *seller* of the FRA, is the notional lender of funds, and has fixed the rate for lending funds. If there is a fall in interest rates the seller will gain, and if there is a rise in rates the seller will pay. Again, the seller may have an actual loan of cash to hedge or be a speculator.

In FRA trading, only the payment that arises as a result of the difference in interest rates changes hands. There is no exchange of cash at the time of the trade. The cash payment that does arise is the difference in interest rates between that at which the FRA was traded and the actual rate prevailing when the FRA matures, as a percentage of the notional amount. FRAs are traded by both banks and corporates and between banks. The FRA market is very liquid in all major currencies and rates are readily quoted on screens by both banks and brokers. Dealing is over the telephone or over a dealing system such as Reuters.

The terminology quoting FRAs refers to the borrowing time period and the time at which the FRA comes into effect (or matures). Hence if a buyer of an FRA wished to hedge against a rise in rates to cover a three-month loan starting in three months' time, he would transact a 'three-against-six month' FRA, or more usually a 3 × 6 or 3-vs-6 FRA. This is referred to in the market as a 'threes-sixes' FRA, and means a three-month loan in three months' time. So a 'ones-fours' FRA (1 v 4) is a three-month loan in one month's time, and a 'threes-nines' FRA (3 v 9) is six-month money in three months' time.

EXAMPLE *6.1*

A company knows that it will need to borrow £1 million in 3 months' time for a 12-month period. It can borrow funds today at Libor + 50 basis points. Libor rates today are at 5% but the company's treasurer expects rates to go up to about 6% over the next few weeks. So the company will be forced to borrow at higher rates unless some sort of hedge is transacted to protect the borrowing requirement. The treasurer decides to buy a 3 × 15 ('threes-fifteens') FRA to cover the 12-month period beginning three months from now. A bank quotes 5.5% for the FRA which the company buys for a notional £1 million. Three months from now rates have indeed gone up to 6%, so the treasurer must borrow funds at 6.5% (the Libor rate plus spread), however he will receive a settlement amount which will be the difference between the rate at which the FRA was bought and today's 12-month Libor rate (6%) as a percentage of £1 million, which will compensate for some of the increased borrowing costs.

Standard forms used in the FRA market

In virtually every market, FRAs trade under a set of terms and conventions that are identical. The British Bankers Association (BBA) compiled standard legal documentation to cover FRA trading. The following standard terms are used in the market. The terms are also illustrated in figure 6.1.

Contract period	The time between the settlement date and maturity date
Fixing date	This is the date on which the *reference rate* is determined, that is, the rate to which the FRA dealing rate is compared (see below)
FRA rate	The interest rate at which the FRA is traded
Maturity date	The date on which the notional loan or deposit expires
Notional sum	The amount for which the FRA is traded
Reference rate	This is the rate used as part of the calculation of the settlement amount, usually the Libor rate on the fixing date for the contract period in question
Settlement date	The date on which the notional loan or deposit of funds becomes effective, that is, is said to begin. This date is used, in conjunction with the notional sum, for calculation purposes only as no actual loan or deposit takes place

Settlement sum   The amount calculated as the difference between the FRA rate and the reference rate as a percentage of the notional sum, paid by one party to the other on the settlement date

Trade date   The date on which the FRA is dealt

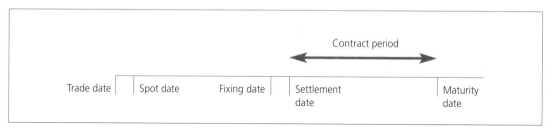

FIGURE 6.1 ■ Key dates in an FRA trade

The spot date is usually two business days after the trade date, however it can by agreement be sooner or later than this. The settlement date will be the time period after the spot date referred to by the FRA terms, for example a 1 × 4 FRA will have a settlement date one calendar month after the spot date. The fixing date is usually two business days before the settlement date. The settlement sum is paid on the settlement date, and as it refers to an amount over a period of time that is paid up front, at the start of the contract period, the calculated sum is discounted. This is because a normal payment of interest on a loan/deposit is paid at the end of the time period to which it relates; since an FRA makes this payment at the *start* of the relevant period, the settlement amount is a discounted figure.

With most FRA trades, the reference rate is the LIBOR fixing on the fixing date.

The settlement sum is calculated after the fixing date, for payment on the settlement date. We may illustrate this with example 6.2.

EXAMPLE *6.2*

Consider a case where a corporate has bought £1 million notional of a 1 v 4 FRA, and dealt at 5.75%, and that the market rate is 6.50% on the fixing date. The contract period is 90 days. In the cash market the extra interest charge that the corporate would pay is a simple interest calculation, and is:

$$\frac{6.50 - 5.75}{100} \times 1,000,000 \times \frac{91}{365} = £1869.86$$

This extra interest that the corporate is facing would be payable with the interest payment for the loan, which (as it is a money market loan) is when the loan matures. Under an FRA then, the settlement sum payable should, if it was paid on the same day as the cash market interest charge, be exactly equal to this. This would make it a perfect hedge. As we noted above though, FRA settlement value is paid at the start of the contract period, that is, the beginning of the underlying loan and not the end. Therefore the settlement sum has to be adjusted to account for this, and the amount of the adjustment is the value of the interest that would be earned if the unadjusted cash value was invested for the contract period in the money market. The amount of the settlement value is given by (6.15).

$$Settlement = \frac{(r_{ref} - r_{FRA}) \times M \times \frac{n}{B}}{1 + (r_{ref} \times \frac{n}{B})} \tag{6.15}$$

where

r_{ref} is the reference interest fixing rate;
r_{FRA} is the FRA rate or *contract rate*;
M is the notional value;
n is the number of days in the contract period;
B is the day-count base (360 or 365).

The expression at (6.15) simply calculates the extra interest payable in the cash market, resulting from the difference between the two interest rates, and then discounts the amount because it is payable at the start of the period and not, as would happen in the cash market, at the end of the period.

In the illustration in example 6.2, as the fixing rate is higher than the dealt rate, the corporate buyer of the FRA receives the settlement sum from the seller. This then compensates the corporate for the higher borrowing costs that he would have to pay in the cash market. If the fixing rate had been lower than 5.75%, the buyer would pay the difference to the seller, because the cash market rates will mean that he is subject to a lower interest rate in the cash market. What the FRA has done is hedge the corporate's exposure, so that whatever happens in the market, it will pay 5.75% on its borrowing.

A market maker in FRAs is trading short-term interest rates. The settlement sum is the value of the FRA. The concept is exactly as with trading short-term interest-rate futures; a trader who buys an FRA is running a long position, so that if on the fixing date $r_{ref} > r_{FRA}$, the settlement sum is positive and the trader realizes a profit. What has happened is that the trader, by buying the FRA, 'borrowed' money at an interest rate, which subsequently rose. This is a gain, exactly like a *short* position in an interest-rate future, where if the price goes down (that is, interest rates go up), the trader realizes a gain. Equally, a 'short' position in an FRA, put on by selling an FRA, realizes a gain if on the fixing date $r_{ref} < r_{FRA}$.

FRA pricing

As their name implies, FRAs are forward rate instruments and are priced using the forward rate principles we established in Chapter 3. Consider an investor who has two alternatives, either a six-month investment at 5% or a one-year investment at 6%. If the investor wishes to invest for six months and then roll-over the investment for a further six months, what rate is required for the roll-over period such that the final return equals the 6% available from the one-year investment? If we view an FRA rate as the break-even forward rate between the two periods, we simply solve for this forward rate and that is our approximate FRA rate. This rate is sometimes referred to as the interest rate 'gap' in the money markets (not to be confused with an interbank desk's *gap risk*, the interest rate exposure arising from the net maturity position of its assets and liabilities).

We can use the standard forward-rate breakeven formula to solve for the required FRA rate; we established this relationship earlier when discussing the calculation of forward rates that are arbitrage-free. The relationship given at (6.16) connects simple (bullet) interest rates for periods of time up to one year, where no compounding of interest is required. As FRAs are money market instruments we are not required to calculate rates for periods in excess of one year,[6] where compounding would need to be built into the equation.

$$(1 + r_2 t_2) = (1 + r_1 t_1)(1 + r_f t_f) \tag{6.16}$$

where

r_2 is the cash market interest rate for the long period;
r_1 is the cash market interest rate for the short period;
r_f is the forward rate for the gap period;
t_2 is the time period from today to the end of the long period;
t_1 is the time period from today to the end of the short period;
t_f is the forward gap time period, or the contract period for the FRA.

This is illustrated in figure 6.2.

The time period t_1 is the time from the dealing date to the FRA settlement date, while t_2 is the time from the dealing date to the FRA maturity date. The time period for the FRA (contract period) is t_2 minus t_1. We can replace the symbol 't' for time period with 'n' for the actual number of days in the time periods themselves. If we do this and then rearrange the equation to solve for r_{FRA} the FRA rate, we obtain (6.17) below.

---

[6] Although it is of course possible to trade FRAs with contract periods greater than one year, for which a different pricing formula must be used, incorporating annual compounding.

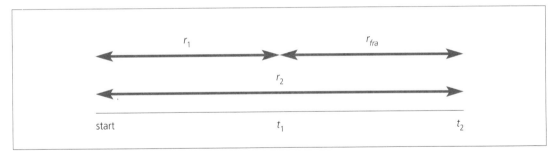

FIGURE 6.2 ■ Rates used in FRA pricing

$$r_{FRA} = \frac{r_2 n_2 - r_1 n_1}{n_{fra}\left(1 + r_1 \frac{n_1}{365}\right)}$$ (6.17)

where

n_1 is the number of days from the dealing date or spot date to the settlement date;

n_2 is the number of days from dealing date or spot date to the maturity date;

r_1 is the spot rate to the settlement date;

r_2 is the spot rate from the spot date to the maturity date;

n_{fra} is the number of days in the FRA contract period;

r_{FRA} is the FRA rate.

If the formula is applied to say, the US money markets, the 365 in the equation is replaced by 360, the day count base for that market.

In practice, FRAs are priced off the exchange-traded short-term interest rate future for that currency, so that sterling FRAs are priced off LIFFE short sterling futures. Traders normally use a spreadsheet pricing model that has futures prices directly fed into it. FRA positions are also usually hedged with other FRAs or short-term interest rate futures.

FRA prices in practice

The dealing rates for FRAs are possibly the most liquid and transparent of any non-exchange traded derivative instrument. This is because they are calculated directly from exchange-traded interest-rate contracts. The key consideration for FRA market makers, however, is how the rates behave in relation to other market interest rates. The forward rate calculated from two period spot rates must, as we have seen, be set such that it is arbitrage-free. If for example the six-month spot rate was 8.00% and the nine-month spot rate was 9.00%, the 6 v 9 FRA would have an approximate rate of 11%. What would be the effect of a change in one or both of the spot rates? The same arbitrage-free principle must apply. If there is an increase in the short-rate period, the FRA rate must decrease, to make the total return unchanged. The extent of the change in the FRA rate is a function of the ratio of the contract period to the long period. If the rate for the long period increases, the FRA rate will increase, by an amount related to the ratio between the total period to the contract period. The FRA rate for any term is generally a function of the three-month LIBOR rate, the rate traded under an interest-rate future. A general rise in this rate will see a rise in FRA rates.

Short-term interest rate futures

Description

A *futures* contract is a transaction that fixes the price today for a commodity that will be delivered at some point in the future. Financial futures fix the price for interest rates, bonds, equities and so on, but trade in the same manner as commodity futures. Contracts for futures are standardized and traded on exchanges. In London, the main futures exchange is LIFFE, although other futures are also traded on for example, the International Petroleum Exchange and the London Metal Exchange. The money markets trade short-term interest rate futures, which fix the rate of interest on a notional fixed term deposit of money (usually for 90 days or three months) for a specified period in the future. The sum is notional because no actual sum of money is deposited when buying or selling futures; the instrument is off-balance sheet. Buying such a contract is equivalent to making a notional deposit, while selling a contract is equivalent to borrowing a notional sum.

The three-month interest-rate future is the most widely used instrument used for hedging interest-rate risk.

The LIFFE exchange in London trades short-term interest rate futures for major currencies including sterling, euros, yen and Swiss franc. Table 6.1 summarizes the terms for the short sterling contract as traded on LIFFE.

TABLE 6.1 ■ Description of LIFFE short sterling future contract

Name	90-day sterling Libor future
Contract size	£500,000
Delivery months	March, June, September, December
Delivery date	First business day after last trading day
Last trading day	Third Wednesday of delivery month
Price	100 minus yield
Tick size	0.005
Tick value	£6.25
Trading hours	0805–1830 (electronic screen trading)

The original futures contracts related to physical commodities, which is why we speak of *delivery* when referring to the expiry of financial futures contracts. Exchange-traded futures such as those on LIFFE are set to expire every quarter during the year. The short sterling contract is a deposit of cash, so as its price refers to the rate of interest on this deposit, the price of the contract is set as:

$$P = 100 - r$$

where P is the price of the contract and r is the rate of interest at the time of expiry implied by the futures contract. This means that if the price of the contract rises, the rate of interest implied goes down, and vice versa. For example, the price of the June 1999 short sterling future (written as Jun99 or M99, from the futures identity letters of H, M, U and Z for contracts expiring in March, June, September and December respectively) at the start of trading on 13 March 1999 was 94.880, which implied a three-month Libor rate of 5.12% on expiry of the contract in June. If a trader bought 20 contracts at this price and then sold them just before the close of trading that day, when the price had risen to 94.96, an implied rate of 5.04%, he would have made 16 ticks profit or £2000. That is, a 16-tick upward price movement in a long position of 20 contracts is equal to £2000. This is calculated as follows:

Profit = ticks gained × tick value × number of contracts
Loss = ticks lost × tick value × number of contracts

The tick value for the short sterling contract is straightforward to calculate, since we know that the contract size is £500,000, there is a minimum price movement (tick movement) of 0.005% and the contract has a three-month 'maturity'.

$$\text{Tick value} = 0.005\% \times £500,000 \times \frac{3}{12}$$

$$= £6.25$$

The profit made by the trader in our example is logical because if we buy short sterling futures we are depositing (notional) funds; if the price of the futures rises, it means the interest rate has fallen. We profit because we have 'deposited' funds at a higher rate beforehand. If we expected sterling interest rates to rise, we would sell short sterling futures, which is equivalent to borrowing funds and locking in the loan rate at a lower level.

Note how the concept of buying and selling interest rate futures differs from FRAs: if we buy an FRA we are borrowing notional funds, whereas if we buy a futures contract we are depositing notional funds. If a position in an interest rate futures contract is held to expiry, cash settlement will take place on the delivery day for that contract.

Short-term interest rate contracts in other currencies are similar to the short sterling contract and trade on exchanges such as Eurex in Frankfurt and MATIF in Paris.

Pricing interest rate futures

The price of a three-month interest rate futures contract is the implied interest rate for that currency's three-month rate at the time of expiry of the contract. Therefore there is always a close relationship and correlation between futures prices, FRA rates (which are derived from futures prices) and cash market rates. On the day of expiry the price of the future will be equal to the Libor rate as fixed that day. This is known as the Exchange Delivery Settlement Price (EDSP) and is used in the calculation of the delivery amount. During the life of the contract its price will be less closely related to the actual three-month Libor rate *today*, but closely related to the *forward rate* for the time of expiry.

Equation (6.16) was our basic formula for money market maturity forward rates, which we adapted to use as our FRA price equation. If we incorporate some extra terminology to cover the dealing dates involved it can also be used as our futures price formula. Let us say that:

T_0 is the trade date;
T_M is the contract expiry date;
T_{CASH} is the value date for cash market deposits traded on T_0;
T_1 is the value date for cash market deposits traded on T_M;
T_2 is the maturity date for a three-month cash market deposit traded on T_M.

We can then use equation (6.18) as our futures price formula to obtain P_{fut}, the futures price for a contract up to the expiry date.

$$P_{fut} = 100 - \left[\frac{r_2 n_2 - r_1 n_1}{n_f \left(1 + r_1 \frac{n_1}{365}\right)} \right] \qquad (6.18)$$

where

P_{fut} is the futures price;
r_1 is the cash market interest rate to T_1;
r_2 is the cash market interest rate to T_2;
n_1 is the number of days from T_{CASH} to T_1;
n_2 is the number of days from T_{CASH} to T_2;
n_f is the number of days from T_1 to T_2.

The formula uses a 365-day count convention which is applies in the sterling money markets; where a market uses a 360-day base this must be used in the equation instead.

In practice, the price of a contract at any one time will be close to the theoretical price that would be established by (6.18) above. Discrepancies will arise for supply and demand reasons in the market, as well as because Libor rates are often quoted only to the nearest sixteenth or 0.0625. The price between FRAs and futures are correlated very closely; in fact, banks will often price FRAs using futures, and use futures to hedge their FRA books. When hedging an FRA book with futures, the hedge is quite close to being exact, because of the two prices track each other almost tick for tick. However, the tick value of a futures contract is fixed, and uses (as we saw above) a 3/12 basis, while FRA settlement values use a 360- or 365-day base. The FRA trader will be aware of this when putting on his hedge.

In our discussion of forward rates in Chapter 3 we emphasized that they were the markets view on future rates using all information available today. Of course a futures price today is very unlikely to be in line with the actual three-month interest rate that is prevailing at the time of the contract's expiry. This explains why prices for futures and actual cash rates will differ on any particular day. Up until expiry the futures price is the implied forward rate; of course there is always a discrepancy between this forward rate and the cash market rate *today*. The gap between the cash price and the futures price is known as the *basis*. This is defined as:

Basis = Cash price − Futures price

At any point during the life of a futures contract prior to final settlement − at which point futures and cash rates converge − there is usually a difference between current cash market rates and the rates implied by the futures price. This is the difference explained above; in fact, the difference between the price implied by the current three-month inter-bank deposit and the futures price is known as *simple basis*, but it is what most market participants refer to as the basis. Simple basis consists of two separate components; *theoretical basis* and *value basis*. Theoretical basis is the difference between the price implied by the current three-month interbank deposit rate and that implied by the theoretical fair futures price based on cash market forward rates, given by (6.18). This basis may be either positive or negative depending on the shape of the yield curve.

Futures contracts do not in practice provide a precise tool for locking into cash market rates today for a transaction that takes place in the future, although this is what they are in theory designed to do. Futures do allow a bank to lock in a rate for a transaction to take place in the future, and this rate is the *forward rate*. The basis is the difference between today's cash market rate and the forward rate on a particular date in the future. As a futures contract approaches expiry, its price and the rate in the cash market will converge (the process is given the name *convergence*). As we noted earlier, this is given by the exchange delivery settlement price, and the two prices (rates) will be exactly in line at the exact moment of expiry.

Hedging using interest-rate futures

Banks use interest rate futures to hedge interest rate risk exposure in cash and OBS instruments. Bond trading desks also often use futures to hedge positions in bonds of up to two or three years maturity, as contracts are traded up to three years maturity. The liquidity of such 'far month' contracts is considerably lower than for near month contracts and the 'front month' contract (the current contract, for the next maturity month). When hedging a bond with a maturity of say two years maturity, the trader will put on a *strip* of futures contracts that matches as near as possible the expiry date of the bond. The purpose of a hedge is to protect the value of a current or anticipated cash market or OBS position from adverse changes in interest rates. The hedger will try to offset the effect of the change in interest rate on the value of his cash position with the change in value of his hedging instrument. If the hedge is an exact one the loss on the main position should be compensated by a profit on the hedge position. If the trader is expecting a fall in interest rates and wishes to protect against such a fall he will buy futures, known as a long hedge, and will sell futures (a short hedge) if wishing to protect against a rise in rates.

Bond traders also use three-month interest-rate contracts to hedge positions in short-dated bonds; for instance, a market maker running a short-dated bond book would find it more appropriate to hedge the book using short-dated futures rather than the longer-dated bond futures contract. When this happens, it is important to calculate accurately the correct number of contracts to use for the hedge. To construct a bond hedge it will be necessary to use a *strip* of contracts, thus ensuring that the maturity date of the bond is covered by the longest-dated futures contract. The hedge is calculated by finding the sensitivity of each cash flow to changes in each of the relevant forward rates. Each cash flow is considered individually and the hedge values are then aggregated and rounded to the nearest whole number of contracts.

Appendix 6.1: Interest rate conversion

To convert an interest rate i quoted on a 365-day basis to one quoted on a 360-day basis (i^*) use the expressions given at (6.1.1).

$$i = i^* \times \frac{365}{360} \qquad (6.1.1)$$

$$i^* = i \times \frac{360}{365}$$

SELECTED BIBLIOGRAPHY AND REFERENCES

Blake, D., *Financial Market Analysis*, Wiley 2000

Chicago Board of Trade, *Interest Rate Futures for Institutional Investors*, CBOT 1987

Choudhry, M., *The Bond and Money Markets: Strategy, Trading, Analysis*, Butterworth-Heinemann 2001, chapter 35

Choudhry, M., *The Repo Handbook*, Butterworth-Heinemann 2001

Figlewski, F., *Hedging with Financial Futures for Institutional Investors*, Probus Publishing 1986

French, K., 'A Comparison of Futures and Forwards Prices', *Journal of Financial Economics* 12, November 1983, pp. 311–342

Hull, J., *Options, Futures and Other Derivatives*, 4th edition, Prentice-Hall Inc. 1999

Jarrow, R., Oldfield, G., 'Forward Contracts and Futures Contracts', *Journal of Financial Economics* 9, December 1981, pp. 373–382

Stigum, M., Robinson, F., *Money Market and Bond Calculations*, Irwin 1996

CHAPTER 7

Hybrid securities

In this chapter we describe in generic form some of the more exotic or structured notes that have been introduced into the fixed income market. The motivations behind the development and use of these products are varied, but include the need for increased yield without additional credit risk, as well as the need to alter, transform or transfer risk exposure and risk-return profiles. Certain structured notes were also developed as hedging instruments. The instruments themselves have been issued by banks, corporate institutions and sovereign authorities. By using certain types of notes, investors can gain access to different markets, sometimes synthetically, that were previously not available to them. For instance, by purchasing a structured note, an investor can take on a position that reflects his views on a particular exchange rate and anticipated changes in yield curve but in a different market. The investment instrument can be tailored to suit the investor's particular risk profile.

We describe a number of structured notes that are currently available to investors today, although often investors will seek particular features that suit their needs, and so there are invariably detail variations in each note. We stress that this is only the tip of the iceberg, and many different types of notes are available; indeed, if any particular investor or issuer requirement has not been met, it is a relatively straightforward process whereby an investment bank can structure a note that meets one or both specific requirements.

Floating-rate notes

Floating-rate notes are not structured notes! We describe them here as a prelude to a discussion on inverse floating-rate notes.

Floating rate notes (FRNs) are bonds that have variable rates of interest; the coupon rate is linked to a specified index and changes periodically as the index changes. An FRN is usually issued with a coupon that pays a fixed spread over a reference index; for example the coupon may be 50 basis points over the six-month interbank rate. An FRN whose spread over the reference rate is not fixed is known as a *variable rate note*. Since the value for the reference benchmark index is not known, it is not possible to calculate the redemption yield for an FRN. Additional features have been added to FRNs, including *floors* (the coupon cannot fall below a specified minimum rate), *caps* (the coupon cannot rise above a maximum rate) and *callability*. There also exist perpetual FRNs. As in other markets, borrowers frequently issue paper with specific or even esoteric terms in order to meet particular requirements or meet customer demand. For example, Citibank recently issued US dollar-denominated FRNs with interest payments indexed to the euribor rate, and another FRN with its day count basis linked to a specified Libor range.

Generally the reference interest rate for FRNs is the London interbank rate; the *offered* rate, that is the rate at which a bank will lend funds to another bank is LIBOR. An FRN will pay interest at LIBOR plus a quoted margin (or spread). The interest rate is fixed for a three-month or six-month period and is reset in line with the LIBOR *fixing* at the end of the interest period. Hence at the coupon re-set date for a sterling FRN paying six-month Libor + 0.50%, if the Libor fix is 7.6875%, then the FRN will pay a coupon of 8.1875%. Interest therefore will accrue at a daily rate of £0.0224315.

On the coupon reset date an FRN will be priced precisely at par. Between reset dates it will trade very close to par because of the way in which the coupon is reset. If market rates rise between reset dates an FRN will trade slightly below par, similarly if rates fall the paper will trade slightly above. This makes FRNs very similar in behaviour to money market instruments traded on a yield basis, although of course FRNs have much longer maturities. Investors can opt to view FRNs as essentially money market instruments or as alternatives to conventional bonds. For this reason, one can use two approaches in analyzing FRNs. The first approach is known as the *margin method*. This calculates the difference between the return on an FRN and that on an equivalent money market security. There are two variations on this, simple margin and discounted margin.

The simple margin method is sometimes preferred because it does not require the forecasting of future interest rates and coupon values. *Simple margin* is defined as the average return on an FRN throughout its life compared with the reference interest rate. It has two components: a *quoted margin* either above or below the reference rate, and a capital gain or loss element which is calculated under the assumption that the difference between the current price of the FRN and the maturity value is spread evenly over the remaining life of the bond. Simple margin is given by (7.1).

$$\text{Simple margin} = \frac{(M - P_d)}{(100 \times T)} + M_q \tag{7.1}$$

where

P_d is $P + AI$, the dirty price;
M is the par value;
T is the number of years from settlement date to maturity;
M_q is the quoted margin.

A quoted margin that is positive reflects yield for an FRN that is offering a higher yield than the comparable money market security.

At certain times the simple margin formula is adjusted to take into account any change in the reference rate since the last coupon reset date. This is done by defining an adjusted price, which is either:

$$AP_d = P_d + (re + M) \times \frac{N_{sc}}{365} \times 100 - \frac{C}{2} \times 100$$

or

(7.2)

$$AP_d = P_d + (re + M) \times \frac{N_{sc}}{365} \times P_d - \frac{C}{2} \times 100$$

where

AP_d is the adjusted dirty price;
re is the current value of the reference interest rate (such as Libor);
$C/2$ is the next coupon payment (that is, C is the reference interest rate on the last coupon reset date plus M_q;
N_{sc} is the number of days between settlement and the next coupon date.

The upper equation in (7.2) ignores the current yield effect: all payments are assumed to be received on the basis of par, and this understates the value of the coupon for FRNs trading below par and overstates the value when they are trading above par. The lower equation in (7.2) takes account of the current yield effect.

The adjusted price AP_d replaces the current price P_d in (7.1) to give an *adjusted simple margin*. The simple margin method has the disadvantage of amortizing the discount or premium on the FRN in a straight line over the remaining life of the bond rather than at a constantly compounded rate. The discounted margin method uses the latter approach. The distinction between simple margin and discounted margin is exactly the same as that between simple yield to maturity and yield to maturity. The discounted margin method does have a disadvantage in that it requires a forecast of the reference interest rate over the remaining life of the bond.

The discounted margin is the solution to equation (7.3) shown below, given for an FRN that pays semi-annual coupons.

$$P_d = \left| \frac{1}{[1 + \frac{1}{2}(re + DM)]^{\text{days/year}}} \right| \cdot \left| \frac{C}{2} + \sum_{t=1}^{N-1} \frac{(re^* + M) \times 100/2}{[1 + \frac{1}{2}(re^* + DM)]^t} + \frac{M}{[1 + \frac{1}{2}(re^* + DM)]^{N-1}} \right| \quad (7.3)$$

where

DM is the discounted margin;
re is the current value of the reference interest rate;

re^* is the assumed (or forecast) value of the reference rate over the remaining life of the bond;

M is the quoted margin;

N is the number of coupon payments before redemption.

Equation (7.3) may be stated in terms of discount factors instead of the reference rate. The *yield to maturity spread* method of evaluating FRNs is designed to allow direct comparison between FRNs and fixed-rate bonds. The yield to maturity on the FRN (rmf) is calculated using (7.3) with both ($re + DM$) and ($re^* + DM$) replaced with rmf. The yield to maturity on a reference bond (rmb) is calculated in the normal fashion. The *yield to maturity spread* is defined as:

Yield to maturity spread = $rmf - rmb$

If this is positive the FRN offers a higher yield than the reference bond.

In addition to plain vanilla FRNs, some of the other types of floating-rate bonds that have traded in the market are:

■ *Collared FRNs.* These offer caps and floors on an instrument, thus establishing a maximum and minimum coupon on the deal. Effectively these securities contain two embedded options, the issuer buying a cap and selling a floor to the investor.

■ *Step-up recovery FRNs.* Where coupons are fixed against comparable longer maturity bonds, thus providing investors with the opportunity to maintain exposure to short-term assets while capitalizing on a positive sloping yield curve.

■ *Corridor FRNs.* These were introduced to capitalize on expectations of comparative interest rate inactivity. A high-risk/high-reward instrument, it offers investors a very substantial uplift over a chosen reference rate. But rates have to remain within a relatively narrow corridor if the interest payment is not to be forfeited entirely.

Inverse floating-rate note

Description

The inverse floating-rate note or *inverse floater* is an instrument that offers enhanced returns to investors that believe the market outlook for bonds generally is positive. An inverse floater pays a coupon that increases as general market rates decline. In other words, it is an instrument for those who have an opposite view to the market consensus. They are suitable in an economic environment of low inflation and a positive yield curve; both these factors would, in a conventional analysis, suggest rising interest rates in the medium term. It is also possible to link the inverse floater's coupon to rates in an environment of a negative yield curve. Such a note would suit an investor who agreed with the market consensus.

The coupon on an inverse floater may be determined in a number of ways. The most common approach involves a formula that quotes a fixed interest rate, minus a variable element that is linked to an index. Coupons are usually set at a floor level, which, in the absence of a floor, will be zero per cent.

Issuers of inverse floaters are usually corporates, although specialized investment vehicles also issue such notes to meet specific client demand.[1]

Table 7.1 illustrates the coupon arrangement on a typical inverse floater, particularly how changes in the Libor rate impact the coupon that is payable on the note.

The inverse floater provides investors with a slightly above-market initial coupon in a yield curve environment that is positive.[2] The above-market initial coupon results from

TABLE 7.1 ■ Terms of an hypothetical inverse floater bond

Nominal value	$100,000,000
Issue date	5 Jan 2000
Maturity date	5 Jan 2003
Note coupon	15.75% − (2 × Libor)
Day-count basis	act/365
Index	6-month Libor
Current Libor rate	5.15%
Rate fixing	Semi-annual
Initial coupon	5.45%
Minimum coupon	0%

GBP Libor	Coupon payable
1.00%	14.75%
1.50%	12.75%
2.00%	11.75%
2.50%	10.75%
3.00%	9.75%
3.50%	8.75%
4.00%	7.75%
4.50%	6.75%
5.00%	5.75%
5.50%	4.75%
6.00%	3.75%
6.50%	2.75%
7.00%	1.75%

[1] By specialized investment vehicles, we mean funds set up to invest in particular areas or sectors. For example, wholly owned subsidiaries of Citigroup such as Centauri or Dorada Corporation issue notes, backed by an AAA-rating, specifically to suit investor demand. For this reason notes issued by such bodies assume a wide variety of forms, often linked with currency or interest-rate swap element, and in a wide range of currencies. As they have an ongoing requirement for funds, notes may be issued at any time, especially when a particular investor requirement is identified.
[2] The sterling yield curve was inverted at this time, but remained slightly positive at the money market maturities, up to seven or eight months.

the swap bank paying this in return for a Libor income, in a swap structure that matches the maturity of the note. The Libor level will be lower than the longer-term swap rate because we assume a positive-sloping yield curve environment. Investors can benefit from an arrangement that provides them with a coupon sensitivity that is twice that of changes in the rate of Libor.

Another interesting feature of inverse floater notes is their high duration, which results from the leveraged arrangement of the coupon. In our hypothetical example, although the note has a calendar maturity of three years, its modified duration will be much higher. This is shown in table 7.2. Inverse floaters have the highest duration values of any instrument traded in the fixed income market. This makes them highly interest-rate sensitive products.

TABLE 7.2 ■ Duration of three-year inverse floater note

Duration of 3-year note with 5.30% coupon	2.218 years
Duration of 3-year inverse floater (× 3)	6.654 years

A number of variations of the inverse floater described have been introduced. It is straightforward to link the notes to any quoted reference index, which would be of interest to investors who had a particular view of short- or long-term interest rate indices, for example the central bank repo rate, 10-year swap rates or a government benchmark. The leverage of the notes can also be altered to reflect the investor's risk preference, and the fixed element may be altered for the same reason. Equally, the fixed element can be set to move upwards or downwards as required. As another possibility, investors who have a particular view on a specific foreign interest-rate market, but who (for one reason or another) are not able to invest in that market's securities, can gain an exposure that reflects their views through the purchase of an inverse FRN that is linked to the foreign index but pays coupon in the domestic currency.

Hedging the note

Borrowers often issue notes in a different currency to the currency they require, and will typically swap the proceeds into the required currency by means of a currency swap. An interest-rate swap arrangement is used to hedge the interest-rate exposure on the inverse floater. The issuer will transact the swap structure with a swap bank, usually a high-rated institution. The swap bank will hedge its own exposure as part of its normal operations in the swap markets. The structure that would apply to the hypothetical note above is shown in figure 7.1.

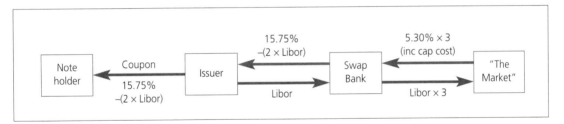

FIGURE 7.1 ■ Inverse floater hedge structure

The swap transacted with the issuer involves:

■ paying fixed at the note coupon level;

■ receiving Libor.

The other side of this transaction for the swap bank is another swap where it pays floating and receives fixed. This is made up of the following:

■ the swap bank pays Libor on the swap;

■ it receives 5.30%, which is the three-year swap rate.

However, the swap bank must also hedge the coupon rate on the note, as this is now his exposure (the issuer being fully hedged by the swap bank and paying Libor, its desired cost of funds). The coupon rate is 15.75% – (2 × Libor), which in effect means that the note holder is receiving 15.75% and paying 2 × Libor. Therefore, the swap bank in order to hedge this cash flow, will pay 2 × Libor and receive two fixed rates of 5.30%. The three rates for the swap total 15.90%. This is higher than the fixed component of the coupon in the note, by 15 basis points. This difference is the cost of fixing a cap, as detailed below.

The inverse floater has a minimum coupon on 0%, and to hedge this element the swap bank will need to purchase an interest-rate cap on Libor with a strike rate of 7.875%. The strike rate is the note coupon on 15.75% divided by two. The cap element of the hedge protects the dealer against a rise in Libor over the set rate. The cap has a cost of 15 basis points, which explains the difference over the coupon rate in the swap structure.

Indexed amortizing note

Description

Another type of hybrid note is the Indexed Amortizing Note or IAN. They were introduced in the US domestic market in the early 1990s at the demand of investors in asset-backed notes known as collateralized mortgage obligations or CMOs. IANs are fixed-coupon unsecured notes issued with a nominal value that is not fixed. That is, the nominal amount may reduce in value ahead of the legal maturity according to the levels recorded by a specified reference index such as six-month Libor. If the reference remains static or its level decreases, the IAN value will amortize in nominal value. The legal maturity of IANs is short- to medium-term, with the five-year maturity being common. The notes have been issued by banks and corporates, although a large volume has been issued by US government agencies. The yield payable on IANs is typically at a premium above that of similar credit quality conventional debt. The amortization schedule on an IAN is linked to the movement of the specified reference index, which is easily understood. This is considered an advantage to certain mortgage-backed notes, which amortize in accordance with less clearly defined patterns such as a *prepayment schedule*.

An issuer of IANs will arrange a hedge that makes the funding obtained more attractive, for example a straight Libor-type exposure. This is most commonly arranged through a swap arrangement that mirrors the note structure. A diagrammatic representation is shown in figure 7.2. In fact it is more common for the swap arrangement to involve a series of options on swaps. The coupon available on an IAN might be attractive to investors when the volatility on *swaptions* is high and there is a steep positively sloping yield curve; under such an environment the option-element of an IAN would confer greatest value.

The terms of an hypothetical IAN issue are given at table 7.3.

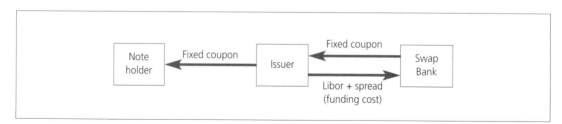

FIGURE 7.2 ■ IAN hedge arrangement

Under the terms of issue of the note summarized in table 7.3, the coupon payable is the current two-year government benchmark plus a fixed spread of 1%. The note has a legal maturity of six years, however, it will mature in three years if the six-month Libor rate is at a level of 6.00% or below two years from the date of issue. If the rate is above 6.00%, the maturity of the note will be extended. The 'lock-out' of three years means that the note has a minimum life of three years, irrespective of what happens to Libor rates. Amortization takes place if, on subsequent rate-fixing dates after the lock-out period, the Libor rate rises. The maximum maturity of the note is six years. If at any time there is less than 20% of the nominal value in issue, the note is cancelled in full.

TABLE 7.3 ■ Hypothetical IAN issue

Issuer	Mortgage agency
Nominal value	$250,000,000
Legal maturity	6 years
Coupon	2-year Treasury plus 100 bps
Interest basis	Monthly
'Lock-out period'	Three years
Reference index	6-month Libor
6m Libor fixing on issue	5.15%
Minimum level of note	20%

Average life sensitivity

Libor rate	Amortization rate	Average life (years)
5.15%	100%	3
6.00%	100%	3
7.00%	21%	4.1
8.00%	7%	5.6
9.00%	0.00%	6

Advantages to investors

The IAN structure offers advantages to investors under certain conditions. If the credit quality is acceptable, the notes offer a high yield over a relatively low term to maturity. The amortization structure is easier to understand than that on mortgage-backed securities, which contain prepayment schedules that are based on assumptions that may not apply. This means that investors will know with certainty how the amortization of the note will proceed, given the level of the reference index at any given time. The 'lock-out' period of a note is usually set at a period that offers investor comfort, such as three years; during this time no amortization can take place.

As with the other instruments described here, IANs can be tailored to meet individual investor requirements. The legal maturity and lock-out period are features that are most frequently subject to variation, with the yield premium decreasing as the lock-out period becomes closer to the formal maturity. The reference index can be a government benchmark or interbank rate such as the swap rate. However, the most common reference is the Libor rate.

Synthetic convertible note

Description

Synthetic convertible notes are fixed-coupon securities whose total return is linked to an external source such as the level of an equity index, or the price of a specific security. The fixed-coupon element is typically at a low level, and the investor has greater exposure to the performance of the external index. A common arrangement has the note redeeming at par, but redeemable at a greater amount if the performance of the reference index exceeds a stated minimum. However, the investor has the safety net of redemption at par. Another typical structure is a zero-coupon note, issued at par and redeemable at par, but redeemable at a higher level if a specified equity index performs above a pre-specified level.

Table 7.4 lists the terms of an hypothetical synthetic convertible note issue that is linked to the FTSE-100 equity index. This note will pay par on maturity, but if the level of the FTSE-100 has increased by more than 10% from the level on note issue, the note will be redeemed at par plus this amount. Note however that this is an investment suitable only for someone who is very bullish on the prospects for the FTSE-100. If this index does not raise by the minimum level, the investor will have received a coupon of 0.5%, which is roughly five percentage points below the level for two-year sterling at this time.

TABLE 7.4 ■ Terms of a synthetic convertible note issue

Nominal value	£50,000,000
Term to maturity	Two years
Issue date	17-Jun-99
Maturity date	17-Jun-01
Issue price	£100
Coupon	0.50%
Interest basis	Semi-annual
Redemption proceeds	Min [100, Formula level]
Formula level	$100 + [100 \times (R(I) - (1.1 \times R(II))/R(II)]$
Index	FTSE-100
$R(I)$	Index level on maturity
$R(II)$	Index level on issue
Hedge terms	
Issuer pays	Libor
Swap bank pays	Redemption proceeds in accordance with formula

Advantages to investors

Similarly to a convertible bond, a synthetic convertible note provides investors with a fixed coupon together with additional market upside potential if the level of the reference index performs above a certain level. Unlike the convertible however, the payoff is in the form of cash.

The reference can be virtually any publicly quoted source, and notes have been issued whose payout is linked to the exchange rate of two currencies, the days on which Libor falls within a specified range, the performance of a selected basket of stocks (say 'technology stocks'), and so on.

Interest differential notes

Description

Interest differential notes or IDNs are hybrid securities which are aimed at investors who wish to put on a position that reflects their view on the interest-rate differential between rates of two different currencies. Notes in the US market are usually denominated in US dollars, whereas Euromarket notes have been issued in a wide range of global currencies.

There are a number of variations of IDNs. Notes may pay a variable coupon and a fixed redemption amount, or a fixed coupon and a redemption amount that is determined by the level or performance of an external reference index. IDNs have also been issued with payoff profiles that are linked to the differentials in interest rates of two specified currencies, or between one currency across different maturities.

EXAMPLE *7.1 Interest differential note*

Here we consider a five-year note that is linked to the differential between US dollar Libor and euro-libor.

The return on this note is a function of the spread between the US dollar Libor rate and euro-libor. An increase in the spread results in a higher coupon payable on the note, while a narrowing of the spread results in a lower coupon payable. Such a structure will appeal to an investor who has a particular view on the USD and EUR yield curves. For instance assume that the US dollar curve is inverted and the euro curve is positively-sloping. A position in an IDN (structured as above) on these two currencies allows an investor to avoid outright yield curve plays in each currency, and instead put on a trade that reflects a view on the relative level of interest rates in each currency. An IDN in this environment would allow an investor to earn a high yield while taking a view that is different to the market consensus.

TABLE 7.5 ■ IDN example

Term to maturity	Five years
Coupon	[(2 × USD Libor) – (2 × EUR Libor) – 0.50%]

Current USD Libor	6.15%
Current EUR Libor	3.05%
Rate differential	2.65%
First coupon fix	5.70%
Current five-year benchmark	4.75%
Yield spread over benchmark	0.95%

Change in Libor spread (bps p.a.)	Libor spread at rate reset	Spread over benchmark
75	4.78%	2.34%
50	3.90%	1.88%
25	3.15%	1.21%
0	2.65%	0.95%
–25	1.97%	0.56%
–50	1.32%	0.34%
–75	0.89%	0.12%
–100	0.32%	–0.28%

When analyzing an IDN, an investor must regard the note to be the equivalent to a fixed-coupon bond together with a double indexation of an interest-rate differential. The effect of this double indexation on the differential is to create two long positions in a five-year USD fixed-rate note and two short positions in a EUR fixed-rate note. The short position in the EUR note means that the EUR exchange-rate risk is removed and the investor has an exposure only to the EUR interest-rate risk, which is the desired position.

The issuer of the note hedges the note with a swap structure as with other hybrid securities. The arrangement involves both USD and EUR interest-rate swaps. The swap bank takes the opposite position in the swaps.

Table 7.5 also illustrates the return profiles possible under different interest-rate scenarios. One possibility shows that the IDN provides 95 basis point yield premium over the five-year government benchmark yield, however this assumes rather unrealistically that the interest differential between the USD and EUR interest rates remains constant through to the final coupon setting date. More significantly, we see that the yield premium available on the note increases as the spread differential between the two rates increases. In a spread tightening environment, the note offers a premium over the government yield as long as the tightening does not exceed 100 basis points each year.

Advantages to investors

IDN-type instruments allow investors to put on positions that reflect their view on foreign interest rate direction and/or levels, but without having to expose themselves to currency (exchange-rate) risk at the same time. The notes may also be structured in a way that allows investors to take a view on any maturity point of the yield curve. For instance the coupon may be set in accordance with the differential between the 10-year government benchmark yields of two specified countries. As another approach, investors can arrange combinations of different maturities in the same currency, which is a straight yield curve or relative value trade in a domestic or foreign currency.

The risk run by a note holder is that the interest-rate differential moves in the opposite direction to that sought, which reduces the coupon payable and may even result in a lower yield than that available on the benchmark bond.

SELECTED BIBLIOGRAPHY AND REFERENCES

Given the nature of this market, with new types of notes being introduced almost all the time, to keep up-to-date ideally one should read banks' own research output. We recommend the 'bible' of fixed-income writing, Fabozzi's *Handbook*, as the ideal start for readers. His edited volume on structured products is also very useful.

Fabozzi, F. (ed.), *Handbook of Fixed Income Securities*, 6th edition, McGraw-Hill 2000.
Fabozzi, F. (ed.), *Handbook of Structured Financial Product*, FJF Associates, 1998.

CHAPTER 8

Securitisation and mortgage-backed securities

The asset-based markets represent a large and diverse group of securities which are suited to a varied group of investors. Often they are the only way for institutional investors to pick up yield while retaining assets with high credit ratings. They are popular with issuers because they represent a cost-effective means of removing assets off the balance sheet, thus freeing up lending lines, and enabling them to have access to lower cost funding. Depending on the nature of the underlying asset backing, there are instruments available that cover the entire term of the yield curve. They are also available paying fixed- or floating-rate coupon. Although the market was developed in the US, there are liquid markets in the UK, Europe, Asia and Latin America. The flexibility of securitisation is its key advantage for both issuers and investors: for instance in the UK it is common for mortgage-backed bonds to have a floating coupon, reflecting the interest basis of UK mortgages, although there have been structures paying fixed rate coupon to suit investor requirements. To arrange this the transaction will include a swap arrangement.

Perhaps the best illustration of the flexibility, innovation, and simple user-friendliness[1] of the debt capital markets is the rise in the use and importance of *securitisation*. For a definition of this technique let us turn to Sundaresan, who says that the approach

> '... simply stated ... is a framework in which some illiquid assets of a corporation or a financial institution are transformed into a package of securities backed by these assets, through careful packaging, credit enhancements, liquidity enhancements and structuring.'   *(Sundaresan, 1997, p. 359)*

The process of securitisation creates *asset-backed bonds*. These are debt instruments that have been created from a package of loan assets on which interest is payable, usually on a floating basis. The asset-backed market was developed in the US and is a large, diverse

---

[1] If readers will permit this expression!

market containing a wide range of instruments. The characteristics of asset-backed securities (ABS) present additional features in their analysis, which are introduced in this chapter. Financial engineering techniques employed by investment banks today enable an entity to create a bond structure from any type of cash flow; the typical forms are high volume loans such as residential mortgages, car loans and credit card loans. The loans form assets on a bank or finance house balance sheet, which are packaged together and used as backing for an issue of bonds. The interest payments on the original loans form the cash flows used to service the new bond issue. The development of the market in securitised bonds is such that these days an investment bank will not think it unusual to underwrite a bond issued secured against any type of cash flow, from the more traditional mortgages and loan assets to cash flows received by leisure and recreational facilities such as heath clubs, public houses and other entities such as nursing homes. The asset class behind a securitised bond issue is significant, and there are distinct classes, each calling for their own methods of analysis and valuation. Traditionally, mortgage-backed bonds are grouped in their own right as mortgage-backed securities (MBS) while all other securitisations are known as asset-backed bonds (ABS).

In this chapter we present an introduction to the basic technique of securitisation. The market is large and diverse, and stretches across a large number of markets and currencies. Readers who need to specialize should consult the bibliography; two good overview titles are the Fabozzi-edited books on structured products and mortgage-backed securities.

Introduction

Reasons for undertaking securitisation

The driving force behind the growth in securitisation was the need for banks to realize value from the assets on their balance sheet. Typically, these assets were residential and commercial mortgages, corporate loans, and retail loans such as credit card debt. What factors might lead a financial institution to securitise a part of its balance sheet?

A bank may wish to reduce the size of its balance sheet for the following reasons:

- if revenues received from assets remain roughly unchanged but the size of assets has decreased, this will lead to an increase in the return on equity ratio;
- the level of capital required to support the balance sheet will be reduced, which again can lead to cost savings or allows the institution to allocate the capital to other, perhaps more profitable, business;
- to obtain cheaper funding: frequently the interest payable on ABS securities is considerably below the level payable on the underlying loans. This creates a cash surplus for the originating entity.

By entering into securitisation, a lower-rated entity can access debt capital markets that would otherwise be the preserve of higher-rated institutions. The growth of the so-called 'credit card banks' in the US, such as MBNA International, would have been severely restricted if a market for the securitised debt of these firms had not been in place.

Market participants

The securitisation process involves a number of participants. In the first instance is the *originator*, the firm whose assets are being securitised. The most common process involves an *issuer* acquiring the assets from the originator. The issuer is typically a company that has been specially set up for the purpose of the securitisation and is known as a *special purpose vehicle* (SPV). It is usually domiciled offshore. The creation of an SPV ensures that the underlying asset pool is held separate from the other assets of the originator. This is done so that in the event that the originator is declared bankrupt or insolvent, the impact on the original assets is minimized. This last is often the responsibility of a *trustee*. The issue trustee is responsible for looking after the interests of bondholders. Its roles include:

■ representing the interests of investors (note holders);

■ monitoring the transaction and issuer to see if any violation of the deal covenants has occurred;

■ enforcing the rights of the note holders in the event of bankruptcy.

The *security trustee* is responsible for undertaking the following duties:

■ holding the security interest in the underlying collateral pool;

■ liaising with the manager of the underlying collateral;

■ acting under the direction of the note trustee in the event of default.

By holding the assets within an SPV framework, defined in formal legal terms, the financial status and credit rating of the originator becomes almost irrelevant to the bondholders. The process may also involved credit enhancements, in which a third-party guarantee of credit quality is obtained, so that notes issued under the securitisation are often rated at investment grade and up to AAA-grade.

Figure 8.1 illustrates in simple fashion the process of securitisation.

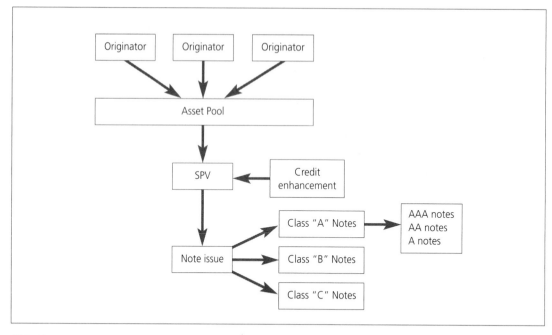

FIGURE 8.1 ■ Securitisation process

Securitising mortgages

Introduction

A mortgage is a loan made for the purpose of purchasing property, which in turn is used as the security for the loan itself. It is defined as a debt instrument giving conditional ownership of an asset, and secured by the asset that is being financed. The borrower provides the lender a mortgage in exchange for the right to use the property during the term of the mortgage, and agrees to make regular payments of both principal and interest. The mortgage lien is the security for the lender, and is removed when the debt is paid off. A mortgage may involve residential property or commercial property and is a long-term debt, normally 25–30 years; however, it can be drawn up for shorter periods if required by the borrower. If the borrower or *mortgagor* defaults on the interest payments, the lender or *mortgagee* has the right to take over the property and recover the debt from the proceeds of selling the property. Mortgages can be either fixed-rate or floating-rate interest. Although in the US mortgages are generally amortizing loans, known as *repayment* mortgages in the UK, there are also *interest only* mortgages where the borrower pays only the interest on the loan; on maturity the original loan amount is paid off by the proceeds of a maturing investment contract taken out at the same time as the mortgage. These are known as *endowment* mortgages and are popular in the UK market, although their popularity has been waning in recent years.

A lending institution may have many hundreds of thousands of individual residential and commercial mortgages on its book. If the total loan book is pooled together and used as collateral for the issue of a bond, the resulting instrument is a *mortgage-backed security*. This process is known as *securitisation*, which is the pooling of loan assets in order to use them as collateral for a bond issue. As we just noted, usually a *special purpose vehicle* (SPV) is set up to serve as the entity representing the pooled assets. This is done for administrative reasons and also sometimes to enhance the credit rating that may be assigned to the bonds. In the UK, some SPVs have a triple-A credit rating, although the majority of SPVs are below this rating, while retaining investment grade status. In the US market certain mortgage-backed securities are backed, either implicitly or explicitly, by the government, in which case they trade essentially as risk-free instruments and are not rated by the credit agencies. In the US a government agency, the Government National Mortgage Association (GNMA, known as 'Ginnie Mae') and two government-sponsored agencies, the Federal Home Loan Corporation and the Federal National Mortgage Association ('Freddie Mac' and 'Fannie Mae' respectively), purchase mortgages for the purpose of pooling them and holding them in their portfolios; they may then be securitised. Bonds that are not issued by government agencies are rated in the same way as other corporate bonds. On the other hand, non-government agencies sometimes obtain mortgage insurance for their issue, in order to boost its credit quality. When this happens, the credit rating of the mortgage insurer becomes an important factor in the credit standing of the bond issue.

Growth of the market

A recent study[2] has suggested the following advantages of mortgage-backed bonds:

■ although many mortgage bonds represent comparatively high quality assets and are collateralized instruments, the yields on them are usually higher then corporate bonds of the same credit quality. This is because of the complexity of the instruments and the uncertain nature of the mortgage cash flows. In the mid-1990s, mortgage-backed bonds traded at yields of around 100–200 basis points above Treasury bonds;

■ the wide range of products offers investors a choice of maturities, cash flows and security to suit individual requirements;

■ agency mortgage-backed bonds are implicitly backed by the government and therefore represent a better credit risk than triple-A rated corporate bonds; the credit ratings for non-agency bonds is often triple-A or double-A rated;

■ the size of the market means that it is very liquid, with agency mortgage-backed bonds having the same liquidity as Treasury bonds;

[2] Hayre, L., Mohebbi, C., Zimmermann, T., 'Mortgage Pass-Through Securities', in Fabozzi, F. (ed.) *The Handbook of Fixed Income Securities*, 5th edition, McGraw-Hill 1998.

■ the monthly coupon frequency of mortgage-backed bonds in the US markets make them an attractive instrument for investors who require frequent income payments; this feature is not available for most other bond market instruments.

In the UK, the asset-backed market has also witnessed rapid growth, and many issues are triple-A rated because issuers create a special purpose vehicle that is responsible for the issue. Various forms of insurance are also used. Unlike the US market, most bonds are floating-rate instruments, reflecting the variable-rate nature of the majority of mortgages in the UK.

Mortgages

In the US market, the terms of a conventional mortgage, known as a *level-payment fixed-rate mortgage*, will state the interest rate payable on the loan, the term of the loan and the frequency of payment. Most mortgages specify monthly payment of interest. These are in fact the characteristics of a level-payment mortgage, which has a fixed interest rate and fixed term to maturity. This means that the monthly interest payments are fixed, hence the term 'level-pay'.

The singular feature of a mortgage is that, even if it charges interest at a fixed rate, its cash flows are not known with absolute certainty. This is because the borrower can elect to repay any or all of the principal before the final maturity date. This is a characteristic of all mortgages, and although some lending institutions impose a penalty on borrowers who retire the loan early, this is a risk for the lender, known as *repayment risk*. The uncertainty of the cash flow patterns is similar to that of a callable bond, and as we shall see later this feature means that we may value mortgage-backed bonds using a pricing model similar to that employed for callable bonds.

The monthly interest payment on a conventional fixed-rate mortgage is given by (8.3), which is derived from the conventional present value analysis used for a annuity. Essentially the primary relationship is:

$$M_{m0} = I \left[\frac{1 - \left[\frac{1}{(1 + r)^n} \right]}{r} \right] \tag{8.1}$$

from which we can derive:

$$I = \frac{M_{m0}}{\left[\frac{1 - \left[\frac{1}{(1 + r)^n} \right]}{r} \right]} \tag{8.2}$$

This is simplified to:

$$I = M_{m0} \left[\frac{r(1 + r)^n}{[(1 + r)^n - 1]} \right] \tag{8.3}$$

where

M_{m0} is the original mortgage balance (the cash amount of loan);
I is the monthly cash mortgage payment;
r is the simple monthly interest rate, given by (annual interest rate/12);
n is the term of the mortgage in months.

The monthly repayment includes both the interest servicing and a repayment of part of the principal. Since a portion of the original balance is paid off every month, the interest payment reduces by a small amount each month, that is, the proportion of the monthly payment dedicated to repaying the principal steadily increases. The remaining mortgage balance for any particular month during the term of the mortgage may be calculated using (8.4),

$$M_{mt} = M_{m0} \left[\frac{[(1 + r)^n - (1 + r)^t]}{[(1 + r)^n - 1]} \right] \tag{8.4}$$

where M_{mt} is the mortgage cash balance after t months and n remains the original maturity of the mortgage in months.

The level of interest payment and principal repayment in any one month during the mortgage term can be calculated using the equations below. If we wish to calculate the value of the principal repayment in a particular month during the mortgage term, we may use (8.5),

$$p_t = M_{m0} \left[\frac{[r(1 + r)^{t-1}]}{[(1 + r)^n - 1]} \right] \tag{8.5}$$

where p_t is the scheduled principal repayment amount for month t, while the level of interest payment in any month is given by (8.6),

$$i_t = M_{m0} \left[\frac{r[(1 + r)^n - (1 + r)^{t-1}]}{[(1 + r)^n - 1]} \right] \tag{8.6}$$

where i_t is the interest payment only in month t.

Some mortgage contracts incorporate a *servicing fee*. This is payable to the mortgage provider to cover the administrative costs associated with collecting interest payments, sending regular statements and other information to borrowers, chasing overdue payments, maintaining the records and processing systems and other activities. Mortgage providers also incur costs when repossessing properties after mortgagors have fallen into default. Mortgages may be serviced by the original lender or another third-party institution that has acquired the right to service it, in return for collecting the fee. When a servicing charge is payable by a borrower, the monthly mortgage payment is comprised of the interest costs, the principal repayment and the servicing fee. The fee incorporated into the monthly payment is usually stated as a percentage, say 0.25%. This is added to the mortgage rate.

Another type of mortgage in the US market is the *adjustable-rate mortgage* (ARM). These loans allow interest payments to be reset at periodic intervals to a short-term interest rate index that has been specified beforehand. The re-sets are at periodic intervals depending on the terms of the loan, and can be on a monthly, six-monthly or annual basis, or even longer. The interest rate is usually fixed at a spread over the reference rate. The reference rate that is used can be a market-determined rate such as the prime rate, or a calculated rate based on the funding costs for US savings and loan institutions or *thrifts*. The cost of funds for thrifts is calculated using the monthly average funding cost on the thrifts' activities, and there are 'thrift indexes' that are used to indicate to the cost of funding. The two most common indices are the Eleventh Federal Home Loan Bank Board District Cost of Funds Index (COFI) and the National Cost of Funds Index. Generally, borrowers prefer to fix the rate they pay on their loans to reduce uncertainty, and this makes fixed-rate mortgages more popular than variable rate mortgages. A common incentive used to entice borrowers away from fixed-rate mortgages is to offer a below-market interest rate on an ARM mortgage, usually for an introductory period. This comfort period may be from two to five years or even longer. ARM mortgages are usually issued with additional features such as an interest-rate cap specified beforehand; such a cap limits the maximum rate that the borrower would have to pay in the event that market rates increase dramatically. ARMs make up more than half the market share in the US domestic mortgage business.[3]

Mortgages in the UK are predominantly *variable rate mortgages*, in which the interest rate moves in line with the clearing bank base rate. It is rare to observe fixed-rate mortgages in the UK market, although short-term fixed-rate mortgages are more common (the rate reverts to a variable basis at the termination of the fixed-rate period).

A *balloon mortgage* entitles a borrower to long-term funding, but under its terms, at a specified future date the interest rate payable is renegotiated. This effectively transforms a long-dated loan into a short-term borrowing. The balloon payment is the original amount of the loan, minus the amount that is amortized. In a balloon mortgage, therefore, the actual maturity of the bonds is below that of the stated maturity.

A *graduated payment mortgage* (GPM) is aimed at lower-earning borrowers, as the mortgage payments for a fixed initial period, say the first five years, are set at lower the level applicable for a level-paying mortgage with an identical interest rate. The later mortgage payments are higher as a result. Hence a GPM mortgage will have a fixed term and

---

[3] Sundaresan (1997), page 366.

a mortgage rate, but the offer letter will also contain details on the number of years over which the monthly mortgage payments will increase and the point at which level payments will take over. There will also be information on the annual increase in the mortgage payments. As the initial payments in a GPM are below the market rate, there will be little or no repayment of principal at this time. This means that the outstanding balance may actually increase during the early stages, a process known as *negative amortization*. The higher payments in the remainder of the mortgage term are designed to pay off the entire balance in maturity.

The opposite to the GPM is the *growing equity mortgage* (GEM). This mortgage charges fixed-rate interest but the payments increase over time; this means that a greater proportion of the principal is paid off over time, so that the mortgage itself is repaid in a shorter time than the level-pay mortgage.

In the UK market it is more common to encounter hybrid mortgages, which charge a combination of fixed-rate and variable-rating interest. For example the rate may be fixed for the first five years, after which it will vary with changes in the lender's base rate. Such a mortgage is known as *fixed/adjustable hybrid mortgage.*

Mortgage risk

Although mortgage contracts are typically long-term loan contracts, running usually for 20–30 years or even longer, there is no limitation on the amount of the principal that may be repaid at any one time. In the US market there is no penalty for repaying the mortgage ahead of its term, known as a mortgage *prepayment*. In the UK some lenders impose a penalty if a mortgage is *prepaid* early, although this is more common for contracts that have been offered at special terms, such as a discounted loan rate for the start of the mortgage's life. The penalty is often set as extra interest, for example six months' worth of mortgage payments at the time when the contract is paid off. As a borrower is free to prepay a mortgage at a time of his choosing, the lender is not certain of the cash flows that will be paid after the contract is taken out. This is known as *prepayment risk.*

A borrower may pay off the principal ahead of the final termination date for a number of reasons. The most common reason is when the property on which the mortgage is secured is subsequently sold by the borrower; this results in the entire mortgage being paid off at once. The average life of a mortgage in the UK market is eight years, and mortgages are most frequently prepaid because the property has been sold.[4] Other actions that result in the prepayment of a mortgage are: when a property is repossessed after the borrower has fallen into default; if there is a change in interest rates making it attractive to refinance the mortgage (usually with another lender); or if the property is destroyed by accident or natural disaster.

---

[4] Source: Halifax plc.

An investor acquiring a pool of mortgages from a lender will be concerned at the level of prepayment risk, which is usually measured by projecting the level of expected future payments using a financial model. Although it would not be possible to evaluate meaningfully the potential of an individual mortgage to be paid off early, it is tenable to conduct such analysis for a large number of loans pooled together. A similar activity is performed by actuaries when they assess the future liability of an insurance provider who has written personal pension contracts. Essentially the level of prepayment risk for a pool of loans is lower than that of an individual mortgage. Prepayment risk has the same type impact on a mortgage pool's performance and valuation as a call feature does on a callable bond. This is understandable because a mortgage is essentially a callable contract, with the 'call' at the option of the borrower of funds.

The other significant risk of a mortgage book is the risk that the borrower will fall into arrears, or be unable to repay the loan on maturity (in the UK). This is known as *default risk*. Lenders take steps to minimize the level of default risk by assessing the credit quality of each borrower, as well as the quality of the property itself. A study has also found that the higher the deposit paid by the borrower, the lower the level of default.[5] Therefore, lenders prefer to advance funds against a borrower's *equity* that is deemed sufficient to protect against falls in the value of the property. In the UK the typical deposit required is 25%, although certain lenders will advance funds against smaller deposits such as 10% or 5%.

Mortgage-backed securities

Overview

Mortgage-backed securities are bonds created from a pool of mortgages. They are formed from mortgages that are for residential or commercial property, or a mixture of both. Bonds created from commercial mortgages are known as *commercial mortgage-backed securities*. There are a range of different securities in the market, known in the US as *mortgage pass-through securities*. There also exist two related securities known as *collateralized mortgage securities* and *stripped mortgage-backed securities*. Bonds that are created from mortgage pools that have been purchased by government agencies are known as *agency mortgage-backed securities*, and are regarded as risk-free in the same way as Treasury securities.

A collateralized mortgage obligation (CMO) differs from a pass-through security in that the cash flows from the mortgage pool are distributed on a prioritized basis, based on the class of security held by the investor. So for example, this might mean that three different securities are formed, with a total nominal value of $100 million each entitled to a pro-rata

---

[5] Brown, S., *et al.*, *Analysis of Mortgage Servicing Portfolios*, Financial Strategies Group, Prudential-Bache Capital Funding 1990.

amount of the interest payments but with different priorities for the repayment of principal. For instance, $60 million of the issue might consist of a bond known as 'class A', that may be entitled to receipt of all the principal repayment cash flows, after which the next class of bonds is entitled to all the repayment cash flow; this bond would be 'class B' bonds, of which say, $25 million was created, and so on. If 300 class A bonds are created, they would have a nominal value of $200,000 and each would receive 0.33% of the total cash flows received by the class A bonds. Note that all classes of bonds receive an equal share of the interest payments; it is the principal repayment cash flows received that differ.

What is the main effect of this security structure? The most significant factor is that, in our illustration, the class A bonds will be repaid earlier than any other class of bond that is formed from the securitisation. It therefore has the shortest maturity. The last class of bonds will have the longest maturity. There is still a level of uncertainty associated with the maturity of each bond, but this is less than the uncertainty associated with a pass-through security.

Stripped mortgage-backed security

The *stripped mortgage-backed security*, as its name suggests, is created by separating the interest and principal payments into individual distinct cash flows. This allows an issuer to create two very interesting securities, the interest only (IO) bond and the principal only (PO) bond. In a stripped mortgage-backed bond the interest and principal are divided into two classes, and two bonds are issued that are each entitled to receive one class of cash flow only. The bond class that receives the interest payment cash flows is known as an *interest-only* or IO class, while the bond receiving the principal repayments is known as a *principal only* or PO class.

The PO bond is similar to a zero-coupon bond in that it is issued at a discount to par value. The return achieved by a PO bondholder is a function of the rapidity at which pre-payments are made; if prepayments are received in a relatively short time the investor will realize a higher return. This would be akin to the buyer of a zero-coupon bond receiving the maturity payment ahead of the redemption date, and the highest possible return that a PO bondholder could receive would occur if all the mortgages were prepaid the instant after the PO bond was bought! A low return will be achieved if all the mortgages are held until maturity, so that there are no prepayments.

Stripped mortgage-backed bonds present potentially less advantage to an issuer compared to a pass-through security or a CMO, however, they are liquid instruments and are often traded to hedge a conventional mortgage bond book.

The price of a PO bond fluctuates as mortgage interest rates change. As we noted earlier, in the US market, the majority of mortgages are fixed-rate loans, so that if mortgage rates fall below the coupon rate on the bond, the holder will expect the volume of pre-payments to increase as individuals refinance loans in order to gain from lower borrowing rates. This will result in a faster stream of payments to the PO bondholder as cash flows are received earlier than expected. The price of the PO rises to reflect this, and also because cash flows in the mortgage will now be discounted at a lower rate. The opposite happens when mortgage rates rise and the rate of prepayment is expected to fall, which causes a PO bond to fall in price.

An IO bond is essentially a stream of cash flows and has no par value. The cash flows represent interest on the mortgage principal outstanding, therefore a higher rate of prepayment leads to a fall in the IO price. This is because the cash flows cease once the principal is redeemed. The risk for the IO bondholder is that prepayments occur so quickly that interest payments cease before the investor has recovered the amount originally paid for the IO bond.

The price of an IO is also a function of mortgage rates in the market, but exhibits more peculiar responses. If rates fall below the bond coupon, again the rate of prepayment is expected to increase. This would lead to the cash flows for the IO to decline, as mortgages were paid off more quickly. This would lead to the price of the IO falling as well, even though the cash flows themselves would be discounted at a lower interest rate. If mortgage rates rise, the outlook for future cash flows will improve as the prepayment rate fall, however there is also a higher discounting rate for the cash flows themselves, so the price of an IO may move in either direction. Thus IO bonds exhibit a curious characteristic for a bond instrument, in that their price moves in the same direction as market rates.

Both versions of the stripped mortgage bond are interesting instruments, and they have high volatilities during times of market rate changes. Note that PO and IO bonds could be created from the hypothetical mortgage pool described above; therefore the combined modified duration of both instruments must equal the modified duration of the original pass-through security.

Cash flow patterns

We stated that the exact term of a mortgage-backed bond structure cannot be stated with accuracy at the time of issue, because of the uncertain frequency of mortgage prepayments. This uncertainty means that it is not possible to analyze the bonds using the conventional methods used for fixed term bonds. The most common approach used by the market is to assume a fixed prepayment rate at the time of issue and use this to project the cash flows, and hence the life span, of the bond. The choice of prepayment selected therefore is significant, although it is also recognized that prepayment rates are not stable and will fluctuate with changes in mortgage rates and the economic cycle. In this section, we consider some of the approaches used in evaluating the prepayment pattern of a mortgage-backed bond.

Prepayment analysis

Some market analysts assume a fixed life for a mortgage pass-through bond based on the average life of a mortgage. Traditionally, a '12-year prepaid life' has been used to evaluate the securities, as market data suggested that the average mortgage has been paid off after the twelfth year. This is not generally favoured because it does not take into account the effect of mortgage rates and other factors. A more common approach is to use a *constant prepayment rate* (CPR). This measure is based on the expected number of mortgages in a pool that will be prepaid in a selected period, and is an annualized figure. The measure for the monthly level of prepayment is known as the *constant monthly repayment*, and measures the expected amount of the outstanding balance, minus the scheduled principal, that will be prepaid in each month. Another name for the constant monthly repayment is the *single monthly mortality rate* or SMM. The SMM is given by (8.7) and is an expected value for the percentage of the remaining mortgage balance that will be prepaid in that month.

$$SMM = 1 - (1 - CPR)^{1/12} \tag{8.7}$$

Constant prepayment rate example

The constant prepayment rate for a pool of mortgages is 2% each month. The outstanding principal balance at the start of the month is £72,200, while the scheduled principal payment is £223. This means that 2% of £71,977, or £1,439 will be prepaid in that month. To approximate the amount of principal prepayment, the constant monthly prepayment is multiplied by the outstanding balance.

In the US market, the convention is to use the prepayment standard developed by the Public Securities Association (PSA),[6] which is the domestic bond market trade association. The PSA benchmark, known as 100% PSA, assumes a steadily increasing constant prepayment rate each month until the 30th month, when a constant rate of 6% is assumed. The starting prepayment rate is 0.2%, increasing at 0.2% each month until the rate levels off at 6%.

For the 100% PSA benchmark we may set, if t is the number of months from the start of the mortgage, that

if $t < 30$, the CPR = 6%.t / 30

while if $t > 30$,

then CPR is equal to 6%.

---

[6] Since renamed the Bond Market Association.

This benchmark can be altered if required to suit changing market conditions. For example, the 200% PSA has a starting prepayment rate and an increase that is double the 100% PSA model, so the initial rate is 0.4%, increasing by 0.4% each month until it reaches 12% in the 30th month, at which point the rate remains constant. The 50% PSA has a starting (and increases by a) rate of 0.1%, remaining constant after it reaches 3%.

The prepayment level of a mortgage pool will have an impact on its cash flows. If the amount of prepayment is nil, the cash flows will remain constant during the life of the mortgage. In a fixed-rate mortgage, the proportion of principal and interest payment will change each month as more and more of the mortgage amortizes. That is, as the principal amount falls each month, the amount of interest decreases. If we assume that a pass-through security has been issued today, so that its coupon reflects the current market level, the payment pattern will resemble the bar chart shown at figure 8.2.

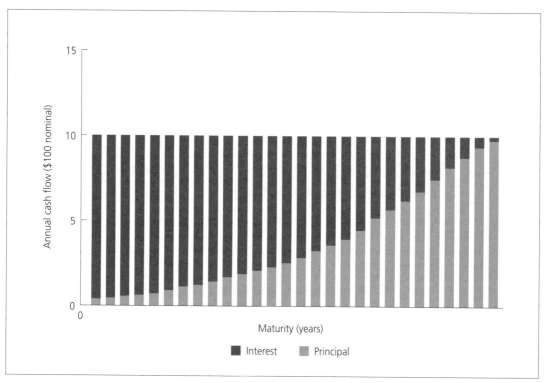

FIGURE 8.2 ■ Mortgage pass-through security with 0% constant prepayment rate

When there is an element of prepayment in a mortgage pool, for example as in the 100% PSA or 200% PSA model, the amount of principal payment will increase during the early years of the mortgages and then becomes more steady, before declining for the remainder of the term; this is because the principal balance has declined to such an extent that the scheduled principal payments become less significant. The example for a prepayment of a single loan at 100% PSA (for a 9% rate 30-year maturity loan) is shown at figure 8.3.

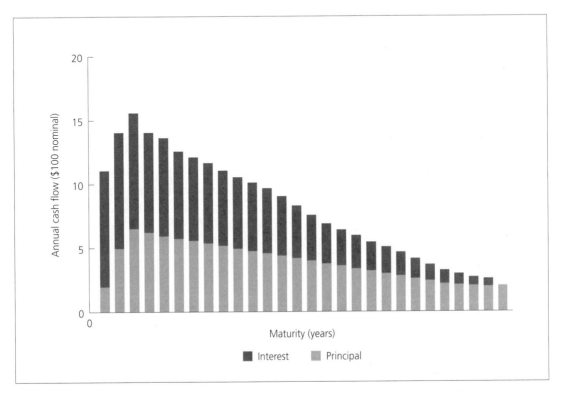

FIGURE 8.3 ▪ 100% PSA model

The prepayment volatility of a mortgage-backed bond will vary according to the interest rate of the underlying mortgages. It has been observed that where the mortgages have interest rates of between 100 and 300 basis points above current mortgage rates, the prepayment volatility is the highest. At the bottom of the range, any fall in interest rates often leads to a sudden increase in refinancing of mortgages, while at the top of the range, an increase in rates will lead to a decrease in the prepayment rate.

The actual cash flow of a mortgage pass-through is dependent on the cash flow patterns of the mortgages in the pool. The projected monthly mortgage payment for a level-paying fixed rate mortgage in any month is given by (8.8),

$$\overline{I}_t = \overline{M}_{mt-1}\left[\frac{r(1 + r)^{n-t+1}}{(1 + r)^{n-t+1} - 1}\right] \tag{8.8}$$

where:

$\bar{I}_t$ is the projected monthly mortgage payment for month t;

$\bar{M}_{mt-1}$ is the projected mortgage balance at the end of month t assuming that prepayments have occurred in the past.

To calculate the interest proportion of the projected monthly mortgage payment we use (8.9) where $\bar{i}_t$ is the projected monthly interest payment for month t.

$$\bar{i}_t = \bar{M}_{mt-1} \cdot i \tag{8.9}$$

Formula (8.9) states that the projected monthly interest payment can be obtained by multiplying the mortgage balance at the end of the previous month by the monthly interest rate. In the same way, the expression for calculating the projected monthly scheduled principal payment for any month is given by (8.10), where $\bar{p}_t$ is the projected scheduled principal payment for the month t.

$$\bar{p}_t = \bar{I}_t - \bar{i}_t \tag{8.10}$$

The projected monthly principal prepayment, which is an expected rate only and not a model forecast, is given by (8.11).

$$\overline{pp}_t = SMM_t(\overline{M}_{mt-1} - \bar{p}_t) \tag{8.11}$$

where $\overline{pp}_t$ is the projected monthly principal prepayment for month t.

The above relationships enable us to calculate values for:

- the projected monthly interest payment;
- the projected monthly scheduled principal payment; and
- the projected monthly principal prepayment.

These values may be used to calculate the total cash flow in any month that a holder of a mortgage-backed bond receives which is given by (8.12) below, where cf_t is the cash flow receipt in month t.

$$cf_t = \bar{i}_t + \bar{p}_t + \overline{pp}_t \tag{8.12}$$

The practice of using a prepayment rate is a market convention that enables analysts to evaluate mortgage-backed bonds. The original PSA prepayment rates were arbitrarily selected, based on the observation that prepayment rates tended to stabilize after the first 30 months of the life of a mortgage. A linear increase in the prepayment rate is also assumed. However, this is a market convention only, adopted by the market as a standard benchmark. The levels do not reflect seasonal variations in prepayment patterns, or the different behaviour patterns of different types of mortgages.

The PSA benchmarks can be (and are) applied to default assumptions to produce a default benchmark. This is used for non-agency mortgage-backed bonds only, as agency securities are guaranteed by one of the three government or government-sponsored agencies. Accordingly, the PSA *standard default assumption* (SDA) benchmark is used to assess the potential default rate for a mortgage pool. For example, the standard benchmark, 100SDA assumes that the default rate in the first month is 0.02% and increases in a linear fashion by 0.02% each month until the thirtieth month, at which point the default rate remains at 0.60%. In month 60, the default rate begins to fall from 0.60% to 0.03% and continues to fall linearly until month 120. From that point the default rate remains constant at 0.03%. The other benchmarks have similar patterns.

Prepayment models

The PSA standard benchmark discussed in the previous section uses an assumption of prepayment rates and can be used to calculate the prepayment proceeds of a mortgage. It is not, strictly speaking, a prepayment *model* because it cannot be used to estimate actual prepayments. A prepayment model, on the other hand, does attempt to predict the prepayment cash flows of a mortgage pool, by modelling the statistical relationships between the various factors that have an impact on the level of prepayment. These factors are the current mortgage rate, the characteristics of the mortgages in the pool, seasonal factors and the general business cycle.

The prevailing mortgage interest rate is probably the most important factor in the level of prepayment. The level of the current mortgage rate and its spread above or below the original contract rate will influence the decision to refinance a mortgage; if the rate is materially below the original rate, the borrower will prepay the mortgage. As the mortgage rate at any time reflects the general bank base rate, the level of market interest rates has the greatest effect on mortgage prepayment levels. The current mortgage rate also has an effect on housing prices, since if mortgages are seen as 'cheap' the general perception will be that now is the right time to purchase; this affects housing market turnover. The pattern followed by mortgage rates since the original loan also has an impact, a phenomenon known as *refinancing burnout*.

Observation of the mortgage market has suggested that housing market and mortgage activity follows a strong seasonal pattern. The strongest period of activity is during the spring and summer, while the market is at its quietest in the winter. The various factors may be used to derive an expression that can be used to calculate expected prepayment levels. For example, a US investment bank uses the following model to calculate expected prepayments:[7]

Monthly prepayment rate =
(Refinancing incentive) × (Season multiplier) × (Month multiplier) × (Burnout)

---

[7] Fabozzi (1997).

Collateralized mortgage securities

A large number of the instruments in the US market are collateralized mortgage obligations (CMOs), the majority of which are issued by government-sponsored agencies and so offer virtual Treasury bond credit quality but at significantly higher yields. This makes the paper attractive to a range of institutional investors, as does the opportunity to tailor the characteristics of a particular issue to suit the needs of a specific investor. The CMO market in the US experienced rapid growth during the 1990s, with a high of $324 billion issued in 1993; this figure had fallen to just under $100 billion during 1998.[8] The growth of the market has brought with it a range of new structures, for example bondholders who wished to have a lower exposure to prepayment risk have invested in *planned amortization classes* (PACs) and *targeted amortization classes* (TACs). The uncertain term to maturity of mortgage-backed bonds has resulted in the creation of bonds that were guaranteed not to extend beyond a stated date, which are known as *very accurately defined maturity* (VDAM) bonds. In the UK and certain overseas markets, mortgage-backed bonds pay a floating-rate coupon, and the interest from foreign investors in the US domestic market led to the creation of bonds with coupons linked to the LIBOR rate. Other types of instruments in the market include interest-only (IO) and principal-only (PO) bonds, also sometimes called Strips, and inverse floating-rate bonds, which are usually created from an existing fixed-rate bond issue.

Main features of US-market CMOs

The primary features of US-market CMOs are summarized below.

Credit quality

CMOs issued by US government agencies have the same guarantee as agency pass-through securities, so may be considered risk-free. These bonds therefore do not require any form of credit insurance or credit enhancement. Whole-loan CMOs do not carry any form of government guarantee, and are rated by credit rating agencies. Most bonds carry a triple-A rating, either because of the quality of the mortgage pool or issuing vehicle or because a form of credit enhancement has been used.

Interest frequency

CMOs typically pay interest on a monthly basis, which is calculated on the current outstanding nominal value of the issue.

---

[8] The source for statistical data in this section is *Asset-Backed Alert* (www.ABalert.com). Used with permission.

Cash flow profile

The cash flow profile of CMOs is based on an assumed prepayment rate. This rate is based on the current market expectation of future prepayment levels and expected market interest rates, and is known as the *pricing speed*.

Maturity

Most CMOs are long-dated instruments, and originally, almost all issues were created from underlying mortgage collateral with a 30-year stated maturity. During the 1990s, issues were created from shorter-dated collateral, including 5–7-year and 15–20-year mortgages.

Market convention

CMOs trade on a yield, as opposed to a price, basis and are usually quoted as a spread over the yield of the nearest maturity Treasury security. The yields are calculated on the basis of an assumed prepayment rate. Agency CMOs are settled on a T+3 basis via an electronic book-entry system known as 'Fedwire', the clearing system run by the Federal Reserve. Whole-loan CMOs also settle on a T+3 basis, and are cleared using either physical delivery or by electronic transfer. New issues CMOs settle from one to three months after the initial offer date.

Originally, mortgage-backed bonds were created from individual underlying mortgages. Agency CMOs are created from mortgages that have already been pooled and securitised, usually in the form of a pass-through security. Issuers of *whole loan* CMOs do not therefore need to create a pass-through security from a pool of individual mortgages, but structure the deal based on cash flows from the entire pool. In the same way as for agency pass-through securities, the underlying mortgages in a whole-loan pool are generally of the same risk type, maturity and interest rate. The other difference between whole-loan CMOs and agency pass-throughs is that the latter are comprised of mortgages of up to a stated maximum size, while larger loans are contained in CMOs. There are essentially two CMO structures, those issues that redirect the underlying pool interest payments and issues redirecting both interest and principal. The main CMO instrument types pay out both interest and principal and are described below.

Whole-loan CMO structures also differ from other mortgage-backed securities in terms of what is known as *compensating interest*. Virtually all mortgage securities pay principal and interest on a monthly basis, on a fixed coupon date. The underlying mortgages however may be paid off on any day of the month. Agency mortgage securities guarantee their bondholders an interest payment for the complete month, even if the underlying mortgage has been paid off ahead of the coupon date (and so has not attracted any interest). Whole-loan CMOs do not offer this guarantee, and so any *payment interest shortfall* will be lost, meaning that a bondholder would receive less than one month's worth interest on the coupon date. Some issuers, but not all, will pay a compensating interest payment to bondholders to make up this shortfall.

CMO structure

CMOs are usually rated AAA/Aaa by rating agencies, and this is because in practice, the cash flows generated by the underlying mortgages or agency securities are well in excess of that required to service the interest obligations of all tranches of the notes. As summarized in Sundaresan (1997, page 389), the general characteristics of CMO structures include the following:

- the high credit rating is ensured by arranging credit insurance via a third party provider, such as a specialist credit guarantee firm;

- there is always considerable excess of underlying collateral as against the nominal value of notes issued; this leads to a significant level of over-collateralization;

- notes issued usually pay coupon on a semi-annual or quarterly basis, although the underlying mortgages pay interest more frequently, say monthly or almost daily. This surplus cash is reinvested in between coupon dates at a money market rate of interest. Issuers usually prefer a guaranteed investment contract (GIC) for their surplus cash, but these are only provided by a few banks and insurance companies, so most issuers have to settle for a money market account. However, the providers will usually accept funds at a much lower level than is usual for interbank deposits, sometimes down to $100,000.

The cash flows that originate from the underlying collateral are separated and allocated to more than one class of notes, known as tranches. Typically, these tranches will pay different rates of interest to appeal to different classes of investors. The two basic CMO structures are *sequential structure* and *planned amortization class* (PAC) structure.

Sequential structure

One of the requirements that CMOs were designed to meet was the demand for mortgage-backed bonds with a wider range of maturities. Most CMO structures redirect principal payments *sequentially* to individual classes of bonds within the structure, in accordance with the stated maturity of each bond. That is, principal payments are first used to pay off the class of bond with the shortest stated maturity, until it is completely redeemed, before being reallocated to the next maturity band class of bond. This occurs until all the bonds in the structure are retired. Sequential pay CMOs are attractive to a wide range of investors, particularly those with shorter-term investment horizons, as they are able to purchase only the class of CMO note whose maturity term meets their requirements.

In addition, investors with more traditional longer-dated investment horizons are protected from prepayment risk in the early years of the issue, because principal payments are used to pay off the shorter-dated bonds in the structure first.

The typical generic CMO sequential structure would have say four tranches, as suggested in table 8.1. The collateral cash flows are allocated to each tranche in specified order, and the first tranche is allotted both its coupon and any prepayments. The remaining tranches do not receive any payments until the first one is fully retired, with the exception of their coupon payments. Essentially each tranche receives successive payments as soon as its immediate predecessor is redeemed. The last tranche is usually known as a *Z-bond* and will receive no cash flows until all preceding tranches have been repaid. In the interim, the face amount of this note will accrue at the stated coupon.

TABLE 8.1 ▪ Generic CMO sequential structure

Tranche	Principal	Coupon	Average life (years)	Yield
A	100	7.00%	2.5	2-year benchmark plus 80 bps
B	250	7.00%	5	5-year benchmark plus 100 bps
C	75	7.00%	10	10-year benchmark plus 120 bps
Z	75	7.00%	20	30-year benchmark plus 150 bps

Planned amortization class

The first issue of PACs was in 1986, after a period of sustained falls in market interest rates led to a demand for less interest-rate volatile mortgage-backed structures. PAC structures are designed to reduce prepayment risk and also the volatility of the weighted average life measure, which is related to the prepayment rate. The securities have a principal payment schedule that is maintained irrespective of any change in prepayment rates. The process is similar to a corporate bond sinking fund schedule, and is based on the minimum amount of principal cash flow that is produced by the underlying mortgage pool at two different prepayment rates, known as *PAC bands*. The PAC bands are set as a low and high PSA standard, for example 50%PSA and 250%PSA. This has the effect of constraining the amount of principal repayment, so that in the early years of the issue the minimum of principal received is at the level of the lower of the two bands, while later in the bond's life, the payment schedule is constrained by the upper PAC band. The total principal cash flow under the PAC schedule will determine the value of PACs in a structure.

A PAC schedule follows an arrangement whereby cash flow uncertainty of principal payment is directed to another class of security known as *companions*, or *support classes*. When prepayment rates are high, companion issues support the main PACs by absorbing any principal prepayments that are in excess of the PAC schedule. When the prepayment rate has fallen, the companion amortization rates are delayed if the level of principal prepayment is not sufficient to reach the minimum level stipulated by the PAC bands. Essentially then the structure of PACs results in the companion issues carrying the prepayment uncertainty, since when prepayment rates are high, the average life of the companions will be reduced as they are paid off, and when prepayment rates are low the companions will see their measure of average life increase as they remain outstanding for a longer period.

The principal cash flows of PACs and companions can be divided sequentially, similar to a sequential-pay structure, which are reviewed in the next section. PACs have a lower price volatility than other mortgage securities, the level of which is relatively stable when the prepayment rates are within the PAC bands. When prepayment rates move outside the bands, the volatility increases by a lower amount than they otherwise would, because the prepayment risk is transferred to the companions. For this reason, PAC issues trade at lower spreads to the Treasury yield curve than other issues of similar average life. The companion bonds are always priced at a higher spread than the PACs, reflecting their higher prepayment risk.

PAC bonds that have a lower prepayment risk than standard PACs are known as *Type II* and *Type III PACs*. A Type II PAC is created from an existing PAC/companion structure, and has a narrower band than the original PAC. This reduced the prepayment risk. If prepayment rates remain within the bands, Type II PACs trade as PACs. If prepayment rates move outside the narrower band, the extra cash flow is redirected to the companion. Type II PACs are second in priority to the PACs and so carry a higher yield. If prepayment rates remain high over a period of time such that all the companions are redeemed, the Type II PACs take over the function of companion, so that they then carry higher prepayment risk. A further PAC with yet narrower bands, created from the same structure, is known as a *Type III PAC*.

The upper and lower bands in a PAC may 'drift' during the life of the CMO, irrespective of the level that actual prepayment rates are at. This drift arises because of the interaction between actual cash prepayments and the bands, and changes in collateral balance and the ratio between the PAC and companion nominal values. The impact of this drift differs according to where the prepayment rate is. The three possible scenarios are as follows.

1. *Prepayment level lies within the current bands.* In this case, the PAC will receive principal in line with the payment schedule, while any prepayments above the schedule amount will be redirected to the companion issue. The effect of this if it continues is that both the lower and upper bands will drift upwards; this is because any prepayment that occurs is within the bands. This causes the upper band to rise, the rationale being that as prepayments have been below it, they have been received at a slower rate than expected, leaving more companion issues to receive future prepayments. The lower band rises as well, the reasoning being that prepayments have been received faster than expected (as they have been above the minimum level) so that a lower amount of collateral is available to generate future principal payments. It has been observed that upper bands tend to rise at a higher rate than the lower rate, so that prepayment levels lying within the bands causes them to widen over time.

2. *Prepayment level lies above the upper band.* Where prepayment rates are above the upper band, the PAC will receive principal in line with the payment schedule until it is paid off. If the prepayment rates stay above the upper band, the two bands will begin to narrow, because the number of companions available to receive faster prepayments will fall. The two bands will converge completely once all the companion bonds have been redeemed, and the PAC will trade as a conventional sequential pay security after that until it is paid off.

3. *Prepayment level lies below the lower band.* If prepayment rates lie below the lower PAC band, the upper band will drift upwards as more companion bonds are available to receive a greater level of prepayments in the future; the lower band may also rise by a small amount. This situation is relatively rare, however, as PACs have the highest priority of all classes in a CMO structure until the payment schedule is back on track.

The band drift process occurs over a long time period and is sometimes not noticeable. Significant changes to the band levels only take place if the prepayment rate is outside the band for a long period. Prepayment rates that move outside the bands over a short time period do not have any effect on the bands.

Targeted amortization class

These bonds were created to cater for investors who require an element of prepayment protection but at a higher yield than would be available with a PAC. Targeted amortization class bonds (TAC) offer a prepayment principal in line with a schedule, providing that the level of prepayment is within the stated range. If the level of principal prepayment moves outside of the range, the extra principal amounts are used to pay off TAC companion bonds, just as with PACs. The main difference between TACs and PACs is that TACs have extra prepayment risk if the level of prepayments falls below the amount required to maintain the payment schedule; this results in the average life of the TAC being extended. Essentially, a TAC is a PAC but with a lower 'PAC band' setting. The preference to hold TACs over PACs is a function of the prevailing interest rate environment; if current rates are low and/or are expected to fall, there is a risk that increasing prepayments will reduce the average life of the bond. In this scenario, investors may be willing to do without the protection against an increase in the average life (deeming it unlikely to be required), and take the extra yield over PACs as a result. This makes TACs attractive compared to PACs under certain conditions, and because one element of the 'PAC band' is removed, TACs trade at a higher yield.

Z-class bonds

We have already alluded to these securities. This type of bond is unique to the domestic US market, and has a very interesting structure. The Z-class bond (or *Z-bond*) is created from a CMO structure and has reallocation of both principal and interest payments. It is essentially a coupon-bearing bond that ranks below all other classes in the CMO's structure, and pays no cash flows for part of its life. When the CMO is issued, the Z-bond has a nominal value of relatively small size, and at the start of its life it pays out cash flows on a monthly basis as determined by its coupons. However at any time that the Z-bond itself is receiving no principal payments, these cash flows are used to retire some of the principal of the other classes in the structure. This results in the nominal value of the bond being increased each month that the coupon payments are not received, so that the principal amount is higher at the end of the bond's life than at the start. This process is known as *accretion*. At the point when all classes of bond ahead of the Z-bond are retired, the Z-bond itself starts to pay out principal and interest cash flows.

In the conventional sequential pay structure, the existence of a Z-bond will increase the principal prepayments in the CMO structure. The other classes in the structure receive some of their principal prepayments from the Z-bond, which lowers their average life volatility. Creating a Z-bond in a CMO structure reduces therefore the average life volatility of all the classes in the structure. Z-bonds are an alternative to investors who might otherwise purchase Treasury zero-coupon bonds, with a similar feature of no reinvestment risk. They also offer the added attraction of higher yields compared to those available on Treasury strips with a similar average life.

Interest-only and principal-only class

Stripped coupon mortgage securities are created when the coupon cash flows payable by a pool of mortgages are split into interest-only (IO) and principal-only (PO) payments. The cash flows will be a function of the prepayment rate, since this determines the nominal value of the collateral pool. IO issues, also known as IO strips, gain whenever the prepayment rate falls, as interest payments are reduced as the principal amount falls. If there is a rise in the prepayment rate, PO bonds benefit because they are discount securities and a higher prepayment rate result in the redemption proceeds being received early. Early strip issues were created with an unequal amount of coupon and principal, resulting in a synthetic coupon rate that was different to the coupon on the underlying bond. These instruments were known as *synthetic coupon pass-throughs*. Nowadays it is more typical for all the interest to be allocated to one class, the IO issue, and all the principal to be allocated to the PO class. The most common CMO structures have a portion of their principal stripped into IO and PO bonds, but in some structures the entire issue is made up of IO and PO bonds. The amount of principal used to create stripped securities will reflect investor demand. In certain cases IO issues created from a class of CMO known as *real estate mortgage investment conduits* (REMICs) have quite esoteric terms. For example, the IO classes might be issued with an amount of principal attached known as the nominal balance. The cash flows for bonds with this structure are paid through a process of amortizing and prepaying the nominal balance. The balance itself is a small amount, resulting in a very high coupon, so that the IO has a multi-digit coupon and very high price (such as 1183% and 3626-12).[9]

Strips created from whole-loan CMOs trade differently from those issued out of agency CMOs. Agency CMOs pay a fixed coupon, whereas whole-loan CMOs pay a coupon based on a weighted average of all the individual mortgage coupons. During the life of the whole-loan issue this coupon value will alter as prepayments change the amount of principal. To preserve the coupon payments of all issues within a structure therefore, a portion of the principal and interest cash flows are stripped from the underlying mortgages, leaving collateral that has a more stable average life. This is another reason that IOs and POs may be created.

IO issue prices exhibit the singular tendency of moving in the same direction as interest rates under certain situations. This reflects the behaviour of mortgages and prepayment rates: when interest rates fall below the mortgage coupon rate, prepayment rates will increase. This causes the cash flow for an IO strip to fall, as the level of the underlying principal declines, which causes the price of the IO to fall as well. This is despite the fact that the issue's cash flows are now discounted at a lower rate. Figure 8.4 shows the price of a sensitivity of a 7% pass-through security compared to the prices of an IO and a PO that have been created from it. Note that the price of the pass-through is not particularly sensitive to a fall in the mortgage rate below the coupon rate of 7%. This illustrates the *negative convexity* property of pass-through securities. The price sensitivity of the two strip issues is very different. The PO experiences a dramatic fall in price as the mortgage rate rises above

---

[9] Ames 1997.

the coupon rate. The IO on the other hand experiences a rise in price in the same situation, while its price falls significantly if mortgage rates fall below the coupon rate.

Both PO and IO issues are extremely price volatile at times of moves in mortgage rates, and have much greater interest rate sensitivity than the pass-through securities from which they are created.

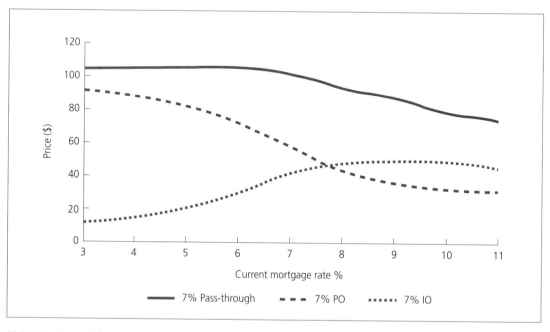

FIGURE 8.4 ■ Price sensitivity of pass-through security, IO and PO to changes in mortgage rate
Price source: Bloomberg

Non-agency CMO bonds

There are no significant differences in the structure and terms of non-agency CMOs compared to agency CMOs. The key feature of non-agency CMOs, however, is that they are not guaranteed by government agencies, and so carry an element of credit risk, in the same way that corporate bonds expose investors to credit risk. To attract investors, therefore, most non-agency CMOs incorporate an element of *credit enhancement* designed to improve the credit standing of the issue. The use of credit enhancement usually results in a triple-A rating, indeed a large majority of non-agency CMOs are triple-A rated, with very few falling below a double-A rating. All of the four main private credit rating agencies are involved in credit analysis and rating of non-agency CMOs. The rating granted to a particular issue of CMOs is dependent on a range of factors, which include:

- the term of the underlying loans;
- the size of the loans, whether *conforming* or *jumbo* (agency mortgages do not include mortgages above a certain stated size, whereas non-agency issues often are comprised of larger size loans known as *jumbo loans*);
- the interest basis for the loans, whether level-pay fixed-rate, variable or other type;
- the type of property;
- the geographical area within which the loans have been made;
- the purpose behind the loans, whether a first purchase or a refinancing.

In this section, we discuss the credit enhancement facility that is used in non-agency CMOs.

Credit enhancements

CMOs are arranged with either an external or internal credit enhancement. An *external* credit enhancement is a guarantee made by a third-party to cover losses on the issue. Usually a set amount of the issue is guaranteed, such as 25%, rather than the entire issue. The guarantee can take the form of a letter of credit, bond insurance or *pool insurance*. A pool insurance policy would be written to insure against losses that arose as a result of default, usually for a cash amount of cover that would remain in place during the life of the pool. Certain policies are set up so that the cash coverage falls in value during the life of the bond. Pool insurance is provided by specialized agencies. Note that only defaults and foreclosures are included in the policy, which forces investors to arrange further cover if they wish to be protected against any other type of loss. A CMO issue that obtains credit enhancement from an external party still has an element of credit risk, but now linked to the fortunes of the provider of insurance. That is, the issue is at risk from a deterioration in the credit quality of the provider of insurance. Investors who purchase non-agency CMOs must ensure that they are satisfied with the credit quality of the third-party guarantor, as well as the quality of the underlying mortgage pool. Note that an external credit enhancement has no impact on the cash flow structure of the CMO.

Internal credit enhancements generally have more complex arrangements and sometimes also affect the cash flow structures of the instruments themselves. The two most common types of internal credit enhancement are *reserve funds* and a senior/subordinated structure.

Reserve funds

There are two types of reserve funds. *A cash reserve fund* is a deposit of cash that has been built up from payments arising from the issue of the bonds. A portion of the profits made when the bonds were initially issued are placed in a separate fund. The fund in turn places this cash into short-term bank deposits. The cash reserve fund is used in the event of default to compensate investors who have suffered capital loss. It is often set up in conjunction with another credit enhancement product, such as a letter of credit. An *excess servicing spread account* is also a separate fund, generated from excess spread after all the payments of the mortgage have been made, that is the coupon, servicing fee and other expenses. For instance if an issue has a gross weighted average coupon of 7.50%, and the service fee is 0.10% and the net weighted average coupon is 7.25%, then the excess servicing amount is 0.15%. This amount is paid into the spread account, and will grow steadily during the bond's life. The funds in the account can be used to pay off any losses arising from the bond that affect investors.

Senior/subordinated structure

This is the most common type of internal credit enhancement method encountered in the market. Essentially, it involves a bond ranking below the CMO that absorbs all the losses arising from default, or other cause, leaving the main issue unaffected. The subordinated bond clearly has the higher risk attached to it, so it trades at a higher yield. Most senior/subordinated arrangements also incorporate a 'shifting interest structure'. This arranges for prepayments to be redirected from the subordinated class to the senior class. Hence it alters the cash flow characteristics of the senior notes, irrespective of the presence of defaults or otherwise.

Commercial mortgage-backed securities

The mortgage-backed bond market includes a sector of securities that are backed by commercial, as opposed to residential, mortgages. These are known as *commercial mortgage-backed securities* (CMBS). They trade essentially as other mortgage securities but there are detail differences in their structure, which are summarized in this section.

Issuing a CMBS

As with a residential mortgage security, a CMBS is created from a pool or 'trust' of commercial mortgages, with the cash flows of the bond backed by the interest and principal payments of the underlying mortgages. A commercial mortgage is a loan made to finance or refinance the purchase of a commercial (business) property. There is a market in direct purchase of a commercial loan book in addition to the more structured CMBS transaction. An issue of CMBS is rated in the same way as a residential mortgage security and usually has a credit enhancement arrangement to raise its credit rating. The credit rating of a CMBS takes into account the size of the issue as well as the level of credit enhancement support.

Classes of bonds in a CMBS structure are usually arranged in a sequential-pay series, and bonds are retired in line with their rating in the structure; the highest-rated bonds are paid off first.

Commercial mortgages impose a penalty on borrowers if they are redeemed early, usually in the form of an interest charge on the final principal. There is no such penalty in the

US residential mortgage market, although early retirement fees are still a feature of residential loans in the UK. The early payment protection in a commercial loan can have other forms as well, such as a prepayment 'lockout', which is a contractual arrangement that prevents early retirement. This early prepayment protection is repeated in a CMBS structure, and may be in the form of call protection of the bonds themselves. There is already a form of protection in the ratings of individual issues in the structure, because the highest-rated bonds are paid off first. That is, the triple-A rated bonds will be retired ahead of the double-A rated bonds, and so on. The highest-rated bonds in a CMBS structure also have the highest protection from default of any of the underlying mortgages, which means that losses of principal arising from default will affect the lowest-rated bond first.

As well as the early retirement protection, commercial mortgages differ from residential loans in that many of them are *balloon* mortgages. A balloon loan is one on which only the interest is paid, or only a small amount of the principal is paid as well as the interest, so that all or a large part of the loan remains to be paid off on the maturity date. This makes CMBSs potentially similar to conventional vanilla bonds (which are also sometimes called 'bullet' bonds) and so attractive to investors who prefer less uncertainty on term to maturity of a bond.

Types of CMBS structures

In the US market there are currently five types of CMBS structure:

- liquidating trusts;
- multi-property single borrower;
- multi-property conduit;
- multi-property non-conduit;
- single property single-borrower.

We briefly describe the three most common structures here.[10]

Liquidating trusts

This sector of the market is relatively small by value and represents bonds issued against non-performing loans, hence the other name of *non-performing CMBS*. The market is structured in a slightly different way to that of ordinary commercial mortgage securities. The features include a *fast-pay structure*, which states that all cash flows from the mortgage pool be used to redeem the most senior bond first, and *overcollateralization*, which is when the value of bonds created is significantly lower than the value of the underlying loans. This overcollateralization results in bonds being paid off sooner. Due to the nature of the asset

---

[10] The structures described in this section are summarized from data contained in Dunlevy (1996), chapter 30 in Fabozzi/Jacob (1996).

backing for liquidating CMBSs, bonds are usually issued with relatively short average lives, and will receive cash flows on only a portion of the loans. A target date for paying off is set and in the event that the target is not met, the bonds usually have a provision to raise the coupon rate. This acts as an incentive for the borrower to meet the retirement target.

Multi-property single borrower

The single borrower/multi-property structure is an important and large-size part of the CMBS market. The special features of these bonds include *cross-collateralization*, which is when properties that are used as collateral for individual loans are pledged against each loan. Another feature known as *cross-default* allows the lender to call each loan in the pool if any one of them defaults. Since cross-collateralization and cross-default links all the properties together, sufficient cash flow is available to meet the collective debt on all of the loans. This influences the grade of credit rating that is received for the issue. A *property release provision* in the structure is set up to protect the investor against the lender removing or prepaying the stronger loans in the book. Another common protection against this risk is a clause in the structure terms that prevents the issuer from substituting one property for another.

Multi-borrower/conduit

A *conduit* is a commercial lending entity that has been set up solely to generate collateral to be used in securitisation deals. The major investment banks have all established conduit arms. Conduits are responsible for originating collateral that meets requirements on loan type (whether amortizing or balloon, and so on), loan term, geographic spread of the properties and the time that the loans were struck. Generally a conduit will want to have a diversified range of underlying loans, known as *pool diversification*, with a wide spread of location and size. A diversified pool reduced the default risk for the investor. After it has generated the collateral the conduit then structures the deal, on terms as similar to CMOs but with the additional features described in this section.

Introduction to evaluation and analysis of mortgage-backed bonds[11]

Term to maturity

The term to maturity cannot be given for certain for a mortgage pass-through security, since the cash flows and prepayment patterns cannot be predicted. To evaluate such a bond, therefore, it is necessary to estimate the term for the bond, and use this measure for any analysis. The maturity measure for any bond is important, as without it it is not

---

[11] The pricing and hedging of mortgage-backed securities is a complex subject and space here does not allow full treatment of it. Interested readers should consult chapter 9 of Sundaresan (1997) or the other relevant references cited in the bibliography. Tuckman (1996) is also a good introduction of pricing models for mortgage securities, see his chapter 18.

possible to assess over what period of time a return is being generated; also, it will not be possible to compare the asset to any other bond. The term to maturity of a bond also gives an indication of its sensitivity to changes in market interest rates. If comparisons with other securities such as government bonds are made, we cannot use the stated maturity of the mortgage-backed bond because prepayments will reduce this figure. The convention in the market is to use other estimated values, which are *average life* and the more traditional duration measure.

The *average life* of a mortgage-pass through security is the weighted-average time to return of a unit of principal payment, made up of projected scheduled principal payments and principal prepayments. It is also known as the *weighted-average life*. It is given by (8.13).

$$\text{Average life} = \tfrac{1}{12} \sum_{t=1}^{n} \frac{t(\text{Principal received at } t)}{\text{Total principal received}} \tag{8.13}$$

where n is the number of months remaining. The time from the term measured by the average life to the final scheduled principal payment is the bond's *tail*.

To calculate duration (or Macaulay's duration) for a bond require the weighted present values of all its cash flows. To apply this for a mortgage-backed bond, therefore, it is necessary to project the bond's cash flows, using an assumed prepayment rate. The projected cash flows, together with the bond price and the periodic interest rate may then be used to arrive at a duration value. The periodic interest rate is derived from the yield. This calculation for a mortgage-backed bond produces a periodic duration figure, which must be divided by 12 to arrive at a duration value in years (or by 4 in the case of a quarterly-paying bond).

Calculating yield and price: static cash flow model

There are a number of ways that the yield on a mortgage-backed bond can be calculated. One of the most common methods employs the *static cash flow model*. This assumes a single prepayment rate to estimate the cash flows for the bond, and does not take into account how changes in market conditions might impact the prepayment pattern.

The conventional yield measure for a bond is the discount rate at which the sum of the present values of all the bond's expected cash flows will be equal to the price of the bond. The convention is usually to compute the yield from the *clean* price, that is excluding any accrued interest. This yield measure is known as the bond's *redemption yield* or *yield-to-maturity*. However, for mortgage-backed bonds it is known as a *cash flow yield* or *mortgage yield*. The cash flow for a mortgage-backed bond is not known with certainty, due to the effect of prepayments, and so must be derived using an assumed prepayment rate. Once the projected cash flows have been calculated, it is possible to calculate the cash flow yield. The formula is given as (8.14).

$$P = \sum_{n=1}^{N} \frac{C(t)}{(1 + ri/1200)^{t-1}} \tag{8.14}$$

Note, however, that a yield so computed will be for a bond with monthly coupon payments,[12] so it is necessary to convert the yield to an annualized equivalent before any comparisons are made with conventional bond yields. In the US and UK markets, the bond-equivalent yield is calculated for mortgage-backed bonds and measured against the relevant government bond yield, which (in both cases) is a semi-annual yield. Although it is reasonably accurate simply to double the yield of a semi-annual coupon bond to arrive at the annualized equivalent,[13] to obtain the bond equivalent yield for a monthly paying mortgage-backed bond, we use (8.15).

$$rm = 2\left[\left(1 + ri_M\right)^6 - 1\right] \tag{8.15}$$

where rm is the bond equivalent yield (we retain the designation that was used to denote yield to maturity in Chapter 4) and ri_M is the interest rate that will equate the present value of the projected monthly cash flows for the mortgage-backed bond to its current price. The equivalent semi-annual yield is given by (8.16).

$$rm_{s/a} = \left(1 + ri_M\right)^6 - 1 \tag{8.16}$$

The cash flow yield calculated for a mortgage-backed bond in this way is essentially the redemption yield, using an assumption to derive the cash flows. As such, the measure suffers from the same drawbacks as it does when used to measure the return of a plain vanilla bond, which are that the calculation assumes a uniform reinvestment rate for all the bond's cash flows and that the bond will be held to maturity. The same weakness will apply to the cash flow yield measure for a mortgage-backed bond. In fact, the potential inaccuracy of the redemption yield measure is even greater with a mortgage-backed bond because the frequency of interest payments is higher, which makes the reinvestment risk greater. The final yield that is returned by a mortgage-backed bond will depend on the performance of the mortgages in the pool, specifically the prepayment pattern.

Given the nature of a mortgage-backed bond's cash flows, the exact yield cannot be calculated, however, it is common for market practitioners to use the cash flow yield measure and compare this to the redemption yield of the equivalent government bond. The usual convention is to quote the spread over the government bond as the main measure of value. When measuring the spread, the mortgage-backed bond is compared to the government security that has a similar duration, or a term to maturity similar to its average life.

As we noted in Chapter 4, it is possible to calculate the price of a mortgage-backed bond once its yield is known (or vice versa). As with a plain vanilla bond, the price is the sum of the present values of all the projected cash flows. It is necessary to convert the bond-equiva-

---

[12] The majority of mortgage-backed bonds pay interest on a monthly basis, since individual mortgages usually do as well; certain mortgage-backed bonds pay on a quarterly basis.
[13] See Chapter 2 for the formulae used to convert yields from one convention basis to another.

lent yield to a monthly yield, which is then used to calculate the present value of each cash flow. The cash flows of IO and PO bonds are dependent on the cash flows of the underlying pass-through security, which is itself dependent on the cash flows of the underlying mortgage pool. Again, to calculate the price of an IO or PO bond, a prepayment rate must be assumed. This enables us to determine the projected level of the monthly cash flows of the IO and the principal payments of the PO. The price of an IO is the present value of the projected interest payments, while the price of the PO is the present value of the projected principal payments, comprising the scheduled principal payments and the projected principal prepayments.

Bond price and option-adjusted spread

The concept of option-adjusted spread (OAS) and its use in the analysis and valuation of bonds with embedded options is considered briefly in Chapter 9, when OAS in discussed in the context of callable bonds. The behaviour of mortgage securities often resembles that of callable bonds, because effectively there is a call feature attached to them, in the shape of the prepayment option of the underlying mortgage holders. This option feature is the principal reason why it is necessary to use average life as the term to maturity for a mortgage security. It is frequently the case that the optionality of a mortgage-backed bond, and the volatility of its yield, have a negative impact on the bondholders. This is for two reasons: the actual yield realized during the holding period has a high probability of being lower than the anticipated yield, which was calculated on the basis of an assumed prepayment level; and mortgages are frequently prepaid at the time when the bondholder will suffer the most, that is, prepayments occur most often when rates have fallen, leaving the bondholder to reinvest repaid principal at a lower market interest rate.

These features combined represent the biggest risk to an investor of holding a mortgage security, and market analysts attempt to measure and quantify this risk. This is usually done using a form of OAS analysis. Under this approach, the value of the mortgagor's prepayment option is calculated in terms of a basis point penalty that must be subtracted from the expected yield spread on the bond. This basis point value is calculated using a binomial model or a simulation model to generate a range of future interest rate paths, only some of which will cause a mortgagor to prepay the mortgage. The interest rate paths that would result in a prepayment are evaluated for their impact on the mortgage bond's expected yield spread over a government bond.[14] As OAS analysis takes account of the option feature of a mortgage-backed bond, it will be less affected by a yield change than the bond's yield spread. Assuming a flat yield curve environment, the relationship between the OAS and the yield spread is given by:

---

[14] The yield spread from OAS analysis is based on the discounted value of the expected cash flow using the government bond-derived forward rate. The yield spread of the cash flow yield to the government bond is based on yields-to-maturity. For this reason, the two spreads are not strictly comparable. The OAS spread is added to the entire yield curve, whereas a yield spread is a spread over a single point on the government bond yield curve.

OAS = Yield spread – Cost of option feature

This relationship can be observed occasionally when yield spreads on current coupon mortgages widen during upward moves in the market. As interest rates fall, the cost of the option feature on a current coupon mortgage will rise, as the possibility of prepayment increases. Put another way, the option feature begins to approach being in-the-money. To adjust for the increased value of the option traders will price in higher spreads on the bond, which will result in the OAS remaining more or less unchanged.

Effective duration and convexity

The modified duration of a bond measures its price sensitivity to a change in yield; the calculation is effectively a snapshot of one point in time. It also assumes that there is no change in expected cash flows as a result of the change in market interest rates. Therefore, it is an inappropriate of interest rate risk for a mortgage-backed bond, whose cash flows would be expected to change after a change in rates, due to the prepayment effect. Hence mortgage-backed bonds react differently to interest rate changes compared to conventional bonds, because when rates fall, the level of prepayments is expected to rise (and vice versa). Therefore, when interest rates fall, the duration of the bond may also fall, which is opposite to the behaviour of a conventional bond. This feature is known as *negative convexity* and is similar to the effect displayed by a callable bond. The prices of both these types of security react to interest rate changes differently compared to the price of conventional bonds.

For this reason the more accurate measure of interest rate sensitivity to use is *effective duration*. Effective duration is the approximate duration of a bond when given by (8.17).

$$D_{app} = \frac{P_- - P_+}{2P_0 (\Delta rm)} \qquad (8.17)$$

where

P_0 is the initial price of the bond;
P_- is the estimated price of the bond if the yield decreases by Δrm;
P_+ is the estimated price of the bond if the yield increases by Δrm;
Δrm is the change in the yield of the bond.

The approximate duration is the effective duration of a bond when the two values P_- and $P+$ are obtained from a valuation model that incorporates the effect of a change in the expected cash flows (from prepayment effects) when there is a change in interest rates. The values are obtained from a pricing model such as the static cash flow model, binomial model or simulation model. The calculation of effective duration uses higher and lower prices that are dependent on the prepayment rate that is assumed. Generally, analysts will assume a higher prepayment rate when the interest rate is at the lower level of the two.

Figure 8.5 illustrates the difference between modified duration and effective duration for a range of agency mortgage pass-through securities, where the effective duration for each bond is calculated using a 20 basis point change in rates. This indicates that the modified duration measure effectively overestimates the price sensitivity of lower coupon bonds. This factor is significant when hedging a mortgage-backed bond position, because using the modified duration figure to calculate the nominal value of the hedging instrument will not prove effective for anything other than very small changes in yield.

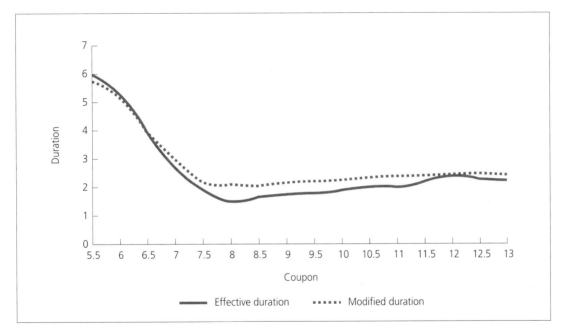

FIGURE 8.5 ■ Modified duration and effective duration for agency mortgage-backed bonds

The formula to calculate approximate convexity (or *effective convexity*) is given below as (8.18); again if the values used in the formula allow for the cash flow to change, the convexity value may be taken to be the effective convexity. The effective convexity value of a mortgage pass-through security is invariably negative.

$$CV_{app} = \frac{P_+ + P_- - 2P_0}{P_0 (\Delta rm)^2} \qquad (8.18)$$

Total return

To assess the value of a mortgage-backed bond over a given investment horizon, it is necessary to measure the return generated during the holding period from the bond's cash flows. This is done using what is known as the *total return* framework. The cash flows from a mortgage-backed bond are comprised of:

- the projected cash flows of the bond (which are the projected interest payments and principal repayments and prepayments);
- the interest earned on the reinvestment of all the payments;
- the projected price of the bond at the end of the holding period.

The first sum can be estimated using an assumed prepayment rate during the period the bond is held, while the second cash flow requires an assumed reinvestment rate. To obtain the projected price of the bond at the end of the holding period, the bondholder must assume first, what the bond equivalent yield of the mortgage bond will be at the end of the holding period, and second, what prepayment rate the market will assume at this point. The second rate is a function of the projected yield at the time. The total return during the time the bond is held, on a monthly basis, is then given by (8.19)

$$\left[\frac{\text{Total future cash flow amount}}{P_m}\right]^{1/n} - 1 \qquad (8.19)$$

which can be converted to an annualized bond-equivalent yield using (8.15) or (8.16).

Note that the return calculated using (8.19) is based on a range of assumptions, which render it almost academic. The best approach to use is to calculate a yield for a range of different assumptions, which then give some idea of the likely yield that may be generated over the holding period, in the form of a range of yields (that is, an upper and lower limit).

Price-yield curves of mortgage pass-through, PO and IO securities[15]

In this section we present an introduction to the yield behaviour of selected mortgage-backed securities under conditions of changing interest rates. To recap, in an environment of high interest rates, the holders of mortgage-backed bonds prefer prepayments to occur. This is because the mortgage will be paying at a low interest rate relative to market conditions, and the likelihood of mortgage prepayment at par results in a higher value for the bond. In the same way when interest rates are low, note holders would prefer that there not be any prepayment, as the bond will be paying interest at a relatively high rate and will therefore be price valuable.

---

[15] This section follows the approach used in Tuckman (1996), pages 254–260 in chapter 18, which is a good introduction to the pricing and behaviour of mortgage-backed securities, and Sundaresan (1997) chapter 9.

Figure 8.6 illustrates the price behaviour of pass-through securities, with nominal coupon of 7%.

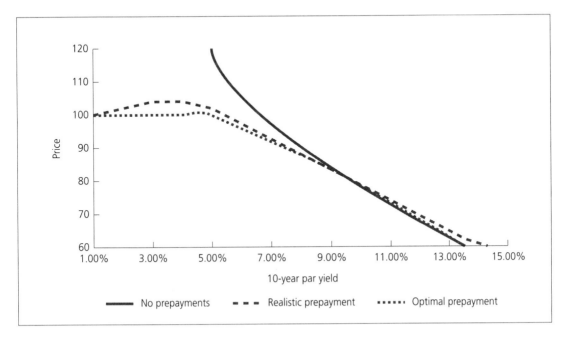

FIGURE 8.6 ■ Hypothetical pass-through securities, 7% coupon

Under conditions of no prepayments, the bond cash flows are certain and the price-yield behaviour resembles that of a conventional bond. Under optimal prepayment, the bond will behave similarly to a callable bond – in a high interest rate environment the bond behaves much like a vanilla bond, while under lower rates the price of the bond is capped at par. However, under what Tuckman calls 'realistic payment' conditions, the price behaviour is somewhat different, as illustrated in figure 8.6. In an environment of very low rates, bond value is higher with the realistic payments assumption than the other two scenarios. This is because there are always a number of mortgage borrowers who will repay their loans irrespective of the level of interest rates, whether rates are low or high. Remember that note holders desire prepayments when interest rates are high, the bond value under the realistic payments model is higher than those of the other two, which predict no prepayments under high interest rate conditions.

As interest rates decrease, certain mortgage borrowers will prepay their loans, but by no means all. As prepayment decreases the value of a mortgage under low interest rates, the fact that not all borrowers prepay under the 'optimal' scenario results in an increase in value of a mortgage to a level greater than its optimal prepaid value. This non-prepayment behaviour can lead to an increase in bond value above par. This is something of an anomaly, as the bond is then priced above the level at which it can theoretically be called. The scenario concludes when eventually all borrowers redeem their mortgages as rates have fallen far enough. This is why the realistic prepayments curve moves down to par at very low levels of rates. The graph shows the existence of *negative convexity* as bond prices fall as interest rates decline, which reflects the behaviour of mortgage borrowers after a long enough period of very low rates. However this does not mean that investors should not buy mortgage-backed bonds at that range of yields when negative convexity applies – as Tuckman notes, the mortgages will be earning rates at above-market levels. It is the total return of the bond over the holding period that is relevant, rather than its price behaviour.[16]

It is also worth commenting on the behaviour of IO and PO securities, which we described earlier. To recap, an IO receives the interest payments of the underlying collateral while the PO receives principal payments. Figure 8.7 illustrates the price behaviour of these instruments, based on a $100 nominal amount for both the underlying mortgage and the IO/PO.

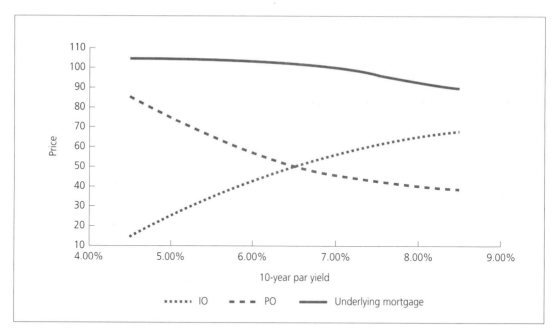

FIGURE 8.7

[16] This is especially true when compared to the performance of other debt market investments. Investment reasoning on price behaviour alone is 'as bad as concluding that premium Treasuries should never be purchased because they will eventually decline in price to par'! (author's exclamation mark; Tuckman 1996, page 256).

Under very high interest rates when prepayments are unlikely, a PO will act as if it is repayable at par on maturity, similar to a zero-coupon bond. As interest rates decline and the level of prepayments increases, the value of the PO will increase. However, other forces are at work that as rates change further, make PO securities more interesting than vanilla strips. These are:

■ the conventional price/yield effect, as lower interest rates cause higher prices;

■ that the PO, again similar to vanilla strips, is very sensitive to the price/yield effect;

■ as the level of prepayments increase, with the expectation of higher levels still, the effective maturity of the PO declines. The effect of this effectively lower maturity is to raise the price of the PO even higher.

The impact of these factors is that PO securities are highly volatile.

The price/yield relationship of the IO is a function of that for the PO, and is obtained by subtracting the value of the latter from that of the underlying mortgage. A significant feature is the high price volatility of the IO under conditions of lower and falling interest rates. This is explained as follows: in a high interest rate environment, with very low prepayment levels, IOs act as vanilla bonds with cash flows known with certainty. This changes as interest rates start to fall, and the cash flows of the IO effectively disappear. This is because as more principal is repaid, the nominal amount of the mortgage on which interest is charged decreases in amount. However, unlike pass-through or other mortgage securities, which receive some principal payment when interest payments decline or cease, IOs receive no cash flow. The impact of a vanishing cash flow is that as interest rates fall, the price of the IO declines dramatically.

As well as purchases by investors, this negative duration property of IOs makes them of use as interest-rate hedging instruments by market makers in mortgage-backed securities.

CASE STUDY *1 Shipshape Residential Mortgages No. 1*

Bristol & West plc is a former UK building society that is now part of the Bank of Ireland group. In October 2000, it issued £300 million of residential mortgage-backed securities through ING Barings. It was the third time that Bristol & West had undertaken a securitisation of part of its mortgage book. The Shipshape Residential Mortgages No. 1 was structured in the following way:

■ a £285 million tranche senior note, rated Aaa by Moody's and Fitch IBCA, with an average life of 3.8 years and paying 25 basis points over three-month Libor;

■ a class 'B' note of £9 million, rated A1 by Moody's and paying a coupon on 80 basis points over three-month Libor. These notes had an average life of 6.1 years;

■ a junior note of £6 million nominal, rated triple-B by Moody's and with an average life of 6.8 years. These notes paid a coupon of 140 basis points over Libor.

CASE STUDY *2 Fosse Securities No. 1 plc*

This was the first securitisation undertaken by Alliance & Leicester plc, another former UK building society which converted into a commercial bank in 1997. The underlying portfolio was approximately 6,700 loans secured by first mortgages on property in the UK. The transaction was a £250 million securitisation via the SPV, named Fosse Securities No. 1 plc. The underwriter was Morgan Stanley Dean Witter, which placed the notes in November 2000. The transaction structure was:

- a senior class 'A' note with AAA/Aaa rating by Standard & Poor's and Moody's, which represented £235 million of the issue, with a legal maturity of November 2032;
- a class 'B' note rated Aa/Aa3 of nominal £5 million;
- a class 'C' note rated BBB/Baa2 of nominal £10 million.

The ratings agencies cited the strengths of the issue as:[17] the loans were *prime* quality; there was a high level of *seasoning* in the underlying asset pool, with average age of 35 months; the average level of the loan-to-value ratio (LTV) was considered low, at 73.5%; and there were low average loan-to-income multiples amongst underlying borrowers.

CASE STUDY *3 SRM Investment No. 1 Limited*

Sveriges Bostadsfinansieringsaktiebolag (SBAB) is the Swedish state-owned national housing finance corporation. Its second-ever securitisation issue was the EUR1 billion SRM Investment No. 1 Limited, issued in October 2000. The underlying asset backing was Swedish residential mortgage loans, with properties being mainly detached and semi-detached single-family properties. The issue was structured and underwritten by Nomura International.

The underlying motives behind the deal were that it allowed SBAB to:

- reduce capital allocation, thereby releasing capital for further lending;
- remove part of its mortgage loan-book off the balance sheet;
- obtain a more diversified source for its funding.

---

[17] Source: ISR, November 2000.

The transaction was structured into the following notes:

■ senior class 'A1' floating-rate note rated AAA/Aaa by S&P and Moody's, issue size EUR755 million, with a legal maturity date in 2057;

■ senior class 'A2' fixed coupon note, rated AAA/Aaa and denominated in Japanese yen, incorporating a step-up facility, legal maturity 2057; issue size JPY20 billion;

■ class 'M' floating-rate note rated A/A2, due 2057; issue size EUR20 million;

■ class 'B' floating-rate note, rated BBB/Baa2, issue size EUR10 million.

The yen tranche reflects the targeting of a Japanese domestic investor base. On issue, the class A1 notes paid 26 basis points over euribor. The structure is illustrated in figure 8.8.

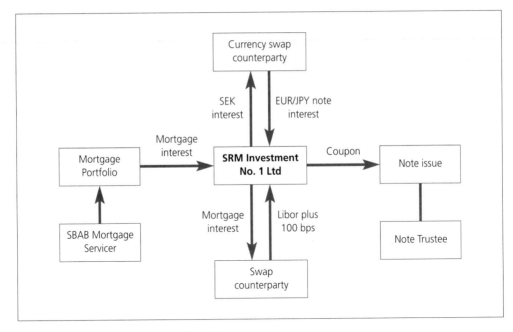

FIGURE 8.8 ■ SRM Investment No. 1 Limited

Source: *ISR*, Thompson Financial. Used with permission.

Collateralized debt obligations

The market in *collateralized bond obligations* (CBOs) and *collateralized loan obligations* (CLOs), which together make up collateralized debt obligations (CDOs) is one of the newest and most exciting developments in securitisation. The origins of the market are generally held to be the repackaging of high-yield debt or loans into higher-rated bonds, which began in the late 1980s. Today, there is great diversity in the different CDO transactions, and the market has expanded into Europe and Asia from its source in the US. Here we introduce the salient features of the main type of CDO, which are known as *cash flow* CDOs. The other main instrument is the market value CDO, for a good description of these see chapter 25 in Fabozzi (1998), which covers CDOs of all types in very accessible fashion.

Both CBOs and CDOs are notes or securities issued against an underlying collateral of assets, almost invariably a diverse pool of corporate bonds or loans, or a combination of both. A transaction with a corporate or sovereign bond asset pool is a CBO, while a CLO

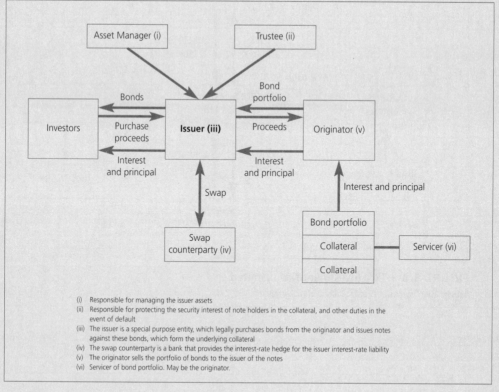

(i)   Responsible for managing the issuer assets
(ii) Responsible for protecting the security interest of note holders in the collateral, and other duties in the event of default
(iii) The issuer is a special purpose entity, which legally purchases bonds from the originator and issues notes against these bonds, which form the underlying collateral
(iv) The swap counterparty is a bank that provides the interest-rate hedge for the issuer interest-rate liability
(v)   The originator sells the portfolio of bonds to the issuer of the notes
(vi) Servicer of bond portfolio. May be the originator.

FIGURE 8.9 ■ Generic arbitrage CBO deal structure

is backed by a portfolio of secured and/or unsecured corporate and commercial bank loans. Cash flow CBOs/CDOs fall into two types; these are *arbitrage* and *balance sheet* CDOs. Some analysts also categorize a third variety known as *emerging market* CDOs.

Arbitrage CDOs form the largest sector of the market. The underlying motivation behind them is a desire to realize the positive yield spread between high-yielding assets and lower-yielding, higher-rated liabilities. Most transactions are CBOs, although there have also been arbitrage CLOs. A generic arbitrage CBO is shown at figure 8.9.

Balance sheet CDOs were introduced because of the desire of banks to reduce their regulatory capital requirement of the assets forming the underlying collateral of the transaction. They were also used to free up lending lines and so increase lending ability, and reduce the funding costs of the originators. As such, most balance sheet deals have been CLOs. A generic balance sheet CLO is shown at figure 8.10.

Another sector of the market is in emerging market sovereign debt which are essentially arbitrage CBOs. Further developments have seen the introduction of *synthetic* CLOs which involve the use of credit derivatives such as credit swaps and credit-linked notes to synthesize the effect of CLO deals without an actual legal

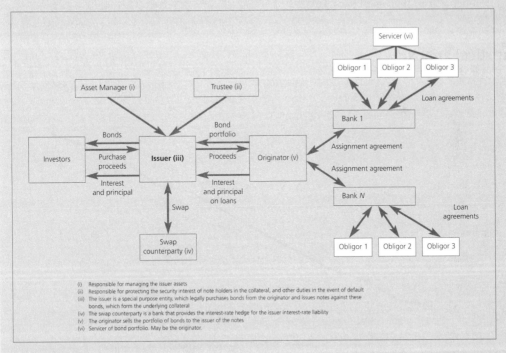

(i)   Responsible for managing the issuer assets
(ii) Responsible for protecting the security interest of note holders in the collateral, and other duties in the event of default
(iii) The issuer is a special purpose entity, which legally purchases bonds from the originator and issues notes against these bonds, which form the underlying collateral
(iv) The swap counterparty is a bank that provides the interest-rate hedge for the issuer interest-rate liability
(v)   The originator sells the portfolio of bonds to the issuer of the notes
(vi) Servicer of bond portfolio. May be the originator.

FIGURE 8.10 ■ Generic balance sheet CLO deal structure

transfer of the underlying assets. The motivations are similar, a desire to reduce capital liability, and so on.

Although they are grouped into a single generic form, there are key differences between CBOs and CLOs. In the first instance, assets such as bank loans have different features to bonds; the analysis of the two will therefore differ. Note also the following:

■ loans are less uniform instruments, and their terms vary widely. This includes terms such as interest dates, amortization schedules, reference rate indices, reset dates, terms to maturity and so on, which impact the analysis of cash flows;

■ the legal documentation for loans is less standardized, in part reflecting the observation above, and this calls for more in-depth legal review;

■ it is often possible to restructure a loan portfolio to reflect changed or changing status of borrowers (for example their ability to service the debt), a flexibility not usually afforded to participants in a CBO;

■ the market in bank loans is far less liquid than that in bonds.

These issues among others mean the analysis of CBOs often presents considerable differences from that used for CLOs.

Statistical annexe

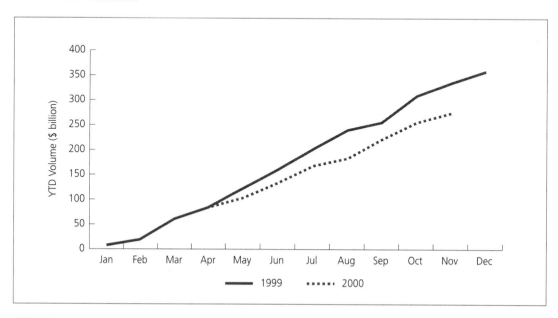

FIGURE 8.11 ■ Worldwide ABS issuance, 1999 and YTD November 2000

Reprinted with permission from Asset-Backed Alert (www.ABAlert.com)

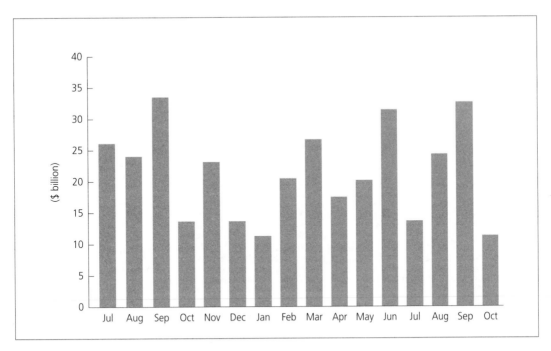

FIGURE 8.12 ■ US ABS Issuance, 15 months to October 2000

Reprinted with permission from Asset-Backed Alert (www.ABAlert.com)

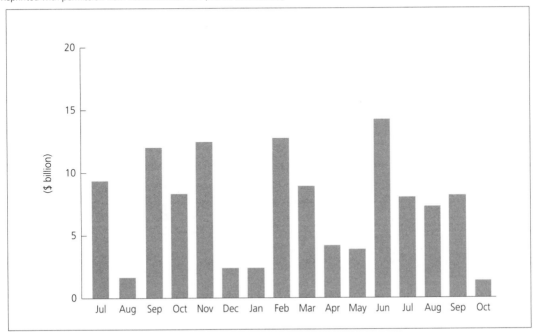

FIGURE 8.13 ■ Non-US ABS issuance, 15 months to October 2000

Reprinted with permission from Asset-Backed Alert (www.ABAlert.com)

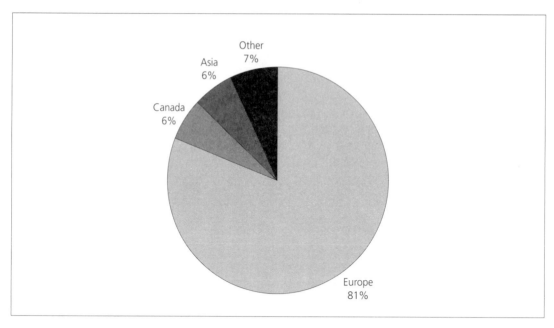

FIGURE 8.14 ■ Geographic spread of non-US ABS issuance, YTD July 2000

Reprinted with permission from Asset-Backed Alert (www.ABAlert.com)

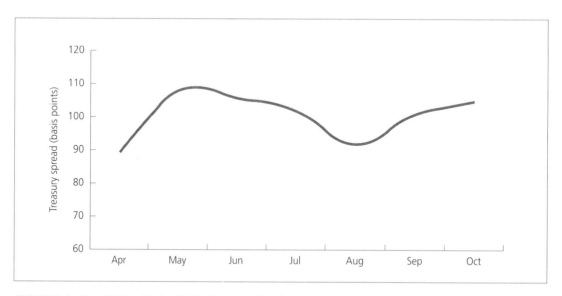

FIGURE 8.15 ■ US Credit Card ABS, five-year fixed rate spreads, six months to October 2000

Reprinted with permission from Asset-Backed Alert (www.ABAlert.com)

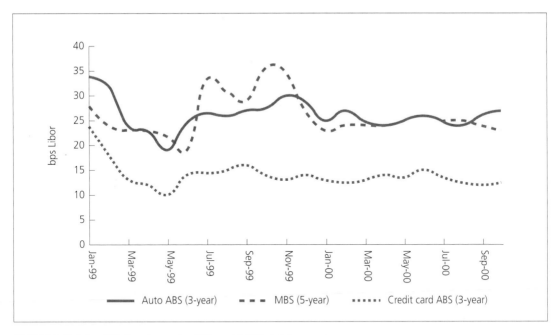

FIGURE 8.16 ■ UK floating-rate ABS and MBS yield spread

Reprinted with permission of International Securitisation Report, a product of Thomson Financial

TABLE 8.2 ■ US ABS spreads, AAA-rated October 2000

		Spread (basis points)		
	Average life	Current	Week-ago	52-week average
Credit card – fixed rate	2.0	+78	+83	+72.0
(versus Treasury)	5.0	+106	+109	+93.4
Credit card – floating rate	2.0	+5	+5	+7.5
(versus 1-month Libor)	5.0	+14	+13	+15.4
Auto loan – pass-through	1.7	+86	+88	+82.8
Auto loan – Tranched	2.0	+84	+86	+75.6
Home equity – Fixed rate/wrapped	2.0	+104	+108	+105.0
(versus Treasury)	5.0	+173	+176	+152.5
Swap spreads	2.0	+74	+78	+66.9
(bid/offer midpoint)	5.0	+98	+101	+86.2
	10.0	+113	+121	+108.3

Reproduced with permission of ABS Alert (www.ABAlert.com)

TABLE 8.3 ■ International asset-backed deals by collateral, Quarter 1 2000

Collateral	US$ amount (millions)	%
Auto loans	18,431	29.2
MBS	17,862	28.3
Credit cards	6,852	10.8
Commercial MBS	6,510	10.3
Leases	4,069	6.5
CLO	1,614	2.7
Student loans	1,309	2.08
Obligations Foncieres	1,213	1.92
Home equity loans	1,075	1.71
Oil receivables	950	1.51
Property loans	604	0.96
Credit rights	460	0.73
Champagne receivables	384	0.61
Pfandbriefe	281	0.45
Shopping loans	279	0.44
Trade receivables	77	0.12
Consumer loans	69.9	0.11
Unknown	984	1.56

Reprinted with permission of International Securitisation Report, a product of Thomson Financial

SELECTED BIBLIOGRAPHY AND REFERENCES

The literature in this area is perhaps not as vast as that of say, term structure modelling, nevertheless, for the reader interested in the US market, it is certainly quite extensive. For a good introduction we recommend the two Fabozzi-edited books, while a good technical introduction is provided in the two articles noted from the June 2000 issue of the *Journal of Fixed Income*. The chapter in Sundaresan (1997), like the rest of his book, is excellent and well worth reading. For a general introduction to the principles of securitisation, see Morris (1990).

Anderson, G., Barber, J., Chang, C., 'Prepayment Risk and the Duration of Default-Free Mortgage-Backed Securities', *Journal of Financial Research* 16, 1993, pp. 1–9
Arora, A., Heike, D., Mattu, R., 'Risk and Return in the Mortgage Market: Review and Outlook', *Journal of Fixed Income*, June 2000, pp. 5–18
Bear Stearns, *Asset-Backed Securities Special Report*, 5 December 1994

Bhattacharya, A., Fabozzi, F. (eds), *Asset-Backed Securities*, FJF Associates, 1996

Fabozzi, F., *The Handbook of Mortgage-Backed Securities*, FJF Associates, 2000

Fabozzi, F. (ed.), *The Handbook of Structured Financial Products*, FJF Associates 1998

Fabozzi, F. (ed.), *Mortgage-Backed Securities: New Strategies, Applications and Research*, Probus Publishing 1987

Fabozzi, F., Jacob, D., *The Handbook of Commercial Mortgage-Backed Securities*, FJF Associates, 1996

Fabozzi, F., Ramsey, C., Ramirez, F., *Collateralized Mortgage Obligations*, FJF Associates, 1994

Hayre, L., Mohebbi, C., 'Mortgage Pass-Through Securities', in Fabozzi, F. (ed.), *Advances and Innovations in the Bond and Mortgage Markets,* Probus Publishing 1989, pp. 259–304

Hayre, L., Chaudhary, S., Young, R., 'Anatomy of Prepayments', *Journal of Fixed Income* June 2000, pp. 19–49

Morris, D., *Asset Securitisation: Principles and Practices*, Executive Enterprise 1990

Schwartz, E., Torous, W., 'Prepayment and Valuation of Mortgage Pass-Through Securities', *Journal of Business* 15(2), 1992, pp. 221–240

Sundaresan, S., *Fixed Income Markets and their Derivatives*, South-Western Publishing 1997, chapter 9

Tuckman, B., *Fixed Income Securities*, Wiley 1996, chapter 18

Waldman, M., Modzelewski, S., 'A Framework for Evaluating Treasury-Based Adjustable Rate Mortgages', in Fabozzi, F. (ed.), *The Handbook of Mortgage-Backed Securities*, Probus Publishing 1985

The analysis of bonds with embedded options

In Chapter 1 we reviewed the yield to maturity calculation, the main measure of bond return used in the fixed income markets. For conventional bonds, the yield calculation is relatively straightforward because the issue's redemption date is fixed. This means that the future cash flows that make up the total cash flows of the bond are known with certainty. As such, data required to calculate the yield to maturity is known with certainty. Callable, put-able and sinking fund bonds, generally termed bonds with *embedded options*, are not as straightforward to analyze. This is because some aspect of their cash flows, such as the timing or the value of their future payments, is uncertain. The term *embedded* is used because the option element cannot be separated from the bond itself. Since callable bonds have more than one possible redemption date, the collection of future cash flows contributing to their overall return is not clearly defined. If we wish to calculate the yield to maturity for such bonds, we must assume a particular redemption date and calculate the yield to this date. The market convention is to assume the first possible maturity date as the one to be used for yield calculation if the bond is priced above par, and the last possible date if the bond is priced below par. The term *yield-to-worst* is sometimes used to refer to a redemption yield calculation made under this assumption; this is the Bloomberg term. If the actual redemption date of a bond is different to the assumed redemption date, the measurement of return will be meaningless and irrelevant.

The market therefore prefers to use other measures of bond return for callable bonds. The most common method of return calculation is something known as *option-adjusted spread analysis* or OAS analysis; a very good account of OAS analysis can be found in Windas (1994). In this chapter we present one of the main methods by which callable bonds are priced. Although the discussion centres on callable bonds, the principles apply to all bonds with embedded option elements in their structure.

Understanding embedded option elements in a bond

Consider an hypothetical sterling corporate bond issued by 'ABC plc'[1] with a 6% coupon on 1 December 1999 and maturing on 1 December 2019. The bond is callable after five years, under the schedule shown at table 9.1. We see that the bond is first callable at a price of 103.00, after which the call price falls progressively until December 2014, after which the bond is callable at par.

TABLE 9.1 ■ Call schedule for 'ABC plc' 6% bond due December 2019

Date	Call price
01-Dec-2004	103.00
01-Dec-2005	102.85
01-Dec-2006	102.65
01-Dec-2007	102.50
01-Dec-2008	102.00
01-Dec-2009	101.75
01-Dec-2010	101.25
01-Dec-2011	100.85
01-Dec-2012	100.45
01-Dec-2013	100.25
01-Dec-2014	100.00

Although our example is hypothetical, this form of call provision is quite common in the corporate debt market. In the rest of this chapter, we review the price behaviour of callable bonds. The basic case can be stated quite easily, however; in our example, the ABC plc bond pays a fixed semi-annual coupon of 6%. If the market level of interest rates rises after the bonds are issued, ABC plc effectively gains because it is paying below-market financing costs on its debt. If rates decline, however, investors gain from a rise in the capital value of their investment, but in this instance, their upside is capped by the call provisions attached to the bond.

The difference between the value of a callable bond and that of an (otherwise identical) non-callable bond of similar credit quality is the value attached to the option element of the callable bond. This is an important relationship and one that we will consider, but first a word on the basics of option instruments.

---

[1] After writing this chapter I discovered that there really was a company called 'ABC plc'! Of course, we refer here to a hypothetical corporate entity.

Basic features of options

An option is a contract between two parties. The buyer of an option has the right, but not the obligation, to buy or sell an underlying asset at a specified price during a specified period or at a specified time (usually the expiry date of the option contract). The price of an option is known as the *premium,* which is paid by the buyer to the seller or *writer* of the option. An option that grants the holder the right to buy the underlying asset is known as a *call* option; one that grants the right to sell the underlying asset is a *put* option. The option writer is short the contract; the buyer is long. If the owner of the option elects to *exercise* his option and enter into the underlying trade, the option writer is obliged to execute under the terms of the option contract. The price at which an option specifies that the underlying asset may be bought or sold is known as the exercise or *strike* price. The expiry date of an option is the last day on which it may be exercised. Options that can be exercised anytime from the time they are struck up to and including the expiry date are called *American* options. Those that can be exercised only on the expiry date are known as *European* options.[2]

The profit/loss profiles for option buyers and sellers are quite different. The buyer of an option has his loss limited to the price of that option, while his profit can, in theory, be unlimited. The seller of an option has his profit limited to the option price, while his loss can in theory be unlimited, or at least potentially very substantial. The profit/loss profiles for the four main types of option positions are abundantly covered in existing literature, see the introduction page for Part III of this book for recommended texts.

The value or price of an option is comprised of two elements, its *intrinsic value* and its *time value.* The intrinsic value of an option is the value to the holder of an option if it were exercised immediately. That is, it is the difference between the strike price and the current price of the underlying asset. The holder of an option will only exercise it if there is underlying intrinsic value. For this reason, the intrinsic value is never less than zero. To illustrate, if a call option on a bond has a strike price of £100 and the underlying bond is currently trading at £103, the option has an intrinsic value of £3. An option with intrinsic value greater than zero is said to be *in-the-money.* An option where the strike price is equal to the price of the underlying is said to be *at-the-money* while one whose strike price is above (call) or below (put) the underlying is said to be *out-of-the-money.*

The time value of an option is the difference between the intrinsic value of an option and its total value. An option with zero intrinsic value has value comprised solely of time value. That is,

---

[2] There are also Bermudan options, and Asian options, but these need not concern us here.

Time value of an option = Option price – Intrinsic value

The time value reflects the potential for an option to move into the money during its life, or move a higher level of being in-the-money, before expiry. Time value diminishes steadily for an option up to its expiry date, when it will be zero. The price of an option on expiry is comprised solely of intrinsic value.

Later in this chapter we will illustrate how the price of a bond with an embedded option is calculated by assessing the value of the 'underlying' bond and the value of its associated option. The basic issues behind the price of the associated option are considered here.[3] The main factors behind the price of an option on an interest-rate instrument such as a bond are:

- the strike price of the option;
- the current price of the underlying bond, and its coupon rate;
- the time to expiry;
- the short-term risk-free rate of interest during the life of the option;
- the expected volatility of interest rates during the life of the option.

The effect of each of these factors will differ for call and put options and American and European options. There are a number of option pricing models used in the market, the most well-known of which is probably the Black-Scholes model. Market participants often use their own variations of models or in-house developed varieties. The fundamental principle behind the Black-Scholes model is that a synthetic option can be created and valued by taking a position in the underlying asset and borrowing or lending funds in the market at the risk-free rate of interest. Although it is the basis for certain subsequent option models and is still used widely in the market, it is not necessarily appropriate for certain interest-rate instruments. For instance, Fabozzi (1997) points out the unsuitability of the Black-Scholes model for certain bond options, based on its underlying assumptions. As a result, a number of other models have been developed for callable bonds analysis.

The call provision

A bond with early redemption provisions essentially is a portfolio containing an underlying conventional bond, with the coupon and maturity date of the actual bond, and a put or call option on this underlying issue. Analysis therefore is interest-rate dependent, it must consider the possibility of the option being exercised when valuing the bond. The value of a bond with an option feature is the sum of the values of the individual elements, that is the underlying bond and the option component. This is expressed at (9.1).

---

[3] For a technical review of option pricing, see the references cited in the bibliography.

$$P_{bond} = P_{underlying} + P_{option} \tag{9.1}$$

Expression (9.1) states simply that the value of the actual bond is composed of the value of the underlying conventional bond together with the value of the embedded option(s). The relationship would hold for a true conventional bond, as the option component value would be zero. For a put-able bond, an embedded put option is an attractive feature for investors as the put feature contributes to its value by acting as a floor on the bond's price. Thus the greater the value of the put, the greater the value of the actual bond. We can express this by rewriting (9.1) as (9.2).

$$P_{pbond} = P_{underlying} + P_{put} \tag{9.2}$$

Expression (9.2) states that the value of a put-able bond is equal to the sum of the values of the underlying conventional bond and the embedded put option. If any of the components of the total price were to increase in value, then so would the value of the out-able bond itself.

A callable bond is viewed as a conventional bond together with a short position in a call option, which acts as a cap on the actual bond's price. This 'short' position in a call option reduces the total value of the actual bond, so we present the bond price in the form (9.3).

$$P_{cbond} = P_{underlying} - P_{call} \tag{9.3}$$

Equation (9.3) states that the price of a callable bond is equal to the price of the underlying conventional bond less the price of the embedded call option. Therefore, if the value of the call option were to increase, the value of the callable bond would decrease. That is, when a bondholder of such a bond sells a call option, he receives the option price; the difference between the price of the option-free bond and the callable bond at any time is the price of the embedded call option. The precise nature of the behaviour of the attached option element will depend on the terms of the callable bond issue. If the issuer of a callable bond is entitled to call the issue at any time after the first call date, the bondholder has effectively sold the issuer an American call option. However, the call option price may vary with the date the option is exercised; this occurs when the call schedule for a bond has different call prices according to which date the bond is called. The underlying bond at the time the call is exercised is comprised of the remaining coupon payments that would have been received by the bondholder had the issue not been called. For ease of explanation the market generally analyzes a callable bond in terms of a long position in a conventional bond and a short position in a call option, as stated by (9.3). Note of course that the option is embedded; it does not trade in its own right. Nevertheless, it is clear that embedded options are important elements not only in the behaviour of a bond but in its valuation as well.

The binomial tree of short-term interest rates

In an earlier chapter we illustrated how a coupon bond yield curve could be used to derive spot (zero-coupon) and implied forward rates. A forward rate is defined as the one-period interest rate for a term beginning at a forward date and maturing one period later. Forward rates form the basis upon which a *binomial* interest-rate tree is built. For an introduction to a binomial process, see appendix 15.1 of Choudhry (2001).

An option model that used implied forward rates to generate a price for an option's underlying bond on a future date would implicitly assume that interest rates implied by the yield curve today for a date in the future would occur with certainty. Such an assumption would essentially repeat the errors associated with yield-to-worst analysis, which would be inaccurate because interest rates do not remain unchanged from a future today to a future pricing date. To avoid this inaccuracy, a binomial tree model assumes that interest rates do not remain fixed but fluctuate over time. This is done by treating implied forward rates, sometimes referred to as *short rates*, as outcomes of a binomial process. In a binomial interest-rate process we construct a binomial tree of possible short rates for each future time period. In the binomial tree we model two interest rates as the possible outcomes of a previous time period, when the interest rate was known.

An introduction to arbitrage-free pricing

Consider a hypothetical situation. Assume that the short-term yield curve describes the following environment:

Six-month rate: 5.00%
One-year rate: 5.15%

Assume further that in six months' time the then six-month rate will be either 5.01% or 5.50%, and that the probability of either new rate is equal at 50% each. Our capital market is a semi-annual one, that is the convention is for bonds to pay a semi-annual coupon, as in the US and UK domestic markets. We can illustrate this state as figure 9.1.

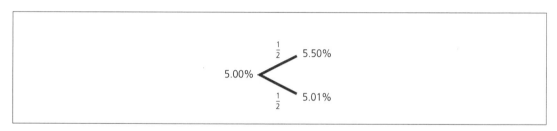

FIGURE 9.1 ■ Binomial interest rate tree

Figure 9.1 is a *binomial interest rate tree* or *lattice* for the six-month interest rate. The tree is called 'binomial' because there are precisely two possibilities for the future level of the interest rate. Using this lattice, we can calculate the tree for the prices of six-month and one-year zero-coupon bonds. The six-month zero-coupon bond price today is given by 100/(1 + [0.05/2]) or 97.56098. The price tree is given at figure 9.2.

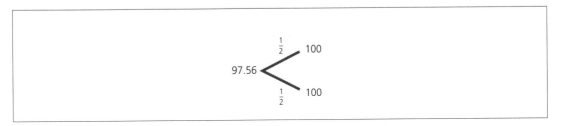

FIGURE 9.2

Period 0 is today; period 1 is the point precisely six months from today. Given that we are dealing with a six-month zero-coupon bond, it is apparent that there is only one *state of the world* whatever the interest rate is in period 1; the maturity value of the bond, which is 100.

The binomial lattice for the one-year zero-coupon bond is given in figure 9.3.

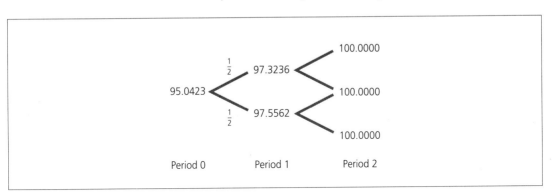

FIGURE 9.3

At period 0 the price of the one-year zero-coupon bond is $100/(1 + [0.0515/2]^2)$ or 95.0423. The price of the bond at period 1, at which point it is now a six-month piece of paper, is dependent on the six-month rate at the time, shown in the diagram. At period 2 the bond matures and its price is 100. The model at figure 9.3 demonstrates that the average or *expected* value of the price of the one-year bond at period 1 is [(0.5 × 97.3236) + (0.5 × 97.5562)] or 97.4399. This is the expected price at period 1, therefore using this the price at period 0 is:

97.4399/(1 + 0.05/2))

or 95.06332

However, we know that the market price is 95.0423. This demonstrates a very important principle in financial economics, that markets do not price derivative instruments on the basis of their expected future value. At period 0 the one-year zero-coupon bond is a more risky investment compared to the shorter-dated bond; in the last six months of its life it will be worth either 97.32 or 97.55 depending on the direction of six-month rates. Investors' preference is for a bond that has a price of 97.4399 at period 1 with certainty. The price of such a bond at period 0 would be 97.4399/(1 + (0.05/2)) or 95.0633. In fact the actual price of the one-year bond at that date, 95.0423, indicates the *risk premium* that the market places on the bond.

We can now consider the pricing of an option. What value should be given to a six-month call option maturing in six months' time (period 1) written on 100 nominal of the six-month zero at a strike price of 97.40? The binomial tree for this option is given at figure 9.4. This shows that at period 1 if the six-month rate is 5.50% the call option has no value, because the price of the bond is below the strike price. If on the other hand the six-month rate is at the lower level, the option has a value of 97.5562 – 97.40 or 0.1562.

How do we calculate the price of the option? Option pricing theory states that to do this one must construct a *replicating portfolio* and find the value of this portfolio. In our example we must set up a portfolio of six-month and one-year zero-coupon bonds today that will have no value at period 1 if the six-month rate rises to 5.50%, but will have a value of 0.1562 if the rate at that time is 5.01%. If we let the value of the six-month and one-year bonds in the replicating portfolio be C_1 and C_2 respectively at period 1, we may set the following equations:

$$C_1 + 0.973236C_2 = 0 \qquad\qquad (9.4)$$

$$C_1 + 0.975562C_2 = 0.1562 \qquad\qquad (9.5)$$

The value of the six-month zero-coupon bond in the replicating portfolio at period 1 is 100 as it matures. In the case of an interest-rate rise, the value of the one-year bond (now

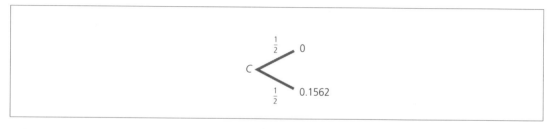

FIGURE 9.4

a six-month bond) at period 1 is 97.3236. The total value of the portfolio is given by the expression (9.4), which states that this value must also be equal to the value of the option. Expression (9.5) gives the value of the replicating portfolio in the event that rates decrease, when the option value is 0.1562.

Solving the expressions above gives us C_1 = –65.3566 and C_2 = 67.1539. What does this mean? Basically to construct the replicating portfolio we purchase 67.15 of one-year zero-coupon bonds and sell short 65.36 of the six-month zero-coupon bond. However, the original intention behind the replicating portfolio was because we wished to price the option: the portfolio and the option have equal values. The value of the portfolio is a known quantity, as it is equal to the price of the six-month bond at period 0 multiplied by C_1 together with the price of the one-year bond multiplied by C_2. This is given by

$$(0.9756 \times -65.3566) + (0.950423 \times 67.1539) = 0.0627$$

That is, the price of the six-month call option is 0.06. This is the *arbitrage-free* price of the option; below this price, a market participant could buy the option and simultaneously sell short the replicating or portfolio and would be guaranteed a profit. If the option was quoted at a price above this, a trader could write the option and buy the portfolio. Note how the probability of the six-month rate increasing or decreasing was not part of the analysis. This reflects the arbitrage pricing logic. That is, the replicating portfolio must be equal in value to the option whatever direction interest rates move in. This means probabilities do not have an impact in the construction of the portfolio. This is not to say that probabilities do not have an impact on the option price – far from it. For example, if there is a very high probability that rates will increase (in our example), intuitively we can see that the value of an option to an investor will fall. However, this is accounted for by the market in the value of the option or callable bond at any one time. If probabilities change, the market price will change to reflect this.

Let us now turn to the concept of *risk neutral* pricing. Notwithstanding what we have just noted about how the market does not price instruments using expected values, there exist risk-neutral probabilities for which the discounted expected value does give the actual price at period 0. If we let p be the risk-neutral probability of an interest rate increase and $(1 - p)$ be the probability of a rate decrease, we may set p such that

$$\frac{97.3236p + 97.5562(1 - p)}{1 + \frac{1}{2}0.05} = 95.0423$$

That is, we can calculate a value for p such that the discounted expected value, using the probability p rather than the actual probability of $\frac{1}{2}$ provides the true market price. The above expression solves to give p = 0.5926.

In our example from the option price tree given the risk-neutral probability of 0.5926 we can calculate the option price to be

$$\frac{(0.5296 \times 0) + (0.4074 \times 0.1562)}{1 + \frac{1}{2} 0.05} = 0.0621$$

This is virtually identical to the 0.062 option price calculated above. Put very simply risk-neutral pricing works by first finding the probabilities that produce prices of the replicating or *underlying* security equal to the discounted expected value. An option on the security it valued by discounting this expected value under the risk-neutral probability.

We can now turn to binomial trees. In the description above, we had a two-period tree, moving to period 2 we might have figure 9.5.

This binomial tree is known as a *non-recombining tree*, because each node branches out to two further nodes. This might seem more logical, and such trees are used in practice in the market. However, implementing it requires a considerable amount of computer processing power, and it is easy to see why. In period 1 there are two possible levels for the interest rate, and at period 2 there are four possible levels. After N interest periods there will be 2^N possible values for the interest rate. If we wished to calculate the current price for a 10-year callable bond that paid semi-annual coupons, we would have over 1 million possible values for the last period set of nodes. For a 20-year bond we would have over 1 trillion possible values. (Note also that in practice binomial models are not used with a six-month time step between nodes, but have much smaller time steps, further increasing the number of nodes.)

For this reason, certain market practitioners prefer to use a *recombining* binomial tree, where the upward-downward state has the same value as the downward-upward state. This is shown in figure 9.6.

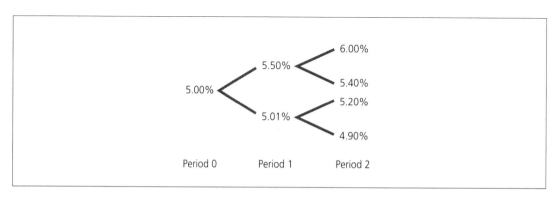

FIGURE 9.5

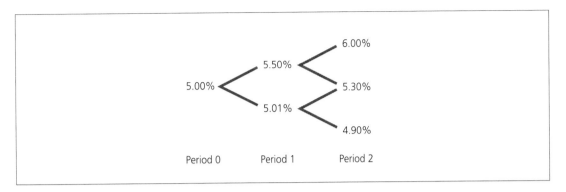

The number of nodes and possible values at the latest time step is much reduced in a recombining tree. For example the number of nodes used to price a 20-year bond that was being priced with one-week time steps would be 52 × 20 + 1 or 1041. Implementation is therefore more straightforward with a recombining tree.

Pricing callable bonds

We can now consider a simple pricing method for callable bonds. We will assume a bino-mial term structure model. It is well worth reading the above text beforehand, especially if one is not familiar with binomial models or the principle of the arbitrage-free pricing of financial instruments. Using the binomial model, we can derive a *risk-neutral* binomial lattice, where each lattice carries an equal probability of upward or downward moves, for the evolution of the six-month interest rate. The time step in the lattice is six months. This model is then used to price a hypothetical semi-annual coupon bond with the terms shown in table 9.2. The tree is shown at figure 9.7.

TABLE 9.2

| Coupon | 6% |
maturity	Three years
Call schedule	
Year 1	103.00
Year 1.5	102.00
Year 2	101.50
Year 2.5	101.00
Year 3	100.00

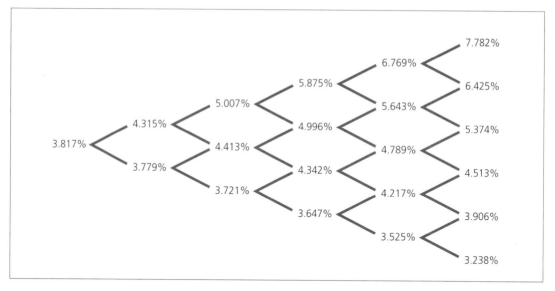

FIGURE 9.7

In the first instance, we construct the binomial tree that describes the price process followed by the bond itself, if we ignore its call feature. This is shown at figure 9.8. Note that the maturity value of the bond on the redemption date is given as 100.00, that is, we perform the analysis on the basis of the bond's ex-coupon value. The final cash flow would of course be 103.00.

We construct the tree from the final date backwards. At each of the nodes at year 3, the price of the bond will be 100.00, the (ex-coupon) par value. At year 2.5 the price of the bond at the highest yield will be that at which the yield of the bond is 7.782%. At this point, the price of the bond after six months will be 103.00 in both the 'up' state and the 'down' state. Following risk-neutral pricing, therefore, the price of the bond at this node is

$$P_{band} = \frac{0.5 \times 103 + 0.5 \times 103}{1 + \dfrac{0.07782}{2}} = 99.14237$$

The same process is used to obtain the prices for every node at year 2.5. Once all these prices have been calculated, we repeat the process for the prices at each node in year 2. At the highest yield, 6.769%, the two possible future values are

$$99.14237 + 3.0 = 102.14237$$

and

$$99.79411 + 3.0 = 102.79411$$

Therefore, the price of the bond in this state is given by

$$P_{bond} = \frac{0.5 \times 102.14237 + 0.5 \times 102.79411}{1 + \dfrac{0.06769}{2}} = 99.11374$$

The same procedure is repeated until we have populated every node in the lattice. At each node the ex-coupon bond price is equal to the sum of the expected value and coupon, discounted at the appropriate six-month interest rate. The completed lattice is shown at figure 9.8.

Once we have calculated the prices for the conventional element of the bond, we can calculate the value of the option element on the callable bond. This is shown in figure 9.9. On the bond's maturity date the option is worthless, because it is an option to call at 100, which is the price the bond is redeemed at in any case. At all other node points a valuation analysis is called for.

The holder of the option in the case of a callable bond is the issuing company. At any time during the life of the bond, the holder will either exercise the option on the call date or elect to hold it to the next date. The option holder must consider:

■ the value of holding the option for an extra period, denoted by P_{Ci};

■ the value of exercising the option straight away, denoted P_C.

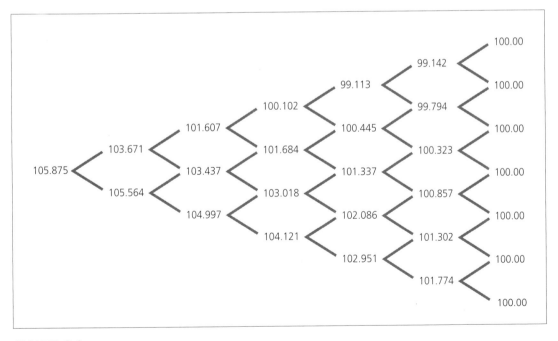

FIGURE 9.8

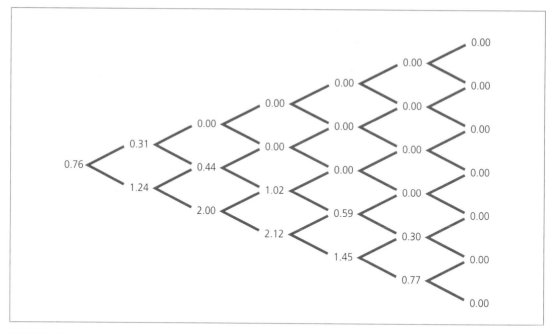

FIGURE 9.9

If the value of the former exceeds that of the latter, the holder will elect to not exercise, and if the value at the exercise date is higher the holder will exercise immediately. At year 2.5 call date for example, there is no value in holding the option because it will be worthless at year 3. Therefore, at any point where the option is in-the-money the holder will exercise.

We can express the general valuation as follows. The value of the option for immediate exercise is V_t; the value if one is holding on to the option for a further period is V_T. Additionally let P be the value of the bond at any particular node, S the call option price, and V_b and V_l the values of the option in the up-state and down-state respectively. The value of the option at any specified node is V. The six-month interest rate at any specified node point is r. We have

$$V_T \frac{0.5V_b + 0.5V_l}{1 + \frac{1}{2}r} \tag{9.6}$$

$$V_t = \max(0, P - S)$$

while the expression for V is $V = \max(V_T, V_t)$.

The rule is as demonstrated above, to work backwards in time and apply the expression at each node, which produces the option value binomial lattice tree.

The general rule with an option is that as they have more value 'alive than dead' it is sometimes optimal to run an in-the-money option rather than exercising straight away. The same is true for callable bonds. A number of factors dictate whether or not an option should be exercised. The first is the asymmetric profile resulting when the price of the 'underlying' asset rises; option holders gain if the price rises, but will only lose the value of their initial investment if the price falls. Therefore, it is optimal to run with the option position. There is also time value, which is lost if the option is exercised early. In the case of callable bonds, it is often the case that the call price decreases as the bond approaches maturity. This is an incentive to delay exercise until a lower exercise price is available. The issue that may influence the decision to exercise sooner is coupon payments, as interest is earned sooner.

To return to our hypothetical example, we can now complete the price tree for the callable bond. Remember that the option in the case of a callable bond is held by the issuer, so the value of the option is subtracted from the price of the bond to obtain the actual value. We see from figure 9.10 that the price of the callable bond today is 105.875 – 0.76 or 105.115. The price of the bond at each node in the lattice is also shown. By building a tree in this way, which can be programmed into a spreadsheet or as a front-end application, we are able to price a callable or putable bond.

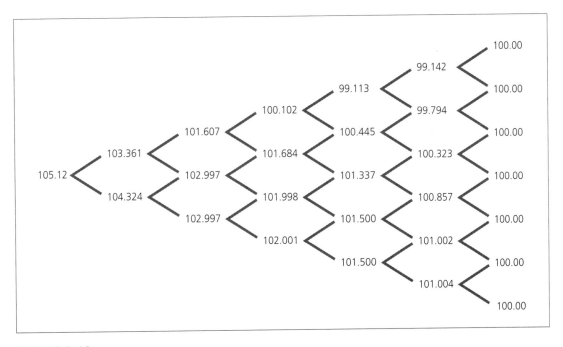

FIGURE 9.10

Price and yield sensitivity

As we saw in an earlier chapter the price/yield relationship for a conventional vanilla bond is essentially convex in shape, while for a bond with an option feature attached, this relationship changes as the price of the bond approaches par, at which the bond is said to exhibit *negative convexity*. This means that the rise in price will be lower than the fall in price for a large change in yield of a given number of basis points. We summarize the price/yield relationship for both conventional and option-feature bonds in table 9.3.

TABLE 9.3

	Value of price change for	
Change in yield	Positive convexity	Negative convexity
Fall of 100 bp	X%	Lower than Y%
Rise of 100 bp	Lower than X%	Y%

The price/yield relationship for a callable bond exhibits negative convexity as interest rates fall. Option-adjusted spread analysis is used to highlight this relationship for changes in rates. This is done by effecting a parallel shift in the benchmark yield curve, holding the spread level constant and then calculating the theoretical price along the nodes of the binomial price tree. The average present value then becomes the projected price for the bond. General results for a hypothetical callable bond, compared to a conventional bond are shown at figure 9.11. In our example, once the market rate falls below the 10% level, the bond exhibits negative convexity. This is because it then becomes callable at that point, which acts as an effective cap on the price of the bond.

The market analyzes bonds with embedded options in terms of a yield spread, with a 'cheap' bond trading at a higher yield spread and a 'dear' bond trading at a lower yield spread. The usual convention is to quote yield spreads as the difference between the redemption yield of the bond being analyzed and the equivalent maturity government bond. This is not accurate because the redemption yield is, in effect, a meaningless number – there is not a single rate at which all the cash flows comprising either bond should be discounted but a set of spot or forward rates that are used for each successive interest period. The correct procedure for discounting, therefore, is to determine the yield spread over the spot or forward rate curve. With regard to the binomial tree, we require the constant spread that, when added to all the short-rates on the binomial tree, makes the theoretical (model-derived) price equal to the observed market price. The constant spread that satisfies this requirement is known as the *option-adjusted spread* (OAS). The spread is referred to as an 'option-adjusted' spread because it reflects the option feature attached to the bond. The OAS will depend on the volatility level assumed in running the model. For any given bond price, the higher the volatility level specified, the lower will

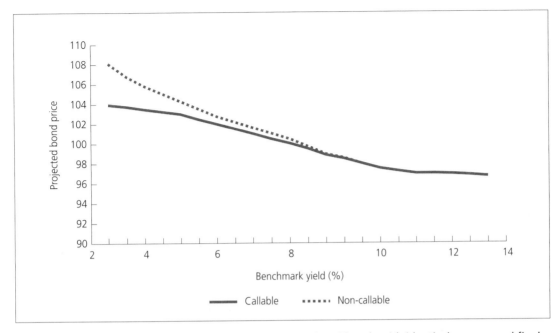

FIGURE 9.11 ▪ Projected prices for callable and conventional bonds with identical coupon and final maturity dates

be the OAS for a callable bond, and the higher for a put-able bond. Since the OAS is calculated usually relative to a government spot or forward rate curve, it reflects the credit risk and any liquidity premium between the corporate bond and the government bond. Note that OAS analysis reflects the valuation model being used, and its accuracy is a reflection of the accuracy of the model itself.

Measuring bond yield spreads

The binomial model evaluates the return of a bond by measuring the extent to which its return exceeds the returns determined by the risk-free short-rates in the tree. The difference between these returns is expressed as a spread and may be considered the *incremental return* of a bond at a specified price. Determining the spread involves the following steps:

▪ the binomial tree is used to derive a theoretical price for the specified bond;

▪ the theoretical price is compared with the bond's observed market price;

▪ if the two prices differ, the rates in the binomial model are adjusted by a user-specified amount, which is the estimate of the spread;

▪ using the adjusted rates a new theoretical price is derived and compared with the observed price;

■ the last two steps are repeated until the theoretical price matches the observed price.

Price volatility of bonds with embedded options

We have reviewed traditional duration and modified duration measures for bond interest-rate risk. Modified duration is essentially a predictive measure, used to describe the expected percentage change in bond price for a 1% change in yield. The measure is a snapshot in time, based on the current yield of the bond and the structure of its expected cash flows. In analyzing a bond with an embedded option, the bondholder must assume a fixed maturity date, based on the current price of the bond, and calculate modified duration based on this assumed redemption date. However, under circumstances where it is not exactly certain what the final maturity is, modified duration may be calculated to the first call date and to the final maturity date. This would be of little use to bondholders in these circumstances, since it may be unclear which measure is appropriate. The problem is more acute for bonds that are continuously callable (or put-able) from the first call date up to maturity.

Effective duration

To recap, the duration for any bond is calculated using (9.7) which assumes annualized yields.

$$D = \frac{\sum_{t=1}^{n} \frac{tC_t}{(1 + rm)^t}}{P} \tag{9.7}$$

Following Fabozzi (1997) the measure can be approximated using (9.8) below.

$$D_{approx} = \frac{P_- - P_+}{2P_0(\Delta rm)} \tag{9.8}$$

where

P_0 is the initial price of the bond;
P_- is the estimated price of the bond is the yield falls by Δrm;
P_+ is the estimated price of the bond if the yield rises by Δrm;
Δrm is the change in the yield of the bond.

The drawbacks of the traditional measure are overcome to a certain extent when OAS analysis is used to measure the *effective duration* of a bond. Whereas traditional duration seeks to predict a bond's price changes based on a given price and assumed redemption date, effective duration is solved from actual price changes resulting from specified shifts in interest rates. Applying the analysis to a bond with an embedded option means that the new prices resulting from yield changes reflect changes in the cash flow. Effective duration may be thought of as a duration measure which recognizes that yield changes may change the future cash flow of the bond. For bonds with embedded options, the difference between traditional duration and effective duration can be significant; for example, for a callable bond the effective duration is sometimes half that of its traditional duration measure. For mortgage-backed securities, the difference is sometimes greater still.

To calculate effective duration using the binomial model and expression (9.8) we employ the following procedure:

■ calculate the OAS spread for the bond;

■ change the benchmark yield through a downward parallel shift;

■ construct an adjusted binomial tree using the new yield curve;

■ add the OAS adjustment to the short-rates at each of the node points in the tree;

■ use the modified binomial tree constructed above to calculate the new value of the bond, which then becomes P_+ for use in equation (9.8).

To determine the lower price resulting from a rise in yields we follow the same procedure but effect an upward parallel shift in the yield curve.

Effective duration for bonds that contain embedded option is often referred to as *option-adjusted spread duration*. There are two advantages associated with using this measure. First, by incorporating the binomial tree into the analysis, the interest-rate dependent nature of the cash flows is taken into account. This is done by holding the bond's OAS constant over the specified interest-rate shifts, in effect maintaining the credit spread demanded by the market at a constant level. This takes into account the behaviour of the embedded option as interest rates change. Second – and possibly more significant – is that OAS duration is calculated based on a parallel shift in the benchmark yield curve, which gives us an indication of the change in bond price with respect to changes in market interest rates rather than with respect to changes in its own yield.

Effective convexity

In the same way that we calculate an effective duration measure for bonds with embedded options, the standard measure of bond convexity we reviewed earlier may not be appropriate for such bonds; this is because the measure does not take into account impact of a change in market interest rates on a bond's future cash flows. As shown in Fabozzi (ibid.) the convexity measure for any bond may be approximated using (9.9).

$$CV = \frac{P_+ + P_- - 2P_0}{P_0(\Delta rm)} \qquad (9.9)$$

If prices input to (9.9) are those assuming that remaining cash flows for the bond do not change when market rates change, the convexity value is that for an option-free bond. To calculate a more meaningful value for bonds with embedded options, the prices used in the equation are derived by changing the cash flows when interest rates change, based on the results obtained from the binomial model. This measure is called *effective convexity or option-adjusted convexity.*

Sinking funds

In some markets, corporate bond issuers set up *sinking fund* provisions. They are more widely used in the US corporate market. For example, consider the hypothetical bond issue described in table 9.4.

TABLE 9.4

Issuer	ABC plc
Issue date	1-Dec-1999
Maturity date	1-Dec-2019
Nominal	£100 million
Coupon	8%
Sinking fund provision	£5 million 1 December 2009 to 2018

In the example of the ABC plc 8% 2019 bond, a proportion of the principal is paid out over a period of time. This is the formal provision. In practice, the actual payments made may differ from the formal requirements.

A sinking fund allows the bond issuer to redeem the nominal amount using one of two methods. The issuer may purchase the stipulated amount in the open market, and then deliver these bonds to the Trustee[4] for cancellation. Alternatively, the issuer may call the required amount of the bonds at par. This is in effect a *partial call*, similar to a callable bond for which only a fraction of the issue may be called. Generally the actual bonds called are selected randomly by certificate serial numbers. Readers will have noticed, however, that the second method by which a portion of the issue is redeemed is

---

[4] Bond issuers appoint a Trustee that is responsible for looking after the interests of bondholders during the life of the issue. In some cases, the Trustee is appointed by the underwriting investment bank or the Issuers' solicitors. Specialized arms of commercial and investment banks carry out the Trustee function, for example Chase Manhattan, Deutsche Bank, Bank of New York, Citibank and others.

actually a call option, which carries value for the issuer. Therefore, the method by which the issuer chooses to fulfil its sinking fund requirement is a function of the level of interest rates. If interest rates have risen since the bond was issued, so that the price of the bond has fallen, the issuer will meet its sinking fund obligation by direct purchase in the open market. However, if interest rates have fallen, the issuing company will call the specified amount of bonds at par. In the hypothetical example given at table 9.4, in effect ABC plc has ten options embedded in the bond, each relating to £5 million nominal of the bonds. The options each have different maturities, so the first expires on 1 December 2009 and subsequent options mature on 1 December each following year until 2018.[5] The decision to exercise the options as they fall due is made using the same binomial tree method that we discussed earlier.

SELECTED BIBLIOGRAPHY AND REFERENCES

The literature on callable bonds and other bonds with embedded options has attracted much attention from academics over the last two decades and, for students of the US dollar market, is rich in variety. For a good introduction we recommend the Fabozzi titles; Questa (1999) is also very accessible, as is Livingstone (1993).

Bodie, Z., Taggart, R., 'Future Investment Opportunities and the Value of the Call Provision on a Bond', *Journal of Finance* 33, 1978, pp. 1187–2000

Choudhry, M., *The Bond and Money Markets*, Butterworth-Heinemann 2001

Fabozzi, F.J., *Fixed Income Mathematics: Analytical and Statistical Techniques*, 3rd edition, McGraw-Hill 1997, chapter 16

Kalotay, A., Williams, G.O., Fabozzi, F.J., 'A model for the Valuation of Bonds and Embedded Options', *Financial Analysts Journal*, May–June 1993, pp. 35–46

Kish, R., Livingstone, M., 'The Determinants of the Call Feature on Corporate Bonds', *Journal of Banking and Finance* 16, 1992, pp. 687–703

Livingstone, M., *Money and Capital Markets*, 2nd edition, NYIOF 1993

Mitchell, K., 'The Call, Sinking Fund, and Term-to-Maturity Features of Corporate Bonds: An Empirical Investigation', *Journal of Financial and Quantitative Analysis* 26, June 1991, pp. 201–222

Narayanan, M.P., Lim, S.P., 'On the Call Provision on Corporate Zero-Coupon Bonds', *Journal of Financial and Quantitative Analysis* 24, March 1989, pp. 91–103

Questa, G., *Fixed Income Analysis for the Global Financial Market*, Wiley, chapter 8

Tuckman, B., *Fixed Income Securities*, Wiley 1996, chapter 17

Van Horne, J.C., *Financial Management and Policy*, Prentice Hall 1986

Windas, T., *An Introduction to Option-Adjusted Spread Analysis*, Bloomberg Publications 1994

[5] The 'options' are European options, in that they can only be exercised on the expiry date.

Part III

Selected derivative instruments

Introduction

In the third part of the book we consider a limited range of derivative instruments, which are not securities, and their application in the bond markets. That the choice has been limited is deliberate, for two reasons: first, the subject matter is a diverse and complex one, and it would not have been possible to cover all derivative products in anything other than superficial detail given the space constraints; second, this area is abundantly covered in the existing literature. Therefore, we concentrate on interest-rate swaps, and how they are used by bond market participants for say, hedging purposes, and an exciting new development of the 1990s, credit derivatives. There is also a chapter on the theory of forward and futures pricing, with a case study featuring the price history and implied repo rate for the LIFFE exchange's long gilt future.

Readers who wish to learn more about derivative instruments have a large selection of titles to choose from. We recommend Blake (2000) as an introductory-level text. This book does a good job of placing all capital market instruments within an integrated context, including the analysis and use of options. Marshall and Bansal (1992) and Levy (1999) are also very good introductory texts that cover a wide range of instruments, including options. Another excellent title is Jarrow and Turnbull (1999), while the author's personal favourite on options and other derivatives is Galitz (1995); this book is well worth purchasing. For an intermediate- to advanced-level treatment the standard text is Hull (2000), but this is not immediately accessible unless one has at least an A-level in mathematics (and taken the exam recently!). Rubinstein (1999) is at the same level, and is very accessible and readable; it is highly recommended. An excellent advanced text on derivatives is Briys *et al.* (1998), which presents the concepts in a way that practitioners will appreciate, whilst remaining academically rigorous. Other advanced treatments that are written in clear and readable style are Pliska (1997) and Elliott and Kopp (1999). An excellent introduction to the mathematics contained in these two texts is given in Ross (1999).

Finally, two references cited elsewhere but worth mentioning again because of their high readability are Questa (1999) and Sundaresan (1997). These are introductory- and intermediate-level treatments respectively, which discuss derivatives and price processes within the context of the fixed income markets. The latter especially is an excellent all-round text.

Recommended reading

Blake, D., *Financial Market Analysis*, 2nd edition, Wiley 2000

Brlys, E., Bellalah, M., Mal, H., de Varenne, F., *Options, Futures and Exotic Derivatives*, Wiley 1998

Elliot, R., Kopp, P., *Mathematics of Financial Markets*, Springer 1999

Galitz, L., *Financial Engineering*, FT Pitman 1995

Hull, J., *Options, Futures and Other Derivatives*, 4th edition, Prentice Hall 2000

Jarrow, R., Turnbull, S., 2nd edition, *Derivative Securities,* South-Western Publishing 2000

Kolb, R., *Futures, Options and Swaps,* 3rd edition, Blackwell 2000

Levy, H., *Introduction to Investments*, 2nd edition, South-Western Publishing 1999

Marshall, J., Bansal, V., *Financial Engineering*, New York Institute of Finance 1992

Pliska, S., *Introduction to Mathematical Finance*, Blackwell 1997

Questa, G., *Fixed Income Analysis for the Global Financial Market*, Wiley 1999

Ross, S., *An Introduction to Mathematical Finance*, Cambridge UP 1999

Rubinstein, M., *Rubinstein on Derivatives*, RISK Books 1999

Sundaresan, S., *Fixed Income Markets and their Derivatives*, South-Western Publishing 1997

CHAPTER 10

Forwards and futures valuation

To begin our discussion of derivative instruments, we discuss the valuation and analysis of forward and futures contracts. A description of interest-rate futures was given in Chapter 6. Here we develop basic valuation concepts. The discussion follows the analysis described in Rubinstein (1999), and is adapted with permission from section 2.2 of that text.[1]

Introduction

A forward contract is an agreement between two parties in which the buyer contracts to purchase from the seller a specified asset, for delivery at a future date, at a price agreed today. The terms are set so that the present value of the contract is zero. For the forthcoming analysis we use the following notation:

P is the current price of the underlying asset, also known as the *spot* price;

P_T is the price of the underlying asset at the time of delivery;

X is the delivery price of the forward contract;

T is the term to maturity of the contract in years, also referred to as the time-to-delivery;

r is the risk-free interest rate;

R is the return of the payout or its *yield*;

F is the current price of the forward contract.

The payoff of a forward contract is therefore given by

$$P_T - X \tag{10.1}$$

with X set at the start so that the present value of $(P_T - X)$ is zero. The payout yield is calculated by obtaining the percentage of the spot price that is paid out on expiry.

---

[1] This is a top book and highly recommended, and for all students and practitioners interested in capital markets, not just those involved with derivative instruments.

Forwards

When a forward contract is written, its delivery price is set so that the present value of the payout is zero. This means that the forward price F is then the price on delivery which would make the present value of the payout, on the delivery date, equal to zero. That is, at the start $F = X$. This is the case only on day 1 of the contract however. From then until the contract expiry the value of X is fixed, but the forward price F will fluctuate continuously until delivery. It is the behaviour of this forward price that we wish to examine. For instance, generally as the spot price of the underlying increases, so the price of a forward contract written on the asset also increases; and vice versa.

At this stage, it is important to remember that the forward price of a contract is not the same as the value of the contract, and the terms of the agreement are set so that at inception the value is zero. The relationship given above is used to show that an equation can be derived which relates F to P, T, r and R.

Consider first the profit/loss profile for a forward contract. This is shown in figure 10.1. The price of the forward can be shown to be related to the underlying variables as

$$F = S(r/R)^T \tag{10.2}$$

and for the one-year contract highlighted in figure 10.1 is 52.5, where the parameters are $S = 50$, $r = 1.05$ and $R = 1.00$.

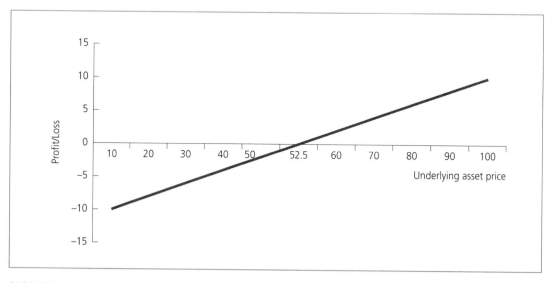

FIGURE 10.1 ■ Forward contract profit/loss profile

Futures

Forward contracts are tailor-made instruments designed to meet specific individual requirements. Futures contracts, on the other hand, are standardized contracts that are traded on recognized futures exchanges. Apart from this, the significant difference between them, and the feature that influences differences between forward and futures prices, is that profits or losses that are gained or suffered in futures trading are paid out at the end of the day. This does not occur with forwards. The majority of trading in futures contracts are always closed out, that is the position is netted out to zero before the expiry of the contract. If a position is run into the delivery month, depending on the terms and conditions of the particular exchange, the long future may be delivered into. Settlement is by physical delivery in the case of commodity futures or in cash in the case of certain financial futures. Bond futures are financial futures where any bond that is in the *delivery basket* for that contract will be delivered to the long future. With both physical and financial futures, only a very small percentage of contracts are actually delivered into as the majority of trading is undertaken for hedging and speculative purposes.

With futures contracts, as all previous trading profits and losses have been settled, on the day of expiry only the additional change from the previous day needs to be accounted for. With a forward contract all loss or gain is rolled up until the expiry day and handed over as a total amount on this day.[2]

Forwards and futures

Cash flow differences

We can now look at the cash flow treatment of the two contracts in greater detail. This is illustrated in table 10.1, which uses F to denote the price of the futures contract as well. The table shows the payoff schedule at the end of each trading day for the two instruments; assume that they have identical terms. With the forward there is no cash flow on intermediate dates, whereas with the futures contract there is. As with the forward contract, the price of the future fixes the present value of the futures contract at zero. Each day the change in price, which at the end of the day is *marked-to-market* at the *close* price, will have resulted in either a profit or gain,[3] which is handed over or received each day as appropriate. The process of daily settlement of price movements means that the

---

[2] We assume the parties have traded only one forward contract between them. If, as is more accurate to assume, a large number of contracts have been traded across a number of different maturity periods and perhaps instruments, as contracts expire only the net loss or gain is transferred between counterparties.
[3] Or no profit or gain if the closing price is unchanged from the previous day's closing price, a *doji* as technical traders call it.

nominal delivery price can be reset each day so that the present value of the contract is always zero. This means that the future and nominal delivery prices of a futures contract are the same at the end of each trading day.

TABLE 10.1 ■ Cash flow process for forwards and futures contracts

Time	Forward contract	Futures contract
0	0	0
1	0	$F_1 - F$
2	0	$F_2 - F_1$
3	0	$F_3 - F_2$
4	0	$F_4 - F_3$
5	0	$F_5 - F_4$
...	0	...
...	0	...
...	0	...
$T-1$	0	$F_{T-1} - F_{T-2}$
T	$P_T - F$	$P_T - F_{T-1}$
Total	$P_T - F$	$P_T - F$

We see in table 10.1 that there are no cash flows changing hands between counterparties to a forward contract. The price of a futures contract is reset each day; after day 1 this means it is reset from F to F_1. The amount $(F_1 - F)$ if positive, is handed over by the short future to the long future. If this amount is negative, it is paid by the long future to the short. On the expiry day T of the contract the long future will receive a settlement amount equal to $P_T - F_{T-1}$ which expresses the relationship between the price of the future and the price of the underlying asset. As significant, the daily cash flows transferred when holding a futures contract cancel each other out, so that on expiry the value of the contract is (at this stage) identical to that for a forward, that is $(P_T - F)$.

With exchange-traded contracts all market participants are deemed to conduct their trading with a central counterparty, the exchange's clearing house. This eliminates counterparty risk in all transactions, and the clearing house is able to guarantee each bargain because all participants are required to contribute to its clearing fund. This is by the process of *margin*, by which each participant deposits an *initial margin* and then, as its profits or losses are recorded, deposits further *variation margin* on a daily basis. The marking-to-market of futures contract is an essential part of this margin process. A good description of the exchange clearing process is contained in Galitz (1995).

This is the key difference between future and forward contracts. If holding a futures position that is recording a daily profit, the receipt of this profit on a daily basis is advantageous because the funds can be reinvested while the position is still maintained. This is not available with a forward. Equally, losses are suffered on a daily basis that are not suffered by the holder of a loss-making forward position.

Relationship between forward and future price

Continuing with the analysis contained in Rubinstein (1999), we wish to illustrate that under certain specified assumptions, the price of futures and forwards written with identical terms must be the same.

This can be shown in the following way. Consider two trading strategies of identical term to maturity and written on the same underlying asset; one strategy uses forward contracts while the other uses futures. Both strategies require no initial investment and are *self-financing*. The assumptions are:

- the absence of risk-free arbitrage opportunities;
- the existence of an economist's perfect market;
- certainty of returns.

Under these conditions, it can be shown that the forward and future price must be identical. In this analysis the return r is the daily return (or instantaneous money market rate) and T is the maturity term in days. Let's look further at the strategies.

For the strategy employing forwards, we buy r^T forward contracts. The start forward price is $F = X$ but of course there is no cash outlay at the start, and the payoff on expiry is

$$r^T(P_T - F).$$

The futures strategy is more involved, due to the daily margin cash flows that are received or paid during the term of the trade. On day 1 we buy r contracts each priced at F. After the close we receive $F_1 - F$. The position is closed out and the cash received is invested at the daily rate r up to the expiry date. The return on this cash is r^{T-1} which means that on expiry we will receive an amount of

$$r(F_1 - F)r^{T-1}.$$

The next day we purchase r^2 futures contracts at the price of F_1 and at the close the cash flow received of $F_2 - F_1$ is invested at the close of trading at r^{T-2}. Again we will receive on expiry a sum equal to

$$r^2(F_2 - F_1)r^{T-2}.$$

This process is repeated until the expiry date, which we assume to be the delivery date. What is the net effect of following this strategy? We will receive on the expiry date a set of maturing cash flows that have been invested daily from the end of day 1. The cash sums will be

$$r^T(F_1 - F) + r^T(F_2 - F_1) + r^T(F_3 - F_2) + \ldots + r^T(P_T - F_{T-1})$$

which nets to

$$r^T(P_T - F)$$

which is also the payoff from the forward contract strategy. Both strategies have a zero cash outlay and are self-financing. The key point is that if indeed we are saying that

$$r^T(P_T - F)_{forward} = r^T(P_T - F)_{future}, \qquad\qquad (10.3)$$

for the assumption of no arbitrage to hold, then $F_{forward} = F_{future}$.

The forward-spot parity

We can use the forward strategy to imply the forward price provided we know the current price of the underlying and the money market interest rate. A numerical example of the forward strategy is given at figure 10.2, with the same parameters given earlier. We assume no-arbitrage and a perfect frictionless market.

What figure 10.2 is saying is that it is possible to replicate the payoff profile we observed in figure 10.1 by a portfolio composed of one unit of the underlying asset, which purchase is financed by borrowing a sum that is equal to the present value of the forward price. This borrowing is repaid on maturity and is equal to $(F/1.05) \times 1.05$ which is in fact F. In the absence of arbitrage opportunity the cost of forming the portfolio will be identical to that of the forward itself. However, we have set the current cost of the forward contract at zero, which gives us

$$-50 + F / 1.05 = 0$$

We solve this expression to obtain F and this is 52.50.

The price of the forward contract is 52.50, although the present value of the forward contract when it is written is zero. Following Rubinstein, we prove this in figure 10.3.

	Cash flows	
	Start date	*Expiry*
Buy forward contract	0	$P_T - F$
Buy one unit of the underlying asset	−50	P_T
Borrow zero present-value of forward price	$F / 1.05$	F
Total	$-50 + F / 1.05$	$P_T - F$
Result		
Set $-50 + F / 1.05$ equal to zero (no-arbitrage condition)		
Therefore $F = 52.5$		

FIGURE 10.2 ▪ Forward strategy

	Start date	Expiry
	0	$P_T - F$
Buy forward contract		
Buy R^{-T} units of the underlying asset	$-PR^{-T}$	P_T
Borrow zero present-value of forward price	Fr^{-T}	$-F$
Total	$-PR^{-T} + Fr^{-T}$	$P_T - F$

Set
$-PR^{-T} + Fr^{-T} = 0$
Therefore
$F = P(r/R)^T$

FIGURE 10.3 ■ Algebraic proof of forward price

What figure 10.3 states is that the payoff profile for the forward can be replicated precisely by setting up a portfolio that holds R^{-T} units of the underlying asset, which is funded through borrowing a sum equal to the present value of the forward price. This borrowing is repaid at maturity, this amount being equal to

$$(Fr^{-T}) \times r^T = F$$

The portfolio has an identical payoff profile (by design) to the forward, this being ($P_T - F$). In a no-arbitrage environment, the cost of setting up the portfolio must be equal to the current price of the forward, as they have identical payoffs and if one was cheaper than the other, there would be a risk-free profit for a trader who bought the cheap instrument and shorted the dear one. However, we set the current cost of the forward (its present value) as zero, which means the cost of constructing the duplicating portfolio must therefore be zero as well. This gives us

$$-PR^{-T} + Fr^{-T} = 0$$

which allows us to solve for the forward price F.

The significant aspect for the buyer of a forward contract is that the payoff of the forward is identical to that of a portfolio containing an equivalent amount of the underlying asset, which has been constructed using borrowed funds. The portfolio is known as the *replicating portfolio*. The price of the forward contract is a function of the current underlying spot price, the risk-free or money market interest rate, the payoff and the maturity of the contract.

To recap then the forward-spot parity states that

$$F = P(r/R)^T \tag{10.4}$$

It can be shown that neither of the possibilities $F > P(r/R)^T$ or $F < P(r/R)^T$ will hold unless arbitrage possibilities are admitted. The only possibility is (10.4), at which the futures price is *fair value*.

The basis and implied repo rate

For later analysis, we introduce now some terms used in the futures markets.

The difference between the price of a futures contract and the current underlying spot price is known as the *basis*. For bond futures contracts, which are written not on a specific bond but a *notional* bond that can in fact be represented by any bond that fits within the contract terms, the size of the basis is given by (10.5).

$$Basis = P_{bond} - (P_{fut} \times CF)$$
(10.5)

where the basis is the *gross basis* and CF is the *conversion factor* for the bond in question. All delivery-eligible bonds are said to be in the *delivery basket*. The conversion factor equalizes each deliverable bond to the futures price.[4] The size of the gross basis represents the cost of carry associated with the bond from today to the delivery date. The bond with the lowest basis associated with it is known as the *cheapest-to-deliver* bond.

The magnitude of the basis changes continuously and this uncertainty is termed *basis risk*. Generally the basis declines over time as the maturity of the contract approaches, and converges to zero on the expiry date. The significance of basis risk is greatest for market participants who use futures contracts for hedging positions held in the underlying asset. The basis is positive or negative according to the type of market in question, and is a function of issues such as *cost of carry*. When the basis is positive, that is $F > P$, the situation is described as a *contango*, and is common in precious metals markets. A negative basis $P < F$ is described as *backwardation* and is common in oil contracts and foreign currency markets.

The hedging of futures and the underlying asset requires a keen observation of the basis. To hedge a position in a futures contract, one could run an opposite position in the underlying. However, running such a position incurs the cost of carry referred to above, which depending on the nature of the asset may include storage costs, opportunity cost of interest foregone, funding costs of holding the asset and so on. The futures price may be analyzed in terms of the forward-spot parity relationship and the risk-free interest rate. If we say that the risk-free rate is

$$r - 1$$

---

[4] For a description and analysis of bond futures contracts, the basis, implied repo and the cheapest-to-deliver bond, see Burghardt *et al.* (1998), an excellent account of the analysis of the Treasury bond basis. Plona (1998) is also a readable treatment of the European government bond basis.

and the forward-spot parity is

$$F = P(r \, / \, R)^T$$

we can set

$$r - 1 = R(F/P)^{1/T} - 1 \tag{10.5}$$

which must hold because of the no-arbitrage assumption.

This interest rate is known as the *implied repo rate*, because it is similar to a repurchase agreement carried out with the futures market. Generally, a relatively high implied repo rate is indicative of high futures prices, and the same for low implied repo rates. The rates can be used to compare contracts with each other, when these have different terms to maturity and even underlying assets. The implied repo rate for the contract is more stable than the basis; as maturity approaches the level of the rate becomes very sensitive to changes in the futures price, spot price and (by definition) time to maturity.

We present an hypothetical illustration of the basis convergence at figure 10.4. The implied repo rate is constant during this time. If we start with

$$F = P(r/R)^T$$

we can derive

$$r = R(F/P)^{1/T}$$

where r is the implied repo rate. The cost of carry is defined as the net cost of holding the underlying asset from trade date to expiry date (or delivery date).

The case study shows the price histories for the LIFFE[5] September 2000 long gilt futures contract.

---

[5] The London International Financial Futures and Options Exchange (LIFFE), pronounced 'life'. The terms of this contract are available at the exchange's website, www.liffe.com which also contains other useful information on contracts traded at the exchange.

LIFFE September 2000 long gilt future contract

In theory, a futures contract represents the price for forward delivery of the underlying asset. Therefore, one should observe a convergence in the price of the future and the price of the underlying as the contract approaches maturity.[6] The gilt price is for the UK Treasury 5.75% 2009, the cheapest-to-deliver gilt for the September 2000 contract throughout the contract's life. However, note that there is in fact no actual convergence of prices; for a bond futures contract, the convergence is best analyzed using the basis, as figure 10.4 shows (the *x*-axis lists the contract days to maturity, which is in fact the dates 29 June 2000 to 27 September 2000, the contract expiry date). The associated yields are shown at figure 10.5, which do demonstrate slight convergence on the very last day of trading. However, the liquidity of bond futures is very low in the delivery month, and decreases further in the last three days of trading up to the expiry Wednesday.

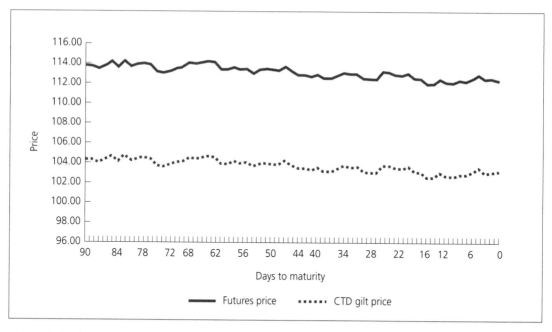

FIGURE 10.4
Source: LIFFE and Bloomberg

---

[6] For example, see the diagram on page 105 of Rubinstein (1999).

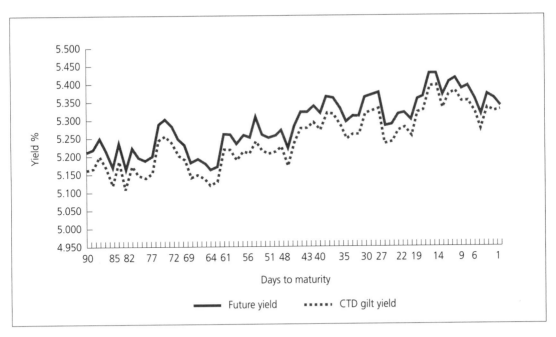

FIGURE 10.5
Source: LIFFE and Bloomberg

The basis history is shown at figure 10.6, which confirms the convergence, as the contract approaches expiry; the dates match those used for figure 10.4. Figure 10.7 shows the stability of the implied repo rate, confirming the analysis we suggested earlier. The spike towards maturity also illustrates the sensitivity of the implied repo rate to very small changes in cash or futures price.

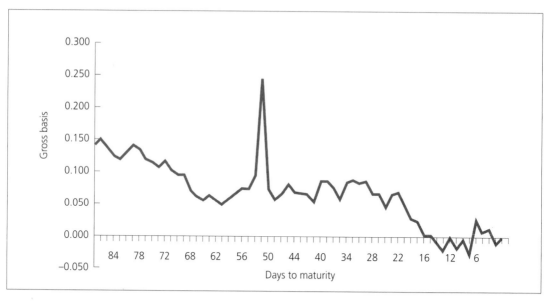

FIGURE 10.6

Source: LIFFE and Bloomberg

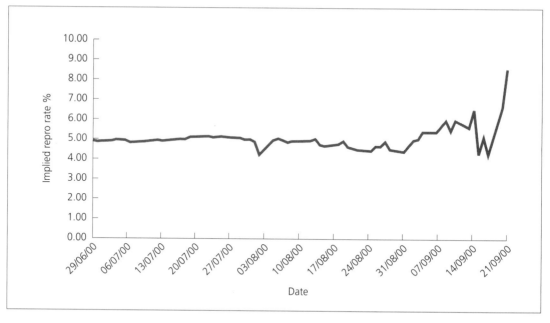

FIGURE 10.7

Source: LIFFE and Bloomberg

SELECTED BIBLIOGRAPHY AND REFERENCES

See chapter 2 in Rubinstein (1999) for the full treatment, very accessibly presented and highly recommended. One of the author's personal favourites is the chapter by Grinblatt and Jegadeesh in Jegadeesh and Tuckman (2000), which is very insightful and well presented. It is quite technical however. Chapter 3 of Kolb (2000) is a standard introductory treatment while chapter 3 of Hull (2000) is an oft-quoted text on futures and forwards and a more quantitative approach than Kolb. The earlier-dated journal references are also well worth reading.

Burghardt, G., *The Treasury Bond Basis*, McGraw Hill 1998

French, K., 'A Comparison of Futures and Forwards Prices', *Journal of Financial Economics* 12, November 1983, pp. 311–342

Galitz, L., *Financial Engineering*, FT Pitman 1995, chapters 3, 4, 6–8

Grinblatt, M., Jegadeesh, N., 'Futures vs. Forward Prices: Implications for Swap Pricing and Derivatives Valuation' in Jegadeesh, N., Tuckman, B., *Advanced Fixed-Income Valuation Tools*, Wiley 2000

Hull, J., *Options, Futures and Other Derivatives*, 4th edition, Prentice Hall 2000

Jarrow, R., Oldfield, G., 'Forward Contracts and Futures Contracts', *Journal of Financial Economics* 9, December 1981, pp. 373–382

Kolb, R., *Futures, Options and Swaps*, 3rd edition, Blackwell 2000

Park, H., Chen, A., 'Differences between Futures and Forward Prices: A Further Investigation of Marking to Market Effects', *Journal of Futures Markets* 5, February 1985, pp. 77–88

Polona, C., *The European Bond Basis*, McGraw-Hill 1997.

Rubinstein, M., *Rubinstein on Derivatives*, RISK Books 1999.

CHAPTER 11

Swaps

Swaps are off-balance sheet instruments involving combinations of two or more basic building blocks. Most swaps currently traded in the market involve combinations of cash market securities, for example a fixed interest rate security combined with a floating interest rate security, possibly also combined with a currency transaction. However, the market has also seen swaps that involve a futures or forward component, as well as swaps that involve an option component. The market in say, dollar, euro and sterling interest rate swaps is very large and very liquid. The main types of swap are interest rate swaps, asset swaps, basis swaps, fixed-rate currency swaps and currency coupon swaps. The market for swaps is organized by the International Swap Dealers Association.

Swaps are now one of the most important and useful instruments in the debt capital markets. They are used by a wide range of institutions, including banks, mortgage banks and building societies, corporates and local authorities. The demand for them has grown as the continuing uncertainty and volatility of interest rates and exchange rates has made it ever more important to hedge their exposures. As the market has matured, the instrument has gained wider acceptance, and is regarded as a 'plain vanilla' product in the debt capital markets. Virtually all commercial and investment banks will quote swap prices for their customers, and as they are OTC instruments, dealt over the telephone, it is possible for banks to tailor swaps to match the precise requirements of individual customers. There is also a close relationship between the bond market and the swap market, and corporate finance teams and underwriting banks keep a close eye on the government yield curve and the swap yield curve, looking out for possibilities regarding new issue of debt.

It is not proposed to cover the historical evolution of the swaps markets, which is abundantly covered in existing literature, nor the myriad of swap products which can be traded today (ditto). In this chapter we review the use of interest-rate swaps from the point of view of the bond market participant; this includes pricing and valuation and its use as a hedging tool. The bibliography lists further reading on important topics such as pricing, valuation and credit risk.

Interest rate swaps

Introduction

Interest-rate swaps are the most important type of swap in terms of volume of transactions. They are used to manage and hedge interest rate risk and exposure, while market makers will also take positions in swaps that reflect their view on the direction of interest rates. An interest rate swap is an agreement between two counterparties to make periodic interest payments to one another during the life of the swap, on a pre-determined set of dates, based on a *notional* principal amount. One party is the fixed-rate payer, and this rate is agreed at the time of trade of the swap; the other party is the floating-rate payer, the floating rate being determined during the life of the swap by reference to a specific market index. The principal or notional amount is never physically exchanged, hence the term 'off-balance sheet', but is used merely to calculate the interest payments. The fixed-rate payer receives floating-rate interest and is said to be 'long' or to have 'bought' the swap. The long side has conceptually purchased a floating-rate note (because it receives floating-rate interest) and issued a fixed coupon bond (because it pays out fixed interest at intervals), that is, it has in principle borrowed funds. The floating-rate payer is said to be 'short' or to have 'sold' the swap. The short side has conceptually purchased a coupon bond (because it receives fixed-rate interest) and issued a floating-rate note (because it pays floating-rate interest). So an interest rate swap is:

- an agreement between two parties;
- to exchange a stream of cash flows;
- calculated as a percentage of a *notional* sum; and
- calculated on different interest bases.

For example in a trade between Bank A and Bank B, Bank A may agree to pay fixed semi-annual coupons of 10% on a notional principal sum of £1 million, in return for receiving from Bank B the prevailing six-month sterling Libor rate on the same amount. The known cash flow is the fixed payment of £50,000 every six months by Bank A to Bank B.

Interest-rate swaps trade in a secondary market so their value moves in line with market interest rates, in exactly the same way as bonds. If a five-year interest-rate swap is transacted today at a rate of 5%, and five-year interest rates subsequently fall to 4.75%, the swap will have decreased in value to the fixed-rate payer, and correspondingly increased in value to the floating-rate payer, who has now seen the level of interest payments fall. The opposite would be true if five-year rates moved to 5.25%. Why is this? Consider the fixed-rate payer in an IR swap to be a borrower of funds; if he fixes the interest rate payable on a loan for five years, and then this interest rate decreases shortly afterwards, is he better off? No, because he is now paying above the market rate for the funds borrowed. For this reason a swap contract decreases in value to the fixed-rate payer if there is a fall in rates. Equally, a floating-rate payer gains if there is a fall in rates, as he can take advantage of the new rates and pay a lower level of interest; hence the value of a swap increases to the floating-rate payer if there is a fall in rates.

A bank swaps desk will have an overall net interest rate position arising from all the swaps it has traded that are currently on the book. This position is an interest rate exposure at all points along the term structure, out to the maturity of the longest-dated swap. At the close of business each day all the swaps on the book will be *marked-to-market* at the interest rate quote for that day.

A swap can be viewed in two ways, either as a bundle of forward or futures contracts, or as a bundle of cash flows arising from the 'sale' and 'purchase' of cash market instruments. If we imagine a strip of futures contracts, maturing every three or six months out to three years, we can see how this is conceptually similar to a three-year interest-rate swap. However in the author's view it is better to visualize a swap as being a bundle of cash flows arising from cash instruments.

Let us imagine we have only two positions on our book:

■ a long position in £100 million of a three-year FRN that pays six-month Libor semi-annually, and is trading at par;

■ a short position in £100 million of a three-year gilt with coupon of 6% that is also trading at par.

Being short a bond is the equivalent to being a borrower of funds. Assuming this position is kept to maturity, the resulting cash flows are shown in table 11.1.

There is no net outflow or inflow at the start of these trades, as the £100 million purchase of the FRN is netted with receipt of £100 million from the sale of the gilt. The resulting cash flows over the three-year period are shown in the last column of table 11.1.

TABLE 11.1 ■ Three-year cash flows

| Period (6mo) | Cash flows resulting from long position in FRN and short position in gilt | | |
	FRN	Gilt	Net cash flow
0	−£100m	+£100m	£0
1	+(Libor × 100)/2	−3	+(Libor × 100)/2 − 3.0
2	+(Libor × 100)/2	−3	+(Libor × 100)/2 − 3.0
3	+(Libor × 100)/2	−3	+(Libor × 100)/2 − 3.0
4	+(Libor × 100)/2	−3	+(Libor × 100)/2 − 3.0
5	+(Libor × 100)/2	−3	+(Libor × 100)/2 − 3.0
6	+[(Libor × 100)/2] + 100	−103	+(Libor × 100)/2 − 3.0

The Libor rate is the six-month rate prevailing at the time of the setting, for instance the Libor rate at period 4 will be the rate actually prevailing at period 4.

This net position is exactly the same as that of a fixed-rate payer in an IR swap. As we had at the start of the trade, there is no cash inflow or outflow on maturity. For a floating-rate payer, the cash flow would mirror exactly a long position in a fixed rate bond and a short position in an FRN. Therefore, the fixed-rate payer in a swap is said to be short in the bond market, that is a borrower of funds; the floating-rate payer in a swap is said to be long the bond market.

Market terminology

Virtually all swaps are traded under the legal terms and conditions stipulated in the ISDA standard documentation. The trade date for a swap is not surprisingly, the date on which the swap is transacted. The terms of the trade include the fixed interest rate, the maturity and notional amount of the swap, and the payment bases of both legs of the swap. The date from which floating interest payments are determined is the *setting date*, which may also be the trade date. Most swaps fix the floating-rate payments to Libor, although other reference rates that are used include the US Prime rate, euribor, the Treasury bill rate and the commercial paper rate. In the same way as for FRA and eurocurrency deposits, the rate is fixed two business days before the interest period begins. The second (and subsequent) setting date will be two business days before the beginning of the second (and subsequent) swap periods. The *effective date* is the date from which interest on the swap is calculated, and this is typically two business days after the trade date. In a *forward*-start swap the effective date will be at some point in the future, specified in the swap terms. The floating interest-rate for each period is fixed at the start of the period, so that the interest payment amount is known in advance by both parties (the fixed rate is known of course, throughout the swap by both parties).

Although for the purposes of explaining swap structures, both parties are said to pay interest payments (and receive them), in practice, only the net difference between both payments changes hands at the end of each interest payment. This eases the administration associated with swaps and reduces the number of cash flows for each swap. The counterparty that is the net payer at the end of each period will make a payment to the counterparty. The first payment date will occur at the end of the first interest period, and subsequent payment dates will fall at the end of successive interest periods. The final payment date falls on the maturity date of the swap. The calculation of interest is given by (11.1).

$$I = M \times r \times \frac{n}{B} \tag{11.1}$$

where I is the interest amount, M is the nominal amount of the swap and B is the interest day-base for the swap. Dollar and euro-denominated swaps use an actual/360 day-count, similar to other money market instruments in those currencies, while sterling swaps use an actual/365 day-count basis.

The cash flows resulting from a vanilla interest rate swap are illustrated in figure 11.1, using the normal convention where cash inflows are shown as an arrow pointing up, while cash outflows are shown as an arrow pointing down. The counterparties in a swap transaction only pay across net cash flows however, so at each interest payment date only one actual cash transfer will be made, by the net payer. This is shown as figure 11.1(iii).

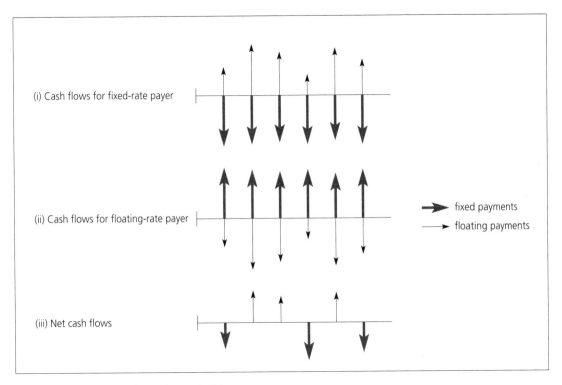

FIGURE 11.1 ■ Cash flows for typical interest rate swap

Swap spreads and the swap yield curve

In the market, banks will quote two-way swap rates, on screens and on the telephone or via a dealing system such as Reuters. Brokers will also be active in relaying prices in the market. The convention in the market is for the swap market maker to set the floating leg at Libor and then quote the fixed rate that is payable for that maturity. So for a five-year swap a bank's swap desk might be willing to quote the following:

Floating-rate payer:	pay 6m-Libor
	receive fixed rate of 5.19%
Fixed-rate payer:	pay fixed rate of 5.25%
	receive 6m-Libor

In this case, the bank is quoting an offer rate of 5.25%, which the fixed-rate payer will pay, in return for receiving Libor flat. The bid price quote is 5.19% which is what a floating-rate payer will receive fixed. The bid-offer spread in this case therefore is 6 basis points. The fixed-rate quotes are always at a spread above the government bond yield curve. Let us assume that the five-year gilt is yielding 4.88%; in this case then the five-year swap bid rate is 31 basis points above this yield. So the bank's swap trader could quote the swap rates as a spread above the benchmark bond yield curve, say 37-31, which is her swap spread quote. This means that the bank is happy to enter into a swap paying fixed 31 basis points above the benchmark yield and receiving Libor, and receiving fixed 37 basis points above the yield curve and paying Libor. The bank's screen on say, Bloomberg or Reuters might look something like table 11.2, which quotes the swap rates as well as the current spread over the government bond benchmark.

TABLE 11.2 ■ Swap quotes

1YR	4.50	4.45	+17
2YR	4.69	4.62	+25
3YR	4.88	4.80	+23
4YR	5.15	5.05	+29
5YR	5.25	5.19	+31
10YR	5.50	5.40	+35

The swap spread is a function of the same factors that influence the spread over government bonds for other instruments. For shorter duration swaps, say up to three years, there are other yield curves that can be used in comparison, such as the cash market curve or a curve derived from futures prices. For longer-dated swaps the spread is determined mainly by the credit spreads that prevail in the corporate bond market. Because a swap is viewed as a package of long and short positions in fixed- and floating-rate bonds, it is the credit spreads in these two markets that will determine the swap spread. This is logical; essentially it is the premium for greater credit risk involved in lending to corporates that dictates that a swap rate will be higher than the same maturity government bond yield. Technical factors will be responsible for day-to-day fluctuations in swap rates, such as the supply of corporate bonds and the level of demand for swaps, plus the cost to swap traders of hedging their swap positions.

We can summarize by saying that swap spreads over government bonds reflect the supply and demand conditions of both swaps and government bonds, as well as the market's view on the credit quality of swap counterparties. There is considerable information content in the swap yield curve, much like that in the government bond yield curve. During times of credit concerns in the market, such as the corrections in Asian and Latin American markets in summer 1998, and the possibility of default by the Russian government regarding its long-dated US dollar bonds, the swap spread will increase, more so at higher maturities. To illustrate this consider the sterling swap spread in 1998/99. The UK swap spread widened from the second half of 1998 onwards, a reaction to bond market volatility around the world. At such times investors embark on a 'flight to quality' that results in yield spreads widening. In the swap market, the spread between two-year and ten-year swaps also increased, reflecting market concern with credit and counterparty risk. The spreads narrowed in the first quarter 1999, as credit concerns brought about by market corrections in 1998 declined. The change in swap spreads is shown in figure 11.2.

Generic swap valuation

Banks generally use *par* swap or *zero-coupon* swap pricing. We will look at this method in the next section; first however we will introduce an intuitive swap valuation method.

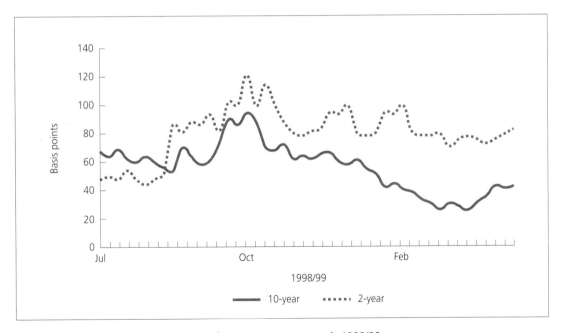

FIGURE 11.2 ▪ Sterling two-year and ten-year swap spreads 1998/99
Source: BoE

Generic swap pricing

Assume we have a vanilla interest-rate swap with a notional principal of N that pays n payments during its life, to a maturity date of T. The date of each payment is on t_i with $i = 1,...n$. The present value today of a future payment is denoted by $PV(0, t)$. If the swap rate is r, the value of the fixed-leg payments is given by (11.2) below.

$$PV_{fixed} = N \sum_{i=1}^{n} PV(0, t_i) \times \left[r \times \left(\frac{t_i - t_{i-1}}{B} \right) \right] \tag{11.2}$$

where B is the money market day base. The term $t_i - t_{i-1}$ is simply the number of days between the ith and the i–1th payments.

The value of the floating-leg payments at the date t_1 for an existing swap is given by

$$PV_{float} = N \times \left[rl \times \frac{t_1}{B} \right] + N - [N \times PV(t_1, t_n)] \tag{11.3}$$

where rl is the LIBOR rate that has been set for the next interest payment. We set the present value of the floating-rate payment at time 0 as follows.

$$PV(0, t_1) = \frac{1}{1 + rl(t_1)\left(\frac{t_1}{B}\right)} \tag{11.4}$$

For a new swap the value of the floating payments is given by

$$PV_{float} = N \left[rl \times \frac{t_1}{B} + 1 \right] \times PV(0, t_1) - PV(0, t_n) \tag{11.5}$$

The swap valuation is then given by $PV_{fixed} - PV_{float}$. The swap rate quoted by a market making bank is that which sets $PV_{fixed} = PV_{float}$ and is known as the par or zero-coupon swap rate. We consider this next.

Zero-coupon swap pricing

So far we have discussed how vanilla swap prices are often quoted as a spread over the benchmark government bond yield in that currency, and how this swap spread is mainly a function of the credit spread required by the market over the government (risk-free) rate. This method is convenient and also logical because banks use government bonds as the main instrument when hedging their swap books. However, because much bank swap trading is now conducted in non-standard, tailor-made swaps, this method can sometimes be unwieldy as each swap needs to have its spread calculated to suit its particular characteristics. Therefore, banks use a standard pricing method for all swaps known as *zero-coupon* swap pricing.

In Chapter 3 we referred to zero-coupon bonds and zero-coupon interest rates. Zero-coupon rates, or *spot rates* are true interest rates for their particular term to maturity. In zero-coupon swap pricing, a bank will view all swaps, even the most complex, as a series of cash flows. The zero-coupon rates that apply now for each of the cash flows in a swap can be used to value these cash flows. Therefore, to value and price a swap, each of the swap's cash flows are present valued using known spot rates; the sum of these present values is the value of the swap.

In a swap the fixed-rate payments are known in advance and so it is straightforward to present-value them. The present value of the floating rate payments is usually estimated in two stages. First the implied forward rates can be calculated using (11.6). We are quite familiar with this relationship from our reading of the earlier chapter.

$$rf_i = \left(\frac{df_i}{df_{i+1}} - 1 \right) N \qquad (11.6)$$

where

rf_i is the one-period forward rate starting at time i;
df_i is the discount factor for the maturity period i;
df_{i+1} is the discount factor for the period $i + 1$;
N is the number of times per year that coupons are paid.

By definition, the floating-payment interest rates are not known in advance, so the swap bank will predict what these will be, using the forward rates applicable to each payment date. The forward rates are those that are currently implied from spot rates. Once the size of the floating-rate payments have been estimated, these can also be valued by using the spot rates. The total value of the fixed and floating legs is the sum of all the present values, so the value of the total swap is the net of the present values of the fixed and floating legs.

While the term *zero-coupon* refers to an interest rate that applies to a discount instrument that pays no coupon and has one cash flow (at maturity), it is not necessary to have a functioning zero-coupon bond market in order to construct a zero-coupon yield curve. In practice, most financial pricing models use a combination of the following instruments to construct zero-coupon yield curves:

■ money market deposits;

■ interest-rate futures;

■ FRAs;

■ government bonds.

Frequently an overlap in the maturity period of all instruments is used; FRA rates are usually calculated from interest-rate futures so it is necessary to use only one of either FRA or futures rates.

Once a zero-coupon yield curve (*term structure*) is derived, this may be used to value a future cash flow maturing at any point along the term structure. This includes swaps: to price an interest-rate swap, we calculate the present value of each of the cash flows using the zero-coupon rates and then sum all the cash flows. As we noted above, while the fixed-rate payments are known in advance, the floating-rate payments must be estimated, using the forward rates implied by the zero-coupon yield curve. The net present value of the swap is the net difference between the present values of the fixed- and floating-rate legs.

Calculating the forward rate from spot rate discount factors

Remember that one way to view a swap is as a long position in a fixed-coupon bond that was funded at Libor, or against a short position in a floating-rate bond. The cash flows from such an arrangement would be paying floating-rate and receiving fixed-rate. In the former arrangement, where a long position in a fixed-rate bond is funded with a floating-rate loan, the cash flows from the principals will cancel out, as they are equal and opposite (assuming the price of the bond on purchase was par), leaving a collection of cash flows that mirror an interest-rate swap that pays floating and receives fixed. Therefore, as the fixed-rate on an interest-rate swap is the same as the coupon (and yield) on a bond priced at par, so that in order to calculate the fixed-rate on an interest-rate swap is the same as calculating the coupon for a bond that we wish to issue at par.

The price of a bond paying semi-annual coupons is given by (11.7), which may be rearranged for the coupon rate r to provide an equation that enables us to determine the par yield, and hence the swap rate r, given by (11.8).

$$P = \frac{r_n}{2} df_1 + \frac{r_n}{2} df_2 + \ldots + \frac{r_n}{2} df_n + Mdf_n \tag{11.7}$$

where r_n is the coupon on an n-period bond with n coupons and M is the maturity payment. It can be shown then that

$$r_n = \frac{1 - df_n}{\dfrac{df_1}{2} + \dfrac{df_2}{2} + \ldots + \dfrac{df_n}{2}}$$

$$= \frac{1 - df_n}{\displaystyle\sum_{i=1}^{n} \frac{df_i}{2}} \tag{11.8}$$

For annual coupon bonds there is no denominator for the discount factor, while for bonds paying coupons on a frequency of N we replace the denominator 2 with N.[1] The expression at (11.8) may be rearranged again, using F for the coupon frequency, to obtain an equation which may be used to calculate the nth discount factor for an n-period swap rate, given at (11.9).

$$df_n = \frac{1 - r_n \sum_{i=1}^{n-1} \frac{df_i}{N}}{1 + \frac{r_n}{N}} \tag{11.9}$$

Expression (11.9) is the general expression for the *boot-strapping* process that we first encountered in Chapter 3. Essentially, to calculate the n-year discount factor we use the discount factors for the years 1 to $n-1$, and the n-year swap rate or zero-coupon rate. If we have the discount factor for any period, we may use (11.9) to determine the same period zero-coupon rate, after rearranging it, shown at (11.10).

$$rs_n = {}^{t_n}\!\sqrt{\frac{1}{df_n}} - 1 \tag{11.10}$$

Discount factors for spot rates may also be used to calculate forward rates. We know that

$$df_1 = \frac{1}{\left(1 + \frac{rs_1}{N}\right)} \tag{11.11}$$

where rs is the zero-coupon rate. If we know the *forward rate* we may use this to calculate a second discount rate, shown by (11.12).

$$df_2 = \frac{df_1}{\left(1 + \frac{rf_1}{N}\right)} \tag{11.12}$$

where rf_1 is the forward rate. This is no use in itself; however, we may derive from it an expression to enable us to calculate the discount factor at any point in time between the previous discount rate and the given forward rate for the period n to $n+1$, shown at (11.13), which may then be rearranged to give us the general expression to calculate a forward rate, given at 11.14.

[1] The expression also assumes an actual/365 day-count basis. If any other day-count convention is used, the $1/N$ factor must be replaced by a fraction made up of the actual number of days as the numerator and the appropriate year base as the denominator.

$$df_{n+1} = \frac{df_n}{\left(1 + \dfrac{rf_n}{N}\right)} \tag{11.13}$$

$$rf_n = \left(\frac{df_n}{df_{i+1}} - 1\right)N \tag{11.14}$$

The general expression for an n-period discount rate at time n from the previous period forward rates is given by (11.15).

$$df_n = \frac{1}{\left(1 + \dfrac{rf_{n-1}}{N}\right)} \times \frac{1}{\left(1 + \dfrac{rf_{n-2}}{N}\right)} \times \ldots \times \frac{1}{\left(1 + \dfrac{rf_n}{N}\right)}$$

$$\tag{11.15}$$

$$df_n = \prod_{i=0}^{n-1} \left[\frac{1}{\left(1 + \dfrac{rf_i}{N}\right)}\right]$$

From the above we may combine equations (11.8) and (11.14) to obtain the general expression for an n-period swap rate and zero-coupon rate, given by (11.16) and (11.17) respectively.

$$r_n = \frac{\displaystyle\sum_{i=1}^{n} \frac{rf_{i-1}\, df_i}{N}}{\displaystyle\sum_{i=1}^{n} \frac{df_i}{N}} \tag{11.16}$$

$$1 + rs_n = \sqrt[t_n]{\prod_{i=0}^{n-1} \left(1 + \frac{rf_i}{N}\right)} \tag{11.17}$$

The two expressions do not tell us anything new, as we have already encountered their results in Chapter 6. The swap rate, which we have denoted as r_n is shown by (11.16) to be the weighted-average of the forward rates. Consider that a strip of FRAs would constitute an interest-rate swap, than a swap rate that is for a continuous period could be covered by a strip of FRAs. Therefore, an average of the FRA rates would be the correct swap rate. As FRA rates are forward rates, we may be comfortable with (11.16), which states that the n-period swap rate is the average of the forward rates from rf_0 to rf_n. To be accurate we must weight the forward rates, and these are weighted by the discount factors for each period. Note that although swap rates are derived from forward rates, interest payments under a swap are paid in the normal way at the end of an interest period, while payments for an FRA are made at the beginning of the period and must be discounted.

Equation (11.17) states that the zero-coupon rate is calculated from the geometric average of (one plus) the forward rates. Again, this is apparent from a reading of the case study example in Chapter 3. The n-period forward rate is obtained using the discount factors for periods n and $n-1$. The discount factor for the complete period is obtained by multiplying the individual discount factors together, and exactly the same result would be obtained by using the zero-coupon interest rate for the whole period to obtain the discount factor.[2]

Illustrating the pricing principles for an interest-rate swap

The rate charged on a newly-transacted interest-rate swap is the one that gives its net present value as zero. The term *valuation* of a swap is used to denote the process of calculating the net present value of an existing swap, when marking-to-market the swap against current market interest rates. Therefore, when we price a swap, we set its net present value to zero, while when we value a swap we set its fixed rate at the market rate and calculate the net present value.

To illustrate the basic principle, we now price a plain vanilla interest rate swap with the terms set out below; for simplicity we assume that the annual fixed-rate payments are the same amount each year, although in practice there would be slight differences. Also assume we already have our zero-coupon yields as shown in table 11.3.

We use the zero-coupon rates to calculate the discount factors, and then use the discount factors to calculate the forward rates. This is done using equation (11.14). These forward rates are then used to predict what the floating-rate payments will be at each interest period. Both fixed-rate and floating-rate payments are then present-valued at the appropriate zero-coupon rate, which enables us to calculate the net present value.

The fixed-rate for the swap is calculated using equation (11.8) to give us:

$$\frac{1 - 0.71298618}{4.16187950}$$

or 6.8963%.

---

[2] Zero-coupon and forward rates are also related in another way. If we change the zero-coupon rate rs_n and the forward rate rf_i into their continuously-compounded equivalent rates, given by $\ln(1+rs_n)$ and $\ln(1+rf_i)$, we may obtain an expression for the continuously-compounded zero-coupon rate as being the simple average of the continuously-compounded forward rates, given by:

$$rs_n' = \frac{1}{t_n} \sum_{i=0}^{n-1} \frac{rf_i'}{N}$$

The terms of the swap are as follows:

Nominal principal	£10,000,000
Fixed rate	6.8963%
Day count fixed	Actual/365
Day count floating	Actual/365
Payment frequency fixed	Annual
Payment frequency floating	Annual
Trade date	31 January 2000
Effective date	2 February 2000
Maturity date	2 February 2005
Term	Five years

TABLE 11.3 ■ Generic interest-rate swap

Period	Zero-coupon rate %	Discount factor	Forward rate %	Fixed payment	Floating payment	Pv fixed payment	Pv floating payment
1	5.5	0.947867298	5.5	689,625	550,000	653,672.9858	521,327.0142
2	6	0.88999644	6.502369605	689,625	650,236.9605	613,763.7949	578,708.58
3	6.25	0.833706493	6.751770257	689,625	675,177.0257	574,944.8402	562,899.4702
4	6.5	0.777323091	7.253534951	689,625	725,353.4951	536,061.4366	563,834.0208
5	7	0.712986179	9.023584719	689,625	902,358.4719	491,693.094	643,369.1194
		4.161879501				2,870,137	2,870,137

TABLE 11.4 ■ Generic interest-rate swap (Excel formulae)

CELL	C	D	E	F	G	H	I	J
21			10000000					
22								
23	Period	Zero-coupon rate %	Discount factor	Forward rate %	Fixed payment	Floating payment	PV fixed payment	PV floating payment
24	1	5.5	0.947867298	5.5	689,625	"(F24*10,000,000)/100	"G24/1.055	"H24/(1.055)
25	2	6	0.88999644	"((E24/E25)-1)*100	689,625	"(F25*10,000,000)/100	"G24/(1.06)^2	"H25/(1.06)^2
26	3	6.25	0.833706493	"((E25/E26)-1)*100	689,625	"(F26*10,000,000)/100	"G24/(1.0625)^3	"H26/(1.0625^3)
27	4	6.5	0.777323091	"((E26/E27)-1)*100	689,625	"(F27*10,000,000)/100	"G24/(1.065)^4	"H27/(1.065)^4
28	5	7	0.712986179	"((E27/E28)-1)*100	689,625	"(F28*10,000,000)/100	"G24/(1.07)^5	"H28/(1.07)^5
			"SUM(E24:E28)				2,870,137	2,870,137

For reference the Microsoft Excel® formulae are shown at table 11.4. It is not surprising that the net present value is zero, because the zero-coupon curve is used to derive the discount factors which are then used to derive the forward rates, which are used to value the swap. As with any financial instrument, the fair value is its breakeven price or hedge cost, and in this case the bank that is pricing the five-year swap shown in table 11.3 could hedge the swap with a series of FRAs transacted at the forward rates shown. If the bank is paying fixed and receiving floating, value of the swap to it will rise if there is a rise in market rates, and fall if there is a fall in market rates. Conversely, if the bank was receiving fixed and paying floating, the swap value to it would fall if there was a rise in rates, and vice versa.

This method is used to price any interest-rate swap, even exotic ones.

Valuation using final maturity discount factor

A short-cut to valuing the floating-leg payments of an interest-rate swap involves using the discount factor for the final maturity period. This is possible because, for the purposes of valuation, an exchange of principal at the beginning and end of the swap is conceptually the same as the floating-leg interest payments. This holds since, in an exchange of principal, the interest payments earned on investing the initial principal would be uncertain, as they are floating rate, while on maturity the original principal would be returned. The net result is a floating-rate level of receipts, exactly similar to the floating-leg payments in a swap. To value the principals then, we need only the final maturity discount rate.

To illustrate, consider table 11.3, where the present value of both legs was found to be £2,870,137. The same result is obtained if we use the five-year discount factor, as shown below.

$$PV_{floating} = (10,000,000 \times 1) - (10,000,000 \times 0.71298618) = 2,870,137$$

The first term is the principal multiplied by the discount factor 1; this is because the present value of an amount valued immediately is unchanged (or rather, it is multiplied by the immediate payment discount factor, which is 1.0000).

Therefore we may use the principal amount of a swap if we wish to value the swap. This is of course for valuation only, as there is no actual exchange of principal in a swap.

Summary of IR swap

Let us summarize the key features of swaps. A plain vanilla swap has the following characteristics:

■ one leg of the swap is fixed-rate interest, while the other will be floating-rate, usually linked to a standard index such as Libor;

■ the fixed rate is fixed through the entire life of the swap;

■ the floating rate is set in advance of each period (quarterly, semi-annually or annually) and paid in arrears;

■ both legs have the same payment frequency;

- the maturity can be standard whole years up to 30 years, or set to match customer requirements;

- the notional principal remains constant during the life of the swap.

Of course to meet customer demand banks can set up swaps that have variations on any or all of the above standard points. Some of the more common variations are discussed in the next section.

Non-vanilla interest-rate swaps

The swap market is very flexible and instruments can be tailor-made to fit the requirements of individual customers. A wide variety of swap contracts have been traded in the market. Although the most common reference rate for the floating-leg of a swap is six-month Libor (for a semi-annual paying floating leg), other reference rates that have been used include three-month Libor, the prime rate (for dollar swaps), the one-month commercial paper rate, the Treasury bill rate and the municipal bond rate (again, for dollar swaps). The term of a swap need not be fixed; swaps may be *extendable* or *putable*. In an extendable swap, one of the parties has the right but not the obligation to extend the life of the swap beyond the fixed maturity date, while in a putable swap, one party has the right to terminate the swap ahead of the specified maturity date.

It is also possible to transact options on swaps, known as *swaptions*. A swaption is the right to enter into a swap agreement at some point in the future, during the life of the option. Essentially a swaption is an option to exchange a fixed-rate bond cash flow for a floating-rate bond cash flow structure. As a floating-rate bond is valued on its principal value at the start of a swap, a swaption may be viewed as the value on a fixed-rate bond, with a strike price that is equal to the face value of the floating-rate bond.

Further types of swap

Constant maturity

A *constant maturity swap* is a swap in which the parties exchange a Libor rate for a fixed swap rate. For example, the terms of the swap might state that six-month Libor is exchanged for the five-year swap rate on a semi-annual basis for the next five years, or for the five-year government bond rate. In the US market the second type of constant maturity swap is known as a *constant maturity Treasury swap*.

Accreting and amortizing swaps

In a plain vanilla swap, the notional principal remains unchanged during the life of the swap. However, it is possible to trade a swap where the notional principal varies during its life. An accreting (*or step-up*) swap is one in which the principal starts off at one level and then increases in amount over time. The opposite, an amortizing swap, is one in which the notional reduces in size over time. An accreting swap would be useful where, for instance a funding liability that is being hedged increases over time. The amortizing swap might be employed by a borrower hedging a bond issue that featured sinking fund payments, where a part of the notional amount outstanding is paid off at set points during the life of the bond. If the principal fluctuates in amount, for example increasing in one year and then reducing in another, the swap is known as a *roller-coaster swap*. Another application for an amortizing swap is as a hedge for a loan that is itself an amortizing one. Frequently, this is combined with a forward-starting swap, to tie in with the cash flows payable on the loan. The pricing and valuation of an amortizing swap is no different in principle to a vanilla interest-rate swap; a single swap rate is calculated using the relevant discount factors, and at this rate the net present value of the swap cash flows will equal zero at the start of the swap.

Libor-in-arrears swap

In this type of swap (also known as a *back-set swap*) the setting date is just before the end of the accrual period for the floating-rate setting and not just before the start. Such a swap would be attractive to a counterparty who had a different view on interest rates compared to the market consensus. For instance in a rising yield curve environment, forward rates will be higher than current market rates, and this will be reflected in the pricing of a swap. A Libor-in-arrears swap would be priced higher than a conventional swap. If the floating-rate payer believed that interest rates would in fact rise more slowly than forward rates (and the market) were suggesting, he may wish to enter into an arrears swap as opposed to a conventional swap.

Basis swap

In a conventional swap, one leg comprises fixed-rate payments and the other floating-rate payments. In a basis swap both legs are floating-rate, but linked to different money market indices. One leg is normally linked to Libor, while the other might be linked to the CD rate say, or the commercial paper rate. This type of swap would be used by a bank in the US that had made loans that paid at the prime rate, and financed its loans at Libor. A basis swap would eliminate the *basis risk* between the bank's income and expense cash flows. Other basis swaps have been traded where both legs are linked to Libor, but at different maturities; for instance one leg might be at three-month Libor and the other at six-month Libor. In such a swap, the basis is different and so is the payment frequency: one leg pays out semi-annually while the other would be paying on a quarterly basis. Note that where the payment frequencies differ, there is a higher level of counterparty risk for one of the parties. For instance, if one party is paying out on a monthly basis but receiving semi-annual cash flows, it would have made five interest payments before receiving one in return.

Margin swap

It is common to encounter swaps where there is a margin above or below Libor on the floating leg, as opposed to a floating leg of Libor flat. If a bank's borrowing is financed at Libor+25bps, it may wish to receive Libor+25bps in the swap so that its cash flows match exactly. The fixed rate quote for a swap must be adjusted correspondingly to allow for the margin on the floating side, so in our example if the fixed-rate quote is say, 6.00%, it would be adjusted to around 6.25%; differences in the margin quoted on the fixed leg might arise if the day-count convention or payment frequency were to differ between fixed and floating legs. Another reason why there may be a margin is if the credit quality of the counterparty demanded it, so that highly rated counterparties may pay slightly below Libor, for instance.

Off-market swap

When a swap is transacted its fixed rate is quoted at the current market rate for that maturity. Where the fixed rate is different to the market rate, this is an off-market swap, and a compensating payment is made by one party to the other. An off-market rate may be used for particular hedging requirements for example, or when a bond issuer wishes to use the swap to hedge the bond as well as to cover the bond's issue costs.

Differential swap

A differential swap is a basis swap but with one of the legs calculated in a different currency. Typically one leg is floating-rate, while the other is floating-rate but with the reference index rate for another currency, but denominated in the domestic currency. For example, a differential swap may have one party paying six-month sterling Libor, in sterling, on a notional principal of £10 million, and receiving euro-Libor, minus a margin, payable in sterling and on the same notional principal. Differential swaps are not very common and are the most difficult for a bank to hedge. The hedging is usually carried out using what is known as a *quanto* option.

Forward-start swap

A forward-start swap is one where the *effective date* is not the usual one or two days after the trade date but a considerable time afterwards, for instance say six months after trade date. Such a swap might be entered into where one counterparty wanted to fix a hedge or cost of borrowing now, but for a point some time in the future. Typically this would be because the party considered that interest rates would rise or the cost of hedging would rise. The swap rate for a forward-starting swap is calculated in the same way as that for a vanilla swap.

Swaptions

Description

A bank or corporate may enter into an option on a swap, which is known as a *swaption*. The buyer of a swaption has the right but not the obligation to enter into an interest rate swap agreement during the life of the option. The terms of the swaption will specify whether the buyer is the fixed- or floating-rate payer; the seller of the option (*the writer*) becomes the counterparty to the swap if the option is exercised. In the market the convention is that if the buyer has the right to exercise the option as the fixed-rate payer, he has traded a *call swaption*, while if by exercising the buyer of the swaption becomes the floating-rate payer he has bought a *put swaption*. The writer of the swaption is the party to the other leg.

Swaptions are to some extent similar to forward start swaps, but the buyer has the *option* of whether or not to commence payments on the effective date. A bank may purchase a call swaption if it expects interest rates to rise, and will exercise the option if indeed rates do rise as the bank has expected.

A company will use swaptions as part of an interest-rate hedge for a future exposure. For example, assume that a company will be entering into a five-year bank loan in three months' time. Interest on the loan is charged on a floating-rate basis, but the company intend to swap this to a fixed-rate liability after they have entered into the loan. As an added hedge, the company may choose to purchase a swaption that gives it the right to receive Libor and pay a fixed rate, say 10%, for a five-year period beginning in three months' time. When the time comes for the company to take out a swap and exchange its interest-rate liability in three months' time (having entered into the loan), if the five-year swap rate is below 10%, the company will transact the swap in the normal way and the swaption will expire worthless. However, if the five-year swap rate is above 10%, the company will instead exercise the swaption, giving it the right to enter into a five-year swap and paying a fixed rate of 10%. Essentially, the company has taken out protection to ensure that it does not have to pay a fixed rate of more than 10%. Hence swaptions can be used to guarantee a maximum swap rate liability. They are similar to forward-starting swaps, but do not commit a party to enter into a swap on fixed terms. The swaption enables a company to hedge against unfavourable movements in interest rates but also to gain from favourable movements, although there is – of course – a cost associated with this, which is the premium paid for the swaption.

Valuation

Swaptions are typically priced using the Black-Scholes or Black option pricing models. These are used to value a European option on a swap, assuming that the appropriate swap rate at the expiry date of the option is lognormal. Consider a swaption with the following terms:

Strike swap rate	r_n
Maturity	n
Start date	t
Pay basis	F
Principal	M

If we imagine that the actual swap rate on the maturity of the swaption is r, the pay-off from the swaption is given by:

$$\frac{M}{F} \max (r - r_n, 0)$$

The cash flows will be received F times per year for n years, on dates $t_1, t_2, \ldots t_{Fn}$. The Black model for the price of an interest-rate option is shown at (11.18).

$$c = P(0, T)[f_0 N(d_1) - X N(d_2)] \tag{11.18}$$

where

c is the price of the call option;
$P(t, T)$ is the price at time t of a zero-coupon bond maturing at time T;
f is the forward price of the underlying asset with maturity T;
f_0 is the forward price at time zero;
X is the strike price of the option;
σ is the volatility of f;

and where

$$d_1 = \frac{\ln(f_0/X) + \sigma^2 T/2}{\sigma \sqrt{T}}$$

$$d_2 = \frac{\ln(f_0/X) - \sigma^2 T/2}{\sigma \sqrt{T}} = d_1 - \sigma \sqrt{T}.$$

Using equation (11.18), the value of the cash flow received at time t_i is given by (11.19).

$$\frac{M}{F} P(0, t_i)[f_0 N(d_1) - r_n N(d_2)] \tag{11.19}$$

where f_0 is the forward swap rate and r_i is the continuously compounded zero-coupon interest rate for an instrument with a maturity of t_i. Using (11.19) then the total value of the swaption is given by (11.20).

$$PV = \sum_{i=1}^{Fn} \frac{M}{F} P(0, t_i)[f_0 N(d_1) - r_n N(d_2)] \tag{11.20}$$

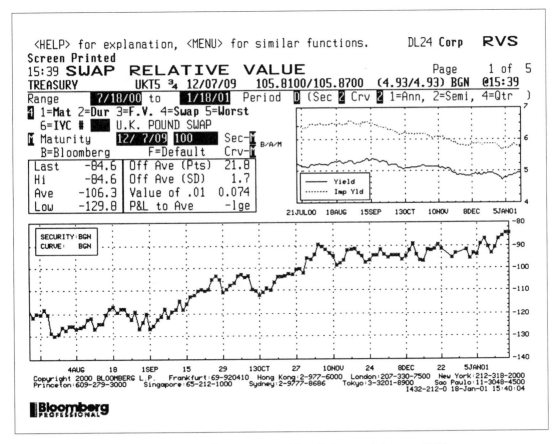

FIGURE 11.3 ∎ Bloomberg chart – gilt versus swap historical spread, January 2001

© Bloomberg L.P. Reproduced with permission

An overview of interest-rate swap applications

In this section we review some of the principal uses of swaps as a hedging tool for bond instruments and also how to hedge a swap book.

Corporate applications

Swaps are part of the over-the-counter (OTC) market and so they can be tailored to suit the particular requirements of the user. It is common for swaps to be structured so that they match particular payment dates, payment frequencies and Libor margins, which may characterize the underlying exposure of the customer. As the market in interest-rate swaps is so large, liquid and competitive, banks are willing to quote rates and structure swaps for virtually all customers, although it may be difficult for smaller customers to obtain competitive piece quotes on notional values below £10 million or £5 million.

Swap applications can be viewed as being one of two main types, asset-linked swaps and liability-linked swaps. Asset-linked swaps are created when the swap is linked to an asset such as a bond in order to change the characteristics of the income stream for investors. Liability-linked swaps are traded when borrowers of funds wish to change the pattern of their cash flows. Of course, just as with repo transactions, the designation of a swap in such terms depends on whose point of view one is looking at the swap. An asset-linked swap hedge is a liability-linked hedge for the counterparty, except in the case of swap market making banks who make two-way quotes in the instruments.

A straightforward application of an interest-rate swap is when a borrower wishes to convert a floating-rate liability into a fixed-rate one, usually in order to remove the exposure to upward moves in interest rates. For instance, a company may wish to fix its financing costs. Let us assume a company currently borrowing money at a floating rate, say six-month Libor +100 basis points fears that interest rates may rise in the remaining three years of its loan. It enters into a three-year semi-annual interest rate swap with a bank, as the fixed-rate payer, paying say 6.75% against receiving six-month Libor. This fixes the company's borrowing costs for three years at 7.75% (7.99% effective annual rate). This is shown in figure 11.4.

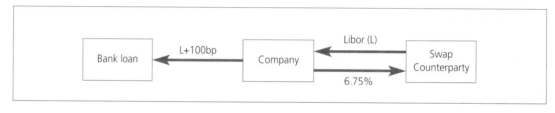

FIGURE 11.4 ■ Changing liability from floating- to fixed-rate

11.1 Liability-linked swap, fixed- to floating- to fixed-rate
exposure

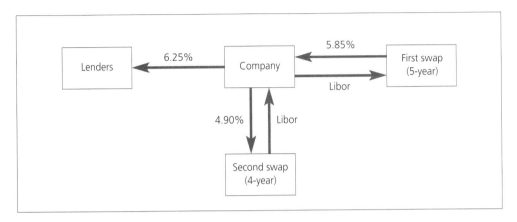

FIGURE 11.5

A corporate borrows for five years at a rate of $6\frac{1}{4}\%$ and shortly after enters into a swap paying floating-rate, so that its net borrowing cost is Libor + 40bps. After one year swap rates have fallen such that the company is quoted four-year swap rates as 4.90–84%. The company decides to switch back into fixed-rate liability in order to take advantage of the lower interest rate environment. It enters into a second swap paying fixed at 4.90% and receiving Libor. The net borrowing cost is now 5.30%. The arrangement is illustrated in figure 11.5. The company has saved 95 basis points on its original borrowing cost, which is the difference between the two swap rates.

Asset-linked swap structures might be required when for example, investors require a fixed interest security when floating-rate assets are available. Borrowers often issue FRNs, the holders of which may prefer to switch the income stream into fixed coupons. As an example, consider a local authority pension fund holding two-year floating-rate gilts. This is an asset of the highest quality, paying Libid minus 12.5bps. The pension fund wishes to swap the cash flows to create a fixed interest asset. It obtains a quote for a tailor-made swap where the floating leg pays Libid, the quote being 5.55–50%. By entering into this swap the pension fund has in place a structure that pays a fixed coupon of 5.375%. This is shown in figure 11.6.

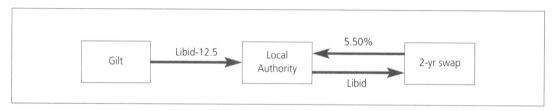

FIGURE 11.6 ■ Transforming floating-rate asset to fixed-rate

Hedging bond instruments using interest-rate swaps

We illustrate here a generic approach to the hedging of bond positions using interest-rate swaps. The bond trader has the option of using other bonds, bond futures or bond options, as well as swaps, when hedging the interest-rate risk exposure of a bond position. However, swaps are particularly efficient instruments to use because they display positive convexity characteristics, that is the increase in value of a swap for a fall in interest rates exceeds the loss in value with a similar magnitude rise in rates. This is exactly the price/yield profile of vanilla bonds.

The primary risk measure we require when hedging using a swap is its present value of a basis point or PVBP.[3] This measures the price sensitivity of the swap for a basis point change in interest rates. The PVBP measure is used to calculate the hedge ratio when hedging a bond position. The PVBP can be given by

$$PVBP = \frac{\text{Change in swap value}}{\text{Rate change in basis points}} \qquad (11.21)$$

which can be written as

$$PVBP = \frac{dS}{dr} \qquad (11.22)$$

Using the basic relationship for the value of a swap, which is viewed as the difference between the values of a fixed coupon bond and equivalent-maturity floating-rate bond (see table 11.1) we can also write

$$PVBP = \frac{d\text{Fixed bond}}{dr} - \frac{d\text{Floating bond}}{dr} \qquad (11.23)$$

which essentially states that the basis point value of the swap is the difference in the basis point values of the fixed-coupon and floating-rate bonds. The value is usually calculated for a notional £1 million of swap. The calculation is based on the duration and modified duration calculations used for bonds[4] and assumes that there is a parallel shift in the yield curve.

---

[3] This is also known as DVBP or dollar value of a basis point in the US market.
[4] See Chapter 2.

Figure 11.7 illustrates how equations (11.22) and (11.23) can be used to obtain the PVBP of a swap. Hypothetical five-year bonds are used in the example. The PVBP for a bond can be obtained using Bloomberg or the MDURATION function on Microsoft Excel. Using either of the two equations above we see that the PVBP of the swap is £425.00. This is shown below.

Calculating the PVBP using (11.22) we have

$$PVBP_{swap} = \frac{dS}{dr} = \frac{4264 - (-4236)}{20} = 425$$

while using (11.23) we obtain the same result using the bond values

$$PVBP_{swap} = PVBP_{fixed} - PVBP_{floating}$$

$$= \frac{1004940 - 995171}{20} - \frac{1000640 - 999371}{20}$$

$$= 488.45 - 63.45$$

$$= 425.00$$

The swap basis point value is lower than that of the five-year fixed-coupon bond, that is £425 compared to £488.45. This is because of the impact of the floating-rate bond risk measure, which reduces the risk exposure of the swap as a whole by £63.45. As a rough rule of thumb, the PVBP of a swap is approximately equal to that of fixed-rate bond that has a maturity similar to the period from the next coupon reset date of the swap through to the maturity date of the swap. This means that a 10-year semi-annual paying swap would have a PVBP close to that of a 9.5-year fixed-rate bond, and a 5.50-year swap would have a PVBP similar to that of a 5-year bond.

Interest rate swap			
Term to maturity	5 years		
Fixed leg	6.50%		
Basis	Semi-annual, act/365		
Floating leg	6-month Libor		
Basis	Semi-annual, act/365		
Nominal amount	£1,000,000		
		Present value £	
	Rate change −10 bps	0 bps	Rate change +10 bps
Fixed coupon bond	1,004,940	1,000,000	995,171
Floating rate bond	1,000,640	1,000,000	999,371
Swap	4,264	0	4,236

FIGURE 11.7 ■ PVBP for interest-rate swap

When using swaps as hedge tools, we bear in mind that over time the PVBP of swaps behave differently to that of bonds. Immediately preceding an interest reset date the PVBP of a swap will be near-identical to that of the same-maturity fixed-rate bond, because the PVBP of a floating-rate bond at this time has essentially nil value. Immediately after the reset date, the swap PVBP will be near-identical to that of a bond that matures at the next reset date. This means that at the point (and this point only) right after the reset the swap PVBP will decrease by the amount of the floating-rate PVBP. In between reset dates the swap PVBP is quite stable, as the effect of the fixed- and floating-rate PVBP changes cancel each other out. Contrast this with the fixed-rate PVBP, which decreases in value over time in stable fashion.[5] This feature is illustrated in figure 11.7. A slight anomaly is that the PVBP of a swap actually increases by a small amount between reset dates; this is because the PVBP of a floating-rate bond decreases at a slightly faster rate than that of the fixed-rate bond during this time.

Hedging bond instruments with interest-rate swaps is conceptually similar to hedging with another bond or with bond futures contracts. If one is holding a long position in a vanilla bond, the hedge requires a long position in the swap: remember that a long posi-

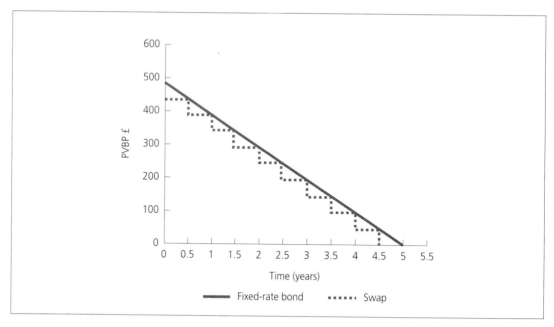

FIGURE 11.8 ■ PVBP of a five-year swap and fixed-rate bond maturity period

[5] This assumes no large-scale sudden yield movements.

tion in a swap is to be paying fixed (and receiving floating). This hedges the receipt of fixed from the bond position. The change in the value of the swap will match the change in value of the bond, only in the opposite direction.[6] The maturity of the swap should match as closely as possible that of the bond. As swaps are OTC contracts, it should be possible to match interest dates as well as maturity dates. If one is short the bond, the hedge is to be short the swap, so the receipt of fixed matches the pay-fixed liability of the short bond position.

The correct nominal amount of the swap to put on is established using the PVBP hedge ratio. This is given as

$$\text{Hedge ratio} = \frac{PVBP_{bond}}{PVBP_{swap}} \tag{11.24}$$

This technique is still used in the market but suffers from the assumption of parallel yield curve shifts and can therefore lead to significant hedging error at times. More advanced techniques are used by banks when hedging books using swaps, which space does not permit any discussion of. Some of these techniques are discussed in the author's forthcoming book on swaps.

SELECTED BIBLIOGRAPHY AND REFERENCES

The swaps market is extensively covered in the academic and practitioner literature. The mother of all swaps books is Das (1994), which contains all one would ever wish to know and is written in a very user-friendly style. Its publication date means that it does not cover the very latest developments, but it is well worth buying. Be warned though, it is a weighty tome. A good general introduction is Decovny (1998), while another accessible and reader-friendly discussion is given in Eales (1995). A superlative overview treatment is given in chapter 14 of Jarrow and Turnbull (2000), and this is a market standard text. Technical aspects are covered in the journal references.

A good account of hedging with swaps can be found in chapter 11 of Fabozzi (1998), which is authored by Shrikant Ramamurthy. For the budding treasury traders amongst you chapter 6 in Gup and Brooks (1993) is a readable introduction to swaps, and asset & liability management.

For the latest on swap trading volumes, and electronic trading on platforms such as *SwapsWire* see the two RISK publications.

---

[6] The change will not be an exact mirror. It is very difficult to establish a precise hedge for a number of reasons, which include differences in day-count bases, maturity mismatches and basis risk.

Bicksler, J., Chen, A., 'An Economic Analysis of Interest Rate Swaps', *Journal of Finance* 41, 3, 1986, pp. 645–655

Brotherton-Ratcliffe, R., Iben, B., 'Yield Curve Applications of Swap Products', in Schwartz, R., Smith, C. (eds), *Advanced Strategies in Financial Risk Management*, New York Institute of Finance, 1993

Das, S., *Swaps and Financial Derivatives*, 2nd edition, IFR Publishing 1994

Decovny, S., *Swaps*, 2nd edition, FT Prentice Hall 1998

Dunbar, N., 'Swaps volumes see euro wane', *Risk*, September 2000

Eales, B., *Financial Risk Management*, McGraw Hill 1995, chapter 3

Fabozzi, F. (ed.), *Perspectives on Interest Rate Risk Management for Money Managers and Traders*, FJF Associates 1998

Gup, B., Brooks, R., *Interest Rate Risk Management*, Irwin 1993

Henna, P., *Interest-rate Risk Management using Futures and Swaps*, Probus 1991

International Swaps and Derivatives Association, *Code of Standard Working, Assumptions and Provisions for Swaps*, New York, 1991

Jarrow, R., Turnbull, S., *Derivative Securities*, 2nd edition, South-Western 2000

Khan, M., 'Online platforms battle for business', *Risk*, September 2000

Kolb, R., *Futures, Options and Swaps*, 3rd edition, Blackwell 2000

Li, A., Raghavan, V.R., 'LIBOR-In-Arrears Swaps', *Journal of Derivatives* 3, Spring 1996, pp. 44–48

Lindsay, R., 'High Wire Act', *Risk*, August 2000

Marshall, J., Kapner, K., *Understanding Swap Finance*, South-Western Publishing 1990

Turnbull, S., 'Swaps: A Zero Sum Game', *Financial Management* 16, Spring 1987, pp. 15–21.

CHAPTER 12

An introduction to credit derivatives and their application in fixed income markets

Unless purchasing what are considered *default-free* instruments such as US Treasuries, Bunds or Gilts, a key risk run by an investor in a bond security is *credit risk*, the risk that the issuer of debt will default on the loan. This might be a default on the servicing of the loans (the coupon payments) or on the principal itself. To meet the need of investors to hedge this risk, instruments known as credit derivatives were introduced. Credit derivatives are a relatively recent innovation, having been introduced in significant volumes only in the mid-1990s. They are financial instruments originally designed to protect banks and other institutions against losses arising from *credit events*. A succinct definition would be that they are instruments designed to lay off or take on credit risk. Since their inception, they have been used to trade credit and for speculative purposes and as hedging instruments.

In this chapter we provide a description of the main types of credit derivatives and how (and why) they are used by participants in the fixed income markets.

Introduction

In an excellent book entitled *Interest Rate Risk Management*,[1] in the chapter on interest-rate swaps, the authors discuss the credit risk of swaps and note that such risk, unlike interest-rate risk, cannot be hedged. The book dates from 1992, and serves to illustrate the rapid growth of the market in credit risk trading, as by 1995/1996 there was a liquid market in instruments designed for just this purpose: hedging credit risk. Credit derivatives allow investors to manage the credit risk exposure of their portfolios or asset holdings, in essence by providing insurance against a deterioration in credit quality of the borrowing

---

[1] On page 140. This book is written in particularly accessible style and is highly recommended. It is an excellent introduction to the subject, particularly for those involved in asset & liability management (ALM) or working on a bank liquidity desk. Its approach is ideal for newcomers to the market. The authors are Benton Gup and Robert Brooks (Irwin 1993), and this author personally would be first in the queue for a second edition!

entity.[2] If there is a technical default by the borrower[3] and the bond is marked down in the market, or an actual default of the loan itself, the losses suffered by the investor can be recouped in part or in full through the payout made by the credit derivative.

Credit risk

Credit risk is the risk that a borrowing entity will default on its loan, either through inability to maintain the interest servicing on the loan or because of bankruptcy or insolvency leading to inability to repay the principal itself. When technical or actual default occurs, bondholders suffer a loss as the value of their asset declines, and the potential greatest loss is that of the entire asset. The extent of credit risk fluctuates as the fortunes of borrowers changes in line with their own economic circumstances and macroeconomic conditions. The magnitude of risk is usually encapsulated by a firm's credit rating, a formal grading assigned to borrowers in the capital markets by firms such as Standard & Poor's, Moody's and FitchIBCA. These ratings agencies undertake a formal analysis of the borrower, after which a rating is announced. The issues considered by the agencies include:

- the financial position of the firm itself, for example its balance sheet position and anticipated cash flows and revenues;
- other firm-specific issues such as the quality of the management and succession planning;
- an assessment of the firm's ability to meet scheduled interest and principal payments, both in its domestic and foreign currencies;
- the outlook for the industry as whole, and competition within it;
- general assessments for the domestic economy.

Appendix 12.1 illustrates the credit ratings awarded by the main rating agencies.

Another measure of credit risk is the credit risk premium, which is the difference between yields on the same-currency government benchmark bonds and corporate bonds. This premium is the compensation required by investors for holding bonds that are not default-free. The credit premium required will fluctuate as individual firms and sectors are perceived to offer improved or worsening credit risk, and the general health of the economy improves. Figures 12.1 and 12.2 illustrate this variability in credit spread premium in the sterling market. The first figure shows the change in yields for ten-year bonds rated AAA, AA and A against the benchmark gilt yield during 1998–2000. The second graph shows spreads for AAA bonds and interbank swaps, also of ten-year maturity.

---

[2] The simplest credit derivative works exactly like an insurance policy, with regular premiums paid by the protection-buyer to the protection-seller, and a payout in the event of a specified credit event.
[3] A technical default is a delay in timely payment of the coupon, or non-payment of the coupon altogether.

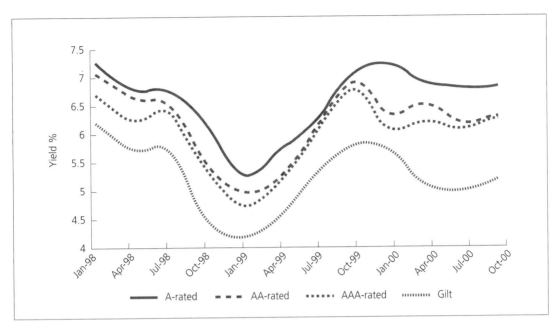

FIGURE 12.1 ▪ Ten-year sterling bond yields

Source: Bank of England and Bloomberg

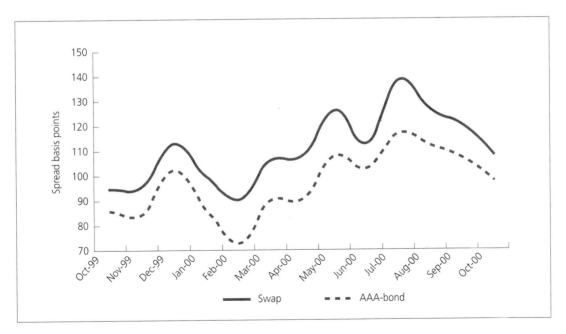

FIGURE 12.2 ▪ Ten-year sterling credit spread

Source: Bank of England and Bloomberg

Credit risk and credit derivatives

Credit derivatives are financial contracts designed to reduce or eliminate credit risk exposure by providing insurance against losses suffered due to credit events. A payout under a credit derivative is triggered by a credit event. As banks define default in different terms, the terms under which a credit derivative is executed usually include a specification of what constitutes a credit event. Typically this can be:

■ bankruptcy or insolvency of the reference asset obligor;

■ a financial restructuring, for example occasioned under administration or as required under US bankruptcy protection;

■ technical default, for example the non-payment of interest or coupon when it falls due;

■ a change in credit spread payable by the obligor above a specified maximum level;

■ a downgrade in credit rating below a specified minimum level.

The principle behind credit derivatives is fairly straightforward. Investors desire exposure to non-default-free sovereign debt because of the higher returns this offers. However, such exposure brings with it concomitant credit risk. This can be managed with credit derivatives. At the same time, the exposure itself can be taken on synthetically if for instance, there are compelling reasons why a cash market position cannot be put on. This is another avenue for the use of credit derivatives. The flexibility of credit derivatives provides users with a number of advantages. As they are OTC products they can be tailor-made to meet specific requirements.

A user of credit derivatives may be any institution that has an exposure to or desires an exposure to credit risk. This includes investment banks and commercial banks, insurance companies, corporates, fund managers, and hedge funds.

Although we have been speaking about credit derivatives as instruments that may be used to manage risk exposure inherent in a corporate or non-AAA sovereign bond portfolio, they may also be used to manage the credit risk of commercial loan books. Indeed it was in this area that credit derivatives were first used. The intense competition amongst commercial banks, combined with rapid disintermediation, meant that banks were forced to evaluate their lending policy, with a view to improving profitability and return on capital. The use of credit derivatives assisted banks with restructuring their businesses, because they allowed banks to repackage and parcel out credit risk, while retaining assets on balance sheet (when required) and thus maintain client relationships. As the instruments isolated certain aspects of credit risk from the underlying loan or bond and transferred them to another entity, it became possible to separate the ownership and management of credit risk from the other features of ownership associated with the assets in question. This means that illiquid assets such as bank loans, and illiquid bonds, can have their credit risk exposures transferred; the bank owning the assets can protect against credit loss even if it cannot transfer the assets themselves.

Some of the advantages of credit derivatives include:

■ the issuer of the original debt (or the obligor of the original loan), known as the *reference entity*, is not required to be a party to the credit risk transfer process (the credit derivative) and in fact is usually not even aware of the transaction; this maintains the client relationship;

■ the credit derivative can be tailor-made to meet the specific requirements of the entity buying the risk protection, as opposed to the liquidity or term of the underlying loan;

■ in theory credit derivatives can be 'sold short' without risk of a liquidity or delivery squeeze, as it is a specific credit risk that is being traded. In the cash market it is not possible to 'sell short' a bank loan, but a credit derivative can be used to establish synthetically the economic effect of such a position;

■ as credit derivatives isolate credit risk from other factors such as client relationships and interest rate risk, they introduce a formal pricing mechanism to price credit issues only. This means a market can develop in credit only, allowing still more efficient pricing, and it becomes possible to model a term structure of credit rates;

■ they are off-balance sheet instruments[4] and, as such, incorporate tremendous flexibility and leverage, exactly like other financial derivatives. For instance, bank loans are not particularly attractive investment for certain investors because of the administration required in managing and servicing a loan portfolio. However, an exposure to bank loans and their associated return can be achieved by say, a total return swap while simultaneously avoiding the administrative costs of actually owning the assets. Hence credit derivatives allow investors access to specific credits while allowing banks access to further distribution for bank loan credit risk.

Why banks use credit derivatives

Credit derivatives can be an important instrument for bond portfolio managers as well as commercial banks, who wish to increase the liquidity of their portfolios, gain from any relative value arising from credit pricing anomalies, and enhance returns. Banks use credit derivatives for a number of reasons. Some of these are summarized below.

---

[4] When credit derivatives are embedded in certain fixed income products, such as structured notes and credit-linked notes, they are of course then part of an on-balance sheet transaction.

Diversifying the credit portfolio

A bank may wish to take on credit exposure by providing credit protection on assets that it already owns, in return for a fee. This enhances income on their portfolio. They may sell credit derivatives to enable non-banking clients to gain credit exposures, if these clients do not wish to purchase the assets directly. In this respect, the bank performs a credit intermediation role.

Reducing credit exposure

Another use of credit derivatives is to reduce credit exposure either for an individual asset or a sectoral concentration, by buying a credit default swap. This may be desirable for assets in their portfolio that cannot be sold for relationship or tax reasons.

Acting as a credit derivatives market maker

A bank may wish to set itself up as a market maker in credit derivatives, that is becoming a credit trader. In this case the trader may or may not hold the reference assets directly, depending on their appetite for risk and the liquidity of the market enabling them to offset derivative contracts as and when required.

Credit derivatives

In this section we review some of the most commonly encountered credit derivative instruments.

Credit default swap

The most common credit derivative, and the simplest, is the *credit default swap, credit swap* or *default swap*. This is a bilateral contract in which a periodic fixed fee or a one-off premium is paid to a *protection seller*, in return for which the seller will make a payment on the occurrence of a specified credit event. The fee is usually quoted as a basis point fee of the nominal value. The swap can refer to a single asset, known as the reference asset or underlying asset, or a basket of assets. The default payment can be paid in whatever way suits the protection buyer or both counterparties. For example, it may be linked to the change in price of the reference asset or another specified asset, it may be fixed at a pre-determined recovery rate, or it may be in the form of actual delivery of the reference asset at a specified price. However it is structured, the credit default swap enables one party to transfer its credit exposure to another party. Banks may use default swaps to trade sovereign and corporate credit spreads without trading the actual assets themselves; for example someone who has gone long a default swap will gain (the protection buyer) if the reference asset obligor suffers a rating downgrade or defaults, and can sell the default swap at a profit if he can find a buyer counterparty. This is because the cost of protection on the reference asset will have increased as a result of the credit event. The original buyer of the default swap need never have owned a bond issued by the reference asset obligor.

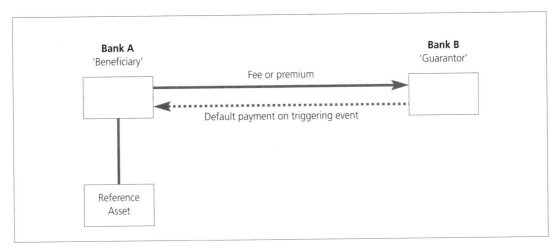

FIGURE 12.3 ■ Credit default swap

The maturity does not have to match the maturity of the reference asset and in most cases does not. On default the swap is terminated and default payment by the protection seller or guarantor is calculated and handed over. The guarantor may have the asset delivered to him and pay the nominal value, or may cash settle the swap contract.

Credit options

Credit options are also bilateral OTC financial contracts. Like other options, a credit option is a contract designed to meet specific hedging or speculative requirements of an entity, which may purchase or sell the option to meet its objectives. A credit call option gives the buyer the right without the obligation to purchase the underlying credit-sensitive asset, or a credit spread, at a specified price and specified time (or period of time). A credit put option gives the buyer the right – without the obligation – to sell the underlying credit-sensitive asset or credit spread. By purchasing credit options, banks and other institutions can take a view on credit spread movements for the cost of the option premium only, without recourse to actual loans issued by an obligor. The writer of credit options seeks to earn fee income.

In many ways, credit options are similar to equity options. A *call* option written on a stock grants the purchaser the right but not the obligation to purchase a specified amount of the stock at a set price and time. A credit option can be used by bond investors to hedge against a decline in the price of specified bonds, in the event of a credit event such as a ratings downgrade. The investor would purchase an option whose payoff profile is a function of the credit quality of the bond, so that a loss on the bond position is offset by the payout from the option.

Again just as with more conventional options, there are both *vanilla* credit options and *exotic* credit options. The vanilla credit option[5] is just that: it grants the purchaser the right but not the obligation to buy (or sell if a *put* option) an asset or credit spread at a specified price (the *strike* price) for a specified period of time up to the maturity of the option. A credit option allows a market participant to take a view on credit only, and no other exposure such as interest rates. As an example, consider an investor who believes that a particular credit spread, which can be that of a specific entity or the average for a sector (such as 'all AA-rated sterling corporates'), will widen over the next six months. The investor can buy a six-month call option on the relevant credit spread, for which a one-off premium (the price of the option) is paid. If the credit spread indeed does widen beyond the strike during the six months, the option will be in-the-money and the investor will gain. If not, the investor's loss is limited to the premium paid.[6]

Exotic credit options are options that have one or more of their parameters changed from the vanilla norm; the same terms are used as in other option markets. Thus a barrier credit option would specify a credit-event that would *trigger* (activate) the option or inactivate it. A digital credit option would have a payout profile that would be fixed, irrespective of how much in-the-money it was on expiry, and a zero payout if out-of-the-money. The variations are virtually endless and so it is prudent to stop here (see footnote 6).

Credit linked note

Another type of credit derivative is the *credit-linked note*. These exist in a number of forms, but all of them contain a link between the return payable on them and the credit-related performance of the underlying asset. A standard credit-linked note is a loan or security, usually issued by an investment-graded entity, that has an interest payment and fixed maturity structure similar to a vanilla bond. The performance of the note, however, including the maturity value, is linked to the performance of specified underlying assets as well as that of the issuing entity. The notes are often used by borrowers to hedge against credit risk, and by investors to enhance the yield received on their holdings. Essentially, credit-linked notes are hybrid instruments that combine a credit derivative with a vanilla bond. The credit-linked note pays regular coupons, although the credit

---

[5] Sometimes referred to as the *standard* credit option.

[6] Depending on whether the option is an American or European one will determine whether it can be exercised before its expiry date or on its expiry date only. For a selection of references that contain all that one would ever wish to know about options (and a lot more besides) see the bibliography at the start of Part III.

derivative element is usually set to allow the issuer to decrease the principal amount if a credit event occurs.

For example, consider an issuer of credit cards that wants to fund its (credit card) loan portfolio via an issue of debt. In order to reduce the credit risk of the loans, it issues a two-year credit-linked note. The principal amount of the bond is 100% as usual, and it pays a coupon of 7.50%, which is 200 basis points above the two-year benchmark. If, however, the incidence of bad debt amongst credit card holders exceeds 10%,[7] the note holders will only receive back £85 per £100 nominal. The credit card issuer has in effect purchased a credit option that lowers its liability should it suffer from a specified credit event, which in this case is an above-expected incidence of bad debts. The credit card bank has issued the credit-linked note to reduce its credit exposure, in the form of this particular type of credit insurance. If the incidence of bad debts is low, the note is redeemed at par. However, if there is a high incidence of such debt, the bank will only have to repay a part of its loan liability.

Why would investors wish to purchase such a note? Because the coupon paid on it will be above what the credit card bank would pay on a vanilla bond it issued, and presumably higher than many other investments in the market. In addition, such notes are usually priced below par on issue. Assuming the notes are eventually redeemed at par, investors will also have realized a substantial capital gain.

An accessible introduction to credit-linked notes is given in Kasapi (1999).

The total return swap

A *total return swap* (TRS), sometimes known as a *total rate of return swap* or *TR swap*, is an agreement between two parties that exchanges the total return from a financial asset between them. This is designed to transfer the credit risk from one party to the other. It is one of the principal instruments used by banks and other financial instruments to manage their credit risk exposure, and as such is a credit derivative.

One definition of a TRS is given in Francis (1999), which states:

> 'A total return swap is a swap agreement in which the *total return* [author's italics] of a bank loan(s) or credit-sensitive security(s) is exchanged for some other cash flow, usually tied to LIBOR or some other loan(s) or credit-sensitive security(s).'
> (*Francis* et al., *1999, p. 29*)

In some versions of a TRS, the actual underlying asset is actually sold to the counterparty, with a corresponding swap transaction agreed alongside; in other versions there is no physical change of ownership of the underlying asset. The TRS trade itself can be to any term to

---

[7] Known as *delinquent* cardholders.

maturity, that is, it need not match the maturity of the underlying security. In a TRS, the total return from the underlying asset is paid over to the counterparty in return for a fixed or floating cash flow. This makes it slightly different from other credit derivatives, as the payments between counterparties to a TRS are connected to changes in the market value of the underlying asset, as well as changes resulting from the occurrence of a credit event.

Figure 12.4 illustrates a generic TR swap. The two counterparties are labelled as banks, but the party termed 'Bank A' may be another financial institution, including cash-rich institutions such as insurance companies and hedge funds. In figure 12.4, Bank A has contracted to pay the 'total return' on a specified reference asset, while simultaneously receiving a Libor-based return from Bank B. The reference or underlying asset can be a bank loan such as a corporate loan, or a sovereign or corporate bond. The total return payments from Bank A includes the interest payments on the underlying loan as well as any appreciation in the market value of the asset. Bank B will pay the Libor-based return; it will also pay any difference if there is a depreciation in the price of the asset. The economic effect is as if Bank B owned the underlying asset, so TR swaps are synthetic loans or securities. A significant feature is that Bank A will usually hold the underlying asset on its balance sheet, so that if this asset was originally on Bank B's balance sheet, this is a means by which the latter can have the asset removed from its balance sheet for the term of the TR swap.[8] If we assume that Bank A has access to Libor funding, it will receive a spread on this from Bank B. Under the terms of the swap, Bank B will pay the difference between the initial market value and any depreciation, so it is sometimes termed the 'guarantor' while Bank A is the 'beneficiary'.

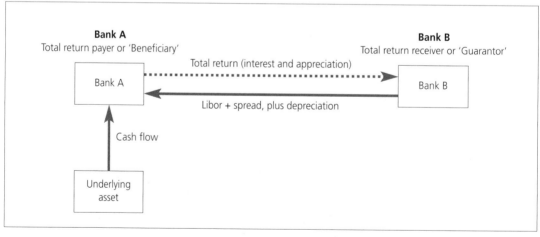

FIGURE 12.4 ■ Total return swap

---

[8] Although it is common for the receiver of the Libor-based payments to have the reference asset on its balance sheet, this is not always the case.

The total return on the underlying asset is the interest payments and any change in the market value if it is an appreciation. The value of an appreciation may be cash settled, or alternatively there may be physical delivery of the reference asset on maturity of the swap, in return for a payment of the initial asset value by the total return 'receiver'. The maturity of the TR swap need not be identical to that of the reference asset, and in fact it is rare for it to do so.

The swap element of the trade will usually pay on a quarterly or semi-annual basis, with the underlying asset being revalued or *marked-to-market* on the re-fixing dates. The asset price is usually obtained from an independent third party source such as Bloomberg or Reuters, or as the average of a range of market quotes. If the *obligor* of the reference asset defaults, the swap may be terminated immediately, with a net present value payment changing hands according to what this value is, or it may be continued with each party making appreciation or depreciation payments as appropriate. This second option is only available if there is a market for the asset, which is unlikely in the case of a bank loan. If the swap is terminated, each counterparty is liable to the other for accrued interest plus any appreciation or depreciation of the asset. Commonly under the terms of the trade, the guarantor bank has the option to purchase the underlying asset from the beneficiary bank, and then dealing directly with loan defaulter.

There are a number of reasons why banks and financial institutions may wish to enter into TR swap arrangements. One of these is to reduce or remove credit risk. Using TR swaps as a credit derivative instrument, a party can remove exposure to an asset without having to sell it. In a vanilla TR swap, the total return payer retains rights to the reference asset, although in some cases servicing and voting rights may be transferred. The total return receiver gains an exposure to the reference asset without having to pay out the cash proceeds that would be required to purchase it. As the maturity of the swap rarely matches that of the asset, the swap receiver may gain from the positive funding or *carry* that derives from being able to roll over short-term funding of a longer-term asset.[9] The total return payer on the other hand benefits from protection against market and credit risk for a specified period of time, without having to liquidate the asset itself. On maturity of the swap, the total return payer may reinvest the asset if it continues to own it, or it may sell the asset in the open market. Thus the instrument may be considered a synthetic repo. A TR swap agreement entered into as a credit derivative is a means by which banks can take on unfunded off-balance sheet credit exposure. Higher-rated banks that have access to Libid funding can benefit by funding on-balance sheet assets that are credit protected through a credit derivative such as a TR swap, assuming the net spread of asset income over credit protection premium is positive.

---

[9] This assumes a positively-sloping yield curve.

A TR swap conducted as a synthetic repo is usually undertaken to effect the temporary removal of assets from the balance sheet. This may be desirable for a number of reasons, for example if the institution is due to be analyzed by credit rating agencies or if the annual external audit is to fall due shortly. Another reason a bank may wish to temporarily remove lower credit-quality assets from its balance sheet is if it is in danger of breaching capital limits in between the quarterly return periods. In this case, as the return period approaches, lower quality assets may be removed from the balance sheet by means of a TR swap, which is set to mature after the return period has passed.

Banks have employed a number of methods to price credit derivatives and TR swaps. Space does not permit an in-depth discussion of these techniques although interested readers may wish to refer to some of the publications listed in the bibliography. Essentially the pricing of credit derivatives is linked to that of other instruments; however, the main difference between credit derivatives and other off-balance sheet products such as equity, currency or bond derivatives is that the latter can be priced and hedged with reference to the underlying asset, which can be problematic when applied to credit derivatives. Credit products pricing uses statistical data on likelihood of default, probability of payout, level of risk tolerance and a pricing model. The basic ingredients of a TR swap are that one party 'funds' an underlying asset and transfers the total return of the asset to another party, in return for a (usually) floating return that is a spread to Libor. This spread is a function of:

- the credit rating of the swap counterparty;
- the amount and value of the reference asset;
- the credit quality of the reference asset;
- the funding costs of the beneficiary bank;
- any required profit margin;
- the capital charge associated with the TR swap.

The TR swap counterparties must consider a number of risk factors associated with the transaction, which include:

- the probability that the TR beneficiary may default while the reference asset has declined in value;
- the reference asset obligor defaults, followed by default of the TR swap receiver before payment of the depreciation has been made to the payer or 'provider'.

The first risk measure is a function of the probability of default by the TR swap receiver and the market volatility of the reference asset, while the second risk is related to the joint probability of default of both factors as well as the recovery probability of the asset.

We have alluded to a number of uses of the TR swap. One other application follows. Assume that a bond trader believes that a particular bond that is not currently on his book is about to decline in price. To reflect this view the trader may do one of the following:

■ Sell the bond in the market and cover the resulting short position in repo. The cash flow out is the coupon on the bond, with capital gain if the bond falls in price. Assume that the repo rate is floating, say Libor plus a spread. However, the trader must be aware of the funding costs of the trade, so that unless the bond can be covered in repo at *general collateral* rates,[10] the funding will be at a loss. The yield on the bond must also be lower than the Libor plus spread received in the repo.

■ As an alternative, the trader may enter into a TR swap in which he pays the total return on the bond and receives Libor plus a spread. If the bond yield exceeds the Libor spread, the funding will be negative, however the trade will gain if the trader's view is proved correct and the bond falls in price by a sufficient amount. If the breakeven funding cost (which the bond must exceed as it falls in value) is lower in the TR swap, this method will be used rather than the repo approach. This is more likely if the bond is special.

Total return swaps are increasingly used as synthetic repo instruments, most commonly by investors that wish to purchase the credit exposure of an asset without purchasing the asset itself. This is conceptually similar to what happened when interest-rate swaps were introduced, which enabled banks and other financial institutions to trade interest-rate risk without borrowing or lending cash funds.

Under a TR swap, an asset such as a bond position may be removed from the balance sheet. In order to avoid adverse impact on regular internal and external capital and credit exposure reporting, a bank may use TR swaps to reduce the amount of lower-quality assets on the balance sheet. This can be done by entering into a short-term TR swap with say, a two-week term that straddles the reporting date. Bonds are removed from the balance sheet if they are part of a sale plus TR swap transaction. This is because legally the bank selling the asset is not required to repurchase bonds from the swap counterparty, nor is the total return payer obliged to sell the bonds back to the counterparty (or indeed sell the bonds at all on maturity of the TR swap).

Selected investment applications

In this section we briefly introduce some typical uses of credit derivatives and applications for bond investment managers.

---

[10] That is, the bond cannot be *special*.

Capital structure arbitrage

A capital structure arbitrage describes an arrangement whereby investors exploit mispricing between the yields received on two different loans by the same issuer. Assume that the reference entity has both a commercial bank loan and a subordinated bond issue outstanding, but that the former pays Libor plus 330 basis points while the latter pays Libor plus 230 basis points. An investor enters into a total return swap in which it effectively is purchasing the bank loan and selling short the bond. The nominal amounts will be at a ratio, for argument's sake let us say 2:1, as the bonds will be more price-sensitive to changes in credit status than the loans.

The trade is illustrated at figure 12.5. The investor receives the 'total return' on the bank loan, while simultaneously paying the return on the bond in addition to Libor plus 30 basis points, which is the price of the TR swap. The swap generates a net spread of 175 basis points, given by $[(100\ bps \times \frac{1}{2}) + (250\ bps \times \frac{1}{2})]$.

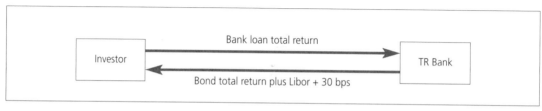

FIGURE 12.5 ■ Total return swap in capital structure arbitrage

Exposure to market sectors

Investors can use credit derivatives to gain exposure to sectors which, for various reasons they do not wish to enter into a cash market transaction for. This can be achieved with an *index* swap, which is similar to a TR swap, with one counterparty paying a total return that is linked to an external reference index. The other party pays a Libor-linked coupon or the total return of another index. Indices that are used might include the government bond index, an high-yield index or a technology stocks index. Assume that an investor believes that the bank loan market will outperform the mortgage-backed bond sector; to reflect this view, the investor enters into an index swap in which he pays the total return of the mortgage index and receives the total return of the bank loan index.

Another possibility is synthetic exposure to foreign currency and money markets. Again we assume that an investor has a particular view on an emerging market currency. If the investor wishes, he can purchase a short-term (say one-year) domestic coupon-bearing note, whose principal redemption is linked to a currency factor. This factor is based on the ratio of the spot value of the foreign currency on issue to that on maturity.

Such currency-linked notes can also structured so that they provide an exposure to sovereign credit risk.

Credit spreads

Credit derivatives can be used to trade credit spreads. Imagine an investor has negative views on a certain emerging market government bond credit spread relative to UK gilts. The simplest way to reflect this view would be to go long with a credit default swap on the sovereign, paying X basis points. Assuming that the investor's view is correct and the sovereign bonds decrease in price as their credit spread widens, the premium payable on the credit swap will increase. The investor's swap can then be sold into the market at this higher premium.

Pricing

A considerable amount of research has been undertaken into credit derivative pricing. Some readable articles are noted in the bibliography. Here we introduce some basic issues.

Asset swap pricing

It is common to see credit default swaps priced using this method, especially by risk management departments who are seeking independently to price such swaps held on a credit trader's book.

A *par asset swap* typically combines the sale of an asset such as a fixed-rate corporate bond to a counterparty, at par and with no interest accrued, with an interest-rate swap. The coupon on the bond is paid in return for Libor, plus a spread if necessary. This spread is the asset swap spread and is the price of the asset swap. In effect, the asset swap allows market participants that pay Libor-based funding to receive the asset swap spread. This spread is a function of the credit risk of the underlying bond asset, which is why it in effect becomes the cornerstone of the price payable on a credit default swap written on that reference asset.

The pricing essentially is:

Asset swap spread = Asset spread over benchmark – interest rate swap spread

The asset spread over the benchmark is simply the bond (asset) redemption yield over that of the government benchmark. The interest-rate swap spread reflects the cost involved in converting fixed-coupon benchmark bonds into a floating-rate coupon during the life of the asset (or default swap), and is based on the swap rate for that maturity.

Credit spread pricing models

Practitioners increasingly model credit risk as they do interest rates and use spread models to price associated derivatives. For example, the Heath-Jarrow-Morton approach (see Chapter 4) has been used, modelling interest-rate risk, default risk and recovery risk.[11] However, spread models do not split the spread elements into default risk and recovery risk, but model the spread as a whole. For example Das (1999) has noted that (12.1) may be used to model credit spreads,

$$ds = k\,(\theta - s)dt + \sigma\,\sqrt{s}dZ \tag{12.1}$$

where

- s is the credit spread;
- k is the mean reversion rate;
- θ is the mean of the spread;
- σ is the volatility.

The standard Brownian motion or Weiner process is indicated as usual by dZ. However, the reader can see that under this approach it would be possible to price credit options in the same way as other option products, modelling the credit spread rather than say, the interest rate. For further information see the bibliography references at the end of this chapter.

---

[11] This is the rate of recovery on a defaulted loan. Bonds rarely descend to 0 in price in the event of default; it is always assumed that there is some residual recovery value still available.

Appendix 12.1: Corporate bond credit ratings

FitchIBCA	Moody's	S&P	Summary description
Investment grade			
AAA	Aaa	AAA	Gilt edged, prime, maximum safety, lowest risk, and when sovereign borrower considered 'default-free'
AA+	Aa1	AA+	
AA	Aa2	AA	High-grade, high credit quality
AA–	Aa3	AA–	
A+	A1	A+	
A	A2	A	Upper-medium grade
A–	A3	A–	
BBB+	Baa1	BBB+	
BBB	Baa2	BBB	Lower-medium grade
BBB-	Baa3	BBB-	
Non-investment grade, speculative grade			
BB+	Ba1	BB+	
BB	Ba2	BB	Low grade; speculative
BB–	Ba3	BB–	
B+	B1		
B	B	B	Highly speculative
B–	B3		
Predominantly speculative, substantial risk or in default			
CCC+		CCC+	
CCC	Caa	CCC	Substantial risk, in poor standing
CC	Ca	CC	May be in default, very speculative
C	C	C	Extremely speculative
		CI	Income bonds only – no interest being paid
DDD			
DD			Default
D		D	

SELECTED BIBLIOGRAPHY AND REFERENCES

Given the relatively recent introduction of this product, there is a surprisingly rich literature on credit derivatives and their applications. Satyajit Das (1997) is an excellent treatment of the subject and strongly recommended, as is Francis *et al.* (1999), which is a high-quality and readable account, with contributions from a number of experienced market practitioners.

The journal articles cited are accessible technical treatises on pricing and valuation issues, and default rates and correlations.

Bessis, J., *Risk Management in Banking*, John Wiley & Sons 1998, pp. 17–18

Crosbie. P., 'Modelling Default Risk', in *Credit Derivatives: Key Issues*, British Bankers Association 1997

Das, Sanjiv, 'Credit Risk Derivatives', *Journal of Derivatives*, Spring 1995, pp. 7–23

Das, Satyajut, *Credit Derivatives: Products, Applications and Pricing*, Wiley 1997

Francis, J., Frost, J., Whittaker, J.G., *The Handbook of Credit Derivatives*, McGraw-Hill 1999

Das, Sanjiv, Tufano, Peter, 'Pricing Credit Sensitive Debt when Interest Rates, Credit Ratings and Credit Spreads are Stochastic', *Journal of Financial Engineering* (5), 1996, pp. 161–198

Jarrow, R., Turnbull, S., 'Credit Risk', in Alexander, C. (ed.), *Handbook of Risk Management and Analysis*, Wiley 1996

Kasapi, A., *Mastering Credit Derivatives*, FT Prentice Hall 1999, chapter 4

Longstaff, F., Schwartz, E., 'Valuing Credit Derivatives', *Journal of Fixed Income*, June 1995, pp. 6–14

Lucas, D., 'Default Correlation and Credit Analysis', *Journal of Fixed Income*, June 1995, pp. 32–41

Pierides, Y., 'The Pricing of Credit Risk Derivatives', *Journal of Economic Dynamics and Control*, volume 5, 1997, pp. 1579–1611

Whittaker, G., Frost, J., 'An Introduction to Credit Derivatives', *Journal of Lending and Credit Risk Management*, May 1997, pp. 15–25

Whittaker, G., Kumar, S., 'Credit Derivatives: A Primer', in Dattatreya, R. (ed.), *Handbook of Fixed Income Derivatives*, Probus 1996

Part IV

Selected market trading considerations

In the last part of this book, which consists of only a single chapter, we present some insights on trading put together by the author during his time working as a gilt-edged market maker and sterling bond proprietary trader. Some sections are based on previously unpublished articles. The entire chapter has been revised and updated for this book.

The topics covered include implied spot yields and market zero-coupon yields, yield curve spread trading and butterfly trading. There are also some observations on the behaviour of the gilt strip market since its introduction in December 1997.

CHAPTER 13

Selected market trading considerations

This chapter examines a number of issues relevant to market participants in the fixed income markets. It is based primarily on unpublished articles written by the author during the time he was working with ABN Amro Hoare Govett in the UK gilt market, with certain sections updated for this book. As it is based on government trading experience, the analysis is confined to generic bonds that are default-free. There is no consideration of factors that would apply to corporate bonds, asset- and mortgage-backed bonds, convertibles and other non-vanilla securities, and issues such as credit risk or prepayment risk.

The chapter considers redemption yield and duration, followed by observations on the implied spot rate and market zero-coupon yields, relative value trading and butterfly trades.

Practical uses of redemption yield and duration

The drawbacks of the traditional gross redemption yield (henceforth referred to simply as 'yield') and duration measures for bond analysis are well documented. That different bonds, even vanilla government securities, can have their yield measured in a number of ways hints, however, at the lack of a satisfactory acceptable measure of return. When assessing the opportunities available in a market, investors will often use the market convention for yield in their analysis. However, the different methods available to calculate yield mean that the comparison of rates of return for different bonds becomes problematic (for example, see figure 13.1(a) and (b) for the alternative yield measures available for a US Treasury security and a UK gilt on the Bloomberg 'YA' page). Duration is another measure that can be defined in more than one way, again making comparison between different bonds an issue.

In this section we look at how the problems inherent in using yield and duration can be mitigated, and how the analysis should proceed when undertaking this.

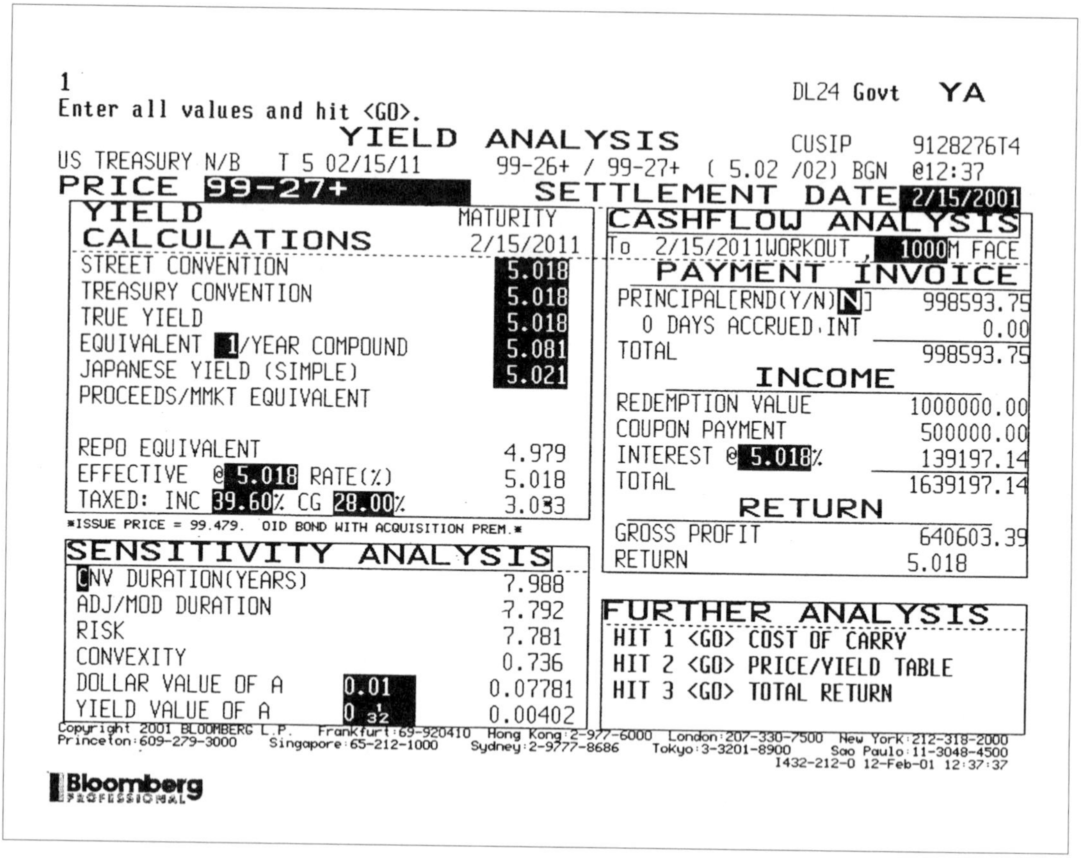

FIGURE 13.1a ■ Yield calculations for US Treasury security on Bloomberg 'YA' page

© Bloomberg L.P. Reproduced with permission

The concept of yield

Ideally the *yield* of an instrument should measure the return achieved from holding it; this would make it a function of the value of the initial investment, the period of the investment and the value of the matured investment. If investment income received during the period is capitalized, this should also be captured by the yield measure, so that we are measuring compounded interest. Under these properties, the yield on a simple instrument such as a T-bill can be defined as follows.

In the sterling market the fixed income interest basis is semi-annual. With this in mind, consider a T-bill with a maturity of m days and a price of P. The true yield rm of the bill is given by

$$P = \frac{100}{\left(1 + \frac{1}{2} rm\right)^n} \tag{13.1}$$

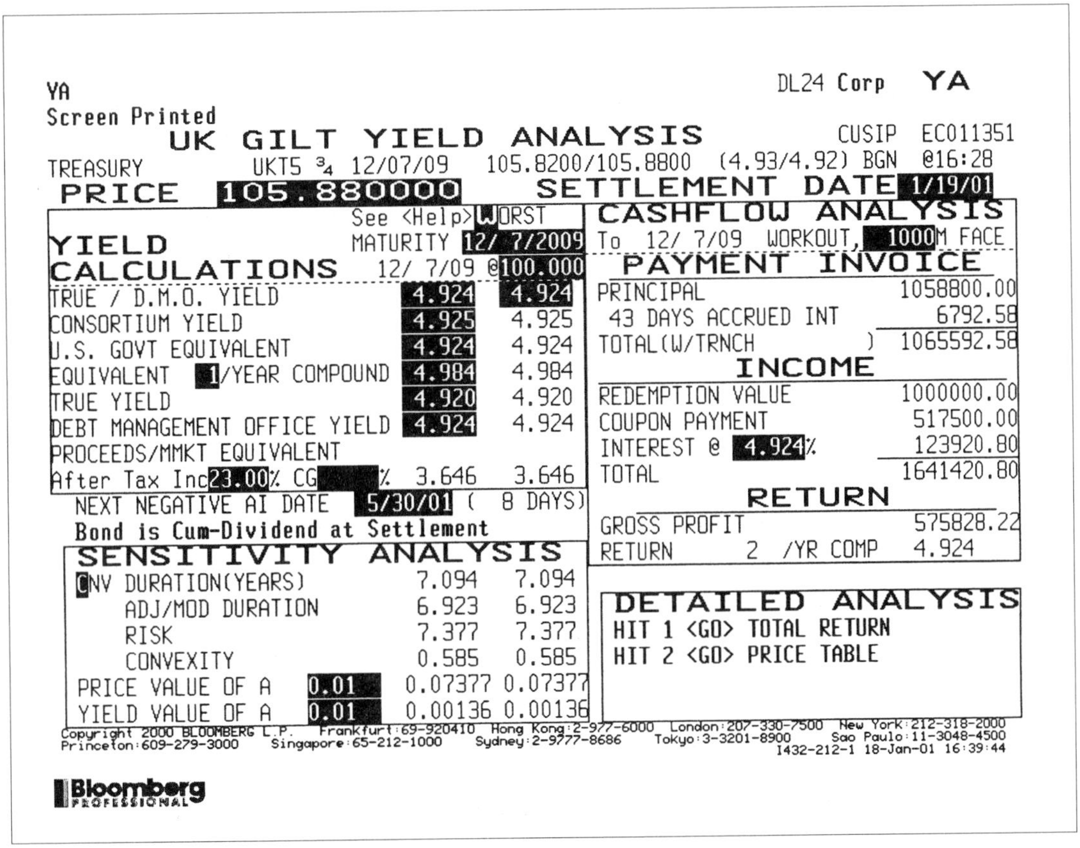

FIGURE 13.1b ▪ Yield calculations for UK gilt on Bloomberg 'YA' page

© Bloomberg L.P. Reproduced with permission

where n is the number of interest periods from value date until maturity. On an actual/365 basis one interest period in the gilt market is a half-year or 182.5 days,[1] so for a 90-day T-bill priced at 98.379, the true yield can be computed by solving

$$98.379 = \frac{100}{\left(1 + \frac{1}{2}rm\right)^{90/182.5}}$$

which gives rm equal to 0.067389 or 6.739%. That said, the yield quoted on T-bills, when computed using the market price, will often differ from the 'true' yield. This is because yield quotes for bills assume simple interest, rather than compound interest in their calculation. Nevertheless we are interested in this definition of the true yield because we wish

---

[1] The accrued basis in the gilt market is of course now actual/actual and not actual/365.

to apply it to longer-dated coupon bonds. Readers are familiar with the definition of bond yield, which involves discounting all the bond's cash flows (its coupons) at a uniform interest rate; yield here then is that interest rate that equates the sum of all the discounted cash flows equal to the observed market price. Let us consider this further.

With a vanilla bond such as a gilt there are m future cash flows of value C, which are the bond interest payments calculated as one-half of the bond coupon rate. The ith payment is termed C_i, with m_i being the days from value date to maturity. The number of interest periods from today to a cash flow date or to maturity is simply the days divided by 182.5 and so is denoted $n_i = m_i/182.5$. At a discount interest rate of r the value of the bond's discounted cash flows would be given by (13.2).

$$PV = \frac{C_1}{\left(1 + \frac{1}{2}r\right)^{n_1}} + \frac{C_2}{\left(1 + \frac{1}{2}r\right)^{n_2}} + \frac{C_m}{\left(1 + \frac{1}{2}r\right)^{n_m}} \qquad (13.2)$$

This leads easily to the true yield definition for the bond, which is the discount interest rate that equates the current market price of the bond to the discounted value of the cash flows. The market price is the *dirty* price, which includes accrued interest. We replace PV in (13.2) with P plus accrued interest, shown at (13.3).

$$P + AI = \frac{C_1}{\left(1 + \frac{1}{2}rm\right)^{n_1}} + \frac{C_2}{\left(1 + \frac{1}{2}rm\right)^{n_2}} + \ldots + \frac{C_m}{\left(1 + \frac{1}{2}rm\right)^{n_m}} \qquad (13.3)$$

We now look at how the true yield for a gilt may differ from the quoted yield.

Yield comparisons from the market

Consider the following market example. Price quotes are in *ticks*, or fractions of 32nds. One-half of a tick is denoted by '+'. On 10 May 1994 the $10\frac{1}{4}\%$ 1995 gilt, with a maturity date of 21 July 1995, was quoted at a price of 104-28+. To calculate the true yield, and indeed any other yield such as the conventional yield, we use the dirty price of the bond together with the discounted value of all remaining cash flows.

The bond pays coupon on 21 January and 21 July. For value 11 May 1994 the accrued will be 109 days, which means that the accrued interest is

$(10.25 \times \frac{1}{2}) \times {}^{109}/_{365}$

or 1.53048. The dirty price of the bond is (104-28+ plus 1.53048) or 106.421105.

The remaining bond cash flows are £5.125 on 21 July 1994 and 21 January 1995, and 105.125 on 21 July 1995. However, 21 January 1995 is a Saturday, so the cash flow will not actually be made until Monday 23 January. The period from value date to receipt of cash flows is

21 July 1994   71 days
23 January 1995   230 days
21 July 1995   436 days

The number of interest periods in this term for each cash flow date is

(71/182.5) or 0.38904
(230/182.5) or 1.26027
(436/182.5) or 2.38904.

Therefore the true yield is computed as follows:

$$106.421105 = \frac{5.125}{\left(1 + \frac{1}{2}rm\right)^{0.38904}} + \frac{5.125}{\left(1 + \frac{1}{2}rm\right)^{1.26027}} + \frac{105.125}{\left(1 + \frac{1}{2}rm\right)^{2.38904}}$$

which solves to give $rm = 0.073241$ or 7.324%.

The conventional yield calculation almost invariably will be different. This is because it ignores delays in the receipt of cash flows when payment dates fall on non-business days, and so the number of interest periods between cash flows are deemed to be in exact one-half-year amounts. So the conventional or *consortium* yield for the same bond would be calculated as

$$106.421105 = \frac{5.125}{\left(1 + \frac{1}{2}rm\right)^{0.38904}} + \frac{5.125}{\left(1 + \frac{1}{2}rm\right)^{1.24932}} + \frac{105.125}{\left(1 + \frac{1}{2}rm\right)^{2.38904}}$$

which solves to give $rm = 0.0732577$ or 7.325%. This shows the true yield to be 0.001% below the consortium yield. This is because under the consortium yield method the cash flows are received earlier than in the true yield treatment. Table 13.1 shows this difference in yields for gilts as at 10 May 1994 for value the next day. Note that the difference in the two measures declines to zero from the 6% 1999 gilt onwards. This is because for longer-dated bonds, the discounting of future cash flows is not materially affected by small delays in the treatment of cash flow receipts, which are only ever a few days if at all, and so there is no difference when computing the true yield.

TABLE 13.1 ■ Gilt yields as at 10 May 1994

Gilt	True yield %	Consortium yield %	Difference
10% 15 November 1996	7.171	7.173	0.002
10.5% 21 February 1997	7.379	7.391	0.012
7.25% 30 March 1998	7.780	7.781	0.001
6% 10 August 1999	7.900	7.900	0.000
9% 3 March 2000	8.191	8.191	0.000
7% 6 November 2001	8.220	8.220	0.000
9.75% 27 August 2002	8.484	8.482	−0.002
8% 10 June 2003	8.359	8.359	0.000
6.75% 26 November 2004	8.243	8.243	0.000

Source: Author's notes; ABN Amro Hoare Govett Sterling Bonds Ltd

Measuring true return on a bond

Although we may be satisfied with our true yield measure, it is not as straightforward as the true yield measure given for the T-bill earlier. With a single cash flow instrument, the actual return generated is straightforward: the maturity value is known, so the return on investment is calculated easily as the increase in value from start to maturity. An investment in a 90-day T-bill at a yield of 5% means that the initial value will increase in value by 5% over 90 days, using semi-annual compounding. We are not able to say this with certainty when confronted with a yield quote for a coupon-bearing bond. A 5% yield on a 90-day T-bill is the return associated with a 90-day maturity, and gives no indications (nor does it attempt to) on the value of the bill after say, 60 days or the yield available for reinvestment on maturity of the bill. Is there a way to view a bond yield in the same fashion as that for a T-bill? Certainly it would assist investors if there was a way to analyze a bond as if the instrument were a single-cash flow security. This is because investors often buy bonds as assets against liabilities that they are required to discharge on known future dates. If the true return on a bond were known, there would be comfort to the investor that the return achieved would meet requirements. Put very simply, this is the concept of *immunization*.

Therefore, if possible we would wish to view bond return in the same way as that for a single-cash flow security: a known initial investment is placed in the market for a set period of time, and the future value of the investment on maturity is calculated. The return on the bond would measure the average rate of capital gain in the investment period. The problem with a bond instrument is that its future value is not known with certainty, and is dependent at the rate at which the investor is able to reinvest interim cash flows; this rate cannot be predicted. There are a number of approaches to get around this problem, which we consider now in simple interest rate environments.

The first scenario assumes, somewhat unrealistically, a flat yield curve environment. Further we expect one movement only in the yield curve, a parallel shift upwards or downwards. A bond instrument is viewed as a package of zero-coupon securities, which would make its theoretical price the sum of the discounted values of each zero-coupon security: this is significant, because each cash flow would then be discounted at the interest rate for that specific term, rather than one single 'internal rate of return'. Under our simple assumptions, we can then measure the return on capital generated from a bond instrument.

The price of the bond, given the redemption yield, is given by (13.3). This is straightforward and conventional. Example 13.1 illustrates the use of this relationship.

EXAMPLE *13.1 Conventional bond pricing*

We have a hypothetical 5% 2002 semi-annual coupon bond that matures on 8 December 2002. For value on 8 December 2000 the bond has precisely four interest periods to maturity and no accrued interest; its cash flows are 2.50, 2.50, 2.50 and 102.50. If the yield curve on 7 December is flat at 5% (using semi-annual compounding) then the price of the bond is given by

$$P + AI = \frac{C_1}{\left(1 + \frac{1}{2}rm\right)^{n_1}} + \frac{C_2}{\left(1 + \frac{1}{2}rm\right)^{n_2}} + \frac{C_3}{\left(1 + \frac{1}{2}rm\right)^{n_3}} + \frac{C_4}{\left(1 + \frac{1}{2}rm\right)^{n_4}}$$

$$= \frac{2.50}{(1 + 0.025)^1} + \frac{2.50}{(1 + 0.025)^2} + \frac{2.50}{(1 + 0.025)^3} + \frac{102.50}{(1 + 0.025)^4}$$

$$= 2.4390 + 2.3879 + 2.3215 + 92.8600$$

$$= 100.00$$

This is the simplest approach, viewing the bond as a bundle of four zero-coupon securities; however, as the yield curve is flat we can use a uniform discount rate. This is shown and, at a rate of 5% the price of the bond is par.

We now assume a one-off parallel shift in the yield curve to a new level of rm_2, which results in a change in the expected future value of the bond. If there are s interest periods from the value date to a specified 'horizon date' this is given by (13.4),

$$P(rm_2, s) = \frac{C_1}{\left(1 + \frac{1}{2}rm_2\right)^{n_1-s}} + \frac{C_2}{\left(1 + \frac{1}{2}rm_2\right)^{n_2-s}} + ... + \frac{C_m}{\left(1 + \frac{1}{2}rm_2\right)^{n_m-s}} \qquad (13.4)$$

which expresses the fact that the ith cash flow contributes

$$\frac{C_i}{\left(1 + \frac{1}{2}rm_2\right)^{n_i-s}}$$

to the future value of the bond. If this cash flow is received ahead of the horizon date then $n_i - s$ will have a negative value, which means we compound C_i to the horizon date at the discount rate rm_2. Otherwise n_i-s will be positive and C_i is discounted backwards to the horizon date at the same rate. So the same rate rm_2 is used to compound or discount payments received ahead of or after the horizon date.

Remember we wish to measure the rate of return, or at best approximate it, for a bond. This return is influenced by changes in the yield curve after initial purchase. Let us consider this now. If we have a short-term horizon period and thus small s, a majority of the bond's cash flows will take place after the horizon date. A higher rate rm_2 will produce a lower future value $P(rm_2, s)$. The opposite occurs if s is large; most of the cash flows will then take place before the horizon date, and a higher value rm_2 will actually increase the value of the cash flows as they can be reinvested at a higher rate of interest. If the value of s is sufficiently high, this reinvestment gain may match and exceed the loss suffered due to revaluation of the bond at the higher rate, which would result in a higher future value $P(rm_2, s)$. The same effect only reversed can occur if $rm_2 < rm$. This is the *reinvestment risk* borne by the bondholder.

There is a horizon date in between the short-term and long-term dates where the net effect of the change in reinvestment rate on the bond's future value is close to zero. At this horizon date the bond behaves like a single cash flow or zero-coupon security, and so its future value can be predicted with more certainty, irrespective of the change in the yield curve after we have purchased it. Let us call this horizon date s_H. At this horizon date the bond will resemble a zero-coupon security that has s_H interest periods to maturity. We denote P_H as the future value of the bond s_H periods after the purchase date. It can be shown that the rate of return on this bond up to this specific horizon date is the value for rm_H that solves (13.5).

$$P + AI = \frac{P_H}{\left(1 + \frac{1}{2}rm_H\right)^{S_H}} \tag{13.5}$$

In (13.5) the market price is given as clean price plus accrued interest as before. It can be shown that the return rm_H is identical to the initial yield value rm. The value that will work for a stable future value is in fact the bond's Macaulay duration value. At this point, under the restrictive assumptions we have listed, the effect of a change in yields will not impact the future value of the bond. At this point the bond's cash flows are said to be *immunized* and the instrument could be used to match a liability that existed at that date.

The restrictions we imposed limit the usefulness of the analysis. We assume one change only in rates after purchase, and this change is uniform across the term structure. Therefore, in practice, an investor must continually adjust his portfolio to maintain its immunization properties. An accessible treatment of the key issues in dynamically managing a portfolio is contained in Fabozzi (1996).

Implied spot rates and market zero-coupon yields[2]

That the duration measure has a number of limitations when used in portfolio management is well known. There are further considerations that limit its use. For instance the limiting value on duration means that most gilts have duration measures of under 12 years.[3] This makes portfolio immunization difficult when liabilities are very long-dated. The need for constant rebalancing of the portfolio also adds to the problem. However, investors in zero-coupon bonds do not face these problems. This makes them potentially very attractive securities for investors. Zero-coupon bonds do not suffer from the duration-based drawbacks of coupon bonds, as their duration value is identical to their term to maturity. This makes portfolio matching easier; a five-year zero-coupon bond has a duration of five years when purchased, and after two years its duration will be three years, irrespective of the change in interest rates in that time. A long-dated zero-coupon bond can then be used to match a long-dated investment liability. However, how should the yield on a zero-coupon bond be compared to that on a coupon bond? It is easy to see that we compare a two-year zero-coupon bond with a coupon bond of two years' duration; however, this becomes impractical when dealing with very long-dated zero-coupon bonds, for which no equivalent coupon gilt is usually available. The way around this can be observed in the US Treasury market, where the technique of *stripping* coupon Treasuries enables us to calculate implied zero-coupon rates with which we can compare actual strip market yields.

In this section we attempt to describe the relationship between spot interest rates, the actual market yields that would be observed on zero-coupon bonds and the yields on coupon bonds. We illustrate how an implied spot rate curve can be derived from the redemption yields and prices observed on coupon bonds, and discuss how this curve may be used to assess relative value in bond yields.

---

[2] This section is based on an unpublished paper originally written in July 1997 when the author was working on the sterling proprietary trading desk in the Treasury division at Hambros Bank Limited, and as first written pre-dates the introduction of zero-coupon strips in the UK gilt market in December 1997. It was updated as part of a guest lecture delivered at City University Business School in 2000.

[3] For instance see Blake (1990) paragraph 5.8.1.

Spot (zero-coupon) yields[4] and coupon bond prices

A gilt is a collection of cash flows, each of which represents an obligation on the part of HM Treasury to service the debt represented by the gilt issue on a semi-annual basis. We can view a gilt as a bundle of individual zero-coupon securities, each maturing on their respective payment date. Viewed in this way, the present value of the gilt becomes the sum of the present values of all the constituent cash flows. Let us consider this first.

Assume that we can observe the spot rates for various maturities and that these rates are $r_1, r_2, r_3, \dots r_N$. If a bond pays coupon C annually from period 1 to period N its present value using the series of spot rates is given by

$$P = \frac{C_1/2}{\left(1 + \frac{1}{2}r_1\right)} + \frac{C_2/2}{\left(1 + \frac{1}{2}r_2\right)^2} + \frac{C_3/2}{\left(1 + \frac{1}{2}r_3\right)^3} + \dots + \frac{C_{N-1}/2}{\left(1 + \frac{1}{2}r_{N-1}\right)^{N-1}} + \frac{C_N/2 + 100}{\left(1 + \frac{1}{2}r_N\right)^N} \qquad (13.6)$$

which is of course different to the conventional redemption yield formula with which we are very familiar. Each cash flow is discounted by the specific spot rate that corresponds to the maturity period of the cash flow. It follows that in order to value a bond in this way, we must know the spot rate term structure. However, this may not always be readily observable. Gilt prices on the other hand are readily observable, and so we may use them to derive spot interest rates. This is examined next.

Deriving the spot rate term structure from gilts prices[5]

We do not require an active strip market in order to construct a spot interest rate curve; we can derive a theoretical or *implied* spot term structure using the yields that are observed on coupon gilts. To illustrate the methodology, we will use a hypothetical set of ten gilts that are trading in a positive yield curve environment. The maturity, price and yield for our ten gilts are shown in table 13.2. Let us assume that these prices are for settlement on 1 March 1999, and that all the bonds have precisely 1, 1.5, 2 and so on years to maturity, that is they mature on 1 March or 1 September of their maturity year. The shortest-dated gilt has no intermediate coupon before it is redeemed, and we can therefore treat it as a zero-coupon bond. All the gilts have no accrued interest because the settlement date is a coupon date.

As we suggested in the previous section, a gilt can be viewed as a bundle of individual zero-coupon securities, so that we may consider its value to be equal to the value of a strip of zero-coupon bonds whose last bond matures at the same time as the coupon bond.

---

[4] The term *spot rate* is usually considered to be synonymous with *zero-coupon rate* and it is common to see this written in textbooks (including this one!). In this chapter the two terms are not used thus, as we make the distinction between a spot rate derived from coupon bond prices and a zero-coupon rate that is observed on a zero-coupon bond trading in the market.
[5] First presented as an internal paper in July 1994.

TABLE 13.2 ▪ Hypothetical gilt prices

Maturity date	Years to maturity	Coupon (%)	Yield to maturity	Price
1 Sep 99	0.5	5.0	6.00	99.5146
1 Mar 00	1.0	10.0	6.30	103.5322
1 Sep 00	1.5	7.0	6.40	100.8453
1 Mar 01	2.0	6.5	6.70	99.6314
1 Sep 01	2.5	8.0	6.90	102.4868
1 Mar 02	3.0	10.5	7.30	108.4838
1 Sep 02	3.5	9.0	7.60	104.2327
1 Mar 03	4.0	7.3	7.80	98.1408
1 Sep 03	4.5	7.5	7.95	98.3251
1 Mar 04	5.0	8.0	8.00	100.0000

Consider the first bond in table 13.2. As it matures in precisely six months' time, it is effectively a zero-coupon bond; its yield of 6% is equal to the six-month spot rate. Given this spot rate we can derive the spot rate for a one-year zero-coupon gilt. The price of a one-year gilt strip must equal the present value of the two cash flows from our 10% one-year coupon gilt. This reflects the principle of no-arbitrage pricing. The cash flows from the one-year coupon gilt are:

1 September 1999	£5
1 March 2000	£5 + £100 = £105

The present value of these cash flows is

$$PV_{Mar00} = \frac{5}{\left(1 + \frac{1}{2}r_1\right)} + \frac{105}{\left(1 + \frac{1}{2}r_2\right)^2}$$

where

r_1 is the six-month theoretical spot rate;
r_2 is the one-year theoretical spot rate.

As we illustrated earlier, in a semi-annual coupon environment we take half of the annual discount rate because we are discounting one-half of the annual coupon.

We have assumed that the six-month spot rate is 6%, based on our decision to treat the six-month gilt as a zero-coupon bond. Therefore the present value of the one-year coupon gilt is

$$PV_{Mar00} = \frac{5}{(1.03)} + \frac{105}{(1 + \frac{1}{2}r_2)^2}$$

As the price of the one-year gilt is 103.5322, which we observe in the market, the following relationship must be true:

$$103.5322 = \frac{5}{(1.03)} + \frac{105}{(1 + \frac{1}{2}r_2)^2}.$$

Using this relationship we are now in a position to calculate the one-year theoretical spot rate as shown below.

$$103.5322 = 4.85437 + \frac{105}{\left(1 + \frac{1}{2}r_2\right)^2}$$

$$98.67783 = 105/\left(1 + \frac{1}{2}r_2\right)^2$$

$$\left(1 + \frac{1}{2}r_2\right)^2 = 105/98.67783$$

$$\left(1 + \frac{1}{2}r_2\right)^2 = 1.064069$$

$$\left(1 + \frac{1}{2}r_2\right) = \sqrt{1.064069}$$

$$\frac{1}{2}r_2 = 0.03154$$

Doubling this yield gives us the annualized bond-equivalent yield of 0.06308, or 6.308%, which is our theoretical one-year spot rate.

Now that we have obtained our theoretical one-year spot rate, we are in a position to calculate the theoretical 1.5-year spot rate. The cash flows for the 7% $1\frac{1}{2}$-year coupon gilt shown in table 13.2 is shown below.

1 September 1999	£3.50
1 March 2000	£3.50
1 September 2000	£103.50

The present value of this cash flow stream is:

$$PV_{Sep00} = \frac{3.50}{\left(1 + \frac{1}{2}r_1\right)} + \frac{3.50}{\left(1 + \frac{1}{2}r_2\right)^2} + \frac{103.50}{\left(1 + \frac{1}{2}r_3\right)^3}$$

where r_3 is the $1\frac{1}{2}$-year theoretical spot rate. We have already established that the six-month and one-year spot rates are 6% and 6.308% respectively, so that r_1 is 0.06 and r_2 is 0.06308. Therefore the present value of the 7% $1\frac{1}{2}$-year coupon gilt is:

$$PV_{Sep00} = \frac{3.5}{(103)} + \frac{3.5}{(1.03154)^2} + \frac{103.5}{\left(1 + \frac{1}{2}r_3\right)^3}.$$

We can see from table 13.2 that the price of the 7% 1½-year gilt is 100.8453; therefore the following relationship must be true:

$$100.8453 = \frac{3.5}{(103)} + \frac{3.5}{(1.03154)^2} + \frac{103.5}{\left(1 + \frac{1}{2}r_3\right)^3}.$$

This equation can then be solved to obtain r_3 which proves to give us a 1½-year theoretical spot rate of 6.407%.

For the two-year implied spot rate, the relationship is:

$$99.6314 = \frac{3.25}{(103)} + \frac{3.25}{(1.03154)^2} + \frac{3.25}{(1.032035)^3} + \frac{103.25}{\left(1 + \frac{1}{2}r_4\right)^4}$$

which solves to give $\frac{1}{2}r_4$ equal to 0.0336 and a 2-year theoretical spot rate of 6.720%.

This process is repeated, using the two-year spot rate and the 8% September 2001 coupon gilt, so that the relationship used to compute the 2½-year theoretical spot rate is:

$$102.4868 = \frac{4}{(103)} + \frac{4}{(1.03154)^2} + \frac{4}{(1.032035)^3} + \frac{4}{(1.0336)^4} + \frac{104}{\left(1 + \frac{1}{2}r_5\right)^5}$$

which solves to give $r_5 = 6.936\%$.

For r_6 the three-year spot rate is 7.394%.

If we carry on the process for the gilts in table 13.2 we will obtain the results shown in table 13.3.

The general relationship used to derive an implied spot rate for the Nth six-month period was given earlier as (13.6), here without the C subscripts.

$$P_n = \frac{C/2}{\left(1 + \frac{1}{2}r\right)} + \frac{C/2}{\left(1 + \frac{1}{2}r_2\right)^2} + \frac{C/2}{\left(1 + \frac{1}{2}r_3\right)^3} + \ldots + \frac{C/2 + 100}{\left(1 + \frac{1}{2}r_N\right)^N} \tag{13.7}$$

We can rewrite this expression as (13.8).

$$P_N = \frac{C}{2} \sum_{t=1}^{N-1} \frac{1}{\left(1 + \frac{1}{2}r_t\right)^t} + \frac{C/2 + 100}{\left(1 + \frac{1}{2}r_N\right)^N} \tag{13.8}$$

where

r_t for $t = 1, 2, \ldots N - 1$ is the theoretical spot rates that are already known. This equation can be rearranged so that we may solve for r_N.

TABLE 13.3

Maturity date	Years to maturity	Yield to maturity (%)	Theoretical spot rate (%)
1 Sep 99	0.5	6.00	6.000
1 Mar 00	1.0	6.30	6.308
1 Sep 00	1.5	6.40	6.407
1 Mar 01	2.0	6.70	6.720
1 Sep 01	2.5	6.90	6.936
1 Mar 02	3.0	7.30	7.394
1 Sep 02	3.5	7.60	7.712
1 Mar 03	4.0	7.80	7.908
1 Sep 03	4.5	7.95	8.069
1 Mar 04	5.0	8.00	8.147

$$r_N = \left[\frac{C/2 + 100}{P_N - \frac{C}{2} \sum_{t=1}^{N-1} \frac{1}{\left(1 + \frac{1}{2}r_t\right)^t}} \right]^{\frac{1}{N}} - 1 \qquad (13.9)$$

Spot yields and bond yields

Following our description of the process by which spot interest rates can be derived from the prices of bonds observed in the market, in this section we illustrate the relationship between such rates and conventional bond yields.

In table 13.4 we show the redemption yields for gilts as at 25 June 1997, together with implied spot rates, and the corresponding graph of these yields at figure 13.2.

The redemption yield curve is a conventional positively-sloping one with a dip at the long end of the term structure at the point of the longest-dated bond. Why do we observe the spread between the two curves? Remember that the spot yield curve is the theoretical return on a zero-coupon instrument, that is one that has no coupons paid during its life. However, the redemption yield curve measures the expected return on instruments that pay a coupon at regular intervals during their life. The rising shape of the curve implies that medium-dated zero-coupon bonds, if they represented actual instruments, would offer a better yield than short-dated zero-coupon bonds. This positively sloping part of the curve influences the relationship between spot yields and

TABLE 13.4 ■ Conventional and spot yields, 25 June 1997

Term (years)	Gilt	Conventional yield %	Spot yield %	Spread %
0.25	8.75% 1/9/1997	6.508	6.508	0.000
1	7.25% 30/3/1998	6.763	6.770	−0.007
1.5	12% 20/11/1998	6.968	6.978	−0.01
2	6% 10/8/1999	6.956	6.972	−0.016
3	8% 7/12/2000	7.133	7.143	−0.01
4	7% 6/11/2001	7.158	7.179	−0.021
5	7% 7/6/2002	7.118	7.131	−0.013
6	8% 10/6/2003	7.173	7.184	−0.011
7	6.75% 27/11/2004	7.151	7.167	−0.016
8	8.50% 7/12/2005	7.188	7.196	−0.008
9	7.50% 7/12/2006	7.189	7.207	−0.018
10	7.25% 7/12/2007	7.170	7.180	−0.01
11	9% 13/10/2008	7.220	7.239	−0.019
12	8% 25/9/2009	7.235	7.271	−0.036
13	6.25% 25/11/2010	7.255	7.312	−0.057
14	9% 12/7/2011	7.254	7.289	−0.035
15	9% 6/8/2012	7.265	7.307	−0.042
16	8% 27/9/2013	7.254	7.289	−0.035
18	8% 7/12/2015	7.222	7.215	0.007
21	8.75% 25/8/2017	7.267	7.318	−0.051
24	8% 7/6/2021	7.209	7.172	0.037

Source: Author's notes; Hambros Bank Limited

bond yields at that part of the curve. For instance the five-year spot rate is 7.131%, so a five-year zero-coupon bond being priced on 24 June 1997 for settlement the following day in theory should pay 7.131%. The actual five-year coupon bond would pay a series of coupons before the final coupon and principal amount on maturity. This last coupon and principal would indeed be valued at 7.131% on 24 June, as they represent what are in effect zero-coupon payments in five years' time.[6] However, the earlier coupon

---

[6] We call this is a 'five-year' bond as it is the benchmark bond for that period, while accepting that the actual maturity is slightly less than five years. An equivalent zero-coupon bond would also be priced on 24 June 1997 for maturity on 7 June 2002 rather than 25 June 2002, although we would call it a five-year security.

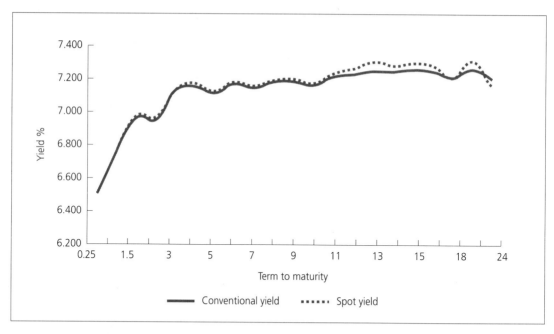

FIGURE 13.2 ▪ Gilt market yields, 25 June 1997

Source: Williams de Broe and Hambros Bank Limited; author's records

payments would be valued at lower spot yields, as given by the positively sloping spot yield curve. We know from earlier in this chapter that the yield on a coupon bond is in effect the average of the yields payable on the bundle spot obligations that constitute the bond, so that the final yield on the bond must be below 7.131% when priced for value on 25 June. The yield is in fact 7.118%. This is why the spot yields lie above the redemption yields at the short to medium end of the curve.

We also note that at the very long end of the curve the demand for bonds is such that the yields are depressed for the 8% 2015 and 8% 2021 gilts. Again these bonds pay regular coupon but, at the longer end their coupons are valued higher by the market, so that these coupons are in effect priced at lower yields. This is confirmed by the implied spot rate curve. The 18- and 24-year spot rates, which would be the theoretical yields on identical-maturity zero-coupon bonds, are 7.215% and 7.172% respectively. However, the 18- and 24-year bonds themselves are priced at 7.222% and 7.209%.

The implication of this property for potential investors in zero-coupon gilts or strips is clear: in a positively sloping yield curve environment there is a yield pickup on similar maturity strips, although these will be instruments of higher modified duration.

Consider now gilt yields for 11 November 1996, shown at table 13.5 and figure 13.3.

TABLE 13.5 ▪ Conventional and spot yields, 10 November 1996

Term (years)	Gilt	Conventional yield %	Spot yield %	Spread %
0.25	T-Bill	6.06	6.060	0.000
1.5	7.25% 30/3/1998	6.71	6.714	−0.004
3	6% 10/8/1999	6.95	6.979	−0.029
4	8% 7/12/2000	7.22	7.255	−0.035
5	7% 6/11/2001	7.31	7.364	−0.054
6	8% 10/6/2003	7.47	7.542	−0.072
8	6.75% 27/11/2004	7.59	7.690	−0.100
9	8.50% 7/12/2005	7.66	7.762	−0.102
10	7.50% 7/12/2006	7.67	7.780	−0.110
15	9% 12/7/2011	7.90	8.129	−0.229
19	8% 7/12/2015	7.91	8.086	−0.176
25	8% 7/6/2021	7.91	8.046	−0.136

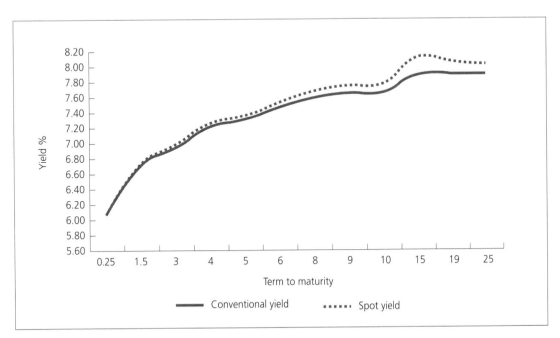

FIGURE 13.3 ▪ Gilt yield curves, 10 November 1996

Source: ABN Amro and Bloomberg, author's notes

At this time the bond yield curve was sloping upwards all the way out to the long-bond. The difference in the yields of the 8% 2015 and 8% 2021 is much less pronounced with the curves for June 1997. The effect of this is that although the implied spot rates decrease at the very long end, they do not fall below the bond yield curve. This means that on this earlier date the market was not placing as high a premium on coupon payments made after 19 years as it would be seen to do several months later. This illustration leads nicely on to the next section, when we look at the yields of strips compared to their theoretical yields.

Implied spot yields and zero-coupon bond yields

In an environment in which there is a liquid market in actual zero-coupon securities or *strips*, we can observe market spot yields from the prices at which the strips are trading. In the previous section we showed how the prices and redemption yields on coupon bonds can be used to derive an implied spot yield curve. But how do these implied rates compare to actual strip yields, and how should we expect them to behave vis-à-vis each other? We discuss some of the key issues in this section.

A spot rate could be said to be the rate of return at purchase on a single-cash flow security held to maturity. It can also, as the previous sections have shown, be viewed as the rate payable on a coupon bond that is viewed as a bundle of individual zero-coupon cash flows, with the bond yield viewed as a complex average of the spot yields on the individual payments. Spot yields cannot actually be observed in the market, and as such are a theoretical construct. Zero-coupon securities on the other hand, are actual market instruments that have been created from stripping individual cash flows from coupon bonds, and trading the resultant cash flows separately.[7] Therefore, the yields observed on zero-coupon bonds will reflect actual market supply and demand for specific securities. This makes zero-coupon yields different from spot yields in practice, notwithstanding the fact that they should be viewed as identical in theory. This reflects how spot yields are derived from other prices and yields, and not observed on market instruments.

How do the two rates differ? If a particular zero-coupon bond is in demand, its price will rise and yield fall. The opposite occurs if the bond is not sought after and is being sold by investors and market makers. The effect of this is that at any time the zero-coupon yield can and does differ from the equivalent-maturity spot yield, be it higher or lower. If investors value an individual zero-coupon bond lower when it is a stripped security compared to when it is part of a package of zero-coupon cash flows (in a coupon bond), the yield on the zero will be higher than the equivalent-maturity spot

---

[7] For more information on this procedure with regard to the gilt strips market, see Choudhry (1999), although no longer in print.

rate. The opposite will happen if investors prefer to hold the zero-coupon security. Despite this reflection of supply and demand, implied spot rates are still important because they allow investors to assess relative value for both zero-coupon bonds and coupon bonds.

Consider table 13.6 and figure 13.4; the latter shows the implied spot yields derived from gilt prices on 2 March 1999, together with the yield for coupon strips and principal strips as at the same date. The yields on principal strips are not joined as a curve, as the comparatively long period between strips would make any conclusions from the resulting curve problematic. These are the yields on the principal or residual cash flow when a bond is stripped. The other cash flows are known as coupon strips.

Two observations are worth making. First that zero-coupon bonds traded cheap to the spot curve throughout the term structure, indicating that investors were not prepared to hold strips without a premium to the theoretical value. This probably reflected the inverted yield curve, which meant that strips would be trading expensive to coupon bonds of the same maturity. However, strips traded expensive to the spot curve at the 11- to 15-year point of the curve. Second, principal strips trade at lower yields than coupon strips of the same maturity. This reflects the liquidity and demand considerations for principal strips, which investors prefer to hold instead of coupon strips.

For reference we graph the curve for the bond yields alongside the spot and zero-coupon yields at figure 13.5.

Determining the value of strips

For the investor to identify relative value it is important to compare curves as we have just described. The three most common ways to calculate the value of a strip are:

■ valuation using the bond curve

■ equivalent duration method

■ theoretical zero-coupon curve construction, also known as *bootstrapping*.

The spread between a strip and a bond with the same maturity is often used as an indicator of strip value. It is essentially a rough-and-ready approach; its main drawback is that two instruments with different risk profiles are being compared against each other. This is particularly true for longer maturities.

When measuring relative value, the equivalent duration method aligning the strip and coupon bond yields on the basis of modified duration will allow for a better comparison. However, the most common approach of determining the value of a strip is via the derivation of a theoretical zero-coupon curve as just described where we illustrated the relationship between coupon and zero-coupon yield. When the curve is flat, the spot

TABLE 13.6 ■ Gilt market gross redemption true yields and implied spot yields on 2 March 1999

Term (years)	Gilt	True yield	Spot yields	Coupon strip yield	Principal strip yield	Modified duration
0.5	6% 10/8/1999	5.033	5.033	5.068		0.43
1.5	8% 7/12/2000*	5.027	4.977	4.973	5.036	1.62
2.5	7% 6/11/2001	4.963	4.927	4.949		2.39
3	7% 7/6/2002*	4.878	4.836	4.91	4.687	2.87
4	8% 10/6/2003	4.845	4.789	4.824		3.6
4.5	6.50% 7/12/2003*	4.735	4.687	4.786	4.691	4.05
5	6.75% 26/11/2004	4.709	4.658	4.798		4.72
6	8.50% 7/12/2005*	4.78	4.728	4.774	4.74	5.23
7	7.50% 7/12/2006*	4.8	4.77	4.781	4.775	5.95
8	7.25% 7/12/2007*	4.759	4.721	4.753	4.723	6.58
9	9% 13/10/2008	4.72	4.644	4.735		6.73
10	5.75% 7/12/2009*	4.604	4.542	4.723	4.518	8.03
11	6.25% 25/11/2010	4.695	4.665	4.711		8.4
12	9% 12/7/2011	4.751	4.721	4.713		8.19
13	9% 6/8/2012	4.787	4.727	4.713		8.71
14	8% 27/9/2013	4.763	4.75	4.71		9.2
16	8% 7/12/2015*	4.711	4.659	4.705	4.670	10.24
18	8.75% 25/8/2017	4.729	4.695	4.682		10.83
22	8% 7/6/2021*	4.679	4.609	4.635	4.612	12.2
29	6% 7/12/2028*	4.537	4.376	4.402	4.365	15.2

* Indicates strippable gilts

Source: Bloomberg

curve will also be flat. When the yield curve is negative, the theoretical zero-coupon curve must lie below the coupon yield curve. This is because the yield on coupon-bearing bonds is affected by the fact that the investor receives part of the cash flow before the maturity of the bond; the discount rates corresponding to these earlier payment dates are higher than the discount rate corresponding to the final payment date on redemption. In addition the spread between zero-coupon yields and bond yields should increase negatively with maturity, so that zero-coupon bonds always yield less than coupon bonds.

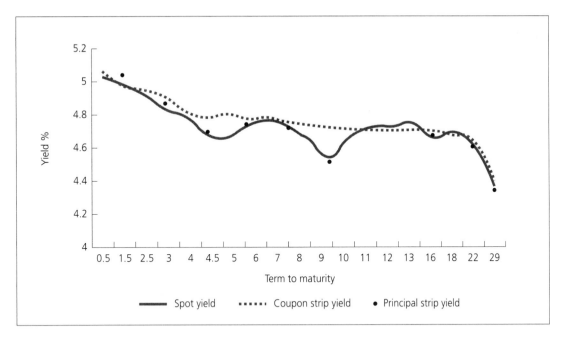

FIGURE 13.4 ■ Spot and strip yields on 2 March 1999

Source: Bloomberg, author's notes

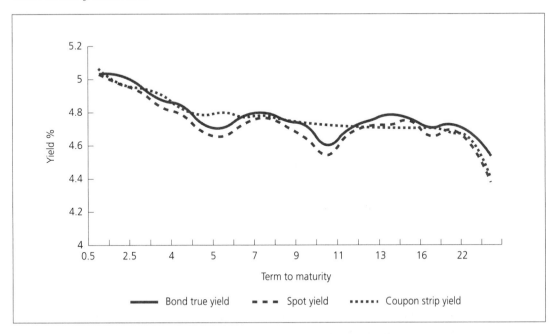

FIGURE 13.5 ■ Gilt bond, implied spot and coupon strip yields, 2 March 1999

Source: Bloomberg, author's notes

In a positively shaped yield curve environment the opposite is true. The theoretical zero-coupon curve will lie above the coupon curve. It is interesting, however, to observe the overall steepness of the curves. In general the steeper the coupon curve is, the steeper the zero-coupon curve will be. It should be remembered that each yearly value of the coupon curve is considered in the derivation of the zero-coupon curve. Hence a yield curve could for example, have exactly one-year, ten-year and thirty-year yields, while the theoretical zero-coupon thirty-year yield could be substantially higher or lower. The derived yield level would depend on whether the points on the term structure in between these maturity bands were connected by a smooth curve or straight line. This argument is sometimes cited as a reason for not using the bootstrapping method, in that the theoretical zero-coupon yields that are obtained are too sensitive for real-world trading. Bond analysts use spline or other curve smoothing techniques to get around this problem, and produce theoretical values that are more realistic. This issue becomes more important when there are few bonds between large points on the term structure, such that linear interpolation between them produces more inaccurate results. For example between the ten-year and thirty-year maturities there are eight liquid gilts; between twenty and thirty years there are only two gilts.

Strips market anomalies

From the start of gilt strips trading the market has observed some long-standing anomalies that mirror observations from other strips markets, such as those in the US and France. These include the following:

Final principal trades expensive

It might be expected that the strip yield curve would behave in a similar fashion to the coupon curve. However, due to supply and demand considerations more weight is always given to the final principal strip, and this is indeed so in the gilt strips market.

Longest maturity is the most expensive

A characteristic seen in all well-developed strip markets is that maturities with the longest duration and the greatest convexity trade expensive relative to theoretical values. Conversely, intermediate maturities tend to trade cheap to the curve. This can be observed when looking at the gilt strips and coupon curves.

Principal strips trade at a premium over coupon strips

Principal strips reflect the premium investors are prepared to pay for greater liquidity and, in some markets, regulatory and tax reasons. This rule is so well established that principal strips will sometimes trade more expensive relative to coupon strips even when their outstanding nominal amount is lower than that of coupon strips.

Intermediate maturity coupons are often relatively cheap

Market makers in the past have often found themselves with large quantities of intermediate maturity coupon strips, the residue of client demand for longer maturities. This has occurred with gilt strips where at certain times coupon strips of three to eight years maturity have traded cheap to the curve.

Very short coupon strips trade expensive

In a positively sloped yield curve environment short strips are often in demand because they provide an attractive opportunity to match liabilities without reinvestment risk at a higher yield than coupon bonds of the same maturity. We have not observed in the gilt strips market to date, as the yield curve has been inverted from before the start of trading. However, in France, for example the short end up to three years is often well bid.

Strips trading strategy

Bond replication through strips

This is the theoretical strategy and the one that first presents itself. The profit potential for a market maker who strips a gilt lies in arbitrage resulting from a mispricing of the coupon bond. Due to the market mechanism requiring that there be no arbitrage opportunity, the bid price of a gilt must be lower than the offer price of a synthetic gilt (a gilt reconstituted from a bundle of coupon and principal strips); equally the offer price of the gilt must be higher than the bid price of a synthetic gilt. Of course if the above conditions are not satisfied, a risk-free profit can be obtained by trading the opposite way in both instruments simultaneously and simply taking the difference.

The potential profit in stripping a gilt will depend on actual gilt yields prevailing in the market and the theoretical spot rate yield curve. To illustrate how a gilt-edged market maker (GEMM) might realize a profit from a coupon stripping exercise, consider a hypothetical five-year, 8% gilt selling at par (and therefore offering a yield to maturity of 8%) trading in the yield curve environment we described earlier, and which was shown in table 13.7. Let us imagine that the market maker buys the gilt at par and strips it, with the intention of selling the resulting zero-coupon bonds at the yields indicated for the corresponding maturities shown in table 13.7.

Table 13.7 shows the price that the market maker would receive for each strip that was created. As we know the price of the coupon gilt is the discounted total present value of all its cash flows using the required market interest rate. Here we can equate it to the total present value of all the cash flows from the strips, each discounted at the yield corresponding to its maturity (from table 13.7). The proceeds received from selling the strips come to a total of £100.4913 per £100 of par value of the gilt originally bought by the GEMM.

We can show why there is an opportunity to realize this profit. Consider the fourth column in table 13.7. This shows us how much the market maker paid for each of the

TABLE 13.7

Maturity date	Years to maturity	Cash flow	Present value at 8%	Yield to maturity (%)	Present value at yield to maturity
1-Sep-99	0.5	4	3.8462	6.00	3.8835
1-Mar-00	1.0	4	3.6982	6.30	3.7594
1-Sep-00	1.5	4	3.5560	6.40	3.6393
1-Mar-01	2.0	4	3.4192	6.70	3.5060
1-Sep-01	2.5	4	3.2877	6.90	3.3760
1-Mar-02	3.0	4	3.1613	7.30	3.2258
1-Sep-02	3.5	4	3.0390	7.60	3.0809
1-Mar-03	4.0	4	2.9228	7.80	2.9453
1-Sep-03	4.5	4	2.8103	7.95	2.8164
1-Mar-04	5.0	104	70.2587	8.00	70.2587
			100.0000		100.4913

cash flows by buying the entire package of cash flows, that is, by buying the bond at a yield of 8%. For instance, let us examine the £4 coupon payment due in three years. By buying the five-year gilt priced to yield 8%, the GEMM pays a price based on 8% (4% semi-annual) for that coupon payment, which is £3.1613. However, if we accept the assumptions in this illustration, investors are willing to accept a lower yield, 7.30% (3.65% semi-annual) and purchase a strip with three years to maturity at the price marked.

Thus investors here are willing to pay £3.2258. On this one coupon payment (now of course a strip versus a coupon payment) the GEMM realizes a profit equal to the difference between £3.2258 and £3.1613, or £0.0645. From all the strips the total profit is £0.4913 per £100 nominal.

Let us now imagine that instead of the observed yield to maturity from table 13.7, the yields required by investors are the same as the theoretical spot rates also shown. Table 13.8 shows that in this case the total proceeds from the sale of zero-coupon gilts would be approximately £100, which being no profit would render the exercise of stripping uneconomical. This shows that where strips prices deviate from theoretical prices, there may be profit opportunities. We have shown elsewhere that there are differences between observed strip yields and theoretical yields, indicating that there are (often very small) differences between derived prices and actual prices. Do these price differences give rise to arbitrage opportunities? Due to the efficiency and transparency of developed country bond markets, the answer is usually no. It is the process of coupon stripping that prevents the price of a

TABLE 13.8

Maturity date	Years to maturity	Cash flow	Present value at 8%	Theoretical spot rate (%)	Present value at spot rate
1-Sep-99	0.5	4	3.8462	6.000	3.8835
1-Mar-00	1.0	4	3.6982	6.308	3.7591
1-Sep-00	1.5	4	3.5560	6.407	3.6390
1-Mar-01	2.0	4	3.4192	6.720	3.5047
1-Sep-01	2.5	4	3.2877	6.936	3.3731
1-Mar-02	3.0	4	3.1613	7.394	3.2171
1-Sep-02	3.5	4	3.0397	7.712	3.0693
1-Mar-03	4.0	4	2.9228	7.908	2.9331
1-Sep-03	4.5	4	2.8103	8.069	2.8020
1-Mar-04	5.0	104	70.2587	8.147	69.7641
			100.0000		~100.0000

gilt from trading at a price that is *materially* different from its theoretical price based on the derived spot yield curve. And where discrepancies arise, any arbitrage activity will cause them to disappear very quickly. As the strips market becomes more liquid, the laws of supply and demand will eliminate obvious arbitrage opportunities, as has already happened in the US Treasury market and is already the norm in the gilts market. However, there will remain occasional opportunities to exploit differences between actual market prices of strips and the theoretical price given by the benchmark (coupon) gilt yield curve.

Gilt strips and cash flow analysis

The following examples illustrate the yield analysis and cash flows for the 5¾% Treasury 2009, which matures on 7 December 2009, its principal strip and a coupon strip maturing on 7 December 2009. The 5¾% 2009 was the 1999 ten-year benchmark gilt. The market information reflects the position for settlement date 11 February 1999. Interest rate and price data was obtained from Bloomberg and Reuters.

Table 13.9 shows the cash flows paid out to a bondholder of £1 million nominal of the 5¾% 2009. On the trade date (10 February 1999, for settlement on 11 February) this bond traded at 113.15, with a corresponding yield of 4.2224%. The convexity of this bond at this time was 0.820. The relevant spot rates at each of the cash flow dates are shown alongside.

TABLE 13.9 ■ Cash flow analysis Treasury 5¾% 2009, yield 4.2224%

Pay date	Cash flow	Spot	Pay date	Cash flow	Spot
7-Jun-99	28,750.00	5.1474	7-Dec-04	28,750.00	4.2746
7-Dec-99	28,750.00	4.9577	7-Jun-05	28,750.00	4.3168
7-Jun-00	28,750.00	4.8511	7-Dec-05	28,750.00	4.3599
7-Dec-00	28,750.00	4.7376	7-Jun-06	28,750.00	4.3738
7-Jun-01	28,750.00	4.6413	7-Dec-06	28,750.00	4.3881
7-Dec-01	28,750.00	4.5481	7-Jun-07	28,750.00	4.3603
7-Jun-02	28,750.00	4.614	7-Dec-07	28,750.00	4.3326
7-Dec-02	28,750.00	4.3962	7-Jun-08	28,750.00	4.2942
7-Jun-03	28,750.00	4.3307	7-Dec-08	28,750.00	4.2548
7-Dec-03	28,750.00	4.2654	7-Jun-09	28,750.00	4.2153
7-Jun-04	28,750.00	4.2696	7-Dec-09	1,028,750.00	4.1759

Nominal	1,000,000	Previous coupon date	7-Dec-98	
Duration	8.33	Accrued interest	10,425.82	
Total cash flow	1,632,500.00	Present value	1,141,925.84	

Source: Bloomberg

The cash flow for the December 2009 principal strip is shown as table 13.10. Note that if calling up this security on the Bloomberg system, the ticker is UKTR, comprising the standard UKT (from 'United Kingdom Treasury') and the suffix R (from 'residual', the Bloomberg term for principal strips). The Bloomberg ticker for coupon strips is UKTS.

The yield on the principal strip at this time was 4.1482%, which corresponds to a price of 64.13409 per £100 nominal. Given that the yield curve was inverted at this time, this is what is expected, a yield lower than the gross redemption yield for the coupon gilt. For a holding of £1 million nominal there is only one cash flow, the redemption payment of £1 million on the redemption date. The convexity for the principal strip was 1.175, which illustrates the higher convexity property of strips versus coupon bonds. Comparing the tables we can see also that duration for the strip is higher than that for the coupon gilt. Note the analysis for the principal strip gives us a slightly different spot curve.

Finally we show at table 13.11 the cash flow analysis for a coupon strip maturing on 7 December 2009. The yield quote for this coupon strip at this time was 4.4263%, corresponding to a price of 62.26518 per £100 nominal. This illustrates the

Table 13.10 ■ Cash flow analysis Treasury 5¾% 2009 principal strip, yield 4.1482%

Pay date	Cash flow	Spot	Pay date	Cash flow	Spot
7-Jun-99	0.00	5.1835	7-Dec-04	0.00	4.2683
7-Dec-99	0.00	4.9577	7-Jun-05	0.00	4.3102
7-Jun-00	0.00	4.8509	7-Dec-05	0.00	4.3529
7-Dec-00	0.00	4.7373	7-Jun-06	0.00	4.3672
7-Jun-01	0.00	4.6411	7-Dec-06	0.00	4.3821
7-Dec-01	0.00	4.5480	7-Jun-07	0.00	4.3571
7-Jun-02	0.00	4.4613	7-Dec-07	0.00	4.3322
7-Dec-02	0.00	4.3952	7-Jun-08	0.00	4.2937
7-Jun-03	0.00	4.3290	7-Dec-08	0.00	4.2543
7-Dec-03	0.00	4.2629	7-Jun-09	0.00	4.2148
7-Jun-04	0.00	4.2651	7-Dec-09	1,000,000.00	4.1753

Nominal	1,000,000	Previous coupon date	7-Dec-98	
Duration	10.82	Accrued interest	0.00	
Total cash flow	1,000,000.00	Present value	641,340.87	

Source: Bloomberg

point on strip prices we referred to earlier; according to a strict interpretation of the law of one price, all strips maturing on the same date should have the same price (the question being asked is, why should an investor have a different yield requirement depending on whether the £100 nominal he receives on maturity was once interest or once principal?). However, as we have already stated, the liquidity differences between principal and coupon strips makes the former easier to trade and also more sought after by investors, hence the difference in yield between principal and coupon strip. The more liquid instrument trades at the lower yield.

TABLE 13.11 ■ Cash flow analysis, December 2009 coupon strip, yield 4.4263%

Pay date	Cash flow	Spot	Pay date	Cash flow	Spot
7-Jun-99	0.00	5.2025	7-Dec-04	0.00	4.3217
7-Dec-99	0.00	5.0151	7-Jun-05	0.00	4.3672
7-Jun-00	0.00	4.8927	7-Dec-05	0.00	4.4136
7-Dec-00	0.00	4.7633	7-Jun-06	0.00	4.4353
7-Jun-01	0.00	4.6881	7-Dec-06	0.00	4.4576
7-Dec-01	0.00	4.6108	7-Jun-07	0.00	4.4299
7-Jun-02	0.00	4.5138	7-Dec-07	0.00	4.4023
7-Dec-02	0.00	4.4450	7-Jun-08	0.00	4.3608
7-Jun-03	0.00	4.3761	7-Dec-08	0.00	4.3183
7-Dec-03	0.00	4.3074	7-Jun-09	0.00	4.2758
7-Jun-04	0.00	4.3141	7-Dec-09	1,000,000.00	4.2333

Nominal	1,000,000	Previous coupon date	7-Dec-98
Duration	10.82	Accrued interest	0.00
Total cash flow	1,000,000.00	Present value	622,651.18

Source: Bloomberg

Yield spread trades[8]

Relative value trades are common amongst investors who do not wish to put on a naked directional position but believe rather that the yield curve will change shape and flatten or widen between two selected points. Such a trade would involve simultaneous positions in bonds of different maturity. Another relative value trade may involve high coupon bonds against low coupon ones of the same maturity, as a tax-related trade. These trades are concerned with the change in yield spread between two or more bonds rather than a change in absolute interest rate level. The key factor is that changes in spread are not conditional upon directional change in interest rate levels; that is, yield spreads may narrow or widen whether interest rates themselves are rising or falling.

Typically spread trades will be constructed as a long position in one bond against a short position in another bond. If it is set up correctly, the trade will only incur a profit or loss if there is change in the shape of the yield curve. This is regarded as being *first-order risk neutral*, which means that there is no interest-rate risk in the event of change in the general level of market interest rates. In this section we examine some common yield spread trades.

---

[8] Originally written by the author in June 1997 as an internal paper when at Hambros Bank Limited. The prices quoted are *tick* prices, that is fractions of a 32nd.

The determinants of yield

The yield at which a fixed interest security is traded is market-determined. This market determination is a function of three factors, the term-to-maturity of the bond, the liquidity of the bond and its credit quality. Government securities such as gilts are default-free and so this factor drops out of the equation. Under 'normal' circumstances the yield on a bond is higher the greater its maturity, this reflecting both the expectations hypothesis and liquidity preference theories. Intuitively we associate higher risk with longer-dated instruments, for which investors must be compensated in the form of higher yield. This higher risk reflects greater uncertainty with longer-dated bonds, both in terms of default and future inflation and interest rate levels. However, for a number of reasons the yield curve assumes an inverted shape and long-dated yields become lower than short-dated ones.[9] Long-dated yields generally are expected to be less volatile over time compared to short-dated yields. This is mainly because incremental changes to economic circumstances or other technical considerations generally have an impact for only short periods of time, which affects the shorter end of the yield curve to a greater extent.

The liquidity of a bond also influences its yield level. The liquidity may be measured by the size of the bid-offer spread, the ease with which the stock may be transacted in size, and the impact of large-size bargains on the market. It is also measured by the extent of any *specialness* in its repo rate. Supply and demand for an individual stock, and the amount of stock available to trade, are the main drivers of liquidity.[10] The general rule is that there is a yield premium for transacting business in lower-liquidity bonds.

In the analysis that follows we assume satisfactory levels of liquidity, that it is straightforward to deal in large sizes without moving the market.

Spread trade risk weighting

A relative value trade usually involves a long position set up against a short position in a bond of different maturity. The trade must be weighted so that the two positions are first-order neutral, which means the risk exposure of each position nets out when considered as a single trade, but only with respect to a general change in interest rate levels. If there is a change in yield spread, a profit or loss will be generated.

A common approach to weighting spread trades is to use the *basis point value* (BPV) of each bond.[11] Table 13.12 shows price and yield data for a set of benchmark gilts for

---

[9] For a summary of term structure theories see Choudhry (2001), chapter 6.

[10] The amount of stock issued and the amount of stock available to trade are not the same thing. If a large amount of a particular issue has been locked away by institutional investors, this may impede liquidity. However, the existence of a large amount at least means that some of the paper may be made available for lending in the stock loan and repo markets. A small issue size is a good indicator of low liquidity.

[11] This is also known as *dollar value of a basis point* (DVBP) or *present value of a value point* (PVBP).

TABLE 13.12 ▪ Gilt prices and yields for value 17 June 1997

Term	Bond	Price	Accrued	Dirty price	Yield %	Modified duration	BPV	Per £1m nominal
2-yr	6% 10/8/1999	98-17	127	100.62	6.753	1.689	0.016642	166.42
5-yr	7% 7/6/2002	100-10	10	100.50	6.922	3.999	0.040115	401.15
10-yr	7.25% 7/12/2007	101-14	10	101.64	7.052	6.911	0.070103	701.03
25-yr	8% 7/6/2021	110-01	10	110.25	7.120	11.179	0.123004	1230.04

Source: Williams de Broe and Hambros Bank Limited; author's notes

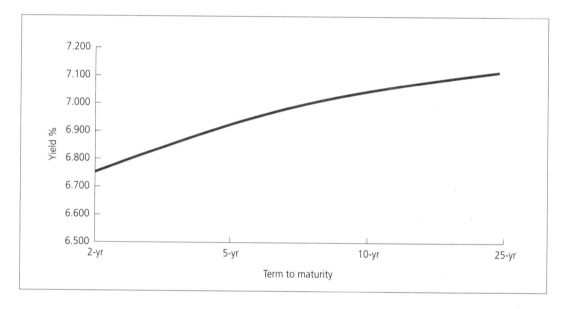

value date 17 June 1997. The BPV for each bond is also shown, per £100 of stock. For the purposes of this discussion we quote mid-prices only and assume that the investor is able to trade at these prices.

An investor believes that the yield curve will flatten between the two-year and ten-year sectors of the curve and that the spread between the 6% 1999 and the 7.25% 2007 will narrow from its present value of 0.299%. To reflect this view the investor buys the ten-year bond and sells short the two-year bond, in amounts that leave the trade first-order risk neutral. If we assume the investor buys £1 million nominal of the 7.25% 2007 gilt, this represents an exposure of £1230.04 loss (profit) if there is a 1 basis point increase (decrease) in yields. Therefore the nominal amount of the short position in the 6% 1999 gilt must equate this risk exposure. The BPV per £1 million nominal of the two-year bond is £166.42, which means that the investor must sell

(1230.04/166.42)

or £7.3912 million of this bond, given by a simple ratio of the two basis point values. We expect to sell a greater nominal amount of the shorter-dated gilt because its risk exposure is lower. This trade generates cash because the short sale proceeds exceed the long buy purchase funds, which are respectively

Buy £1m 7.25% 2007	–£1,102,500
Sell £7.39m 6% 1999	+£7,437,025

What are the possible outcomes of this trade? If there is a parallel shift in the yield curve, the trade neither gains or loses. If the yield spread narrows by say, 15 basis points the trade will gain either from a drop in yield on the long side or a gain in yield in the short side, or a combination of both. Conversely, a widening of the spread will result in a loss. Any narrowing spread is positive for the trade, while any widening is harmful.

The trade would be put on the same ratio if the amounts were higher, which is *scaling* the trade. So for example is the investor had bought £100 million of the 7.25% 2007, he would need to sell short £739 million of the two-year bonds. However, the risk exposure is greater by the same amount, so that in this case the trade would generate 100 times the risk. As can be imagined, there is a greater potential reward but at the same time a greater amount of stress in managing the position.

Using BPVs to risk-weight a relative value trades is common but suffers from any traditional duration-based measure because of the assumptions used in the analysis. Note that when using this method the ratio of the nominal amount of the bonds must equate the reciprocal of the bonds' BPV ratio. So in this case the BPV ratio is

(166.42/1230.04)

or 0.1353, which has a reciprocal of 7.3912. This means that the nominal values of the two bonds must always be in the ratio of 7.39:1. This weighting is not static however; we know from Chapter 2 that duration measures are a snapshot estimation of dynamic properties such as yield and term to maturity. Therefore, for anything but very short-term trades the relative values may need to be adjusted as the BPVs alter over time.

Another method to weigh trades is by duration-weighting, which involves weighting in terms of market values. This compares to the BPV approach which provides a weighting ratio in terms of nominal values. In practice the duration approach does not produce any more accurate risk weighting.

A key element of any relative value trade is the financing cost of each position. This is where the repo market in each bond becomes important. In the example described above, the financing requirement is:

■ repo out the 7.25% 2007, for which £1.1 million of cash must be borrowed to finance the purchase; the trader pays the repo rate on this stock;

■ reverse repo the 6% 1999 bond, which must be borrowed in repo to cover the short sale; the trader earns the repo rate on this stock.

If the repo rate on both stocks is close to the general repo rate in the market, there will be a bid-offer spread to pay but the greater amount of funds lent out against the 6% 1999 bond will result in a net financing gain on the trade whatever happens to the yield spread. If the 7.25% 2007 gilt is special, because the stock is in excessive demand in the market (for whatever reason) the financing gain will be greater still. If the 6% 1999 is *special*, the trade will suffer a financing loss.

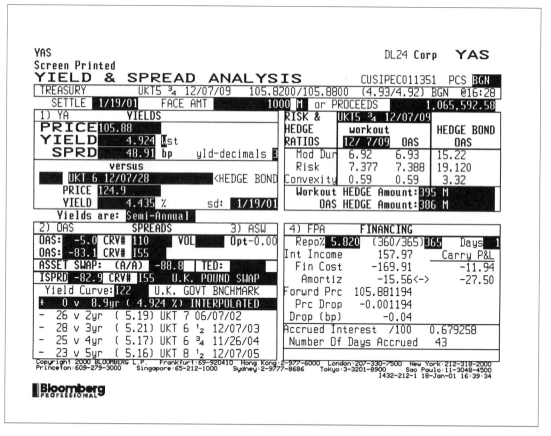

FIGURE 13.6 ■ Bloomberg yield spread analysis page, $5\frac{3}{4}$% 2009 versus 6% 2028, 19 January 2001
© Bloomberg L.P. Used with permission.

A detailed account of the funding issues involved is in chapter 34 of Choudhry (2001).

Identifying yield spread trades

Yield spread trades are a type of relative value position that a trader can construct when the objective is to gain from a change in the spread between two points on the yield curve. The decision on which sectors of the curve to target is an important one and is based on a number of factors. An investor may naturally target say, the five- and ten-year areas of the yield curve to meet investment objectives and have a view on these maturities. Or a trader may draw conclusions from studying the historical spread between two sectors.

Yield spreads do not move in parallel however and there is not a perfect correlation between the changes of short-, medium- and long-term sectors of the curve. The money market yield curve can sometimes act independently of the bond curve. Table 13.13 shows the change in benchmark yields during 1996/1997. There is no set pattern in the change in both yield levels and spreads. It is apparent that one segment of the curve can flatten while another is steepening, or remains unchanged.

TABLE 13.13 ■ Yield levels and yield spreads during November 1996–November 1997

| | *Changes in yield levels* | | | | | |
	3-month	*1-year*	*2-year*	*5-year*	*10-year*	*25-year*
10/11/96	6.06	6.71	6.83	7.31	7.67	7.91
10/7/97	6.42	6.96	7.057	7.156	7.025	6.921
Change	0.36	0.25	0.227	−0.154	−0.645	−0.989
10/11/97	7.15	7.3	7.09	6.8	6.69	6.47
Change	0.73	0.34	0.033	−0.356	−0.335	−0.451
	Changes in yield spread					
	3m / 1y	*1y / 2y*	*2y / 5y*	*5y / 10y*	*5y/25y*	*10y/25y*
10/11/96	−0.65	−0.12	−0.48	−0.36	−0.6	−0.24
10/7/97	−0.54	−0.457	−0.099	0.131	0.235	0.104
Change	0.11	−0.337	0.381	0.491	0.835	0.344
10/11/97	−0.15	0.21	0.29	0.11	0.33	0.22
Change	0.39	0.667	0.389	−0.021	0.095	0.116

Source: ABN Amro Hoare Govett Sterling Bonds Ltd, Hambros Bank Limited, Tullett & Tokyo; author's notes

Another type of trade is where an investor has a view on one part of the curve relative to two other parts of the curve. This can be reflected in a number of ways, one of which is the butterfly trade, considered in the next section.

Coupon spreads[12]

Coupon spreads are becoming less common in the gilt market because of the disappearance of high-coupon or other exotic gilts and the concentration on liquid benchmark issues. However, they are genuine spread trades. The basic principle behind the trade is a spread of two bonds that have similar maturity or similar duration but different coupons.

Table 13.14 shows the yields for a set of high coupon and low(er) coupon gilts for a specified date in May 1993 and the yields for the same gilts six months later. From the yield curves we see that general yield levels declines by approximately 80-130 basis points. The last column in the table shows that, apart from the earliest pair of gilts (which do not have strictly comparable maturity dates), the performance of the lower coupon gilt exceeded that of the higher coupon gilt in every instance. Therefore buying the spread of the low coupon versus the high coupon should in theory generate a trading gain in an environment of falling yields. One explanation of this is that the lower coupon bonds are often the benchmark, which means the demand for them is higher. In addition, during a bull market, more bonds are considered to be 'high' coupon as overall yield levels decrease.

TABLE 13.14 ■ Yield changes on high and low coupon gilts from May 1993 to November 1993

Stock	Term	10-May-93	12-Nov-93
Gilt	1	5.45	5.19
10Q95	2	6.39	5.39
10 96	3	6.94	5.82
10H 97	4	7.13	5.97
9T 98 and 7Q 98	5	7.31	6.14
10Q 99	6	7.73	6.55
9 00	7	7.67	6.54
10 01	8	8.01	6.82
9T 02	9	8.13	6.95
8 03	10	8.07	6.85
9 08	15	8.45	7.18
9 12	20	8.55	7.23
8T 17	30	8.6	7.22

[12] First presented by the author as an internal paper in April 1995.

TABLE 13.14 ■ Continued

Gilt	Maturity	Yield 10/05/1993	Yield 12/11/1993	Yield change %
10Q 95	21-Jul-95	6.393	5.390	−1.003
14 96	10-Jan-96	6.608	5.576	−1.032
15Q 96	3-May-96	6.851	5.796	−1.055
13Q 96	15-May-96	6.847	5.769	−1.078
13Q 97	22-Jan-97	7.142	5.999	−1.143
10H 97	21-Feb-97	7.131	5.974	1.157
7 97	6-Aug-97	7.219	6.037	−1.182
8T 97	1-Sep-97	7.223	6.055	−1.168
15 97	27-Oct-97	7.294	6.113	−1.161
9T 98	19-Jan-98	7.315	6.102	−1.213
7Q 98	30-Mar-98	7.362	6.144	−1.218
6 99	10-Aug-99	7.724	6.536	−1.188
10Q 99	22-Nov-99	7.731	6.552	−1.179
8 03	10-Jun-03	8.075	6.854	−1.221
10 03	8-Sep-03	8.137	6.922	−1.215

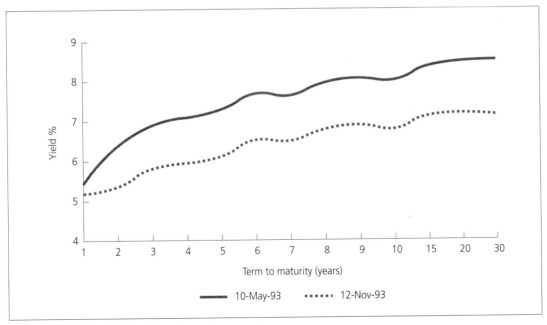

Source: ABN Hoare Govett Sterling Bonds Ltd; Bloomberg; author's notes

The exception noted in table 13.14 is the outperformance of the 14% Treasury 1996 compared to the lower-coupon 10¼% 1995 stock. This is not necessarily conclusive, because the bonds are six months apart in maturity, which is a significant amount for short-dated stock. However, in an environment of low or falling interest rates, shorter-dated investors such as banks and insurance companies often prefer to hold very high-coupon bonds because of the high income levels they generate. This may explain the demand for the 14% 1996 stock[13] although the evidence at the time was only anecdotal.

Butterfly trades[14]

Butterfly trades are another method by which traders can reflect a view on changing yield levels without resorting to a naked punt on interest rates. They are another form of relative value trade; amongst portfolio managers they are viewed as a means of enhancing returns. In essence a butterfly trade is a short position in one bond against a long position of two bonds, one of shorter maturity and the other of longer maturity than the short-sold bond. Duration-weighting is used so that the net position is first-order risk-neutral, and nominal values are calculated such that the short sale and long purchase cash flows net to zero, or very closely to zero.

This section reviews some of the aspects of butterfly trades.

Basic concepts

A butterfly trade is par excellence a yield curve trade. If the average return on the combined long position is greater than the return on the short position (which is a cost) during the time the trade is maintained, the strategy will generate a profit. It reflects a view that the short end of the curve will steepen relative to the 'middle' of the curve while the long end will flatten. For this reason higher convexity stocks are usually preferred for the long positions, even if this entails a loss in yield. However, the trade is not 'risk-free', for the same reasons that a conventional two-bond yield spread is not. Although in theory a butterfly is risk-neutral with respect to parallel changes in the yield curve, changes in the shape of the curve can result in losses. For this reason the position must be managed dynamically and monitored for changes in risk relative to changes in the shape of the yield curve.

In a butterfly trade the trader is long a short-dated and long-dated bond, and short a bond of a maturity that falls in between these two maturities. A portfolio manager with a constraint on running short positions may consider this trade as a switch out of a long

---

[13] This stock also has a special place in the author's heart, although he was Number 2 on the desk when the head of Treasury put on a very large position in it …!

[14] Revised and updated version of a paper first presented internally to head of Cash-OBS desk, Treasury division, at Hambros Bank Limited in June 1997.

position in the medium-dated bond and into duration-weighted amounts of the short-dated and long-dated bond. However, it is not strictly correct to view the combined long position to be an exact substitute for the short position, as due to liquidity and other reasons the two positions will behave differently for given changes in the yield curve. In addition one must be careful to compare like for like, as the yield change in the short position must be analyzed against yield changes in *two* bonds. This raises the issue of portfolio yield.

Putting on the trade

We begin by considering the calculation of the nominal amounts of the long positions, assuming a user-specified starting amount in the short position. In table 13.15 we show three gilts as at 25 April 1997. The trade we wish to put on is a short position in the five-year bond, the 7% Treasury 2002 against long positions in the two-year bond, the 6% Treasury 1999 and the ten-year bond, the $7\frac{1}{4}$% Treasury 2007. Assuming £10 million nominal of the five-year bond, the nominal values of the long positions can be calculated using duration, modified duration or basis point values (the last two, unsurprisingly, will generate identical results). The more common approach is to use basis point values.

TABLE 13.15 ■ Bond values for butterfly strategy, June 1997

	2-year bond	*5-year bond*	*10-year bond*
Gilt	6% 1999	7% 2002	7.25% 2007
Maturity date	10 Aug 1999	07 Jun 2002	07 Dec 2007
Price	98-08	99-27	101-06
Accrued interest	2.30137	0.44110	0.45685
Dirty price	100.551	100.285	101.644
GRY %	6.913	7.034	7.085
Duration	1.969	4.243	7.489
Modified duration	1.904	4.099	7.233
Basis point value	0.01914	0.0411	0.07352
Convexity	0.047	0.204	0.676

Source: author's notes

In a butterfly trade the net cash flow should be as close to zero as possible, and the trade must be basis point value-neutral. Using the following notation,

P_1 the dirty price of the short position;
P_2 the dirty price of the long position in the two-year bond;
P_3 the dirty price of the long position in the ten-year bond;
M_1 the nominal value of short-position bond, with M_2 and M_3 the long-position bonds;
BPV_1 the basis point value of the short-position bond

if applying basis point values, the amounts required for each stock are given by

$$M_1 P_1 = M_2 P_2 + M_3 P_3 \tag{13.10}$$

while the risk-neutral calculation is given by

$$M_1 BPV_1 = M_2 BPV_2 + M_3 BPV_3. \tag{13.11}$$

The value of M_1 is not unknown, as we have set it at £10 million. The equations can be rearranged therefore to solve for the remaining two bonds, which are

$$M_2 = \frac{P_1 BPV_3 - P_3 BPV_1}{P_2 BPV_3 - P_3 BPV_2} M_1 \tag{13.12}$$

$$M_3 = \frac{P_2 BPV_1 - P_1 BPV_2}{P_2 BPV_3 - P_3 BPV_2} M_1$$

Using the dirty prices and BPVs from table 13.15, we obtain the following values for the long positions. The position required is short £10 million 7% 2002 and long £5.347 million of the 6% 1999 and £4.576 million of the 7¼% 2007. With these values the trade results in a zero net cash flow and a first-order risk neutral interest-rate exposure. Identical results would be obtained using the modified duration values, and similar results using the duration measures. If using Macaulay duration the nominal values are calculated using

$$D_1 = \frac{MV_2 D_2 + MV_3 D_3}{MV_2 + MV_3} \tag{13.13}$$

where D and MV represent duration and market value for each respective stock.

Yield gain

We know that the gross redemption yield for a vanilla bond is that rate r where

$$P_d = \sum_{i=1}^{N} C_i e^{-rn}. \tag{13.14}$$

The right-hand side of (13.14) is simply the present value of the cash flow payments C to be made by the bond in its remaining lifetime. Expression (13.14) gives the continuously compounded yields to maturity; in practice users define a yield with compounding interval m, that is

$$r = (e^{rmn} - 1)/m. \tag{13.15}$$

Treasuries and gilts compound on a semi-annual basis.

In principle we may compute the yield on a portfolio of bonds exactly as for a single bond, using (13.14) to give the yield for a set of cash flows which are purchased today at their present value. In practice the market calculates portfolio yield as a weighted average of the individual yields on each of the bonds in the portfolio. This is described for example in Fabozzi (1993), and his description points out the weakness of this method. An alternative approach is to weight individual yields using bonds' basis point values, which we illustrate here in the context of the earlier butterfly trade. In this trade we have

■ short £10 million 7% 2002;

■ long £5.347 million 6% 1999 and £4.576 million 7¼% 2007.

Using the semi-annual adjusted form of (13.14), the true yield of the long position is 7.033%. To calculate the portfolio yield of the long position using market value weighting, we may use

$$r_{port} = \left(MV_2/MV_{port}\right)r_2 + \left(MV_3/MV_{port}\right)r_3 \tag{13.16}$$

which results in a portfolio yield for the long position of 6.993%. If we weight the yield with basis point values we use

$$r_{port} = \frac{BPV_2 M_2 r_2 + BPV_3 M_3 r_3}{BPV_2 M_2 + BPV_3 M_3}. \tag{13.17}$$

Substituting the values from table 13.15 we obtain

$$r_{port} = \frac{(1,914)(5.347)(6.913) + (7,352)(4.576)(7.085)}{(1,914)(5.347) + (7,352)(4.576)}$$

or 7.045%.

We see that using basis point values produces a seemingly more accurate weighted yield, closer to the true yield computed using the expression above. In addition, using this measure, a portfolio manager switching into the long butterfly position from a position in the 7% 2002 would pick up a yield gain of 1.2 basis points, compared to the 4 basis points that an analyst would conclude had been lost using the first yield measure.[15]

The butterfly trade therefore produces a yield gain in addition to the capital gain expected if the yield curve changes in the anticipated way.

Convexity gain

In addition to yield pick-up, the butterfly trade provides in theory a convexity gain which will outperform the short position irrespective of which direction interest rates moved in, provided we have a parallel shift. This is illustrated in table 13.16. This shows that the changes in value of the 7% 2002 as interest rates rise and fall, together with the change in value of the combined portfolio.

TABLE 13.16 ■ Changes in bond values with changes in yield levels

Yield change (bps)	7% 2002 value (£)	Portfolio value* (£)	Difference (£)	BPV 7% 2002 (5-year)	BPV 6% 1999 (2-year)	BPV 7.25% 2007 (10-year)
+250	9,062,370	9,057,175	−5,195	0.0363	0.0180	0.0584
+200	9,246,170	9,243,200	−2,970	0.0372	0.0182	0.0611
+150	9,434,560	9,435,200	640	0.0381	0.0184	0.0640
+100	9,627,650	9,629,530	1,880	0.0391	0.0187	0.0670
+50	9,825,600	9,828,540	2,940	0.0401	0.0189	0.0702
0	**10,028,500**	**10,028,500**	**0**	**0.0411**	**0.0191**	**0.0735**
−50	10,236,560	10,251,300	14,740	0.0421	0.0194	0.0770
−100	10,450,000	10,483,800	33,800	0.0432	0.0196	0.0808
−150	10,668,600	10,725,700	57,100	0.0443	0.0199	0.0847
−200	10,893,000	10,977,300	84,300	0.0454	0.0201	0.0888
−250	11,123,000	11,240,435	117,435	0.0466	0.0204	0.0931

*Combined value of long positions in 6% 1999 and 7.25% 2007. Values rounded. Yield change is parallel shift

[15] The actual income gained on the spread will depend on the funding costs for all three bonds, a function of the specific repo rates available for each bond. Shortly after the time of writing, the 6% Treasury 1999 went special, so the funding gain on a long position in this stock would have been excessive. However, buying the stock outright would have necessitated paying a yield premium, as demand for it increased as a result of it going special. In the event the premium was deemed high, an alternative stock was nominated, the 10¼% Conversion 1999, a bond with near-identical modified duration value.

We observe from table 13.16 that whatever the change in interest rates, up to a point, the portfolio value will be higher than the value of the short position, although the effect is progressively reduced as yields rise. The butterfly will always gain if yields fall, and protects against downside risk if yields rise to a certain extent. This is the effect of convexity; when interest rates rise, the portfolio value declines by less than the short position value, and when rates fall, the portfolio value increases by more. Essentially the combined long position exhibits greater convexity than the short position. The effect is greater if yields fall, while there is an element of downside protection as yields rise, up to the +150 basis point parallel shift.

Portfolio managers may seek greater convexity whether or not there is a yield pick up available from a switch. However, the convexity effect is only material for large changes in yield, and so if there was not a corresponding yield gain from the switch, the trade may not perform positively. As we noted, this depends partly on the funding position for each stock. The price/yield profile for each stock is shown at figure 13.7.

Essentially, by putting on a butterfly as opposed to a two-bond spread or a straight directional play, the trader limits the downside risk if interest rates fall, while preserving the upside gain if yields fall.

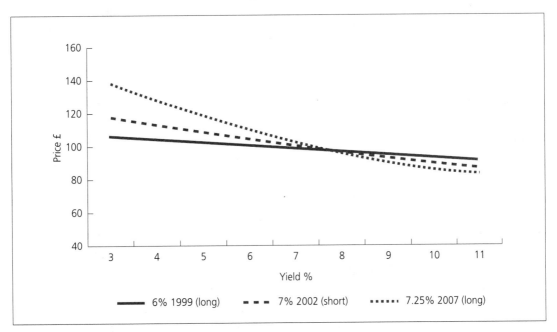

FIGURE 13.7 ■ Illustration of convexity for each stock in butterfly trade, 27 June 1997

Analysis using Bloomberg screen 'BBA'

To conclude the discussion of butterfly trade strategy, we describe the analysis if using the 'BBA' screen on Bloomberg. The trade is illustrated at figure 13.8.

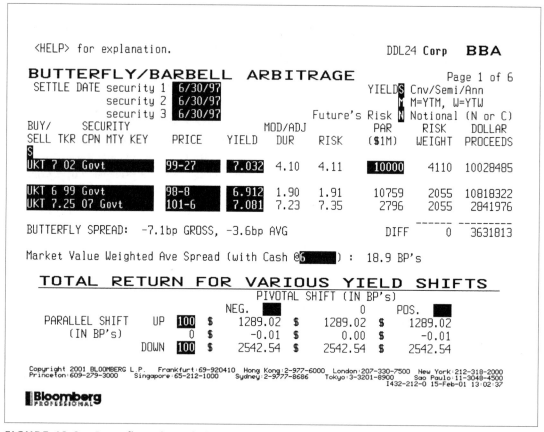

FIGURE 13.8 ■ Butterfly trade analysis on 27 June 1997, on screen BBA

© Bloomberg L.P. Reproduced with permission

Using this approach, the nominal values of the two long positions are calculated using BPV ratios only. This is shown under the column 'Risk Weight', and we note that the difference is zero. However, the nominal value required for the two-year bond is much greater, at £10.76 million, and for the ten-year bond much lower at £2.8 million. This results in a cash outflow of £3.632 million. The profit profile is in theory much improved however; at the bottom of the screen we observe the results of a 100 basis point parallel shift in either direction, which is a profit. Positive results were also seen for 200 and 300 basis point parallel shifts in either direction. This screen incorporates the effect of a (uniform) funding rate, input on this occasion as 6.00%.[16] Note that the screen allows the user to see the results of a pivotal shift, however, in this example a 0 basis point pivotal shift is selected.

---

[16] In reality the repo rate will be slightly different for each stock, and there will be a bid-offer spread to pay, but as long as none of the stocks are special the calculations should be reasonably close.

This trade therefore created a profit whatever direction interest rates moved in.

The spread history for the position up to the day before the trade is shown at figure 13.9, a reproduction of the graph on Bloomberg screen BBA.

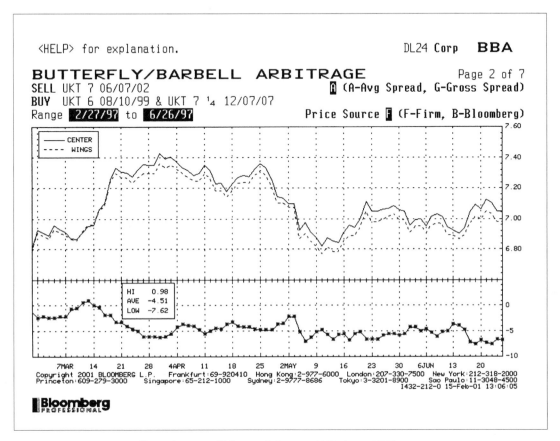

FIGURE 13.9 ▪ Butterfly trade spread history, February 1997–June 1997

© Bloomberg L.P. Reproduced with permission

SELECTED BIBLIOGRAPHY AND REFERENCES

Blake, D., *Financial Market Analysis*, McGraw Hill 1990

Choudhry, M., *Introduction to the Gilt Strips Market*, Securities Institute (Services) Limited, 1999

Choudhry, M., *The Repo Handbook*, Butterworth-Heinemann 2001

Choudhry, M., *The Bond and Money Markets: Strategy, Trading, Analysis*, Butterworth-Heinemann 2001

Fabozzi, F., *Fixed Income Mathematics*, McGraw-Hill, 1993, chapter 6

Fabozzi, F., *Bond Portfolio Management*, FJF Associates 1996, chapters 10–14

Basic tools

In this appendix we provide a very brief summary overview of some of the main arithmetic tools that are mentioned in the text. There is no derivation or proof, and interested readers can access any number of textbooks on econometrics.

Summation and product operators

Summation is indicated by the use of the Greek capital letter Σ, pronounced sigma. Thus we have

$$\sum_{i=1}^{N} x_i = x_1 + x_2 + x_3 + \ldots + x_N$$

The double summation operator is also used, thus

$$\sum_{i=1}^{n} \sum_{j=1}^{m} x_{ij} = \sum_{i=1}^{n} (x_{i1} + x_{i2} + \ldots + x_{im})$$

The product operator is given by

$$\prod_{i=1}^{n} x_i = x_1 \cdot x_2 \cdot x_3 \cdot \ldots \cdot x_n$$

The integral calculus

The process of differentiation is demonstrated by

$$y = 6x^3 + 2x^2 + 3x$$

where

$$\frac{dy}{dx} = 18x^2 + 4x + 3$$

The reverse of this process is *integration*, indicated by

$$\int 18x^2 + 4x + 3 \mathrm{d}x$$

where $\mathrm{d}x$ is used to indicate the original differentiation with respect to x.
If we know that

$$\int g\,(x)\mathrm{d}x = f\,(x)$$

then

$\int_a^b g(x)\mathrm{d}x$ is defined as $f(a) - f(b)$ and is the definite integral between a and b of the
function $g(x)$.

Figure A.6 shows part of the function $y = f(x)$ between the points a and b on the x-axis.
Imagine that we wish to find the area A between the curve, the x-axis and the lines $x = a$
and $x = b$. We divide the area A into strips of width δx and height y. These strips are
approximately rectangles.

Again approximating, we can say that the area of each strip $\delta A = y\delta x$, so that

$$\frac{\delta A}{\mathrm{d}x} \approx y$$

As the value of δx becomes progressively smaller and approaches (but does not reach)
zero, any strips becomes closer to a rectangle and the approximation given by the above
equation approaches an equality, so that we then get

$$\frac{\mathrm{d}A}{\mathrm{d}x} = y$$

However $y = f(x)$, which means we can state

$$\frac{\mathrm{d}A}{\mathrm{d}x} = f(x)$$

Therefore we can state

$$A = \int f\,(x)\mathrm{d}x$$

We let the integral be

$$A = g(x)$$

At the point a on the x-axis $A = 0$, which also means that $g(a) = 0$, and at the point b on
the x-axis we would have A equal to the whole area, which would allow us to set
$A = g(b)$. But as $g(a) = 0$ at this point, we can set

$$A = g(b) - g(a)$$

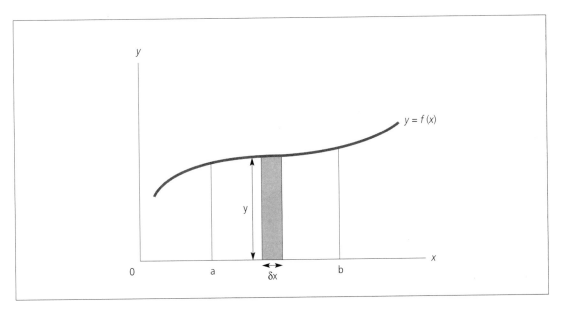

FIGURE A.1

The expression is actually

$$\int_a^b f(x)dx$$

which is usually written

$$\int_a^b y\,dx$$

Hence using the definite integral allows us to calculate the area under the graph.

Stochastic integrals

If X is a generalized Brownian motion described by

$$X_t = X_0 + bt + \sigma Z_t$$

at time t, for the time interval $t_0 = 0 < t_1 < t_2 < \,....\, < t_{A-1} < t_A = t$ we have

$$X_t = X_0 + \sum_{i=1}^{A} [b(t_i - t_{i-1}) + \sigma(Z_{ti} - Z_{ti-1})]$$

At the limit where A goes to infinity we obtain

$$X_t = X_0 + \sum_0^T (bdt + \sigma dZ_t)$$

If the variables b and Σ are functions of t and X_t and are not constant then the process X can be shown to be defined as

$$X_t = X_0 + \sum_0^T [b(t, X_t) \, dt + \sigma(t, X_t) \, dZ_t]$$

which describes the limit position as A approaches infinity. At this point we have

$$dX_t = b(t, X_t) \, dt + \sigma(t, X_t) \, dZ_t$$

and X is described as a *diffusion* process. This process has the following properties

- the value of the process at time $t = 0$ is X_0;
- the instantaneous *drift* of the process at time t is given by $b(t, X_t)$;
- the instantaneous standard deviation or *volatility* of the process at time t is given by $\sigma(t, X_t)$.

The integral $\sum_0^T \sigma(t, X_t) \, dZ_t$ is called a stochastic integral.

Index